This Book may

# 1848
## CHAPTERS OF GERMAN HISTORY

# 1848

## CHAPTERS OF GERMAN HISTORY

by
VEIT VALENTIN

Translated by
Ethel Talbot Scheffauer

LONDON
GEORGE ALLEN AND UNWIN LTD

943.07
V23e

FIRST PUBLISHED IN 1940

35907
Jan. 1958

PRINTED IN GREAT BRITAIN
in 12-Point Bembo Type
BY UNWIN BROTHERS LIMITED
WOKING

# CONTENTS

## PART ONE

## PART TWO

9

# PART I

## CHAPTER ONE

# THE AUSTRIAN IMPERIAL STATE

O N THE 5th of May, 1847, Count Dietrichstein, premier Court Chamberlain, delivered the dead body of Archduke Karl into the hands of the Guardian Father of the Monastery of the Capuchians with the words:

"Receive, most venerable Guardian, the corpse of His Imperial Highness, the most illustrious lord, Archduke Karl of Austria, that chivalrous prince without fear and without reproach, whose high virtues were an occasion of universal love and admiration and whose heroic and glorious feats of arms will cause his memory to endure immortal for ever in the grateful hearts of all subjects of the Imperial Realm and in the hearts of all Germans."

The obsequies of Archduke Karl were the last great occasion of pomp and ceremony in the old Empire of Austria. Already a new element was making itself felt: the peoples of the Empire.

Archduke Karl, the victor of Aspern, had been the defeated of Wagram; but his name had continued to diffuse a radiance over all Austria's hopes, those of Germany, of all Europe. He should have been Emperor instead of the stiff-necked Francis; he saw in absolutism a form of government that had outlived its hour; he would fain have reconciled his Austria with the spirit of the age. In vain had he set himself against slackness and lack of organization—he remained without influence, always thrust aside and treated with suspicion. Ever since the days of Maria Theresa and Emperor Josef II there had always been men who were filled with the sacred fire of creation and the wish to reform. But no creative spirit had again become Emperor. Emperor Franz, a bigoted despot, won the hearts of comfortable citizens by his cosy Viennese charm —but under his pettifogging, anxious, narrow-minded guidance, all grew cold and petty, rigid and lame; and his successor, Emperor Ferdinand, was a tattling, but by no means inocuous simpleton, who, as a symbol of monarchy turned the Crown into a laughing-stock. He was an epileptic and should never have been allowed to succeed to the throne; but for that Austro-German quality of patience and good-humour which had so often been tried and proven, nothing could have preserved the monarchy intact.

"Good Heavens," wrote the Empress of Russia, after making Emperor Ferdinand's acquaintance, "I had heard much of him, of his puny, wizened figure, his great head devoid of any expression save stupidity, but the reality transcends all description."

It was neither Franz nor Ferdinand who determined Austria's destiny. The fate of Austria, of Germany, of all Europe was summed up for many a year in the one name—Metternich. The revolutionary movement of 1848–49 can only be understood in the light of this man's work and personality. It was directed against the very nature of the man, against his spirit, his principles, his "system." He who defends Metternich, condemns the Revolution. To defend the Revolution is to damn him. Both need to be *understood*.

Two generations of German, Italian, Slavonic youth hated under the name of Metternich everything which seemed to them deserving of hatred. The curses of Grillparzer and Lenau were levelled against his system. Until our own day he was in the company of the damned. The new European feeling of the post-war period sought to reinstate him. What is the truth about Metternich?

14

"The Rhine flows in my veins," wrote the old prince, as he looked down from the heights of his home on the Johannis hill for the last time, shortly before his death. Even in Vienna, despite all the grave dignity that encompassed a State chancellor, he had remained a Rhinelander of the cold country: charming, easygoing, tasteful, fond of conversation—in politics, a cosmopolitan European. His comrades at the University had had a nickname for him—"Fin, faux, fanfaron"—he was agreeable, complacent to a fault, a man of talents, but even more vain than gifted. The French Revolution of 1789 had robbed the princely house of Metternich, like many another, of home and property: was it not inevitable that he should hate this revolution? Must he not love a conservative stability, such as he found in England? In self-determination of peoples, freedom of nations, democracy, he saw only the destruction of what had been and a hindrance to quiet development: there was only one answer to revolutionary demands and all their militant unrest, and his professors had already taught young Metternich that answer: *Pax Christiana*, European Republic.

Metternich conquered Napoleon. Determined, polished, and without prejudice, quietly crafty, he studied the man of destiny of his epoch. He did not suffer, nor rise up against him with heroic imprudence, full of wrath against the Emperor, as Freiherr vom Stein had done. Early in life, Metternich was already a master of preparing the next step, he was neither particularly courageous nor especially energetic. He liked to talk in riddles and to employ roundabout methods; he revered the power of money and high position, and above all he had confidence in himself. He temporized, employed finesse of every kind, played against Napoleon, with him and round about him for a long time—too long, for at last no one knew who was the cheat and who the cheated.

But he conquered the heroic man of blood; he, the fine gentleman, squire of dames, frivolous, playful tactician, a man who was hated by all serious moralists and upright men to whom their politics were a matter of faith. But it was he who achieved his end and not they: a powerful Austrian Imperial State, soaring high over the heads of Germany, Italy, and the Slavs, heart of an anti-revolutionary Central Europe, allied with Russia and with England, determined to hold off France and keep Prussia small and feeble. Undisturbed, Metternich allowed France to swallow Alsace and Lorraine, indifferently he renounced the Rhenish influence accruing from of old to the House of Hapsburg: he thought concentration more important. The Imperial State was a little Europe in itself and the German Federation and the Holy Alliance made this little Europe an axis of the greater Europe beyond its borders. The imperial name continued to carry on the universalism of the old in a new form. The old empire had been "holy" and "Roman"; the new system of the Imperial State of Austria was holy and Roman in a peculiar new manner of its own; it was the very embodiment of counter-revolution.

Metternich took pleasure in observing spiders and admired the cruel cleverness of their cross-threads. He wove his own nets over all that made up his world. He was the first Court- and State-Chancellor since Prince Kaunitz: noble and nonchalant, finest flower of his time and his class, an eternal fixed smile upon his lips. When he laughed, which was seldom, people were horrified at the Mephistophelian leer that turned his features to a grimace. His mild blue eye seldom darted a sudden lightning out of that polite mask; his nasal voice had no resonance; as he grew old he was always lecturing in long perorations. In extreme old age he had almost acquired the "Hapsburg lip."

Metternich achieved all that could be achieved by *esprit* and *raison*, in which the eighteenth century always excelled the nineteenth. He was always busy, business was to him a living thing. How easily he apprehended everything, not only its material content, but the very thoughts of those who reported to him! He at once, all too quickly, visualized the whole situation in agreeable fashion; he was fond of improvizing and did it well, and so, in spite of his many activities, he always had plenty of time, time for people and for good stories, for travel, books, enjoyment of every kind, for rarities, even for the serious study of natural sciences; he loved to lard his talk with scientific idiom. He was most successful and this seemed to him to prove that he was always right; thus the master diplomatist fancied himself also a master strategist and historian; the naïveté of this over-estimation of his powers marks the boundaries of his personality. Sensual and sly, he took what he could get, but poured forth edifying talk about his warmth of heart. In essence he was a genius of cool reason, a cold and mighty prosaist of conservatism, an arrogant man of possessions who protected and revered all men of property, an enlightened great lord, whose soul revolted against everything warm and young, everything mysterious and mystical, everything spectacularly heroic, all simple faith, the oppresesd and the fanatical.

Metternich was no "Social Conservative" as were Disraeli and Bismarck in a later age, but a reactionary, although the most brilliant and elegant of all reactionaries of his day. He led the great counterblast against the revolutionary movement. But the Revolution hit back and swept him away. He may have patronized technical progress, economic development, and the spread of communications—but he did it as a descendant of the old police state. Everything new in Austria was suppressed wherever possible—although the new was too many-coloured and powerful to be capable of suppression.

Metternich's foreign policy preserved the peace, they say. But it reached its height before the July revolution. When one congress followed on the heels of the last, in the 'twenties, Europe was politically active, legitimist, united against every national and liberal tendency. The turning-point was Greece's fight for freedom. England turned her back on the "system."

Then Metternich, acting upon a correct instinct, proposed to make war upon the France of the July revolution. Archduke Karl proved that a war would be impossible for Austria, with her financial deficit and her neglected army. It was at this point that Metternich's system might really be considered as shattered to the core. The period until the outbreak of the Revolution of 1848 was the merciful interregnum of an aristocratic façade hiding an actual state of bankruptcy. It was a period rich in humiliations and defeats, alternating with momentary successes. A keen observer such as Count Arnim, the Prussian minister, could not fail to observe the deep internal weakness of Metternich and his system. He wrote thus, six months before the outbreak of the Revolution of 1848:

"The man in whom the power of Austria is centralized, has one foot in the grave. His old intellectual strength is broken, and although as a diplomatist he is still apparently at his height, he is no longer statesman enough, nor has he the State sufficiently firm in hand to master the present state of things. He has had to endure many a mortification of late, plans have gone astray, old opponents, among them Count Kolowrat, have been singled out by the Emperor and honoured by visits and so on—all this has embittered the last days of his glorious career and broken him up more quickly than would otherwise have been the case."

Metternich attempted to comfort himself and others for the mighty innovations which were sweeping Europe, including Austria, by setting up a number of precepts, threadbare though they were. Apparently as calm and dignified as ever, still impressive as a highly-cultivated man of the world, he hoped to be able to maintain his position by means of his studied carelessness, his supple cleverness, a tactician turning weakness to a weapon. His contemporaries undoubtedly suspected the pettiness of the mighty man, although he understood so admirably how to mask it behind great principles.

18

Metternich's Austrian Imperial State was a little Europe which aspired to be the heart of Greater Europe—a small Europe led by Germany under the visible sign of German claims to hegemony. Metternich could preserve his European position only as long as he could succeed in keeping all Germany at his back. If Germany were to set herself up against the Imperial State of Austria, the crisis would have come. In July 1847, the Chancellor expounded his view of things very characteristically to Count Arnim, the Prussian minister. "The French cabinet has called Austria an Italian power and deduces from this an eventual right to intervene. Austria has Italian provinces, to be sure, but she is not an Italian power." There were only three nationalities, said the Prince, the Germanic, the Latin, and the Slavonic. "Austria is a realm which embraces peoples of various nationalities under its sovereignty, but as realm she has only one nationality. This is the German—she is German as a matter of history, as the point of junction of all her provinces and by virtue of her civilization."

If all the vital powers in the Imperial State must turn against the patriarchal central guardianship, then they were at the same time warring against the German element which it represented. And if the German element desired freedom, it must shatter the basis of the Imperial State. In this tangle of contradictions we have at once the bitterest denunciation and the only justification of Metternich and his system.


In his day, Ludwig Börne compared Austria and China. An Austrian aristocrat, who certainly knew more about Austria than about China, took up the simile in the 'forties. He said: "Austria has the same relation to Europe that China has to Asia." The sentence occurs in a booklet entitled *Austria and Her Future*, published anonymously in Hamburg in 1843; the author was Baron Victor von Andrian-Werburg, a scion of an ancient and wealthy South German noble family, and holder of various State offices. "Austria is not a country which is an entity in itself (for it represents no idea which unites all its citizens), the Austrians do not constitute a nation; Austria is a complex of nations which will fall apart unless it receives aid from without. Enough of too much government, of printed regulations! The professions must have representation, not only the aristocrats but also the plain citizens, in order to combat the deadly routine of an all-powerful bureaucracy. The people must be awakened as a whole and take shape in autonomous provinces and districts. State and people have never yet formed a unity: the governed have no part in the government and therefore no love for it; the administration with its one hundred and forty thousand officials resembles a mummy; finances are in a rotten state, the system of taxation imposes too great a burden upon the small man. The middle classes have certainly made material progress; they suffer the more under the pressure exerted by police and censorship, under mismanagement, grandmotherly legislation, and malicious fussiness." Andrian recommends the replacement of this system while there is yet time by developing the trade and professional bodies into a house of representatives and on this basis the creation of an upper house of peers from the ranks of the wealthy nobility. Here is an admirable fragment from Andrian's book: "The citizen may be as jolly as he likes, get drunk, tell obscene stories, read a snippet theatrical journal, even found a cotton factory—but he must show no interest in his parish, his province or the state, or in the important questions of the day, however nearly they may affect his pocket or menace his very existence—he must ignore all this, for fear of causing the gentlemen of the government any inconvenience." Andrian was naturally put under police supervision. His book still rises high above the flood of critical ephemera treating of Austrian conditions, as a remarkable monument of statesmanlike insight. It was obviously influenced by English example and by de Tocqueville, but was not manufactured in dogmatic fashion; rather did it grow out of real patriotism and a true feeling for the needs of an Austro-German State. It had a great effect and undoubtedly influenced the movement for representation, but it did not succeed in leading to such an upheaval of conditions as to produce autonomous self-government. Paralysis had already gone too far.

To be sure, observers who judged Vienna from outside appearances noticed little amiss: the most gracious of all German cities was then the only capital city on the Continent in which European thought was combined with real tradition and an amiable enjoyment of life's pleasures. Old Vienna presented itself as a model to be followed by all other Austrian cities; it was a market-place of races, propagating the Austrian conception of a State. It has grown to greatness as an imperial city and remained one with its "naïve centralism." The court and the nobles spent lavishly; there was no other aristocracy resembling this, the "first specifically Austrian class of humanity." The names were German, Burgundian, Walloon, Polish, Italian, Hungarian or what not. Their owners had possessions and ancestral castles somewhere in the Emperor's dominions, usually in various provinces, so that they were at home everywhere, mixed with one another, were mutually related, matted into a veritable family clique, attached to the Imperial city of Vienna by their style of life, their delight in city pleasures, in German music, and by the dignity of office at court, in the army or the diplomatic service. It was only in this most German court city that the real European cavalier could maintain himself through all change and chance. The Viennese citizen, governed by a mayor who had not been elected but nominated, looked up with reverence to the Imperial house and to this aristocracy; he profited greatly by the generous way of life affected by these great gentlemen and could not take objection to them; he was himself rather a spendthrift than a miser. The Viennese liked to think of himself as free and enlightened; he had to grumble outrageously in any case and talk scandal at his café and the theatre. Educated young men intoxicated themselves with daring witticisms and satirical verses. Everyone was cultivated to the finger-tips, no one had any confidence in the State. In one of his reports, the Bavarian Ministerial Councillor von Herrmann expressed astonishment at the flippancy of the Viennese as regards religion, and at the persistence of the spirit of Josephinism among the middle classes. To be sure, the Court, especially the Imperial princesses, part of the nobility, Prince Metternich himself, thought that more concessions should again be made to the Church. We may well say that Prince Metternich regarded the Neo-Roman movement as a political ally. Although Vienna treated only of ecclesiastical matters with the South German courts of Munich and Stuttgart in the 'forties, yet Austrian policy gained thereby a useful opportunity of interfering in the internal home affairs of these German neighbours. Vienna remained constantly in touch with the higher dignitaries of the Catholic Church there. But it was significant that Prince Metternich preferred extreme "Ultramontanes" to be in Bavaria or anywhere else rather than in Austria; abroad they were graciously encouraged, but it was not unknown for them to be refused a passport to Austria. The Imperial State gladly served the Roman Church, but only inasmuch as she could also be of service to it. The Jesuits, who were given preference in educational posts, were not popular with the middle and lower classes. Things looked ill for the petty citizen and the working-classes, who were just beginning to acquire some education. In 1845, in Vienna, the taxes had to be extorted from more than half the taxpaying artisans by military force. In 1847, the Vienna Penny Club (Kreuzerverein) was founded to secure loans, tools, and raw materials for the small craftsman. There were working-class riots in the hunger years of 1846–47, not only in Vienna, but in several Bohemian cities. The Boys in Caps (Kappelbuben), as the young unemployed were called, were up to ugly tricks in the very heart of the city. The starving and homeless slept in the sewers and in the midst of the thickly-populated district of Mariahilf, it was possible for people to collapse owing to hunger in the open street. There were many educated people, writers, teachers, minor officials, and lawyers' clerks who lived the lives of impoverished working-men. There was a strong Jewish element. Until March 1848 there was a "Jewish Bureau" in Vienna, where Jews strange to the town must report after three days and pay a poll-tax every fortnight. Jews were not allowed at all in the mountain districts and consequently many foregathered in the capital, most of them living in misery and in opposition to all authority. There were terrible memories of the bad times thirty years before, the famine years of 1816–17. At that time, people had endured the scarcity patiently as a dispensation of Providence, without any attempt to rebel against authority and property. Now such crises provoked the spread of Communistic doctrines among the lower classes. In order to secure the food supply in Bohemia, in spite of unemployment and the cessation of work in the factories, Archduke Stephan, then Governor of Bohemia, put through a complete ban on the export of grain—in support of the popularity he so carefully cultivated, "in defiance of all caution." These Austrian export bans of the hunger year 1846–47 deepened the economic gulf that yawned between the Imperial State and the neighbouring German States of the Zollverein (Customs League). Saxony entered a formal protest against the ban and was supported by Prussia. Württemberg, which had already made large purchases of grain in Hungary and wished to get them out of the country in spite of the ban, sent a special Ministerial Councillor to Vienna to negotiate.

Taking it all in all, the social and economic conditions were wretched to the core. Privilege, convention, and prejudice reigned; citizen and peasant were crushed by bureaucracy, a bureaucracy which Metternich himself had once compared to a gimlet: the official bored his way through documents, he perforated them instead of absorbing them. The Land tax, the foundation of the whole system of taxation, had not since 1828 been capable of covering the national debt, the budget for army expenses was nothing like defrayed by it. On account of the prevailing insecurity, capital fled to real estate as an object of speculation and thus the social character of the provincial Diets altered more and more. Many wholesale business men appeared in them, there were also honorary members; on the other hand, the factory workers already made up 9 per cent of the population, in Lower Austria the rate was considerably higher.

The dissemination of communistic teachings was forbidden on pain of death. Nevertheless, W. Weitling was in Vienna as early as 1834 and 1836, but he proceeded with great caution. In a confidential report to Metternich on May 21, 1842, he is described as a good observer, adroit, and adaptable. His writings were, of course, suppressed. Two of his disciples, who as members of the "League of Just Men" (Bund der Gerechten) sought to transform all Germany into a communistic republic, were condemned to death for high treason in Vienna, but reprieved. Metternich was kept in constant touch with the work of the Communist leaders and the closely-woven net of their connections all over Central and Western Europe down to the last detail by his "Naderer," the much-feared police spies.

Up to 1848 there had been two great categories of Austrians —and even the influence of Maria Theresa and Josef II did but little to alter this. The first group, small in numbers, comprised the men who were entitled by birth to a share in the government. The higher official positions belonged by natural right to members of the old aristocratic families—they rose with ease and reached positions of high and universal

influence at an early age. The carrying out of the emancipation of the peasants, for instance, was prevented by the
high aristocracy with landed property because it ran contrary
to their economic interests. It was rare for persons of the
middle classes to reach high position. The upper middle
classes, usually with a freshly-baked title, but socially rele-
gated severely to the "second-class" by the real nobility, were
proud to be allowed to take secondary and minor official
positions; they grumbled in a loyal spirit and hoped one day
to become Court Councillor. A career such as that of Baron
Kübeck or Count Prokesch-Osten was unusual, worthy of
reverent admiration and explicable only by a combination
of unusual good fortune and unusual talents. The second
group in Austria was made up of the hundreds of thousands
who were permitted only "to work, pay taxes, obey the
laws, and put up with ordinances." The great fact of the
last pre-Revolution years is only the conviction: this division
is thoroughly out of date, something new must come. The
opposition had a thousand faces. It lived in the ambitions of
archdukes and in the hatred of struggling workers for grain
and rent profiteers. It created an organ for itself in the Juristic
Political Reading Society, which united all that was vital in
Vienna in the sphere of politics, intellect, learning, and economics and which, with its lectures and discussions grew to be
a kind of parliament of notables. This opposition penetrated
even to the almighty State conference, where Count Kolowrat
was battling against Metternich and his system.

In the year 1813, Emperor Franz, like the fearsome pedant
that he was, had struck out the word "Fatherland" on the
call to his subjects with his own hand and substituted the
word "Emperor." It was a fact that the Emperor owned the
land, it was the family property of the house of Hapsburg-
Lorraine: he thought he could make short shrift with the
"liberty" of the aristocratic classes—and from the ranks of

their relations he would make the "State"—that is, the "police" for internal administration and the army to keep thing together against attacks from without. He who wore the Emperor's coat was the Emperor's property and he had no concern with the nationality, the people, the subject, the citizen in this country which was still nine-tenths agrarian. This Austria, the Great Power of the European East, had grown up in the sign of the Great Power of Turkey—it was not a German unity, as Emperor Josef II had dreamed, but a monarchistic class union, not rationalized as a compound State, but held together as long as might be by the necessities of its component parts, the nimbus of the imperial crown, the raising of "stability" to the status of a vital principle, held together by cunning, by tricks, by a sly compound of laxity and brutality. When once the subjects began to be a people chaos would set in. The Revolution of 1848 was to break the power of the Imperial State—for the first time.

## CHAPTER TWO

# PRUSSIA AS A GREAT POWER

"**P**RUSSIA'S position is very different from that of Austria and Russia, which are independent entities, whereas Prussia is a hybrid, an upstart, and therefore employs the means |by which such upstarts commonly obtain abundant elbow room. The difference in position resembles that between the simple honest citizen and the adventurer, which permits the latter to seek his advantage *per fas et nefas* wherever he can find it."

Prince Metternich used these words in a marginal note on the report submitted to him by Count Trauttmansdorff, Austria's envoy to Berlin, on August 9, 1847. They referred to the action taken by Prussia against her Polish subjects in the matter of the great Polish lawsuit. But they may well be considered as an observation of general application.

If Metternich referred to the Prussian State as an upstart, Prussian policy had for decades furnished him with every excuse. Maria Theresa had honestly detested young Frederick the Great as a kind of adventurer, to whom *fas* and *nefas* were all one, Emperor Josef had doubtless honestly admired Frederick in his old age. But Frederick's Prussia gave Prince Kaunitz a worse time of it than Metternich had later. The position in which the Vienna Congress left Prussia was already somewhat weaker, regarded purely as a potentiality, than that which Frederick had grasped for her. The power of a strong personality could certainly have made good this loss. Only after the experience of the Wars of Liberation did this somewhat colonial and aloof Prussianism become really German. It was the sensation of belonging to the great family of German blood which transformed loyal Prussian subjects into self-sacrificing energetic believers in a State—which, to be sure, existed as yet only in the longing hopes of patriotic hearts.

It is a strange trick of fate that this North-Easterly State organism which against its will became Germany's destiny, should have borne the name of an Eastern European heathen tribe which at some time far back in the dawn of history had been half exterminated and half converted.

They who lived in the heart of the old dominions, in Lower Saxony or Suebia, along the shores of the Rhine or the Main, thought of the Prussians only as a species of Lithuanians or Masurians. The Electors of Brandenburg had purposely set one foot outside their boundaries—they hoped by alliance with Prussia to achieve the same effect as Electoral Saxony had achieved by alliance with Poland: a sovereignty of European significance. We might say that the Brandenburgians came from the old realm to the new by way of Prussia. But it was a roundabout way, and they found it all too difficult and protracted.

If Austria had become a little Europe after 1815, Prussia had become a little Germany. Its hybrid nature had remained, it had in fact become even more indefinite. The actual Prussia, later divided into East and West Prussia and Prussian Poland, known as "the Grand Duchy of Posen," belonged as little to the German Confederation as she had formerly belonged to the old Realm. But through the Saxons, Westphalians, and Rhenish Franconians, the heart of the Frederician great power had received an invaluable success of Germanic thought and strength. The territorial superiority of the Eastern section of the State of Prussia was more than compensated for in the

Western half by a more vital and economically more developed population. Prussia's history in the nineteenth century is that of a battle between West and East, between the German people and princely power and predominance, between the creative citizen spirit and militaristic-bureaucratic commandos, between the democratic will to work and feudal reaction. This must not be understood to mean that the spirit of living development was present only in the west—it was very strongly marked precisely in the further east; but it found more congenial ground and continuous support in the west.

The Imperial State of Austria existed beside Germany and towered above her. But in order to dominate Germany she must necessarily avoid any contact with the idea of German freedom, of German unity. Were these ideas to spread to the numerically superior Slavonic subjects of the Imperial State, it would precipitate the crisis. But it was through assimilating ideas of German freedom and German unity that Prussia had regained her status after her collapse in Napoleonic days. The Prussians had become a people only because they felt themselves to be a living component part of the German nation. The non-German elements in Prussia were not numerically considerable. All the new Prussians of 1815 could only be won permanently for the Prussian State ideal if they were allowed to help bear the burden of the State in peaceful self-determination. The Hohenzollern dynasty could also feel most secure when this was accomplished: the broad masses who shed their blood on the French and German battlefields fought for their own freedom just as much as for the King who had summoned them to battle. There were no more loyal Monarchists than these Prussian Germans. They sacrificed everything for the dynasty; was it too much to expect that the dynasty would now sacrifice something for them?

Emperor Franz had never promised his peoples to grant them a constitution—he therefore had no need to break a pledged word. The events of the Revolution of 1848–49 proved conclusively enough what difficulties lay in the way of creating a comprehensive constitution for the unique political formation known as Austria—difficulties of politics, of race and even of speech which must hinder its operating successfully. Prussia was in a different case. She had been promised a comprehensive constitution, not once, but repeatedly. The great financial edict of October 27, 1810, contained the King of Prussia's first public pledge; the new financial edict of September 7, 1811, contained the second. As early as February 23, 1811, the *Landesdeputiertenversammlung*, the Assembly of Provincial Deputies, was opened as a preliminary to Imperial Diets. From April 1812 to May 1813, from February 1814 to July 1815, the members of the General Commission for the Regulation of the Provincial and Communal War Debts met in Berlin. This body was chosen by the diets of the separate provinces. It begged that a constitution might be granted giving suitable representation to all citizens of all classes. The Cabinet order of June 5, 1814, again, for the third time, promised to grant a constitution and proportional representation. The fourth promise was given in the famous Edict issued by the King on May 22, 1815, published on July 8, 1815, after the Battle of Waterloo. The King solemnly pledged himself for the fifth and last time to call representatives to the Imperial Diets in the edict of January 17, 1820.

As we know, Frederick William III never fulfilled this fivefold promise, in spite of all the efforts of Hardenberg, Humboldt, and Boyen. The first reason for this lay in the King's own nature. Friedrich Wilhelm III had many traits in common with the Kaiser Franz: he, too, felt himself to be the father of his country, and in any case much better able to further the well-being of his subjects than they could judge or even be aware of. Like the Austrian, he was a pedant, who liked to stress the importance of little things, because he had no sympathy with or understanding of, greatness. But Emperor

30

Franz was more artful and more energetic; everything Friedrich Wilhelm the Prussian did was done as slowly as possible;
sometimes he actually hit the mark. People of talent whose
instinct drove them to do the right thing, irritated his monarchical sensibilities and aroused his obstinacy, against which
it was practically impossible to do anything. Absolutism was
in the very blood of this royal philistine: he amused himself
well enough in his sober way, but spoilt other people's enjoyment by his grumbling—often enough the victim was his
first wife, Queen Louise, a splendid woman, full of South
German warmth and fire. He demanded loyalty, obedience,
and self-sacrifice as a matter of course, and treated men of
the people better than his own "servants of the State." As he
grew older his one desire was to be left alone. He was not
really religious, nor conscientious; he had no true sense of
responsibility, political or otherwise; his nature was difficult
and stunted, he was ill-tempered and grumpy. He had nothing
in common with the spirit of the great age of the German
awakening—he came of a different and more unlovely world.
His good subjects would have long enough to wait. He was a
king who thought all ideas of liberty fantastic and Jacobin-
istic; how it delighted him, at Aix-la-Chapelle in 1818, to
read that pronouncement of Prince Metternich in which he
proved that national representation would mean the dissolution of the Prussian State! The Cabinet order of June 11,
1821, decreed a limitation to "Provincial Diets." Something
new was created, both in its constituent parts and in its powers
—not a revival of the old class representation, which would
still have provided something vital, but a representation of
cliques, conventionalized in the most old-fashioned way, an
entirely new body in which aristocrats had an absolute predominance, especially in the Eastern provinces. The condition
of representation was ownership of land! Even in the Rhineland there were fifty-five representatives of the countryside
as against twenty-five from the cities. The family right of

entail was reintroduced in 1826 by a Cabinet order—the educated rising middle class was completely ignored!

Thus Prussia was once again separated from the rest of Germany. No one had a greater interest in this than Metternich's Austrian Imperial State. It was his masterpiece to set Prussia in permanent opposition to the idea of freedom, to the idea of a German Nation. His allies were the Prussian feudal aristocracy and the bureaucracy. The desire for power which consumed the Brandenburgian and Pomeranian squires is probably the decisive and most important factor in the anti-constitutional development of Prussia. Here certainly lay the core of Electoral Brandenburg's strength. In olden days the dynasty had demanded much of them, as did dynasties everywhere, and in return they had demanded and obtained the most important posts in army and administration, and had led the aristocrats of the other provinces along the same track. There was no denying that Prussia owed her position as a great power, a difficult position in itself and very open to attacks from without, mainly to the army. By means of the army, this State had again and again been thrust up and forward beyond its actual possibilities. In Austria, the nobles, the administration, and the army accounted for practically all that was Austrian; there could not very well be an entire Austrian people. In Prussia the nobles, administration, army, being specifically emanations of the old-fashioned Prussian spirit, deliberately prevented the liberating and refreshing alliance with a neo-Prussian-German patriotism.

This aristocracy was not composed of men of the world as was the Austrian, but its roots were more deeply embedded in the soil; the nobles were not at all cosmopolitan and many of them were, in fact, exceedingly provincial; the actual Junkers of Brandenburg and Pomerania understood but little of the German spirit; it was another matter in the Province of Prussia, in Silesia, and especially in the west. The administration was more productive than in Austria, but harder, less imaginative and efficient rather than in any way agreeable. A certain Colonial tone which came from the east pervaded the entire State of Prussia; in Prussian Saxony, but especially in Westphalia and on the Rhine, it was felt that these much schooled and examined lovers of documents were too abrupt, too self-confident, too super-clever; people preferred to be treated more diplomatically, with more regard to their feelings. Even those who respected the sober solidity of these bureaucrats could not with the best will in the world think them amiable. They took themselves seriously with their eternal administration, and it was no joke for anyone else either; they often sought to dissipate their own feeling of inferiority by a boastfulness that was in the worst of taste. The system of secret orders and instructions, the underhand investigations into people's private opinions, and the maddening insistence on petty details, deeply wounded every impulse to free and independent citizenship. The Prussian nobility, being in an absolute majority in all branches of State administration, could retain a relative freshness by a higher standard of living and occasional blood transfusions by marriage; but the petty representatives of the State in army and administration were often especially insufferable—stiff and unteachable, irritating and tactless. There were many, on the other hand, who had a good head on their shoulders, some from non-Prussian courses, sons of the upper middle class, and their administration was fruitful and upright.

A constitution with even approximate popular representation could have smoothed out these differences while there was yet time, could have mitigated much that was harsh and reconciled the spirit of provincialism with the idea of the Prussian State as a whole! Instead of this, the provinces were artificially kept apart. Instead of a unified economic policy which would have used West and East to complement one another, separate interests were encouraged. The financial strength of the State was not utilized to the full. Rising forces were repressed and thus deeply embittered, and everything was done to enhance the arrogance of the ruling classes. The principle of grandmotherly legislation from above was systematically promulgated and so deeply imbued that it took generations to eradicate it.

In spite of having broken his fivefold promise, Frederick William III retained his patriarchal good conscience to the end, upheld by the inborn royal self-assurance with which he supplemented his lack of talent. No patriot could ignore this matter of the constitution. It was the worst factor of the inheritance to which Frederick William IV was now to succeed.

> Grey tomb of German cathedral stone
> Shuts in the high-minded dreamer alone:
> Who hated the facts, as his sword of state
> And paled, as his people waxed and grew great.

Thus Fritz von Unruh, the poet-dramatist, speaks of a "romantic king," in a tomb of rock, where coffins of kings stand side by side.

If Prince Metternich was the destiny of Germany in the days before the Revolution of 1848–49, the Prussian King, Frederick William IV, became Germany's destiny during the Revolution itself. Only with a certain mournful hesitation does the historian touch upon the figure of this unhappy man. Even his contemporaries quarrelled passionately over him; research is still less able to agree.

"You are still, as your sainted mother once described you to me, a prey of the mighty passing moment, and this one fault of yours explains all your other faults," Ancillon once wrote to the young Crown Prince. This Ancillon was that theologian of the French Reformed Church who later, to the delight of Metternich, rose to be Prussian Minister of Foreign Affairs.

"Prey of the mighty passing moment"—it was a fitting

definition. The urge of the moment was always stronger in Frederick William IV than the best impulses in his nature. He allowed himself to be overwhelmed and overpowered by the influences which streamed in upon him—he then felt lifted above himself. Therefore his spoken word was so moving, his letters so spontaneous, warm, and arresting. Every man of feeling discerned a power in this man, the glorious, convincing power of personality. But then came the reaction—after the powerful moment, the powerless one. The same man was then capable of feeble quibbling with himself and others; complainingly he would flee from himself and all his duties, and abandon himself to the pleasure of self-forgetfulness.

This was a king whose rule never extended to his own person. He could be violent, full of noisy wrath, insulting his family and faithful servants, uncontrolled to the point of brutality in word and gesture—and then once more charming, amiable, expansive, scintillating with wit, compelling the admiration even of the serious critic.

It has been pointed out with much justice that the personality of Frederick William IV has features "which the psychiatrist finds in the diagnosis of a reactively labile neurotic." It would certainly be an excellent idea to allow historians and physicians access to contemporary documents and letters about the young Crown Prince, as has been suggested. There have been many neurotics in history and especially on thrones. The physician would simply see in them confirmatory additional matter for his case-book. Rarely does a neurosis such as was discernible from the beginning in the case of Frederick William IV culminate in a mental collapse—for which, in the King's case, there were specific causes. It is enough for the historian to know that Frederick William's nature early caused anxiety to those of his entourage who were capable of forming a judgment upon it; but that really serious symptoms could only be established at a relatively advanced stage. Until after the Revolution period he was merely an eccentric normal person, one of those many border cases which are common enough in the everyday world; people who often achieve astonishing results in intellectual fields, but in spite of the tremendous energy they dissipate, are invariably a fatal influence in business and still more so in politics. Old royal families, like all old families, are particularly rich in such symptoms of intellectual and spiritual degeneration—a fact which has caused much serious reflection in the minds of even convinced monarchists. That Germany's history before the Revolution of 1848–49 and especially during its course, was so largely determined by a royal neurotic, is a tragic historical fact which we are not here to deplore, but rather to expound in all its consequences.

A particularly fruitful source of investigation into the true nature of Frederick William IV is his correspondence with King John of Saxony. King John, who translated Dante under the pseudonym of Philaletes, was probably the only friend Frederick William possessed who was his equal both in rank and intellect. The quick power, the dazzling firework quality of his nature finds expression here as perhaps nowhere else. We of a later generation seem to meet this extraordinary being almost in the flesh in these letters: we see his glittering wit spring breathlessly from one theme to another, pictures and puns tumble over one another until writing is too slow for him and his pen flows into pictures—in charming self-irony he signs his letter with a drawing of a complacent turbot, as symbol of his own broad and clumsy person, ready, however, to roll in homage at a fair lady's feet. This unexampled fertility of feeling and observation continually sought new forms of expression, passing from one language to another, English, Italian, Dutch, even Sanscrit—above all, of course, the courtly French of the period mixed with his own scintillating, breathless German. He delights in witticisms, more delicately pointed than the merciless cockney humour of his coquettishly ironic Berlin dialect jokes are the malicious arrows of wit which he launches, cruelly enough, at all manner of persons and things. Does this man take anything seriously?—we ask ourselves at last, not without a certain perturbation. There is something, however—the great and ancient in history and art.

Things must become venerable by reason of age; a new, lofty truth must come clothed in the pomp of distance, otherwise Frederick William could neither love nor venerate. His relation to art, history, and antiquity was a flight from the present—the world of utilitarian, the "man with a good business head," all that was practical and everyday was to him insufferably tiresome. He was incapable of believing that this dim past had once been a simple everyday world, full of petty toil and tribulation for the men of its age. The false view of the world and of history translated to him by the romantic learning of his day, was to him an urgent spiritual necessity. He never had any conception of true statesmanship. He simply could not understand politics. When Emperor Francis died, in 1835, this Prussian crown prince mourned for "dear, splendid Franz, sometime Roman Emperor and (to my mind something far more inexpressible), the last King of the Teutons." Even as early as this he expressed the idea of reviving the Holy Roman Empire and allying it with the Austrian territories. The French Revolution of 1789 was not a historical event like any other to these princes; truly not the first European revolution and certainly not the last, but something entirely new, an apocalyptic monster, sinning against the established order of the world, disturbing it for the first time since the Creation, churning things up in a most blasphemous manner. The terroristic excesses of the French Revolution had actually aroused such horror in aristocratic Europe that even the younger generation to which Frederick William belonged, never got over it. The idea of a democratic State was wittingly or unwittingly held responsible, averse as democrats were to terror of any kind; as long as he lived, the idea of a democratic State constitution seemed to Frederick William nothing more than a French atrocity, which should be confronted by something firmly rooted in German soil. No German patriotism prevented the German princes of their day from slavishly and abjectly copying the absolutism of Louis XIV. Why should not the middle classes learn something from France in their turn? In reality, however, democracy was a European phenomenon, just as much as absolutism, or as feudalism had been in its day; these were forms of political common life at which all European peoples had laboured, each transforming the fundamental idea according to its own national conception. Frederick William IV had no idea that the democratic idea which he attacked so hotly was considerably more "Christian-Germanic" than the Divine Right of Kings of which he felt himself to be such an enthusiastic representative.

Frederick William IV was defenceless against all complicated political individual problems. He revelled in generalities and generalizations. At first he busily attacked the whole mass of work, but was impatient of detail and so repelled by the actual business aspects that he thrust the whole thing aside, hastily and fearfully. He never took the trouble to think anything out, but took refuge in impromptu which were usually brilliant rather than wise. Just as he would try to remedy the lack of clarity in his letters by his notorious habit of underlining, so in conversation he resorted to gestures and embraces. He liked to discuss things with far too many people, gave credence to contradictory points of view and finally took some action for which neither he nor anyone else was prepared and yet adhered to his original opinion, the more firmly, the more impossible its practical realization. Leopold von Gerlach wrote of him in 1847: "He sticks to his principles, never gives them up and trusts to them so firmly that he is completely indifferent as to when, how or by whom they

are put into execution." It never occurred to any of his contemporaries to mistake this sterile obstinacy for statesmanlike
energy. On the contrary, it was the best proof of the helplessness of the King when brought up against anything concrete
and practical; his weakness, sometimes almost pathetic, when
confronted with the necessity of making a decision, took
refuge in the world of ideas in which he was at home, and
he helped himself out of the dilemma by preaching and
writing fulsomely about this sacred *Weltanschauung*. Thus in
all his sparkling variations of thought he continually returned
to the same point, to the horror of practical politicians. This
habit of fleeing the commonplace must necessarily lead him
into the fault of self-deception. The worldly-wise Prince
Metternich remarked pointedly enough that the King's
enthusiasm was more dangerous to himself than to others.
Thus he lived happily enough in a world that was more and
more of his own creation, soaring above the trivial and
more annoyed by some disturbing truth than by the pious-
impious deception practised upon him by those who suited
themselves to his mood. All research has always emphasized
the artist in the man; but we need only compare this tasteful
rhetorician and sketcher with a true creative artist, to realize
the difference. He possessed neither seriousness, concentration
nor energy directed to a definite end. He never gave himself
wholly and without reserve to any great matter. It seemed
quite natural to him that people should devote themselves to
him, that Germany should believe as he did and do as he
would; he expected nothing else and felt misunderstood
if it failed to happen. Frail as he was, his self-confidence
never failed him; he was at once stubborn and elastic. His
words were fiery, but when he was misunderstood he
could be as hard and malicious as a creator destroying
his imperfect creation. Continually occupied with his own
complicated person, he confounded State and monarch
more completely than any absolutist, and thus his hyper-

sensitive dynastic vanity regarded every idea of reform as high treason.

Whether this highly-gifted man was best at speech-making, letter-writing or sketching it is hard to say. Thousands of his drawings are preserved in the Berlin Castle Library—for the most part southern landscapes, done in the cool north with a pen inspired by longing—pseudo-antique renaissance, "ideal" scenes, full of temples, fountains, and sacred groves, complete with altar and sphinx—expanses of clear sky, wide stretches of sea: the visions of a restless brain, striving to escape from the hideousness of everyday. He was fond of building and his deepest preoccupation was his cathedral—the cathedral he imagined but never finished building, an edifice which was to soar from the shore of the river Spree in Berlin and dominate its entire surroundings, a "church city" like St. Peter's in Rome. It was to be a symbol of Christian universality, constructed of course with an eye to the past, with basilica, cupola, campo santo, majestic plethora of pillars, with triumphant arches over the vaulted apse.

The natural self-consciousness of an intellectually brilliant Crown Prince, who found it particularly easy to shine in his sober Prussian surroundings, swelled in him after he became king into an inflated faith in the revelation of majesty so that Frederick William IV was separated to an unearthly and completely unhealthy degree from the facts of the nineteenth century. It has rightly been emphasized that this fervent faith in Divine Right was confined to his period of kingship—it was not just a theory, but so dangerous and irrefutable precisely because it endured and perpetuated itself as a spontaneous spiritual emotion. Thus this man, personally of simple tastes and no friend of ceremony, cultivated a belief that since he was now "the Lord's Anointed," things must be known to him which he had not known as Crown Prince. He therefore treated his ministers with studied contempt as irresponsible tools, believed himself to be always in the right, in spite of all patent lack of success, and imagined that whatever he did, however contradictory, must somehow be mystically imbued with meaning and sure of a deeper effectiveness. He enjoyed being a king and resented grumbling criticism.

"Perhaps he had more feeling than a State can stomach," said Leopold von Ranke, in his biography of Frederick William IV in the *Allgemeine Deutsche Biographie*, and this shows how even the critically-minded may be blinded by the magic spell of this mysteriously shimmering personality. Feeling, strong receptivity for the eternal values of humanity, was for Frederick William predominantly a matter of intellect and taste; he was warm-hearted and emotional, to be sure, but of too divided a mind to be genuine in his feelings. There was always something unearthly about him, an element of the incalculable; and though he loved to feel cosy and comfortable, other people seldom had such emotions in his presence. His charity towards the lower orders certainly deserves to be warmly recognized. "You cannot tread these people underfoot," he once said. But in 1830, at the time of the troubles in Dresden, he advised his friend Johann to have nothing to do with the "rabble" and to suppress the "canaille" by military measures. There was a good deal of arrogance in his form of welfare work—the people were to feel the King's gracious mercy, but to remain properly humble. What the "people" were really like and what they wanted, Frederick William IV never understood.

Treitschke called him the greatest of all amateurs. Real amateurs are usually less mischievous than this monarch. One cannot even say that he naïvely overrated any of his numerous talents. His mastery as an orator, sketcher and letter-writer was far above all amateur standards. A current of human energy pulsed in him as in few of his contemporaries. The effect of his personality was always electrifying, even upon convinced opponents. Everything that characterized the amateur—pathetic helplessness, restless gratefulness for indulgent recognition, foolish pride—was lacking in him. Whatever happened the King always made a relatively rapid recovery; he could throw off unpleasant experiences as if they were bad dreams. "I'm looking for the King," his clever, kindly wife, Bavarian Elisabeth, used to say, whenever he lost his balance, as he so often did. It was hard to see the monarch in him then—he alone never ceased to believe in the superiority of his kingship.

Frederick William IV has often been compared with a later Hohenzollern sovereign, and the contemporaries who in 1894 first read the splendid fifth volume of the *Deutsche Geschichte*, thought they had discovered a most destructive indictment of the young Emperor Wilhelm II. Treitschke may have wished to draw a certain analogy: but the comparison is unjust to both princes. Only the outward outline of an eternal urge to speech-making and increasing inability to work is common to both of them. Frederick William IV had a much richer, deeper nature than William II, he had an inborn artistic taste and fascinated important personalities of every kind when he chose to be amiable, because he was himself a man of personality. William II, on the contrary, may have had better political instinct, but unfortunately he had neither the courage of his own opinions nor respect for superiority in others. He differs from Frederick William IV as the technician from the artist; he was narrower, more one-sided and actually blighted with the curse of the eternally dissatisfied amateur, whose unfruitful flurry he sought to conceal behind grandiose royal gestures. Politically, Frederick William IV was far more unfortunate than William II; for whereas the last German Emperor had practically retired long before the World War and allowed men and things to take their course as they would, Frederick William IV always attempted to do everything himself, right up to the time of his mental breakdown, and really took his own decisions; Wilhelm II's later reign was more like a regency.

The best thing in Frederick William IV was undoubtedly his artistic sympathies. But his taste was historical rather than creative. His soundest piece of architecture was his little castle of Charlottenhof, which he built as Crown Prince. It is more harmonious than its creator, who was always endangered by the dark forces latent within him. His later buildings were loud, empty, prone to false pomp. In his buildings a prince betrays his own character. What he did for art and intellect was not done in any modern spirit. Cornelius, Tieck, Schelling were long past their best in the 'forties. That old Arndt was dug out of his retreat and given his professorship at Bonn once more was certainly rather the fulfilment of a duty of respect than a contribution to learning. But we owe warm thanks to the King for his patronage of Dahlmann and the Brothers Grimm, of Lepsius, and the founding of the Verdun prize for Art and Science; but this again is outweighed by such acts of intolerance as the removal from office of the patriotic poet, Hoffmann von Fallersleben and the persecution of Nauwerck on account of his political convictions. Frederick William IV referred to this progressive philosopher as a "patented revolutionary" and decreed: "In Prussia no revolutionary can find a refuge under the wings of the government."

Frederick William IV had many pietists among his personal friends and probably considered himself to be a deeply religious man. At least he took pains to be thought so. But the malicious satirist who played so lightheartedly with the feelings of others and with all they held sacred, who had so little regard for the personal dignity of his fellow men, must certainly be set free from any suspicion of being truly religious. Naturally this does not prevent his having been an energetic reformer of the Church, in fact it seems to be a natural corollary. He dreamed of a New Evangelical Church with the Prince-Bishop of Magdeburg as Primas Germaniae and about three hundred and fifty Prussian bishops. This church of the future was to serve the General Synod which he proposed to create. In reality, Frederick William IV was never touched by the real spirit of Protestantism. He took pleasure in tangled theological studies and projects, buried himself in the problematics of apostolic Christianity and completely lost touch with the problems and troubles of his own time. But he felt himself so inspired by the consciousness of his Divine Right, so close to Deity, that he could envisage himself as creator of a divinely-ordered State, administered by the children of light. Such fantastic dreams could only harm the true historic spirit of Protestantism. Towards the Catholic Church the King, blinded by its organization and its artistic splendours, was all too indulgent and uncritical. The "Catholic Section" in the Ministry of Culture (1841) was the fruit of this attitude.

Frederick William IV was the first monarch since Frederick the Great to live again in Sanssouci—no Hohenzollern dared it again after him and it was mockingly said of him that he was "trying to imitate Old Fritz." In reality no stronger contrast could be imagined. The cold, proud agnosticism of the great king, his hard, ruthless policy of conquest were alien to Frederick William's very soul. His final dream was of a universal Europe and in this Europe, organized and made peaceful on a Christian plan, there was to be a great, mighty Germany, rejuvenating under an emperor, who was to compel the world to peace without bloodshed. This Prussian king had an unmilitary nature and was the only Hohenzollern monarch who did not pose as an army chieftain. During manoeuvres as Crown Prince, to be sure, he could be so fiery that the old generals protested; but when it came to criticism, he was as brilliant as ever. He loved military music, glittering weapons and salvos of salutes; but the thunder of the cannon must be suitably remote from his delicate nervous system. He once persisted with his manœuvres right into the streets of Berlin, so that hundreds of window-panes were shattered by the concussions. After he became king, he was less and less interested in the military, not only because it "bored" him, but also because he was willing to cede this field of activity to the jealous Prince of Prussia. His wing-adjutant von Manteuffel

once endeavoured to persuade him to take more interest in
military affairs, whereupon he retorted: "Would you have
me break with Wilhelm altogether?" His political view of the
world was based upon a false conception of mediaevalism.
If he thought to assign to the King of Prussia the rôle of
Grand Field-Marshal of Germany in this neo-ancient Europe,
this was really over-modest in face of the Austrian Imperial
State which stood in such power beside and above Germany.
But the other German princes were inclined to find it all too
ambitious. Frederick William IV never realized that any
strong German policy of that day must necessarily be directed
primarily against Russia and then against Austria. German
policy in the middle of the century was not only a home but
also a foreign problem. Metternich conducted it as a policy
of reaction and the holy alliance. If Prussia continued to bow
to this she could not mean much more as a State than Bavaria
or Hanover.

Liberalism, the great opponent of Metternich in Europe,
was as terrible to Frederick William IV as the Scarlet Woman
of the Apocalypse; it was therefore practically impossible for
the Prussian king to undertake a change of foreign policy,
such as an alliance with England against Russia, in accordance
with the ruling oppositional forces in world policy, although
he was fond of playing with such a possibility. Here we find
the foreign and home policy of the revolutionary period
entwining into a significantly unique complex of conflicting
forces.

These circumstances also gave the constitutional problem
in Frederick William's Prussia such unusual weight. Anti-
constitutional Prussia was a sure ally of Russo-Austrian policy.
Any concession to the "spirit of the age" must endanger the
"system." The Prussian king was bound to Nicholas I, his
brother-in-law, by a warm feeling of friendship, consolidated,

after the fashion of the time, by a solemn vow of loyalty taken in 1818. After the death of the old King Frederick William III, the correspondence of the two brothers-in-law, which had been subject to long pauses, acquired a new political significance. Nicholas I began to regard himself as the guardian of "Papa's" political inheritance and tried to influence the new king in this spirit. Frederick William III had attempted to nullify his fivefold public promise to create a constitution by a clause in his will, written in his own hand, but neither signed nor corrected. It therefore could only have the character of a draft. The old king ordered that any alteration in political conditions should only be undertaken with the agreement of all his agnates and that the promised "National diets" should if necessary be replaced by a commission composed of thirty-two representatives of the provincial diets and thirty-two members of the National Council! This truly reactionary statute of Frederick William III was a useful weapon in the hand of the Russian emperor against the filial-minded son. He demanded the publication of the "testament"; he protested against Frederick William's plan of developing the provincial diets into national diets, and he succeeded in procrastinating the course of matters to a dangerous extent. In his letter of December 31, 1844, the King tried to convince his imperial brother-in-law of his own wishes: no constitution, no periodical diets, no elections. Frederick William declared that he was bound by none of the former promises, except the statute of the national debt of 1820, which he called the *grand malheur*, but of which they must take the consequences. His purpose was: to abolish the law of 1815 and all that was inconvenient in the law of 1820 by royal proclamation; to unite the eight provincial diets and grant important rights to this body, "these rights to be circumscribed by the inviolable and unalterable barrier of the rights of the Crown." At the close of this letter, Frederick William raised the question: "What have I to gain?" He thought he perceived a double advantage: "(1) What every human being must gain by an act of justice"—(for in the old kingdom the diets had the right to grant taxes, in Westphalia as late as 1806)—and (2) The pacification of public opinion—in that the promises given formerly will now be fulfilled: the sickness, caused by the "mad Hardenberg legislation" must be healed, "the medicine swallowed."

Nowhere else did Frederick William IV speak out so plainly as to his actual motives. Repugnant as all this was to him, and however he might try to find new interpretations—he could not and would not deny the compulsion of the old obligation. The provincial diets were there, apparently awakened to new life; in reality they were a new creation, romantically linked to shadowy institutions of olden days; to unite them was something entirely new, it was a kind of repetition of historical developments of centuries before—nothing could be more satisfactory to the King of Prussia. He imagined that he had found a unique way out, suitable to the peculiar character of the Prussian State.

When the Federal Diet (*Vereinigte Landtag*) first met, great hopes were set upon Count Arnim-Boitzenburg, formerly Minister of the Interior, with whom the King had parted because he wished to take a clear path in constitutional policy. Now, too, he declined the office of President of the Landtag, because he still considered a representative assembly with two chambers to be the only possible and desirable system. Arnim was not by any means a liberal, as he had often proved during his periods of office; but he had the political instinct and told himself from the beginning that the King would never be able to carry out the work he had begun unless he made concessions. At the beginning of the negotiations it seemed as if this high official (who was nothing if not official) had "the Diet in his pocket." He was adroit in the employment of formalities and thus likely to win the inexperienced assembly to his side. But it soon appeared that his continual attempts at mediation, his sleek arguments, retarded rather than accelerated the political impetus of the *Landtag*. He tired the members out, he bored them and his prestige waned. His epigrams and aphorisms merely gave the impression that he was wasting his considerable talent.

"Among the few speakers who took the Government view and represented the King's will as expressed in the Patent, a young man named von Bismarck distinguished himself most conspicuously and was noted as likely to prove a prominent figure in later assemblies. His firm and vigorous dialectics deeply wounded Herr von Vincke, for instance, and actually led to a challenge, which was, however, abortive, as the matter was settled by mediation." These words, written home on June 6, 1847, by General von Schäffer-Bernstein, the Berlin Chargé d'Affaires of the Grand Duchy of Hesse, are a remarkable witness to the personal impression created by young Otto von Bismarck-Schönhausen, member of the second Curie. He was destined politically to decorate his victories with the very ideas which he was at this time attacking so energetically. Indeed, it cannot be said that this hot-headed manner of combat did the King's cause much good; the King felt this himself, and quite rightly. Bismarck's bizarre subjectivity rather tended to steel the liberal leaders in their belief in the mighty demands raised by the age which they served.

Bismarck earned from his friends the honourable title of "the Vincke-biter." The Westphalian leader Georg von Vincke, an aristocrat like himself, was perhaps the strongest figure in the Federal Diet, a defender of right against might, a figure of power and true manliness such as Germany has seldom seen; personally he was hot-tempered, touchy and difficult, not adaptable enough to command speedy successes, but a born people's representative, a man carved out of oak; like a rugged bit of Gothic in real life. His massive, stocky figure revealed a man who enjoyed the good things of life;

there was a sly twinkle in his light, keen eyes, he was always ready to spring to the attack upon lack of clarity, sentimentality, prattle, and above all, injustice. To borrow one of his own excellent metaphors, he "ploughed the field of justice" as no one else could. The spirit of the War of Liberation was still alive in this man—indeed it seemed to have been re-kindled in the ranks of the United *Landtag*. This time the King had not had any intention of summoning the people, but the people had come. They spoke from the lips of a man like Vincke, whose ancestors had lived with the people and for the people for hundreds of years; inheritance, tradition, a given word and their native customs were sacred powers to them, now urging upward to take on new forms. Vincke's eloquence poured from him in a sparkling stream, rapid, often too voluble even for this long-suffering age, but coloured, powerful, persuasive. Proud and pliable, a fighter and a prophet, a daring mocker and a solemn judge, Vincke was great and independent, rather an inspiring force and a leader than a creator. A nobleman shaken out of his traditions by the spirit of history to become a citizen of the State, he was a real old German personality, full of contradictions, a stranger to Prussia and doomed to a final infertility. In this he reminds us of Freiherr von Stein, whom he quoted in a famous speech at the Westphalian Provincial Diet of 1845, when demanding National Diets. He said that to offer the excuse that National Diets had been promised, but no time set for their establishment, was, in Stein's own words, "a revolting piece of Machiavellism."

Vincke worked with the Rhinelanders, but often against them; he was a man in his own right and not a tool of Rhenish activities. The Court and bureaucracy of Berlin were doubtless somewhat astonished at being confronted for the first time by considerable burghers who were sure of themselves, full of knowledge, industrious, and successful. There was Camphausen, thoughtful and brooding, a good calculator, enterprising, cautious and just, thorough and accurate, a man who acted according to the lessons of experience, full of strength and originality, independent of doctrines, regarding men and their talk with a certain scepticism, moving forward with a sure but careful step, a tall upright figure, still lit with a gleam of the philosophic age, but already in the happy beginnings of creative civic toil. He saw, plain and close before him, the goal of a free German citizenship: everything he did for the development of railways, of customs duties, of the freedom of the press, was really directed towards this end. He was full of dignity, a figure to command respect, standing for the useful and the purposeful, a patriot with fine feelings, moved to demand the right of a State to develop individuality; therefore he wished that Prussia should stand on her own feet, but in harmony with Europe and with the spirit of the age. What Camphausen said was always clear and firm, deliberate but significant and assured, to the point, a little pallid like his own calm features, sometimes a little sharp, but always proud and therefore not enkindling and powerful. Only a touch was missing to have made a statesman of Camphausen, but it was the decisive touch: the spark of passion from the deeps which can move men to the highest.

A man who was practical in quite another fashion than Ludolf Camphausen was David Hansemann: he, also a successful merchant, was made of sterner stuff. He was the type, just being developed, of a lord of industry, used to resolute issuing of orders, a sober thinker, always reckoning, risen to power through calculation and speculation and therefore inclined to present his bill to the State. Hansemann was a lively orator, quite free of the prevailing style, which had inherited from literature a tendency to pomposity. He rattled along in somewhat slovenly fashion, made jokes, appeared more comprehensible and good-natured than he really was, enjoyed clever and witty opposition. He was carefree and decisive, a convincing realist, a utilitarian, always ready to compromise in order to achieve a real result. His energy and cleverness were often a blessing to the Diet; he was a master of proverbial phrases and liked to appeal to common sense. Hansemann knew Western Europe well and on account of his book *Prussia and France*, he was supposed to be a one-sided friend of the institution and way of living favoured by the July King. This was an injustice to this sharp-witted connoisseur of international finance; he had a fine sense of psychological distinctions and showed his instinct for politics by warning Prussia to abandon her isolated position as fifth European great power, and become instead the protector of the smaller Central European states, while preserving a defensive attitude towards the others. Naturally he was in favour of a straightforward constitutional system; he had been for rejecting the patent of February 3rd altogether and having nothing to do with the *Vereinigten Landtag*. His sense of precision, practical work, solid comprehensibility, was deeply wounded. Nevertheless, he was one of the most frequent speakers in the Diet—no orator with great principles to defend or a very scholarly programme, but master of terse, pithy remarks and adroit amendments, a parliamentary tactician of a high order who liked to impart information in a humorous way and always held the ear of the house. His pamphlet addressed to Frederick William IV in 1830, demanding parliamentary usages, proves that he was also a man of courage. It was printed as a manuscript for the members of the 8th Rhenish Provincial Diet in 1845.

Prince Felix Lichnovsky held a curious position in the Federal Diet. He was the scion of an Austrian family which had always been rich in unusual personalities, the son of a Hungarian mother. An amusing chatterer, an author, man of the world and philanderer, he was really out of place in a Prussian atmosphere. Being a Silesian landowner, he took the part of the unfortunate and persecuted weavers in the Diet; knowing the ways of most Western European parliaments, he became the Diet's master of ceremonies; a Catholic on the best terms with the Vatican, a Legitimist in the Spanish Civil War, he enjoyed being in the opposition; his interpolations, always elegantly couched, were often expertly informed, always wittily phrased and full of interest. He was extremely friendly with the Duchess of Sagan, a clever woman of great political gifts, with whom the King at one time also enjoyed discussing serious questions; such a friendship must necessarily be useful, especially for a man about whom a nimbus of adventure shone and who, in his own daring fashion, did everything possible to preserve the belief that he was a dangerous character. With but few exceptions, the diplomatic corps refused to have anything to do with the prince; but this did not trouble him, he passed from one group to another, feeling himself first everywhere and exceeding even his vanity by his inborn gracious charm. He was a man of many talents and many languages, could do many things well and dispose easily of cheap criticism, but he never succeeded in being taken as seriously as he deserved.

We have no intention of recounting the history of this United Diet; its life began with a lack of harmony; soon there was open hostility; only with difficulty could the rupture between Crown and Diet be avoided. There were quarrels about finance, about the Crown's broken promises—the Government certainly did much to facilitate the task of the Opposition. As Metternich wrote sarcastically: "Why did the King ever bring the thing to life? Was it so that it might hear his will? He had no need to summon a class diet for that. As matters are, the summoning of the diet seems to be in the nature of a bad joke."

Only a decisive move towards true constitutionalism could perhaps have saved Prussia from the shock of revolution.

While the Federal Diet was entertaining Berlin as it had

never been entertained before, with brilliant pageants, the splendour of the Court, receptions, balls, "assemblies" and other festive occasions—all this time social conditions among the lower classes in the growing capital were such that the so-called "Potato Revolution" broke out.

On April 21st, the President issued a decree postponing the payment of the milling tax temporarily until August 1st on account of "the quite extraordinary rise in prices." Before this fact had become known, there had been scenes of disorder at the markets. The potato merchants abused the public because people refused to buy on account of the high prices. Plundering took place and the excited crowd also began to loot shops. Police and military patrols seemed to be powerless: then the Alexander Regiment, a battalion of the Franz Regiment and the curassiers of the guard were called out. The cavalry were supposed to use only the flat of their swords but, irritated by stone-throwing, they began to use their blades on the crowds. In the morning of April 22nd, whole processions from the suburbs streamed into the centre of the city, shouting "Revolution!" and plundering shops of every kind. No work was done, business was at a standstill, schools and theatres remained closed. The Prince of Prussia called a council of war in his palace: a regular plan for the military occupation of the city was contemplated. The crowd smashed windows and mirrors at the Prince's palace. But the actual military headquarters were at the Castle. The whole garrison were mobilized, except the artillery. General von Prittwitz was in command. A barricade had been set up in Bischof's Street and the fusiliers took it by storm. Up to the 24th, military patrolled the city. Gradually things quietened down again. The weekly open-air markets were held under military protection—an odd spectacle. Herr von Puttkamer, the police-president, who really could not have accomplished much with his force of thirty gendarmes, was roundly abused by the Prince of Prussia and dismissed on the grounds that he had been lacking in initiative and decision. The citizens had, with a few exceptions, put up with a good deal—they feared organized rebellion of the workers, were excited by political speeches, and a great many doubtless sympathized with the rioters, whose main incentive was obviously hunger. The city authorities had furnished certain citizens with white armlets and they had attempted to pacify the crowds. Mayor Naunyn even proposed to one of the ministers, von Bodelschwingh, that the inefficient police should be supplemented by "constables" with white armlets and strong cudgels as permanent organs to protect persons and property in the event of attack. The official curtly rejected the well-meant plan; the mayor pointed out that this uncompromising attitude could lead to no good and that the minister was taking a great responsibility upon himself. The Police-president's mediation did not help. The police state feared to jeopardize its monopoly of power by granting even a modest measure of independent self-government to its citizens. Yet the Mayor of Berlin had emphasized with almost exaggerated loyalty that the citizens wished to act "in the most complete co-operation with the government and the police"; it was a matter of providing "protection for the propertied class against those without property"—in other words, against the proletariate.

How many proletarians were there in Berlin at this time? From 1815–47, the population of Berlin had risen from one hundred and eighty thousand inhabitants to over four hundred thousand—as many as in Vienna, but less than London, Paris, Constantinople, and St. Petersburg. The number of factory workers of both sexes, casual labourers and merchants' apprentices is stated to have been about forty to fifty thousand. There were about twenty thousand apprentices to handicrafts and rather more domestic servants of both sexes; the garrison was about fifteen thousand. The royal residential capital with strong military admixture which had been Berlin's aspect at the beginning of the nineteenth century had thus already been transformed. To be sure, anyone going from the Castle down unter den Linden still saw the little old city—a larger Potsdam, a smaller St. Petersburg, dynastic, stiffly erect, somewhat cold and cuttingly arrogant, but elegant, refined after its fashion and a complete world in itself, seat of the Prussian ruling dynasty with the somewhat strained and self-conscious stiffness of the Frederick the Great tradition.

Vienna at this period had far more unity of bourgeois character. Berlin was a special case of a great city. Different classes lived by themselves, as much strangers to and suspicious of one another as the quarters in which they lived. The spirit of the old State was antagonistic to a plan, to admixture, to growing up together. What a gulf yawned between the porcelain elegance of the wide street under the linden-trees with the elegant carriages enamelled in various colours, from a glance at which every errand-boy could recognize the aristocratic family within—with the well-drilled watch parade, its fashionable Kranzler café where the great world took cakes and coffee—and the starchy military quiet of the Kreuzberg, or the terrible blocks of slum tenements in the North of the city where the poor cloth-weavers lived. Berlin was a melting-pot for the Eastern provinces—there was something of Stettin, Königsberg, Posen, Breslau about the city; it attracted the population from the eastern provinces of Prussia, while a feeling of estrangement from the capital began as far north as Prussian Saxony and increased to direct dislike in the western half of the kingdom. Very little migration from the west came to the capital at this period and scarcely any at all from the south. They who came from the heart of Germany to this quickly-swollen city could feel all the gaps in its development; something sudden, artificial, trashy, loud, parvenu, a painfully evident mixture of the pretentious and the threadbare. The public buildings were imposing, to be sure, or at least solid, respectable buildings—the palaces in the Linden quarter, the splendid Schinkel architecture, the older churches, especially the Protestant cathedral—what a contrast they were to the cheap and tasteless building that went on in the north and east, where dull, straight rows of streets, badly paved, seldom cleaned and without a trace of green petered out into barren wastes of sand. In between there were still occasional charming quiet corners left over from former days. Characteristic of this lack of steady natural growth was the rarity of good inns in Berlin. There were a few relatively luxurious and splendid hotels—and then plenty of small inns and taverns of very poor quality. There was a lack of good, comfortable old hostelries with a tradition of good service and cosy hospitality. There were innumerable shoddy furnished rooms. The restaurants were in somewhat better case. Jagor was famous, Lutter and Wagner still flourished, but the old-fashioned beer-halls, where Berlin's native "white beer" was dispensed, were being displaced by the growing popularity of Bavarian beers.

Berlin was an Eastern capital, on the periphery of all things German, often visited in passing by the Prussian nobility, but permanently lived in by very few of them. It was the home of a small class of merchants and tradespeople who were steadily growing richer and more prosperous, but burdened more and more heavily by terrible poverty among the masses which set the city administration many a difficult problem. The number of the inhabitants rose by 30 per cent from 1841–50, but the expenses of the poor-box by 63 per cent. Looking after the poor swallowed up nearly 40 per cent of the city's budget. Over six thousand people received alms in the course of a year, the annual grant to each being twenty-four thalers and fourteen silver groats. In addition to this, soup was distributed as well as bread tickets and free grants of land for growing potatoes. There were also charitable societies. But the impoverishment of the small craftsman could not be checked by such means. It was the outcome of a deep-seated redistribution of society which was felt in Berlin with peculiar severity. A proposal was once made in the Berlin City Council that an attempt should be made to discourage destitute workmen from coming to Berlin by making citizenship a condition of permission to carry on a trade—a proposal characteristic of the difficulties in which the great city was becoming more and more involved.

"Berlin is a magnet which attracts poverty," wrote the *Allgemeine Zeitung* on May 9, 1847. Thus the Prussian capital became the home of crass contrasts; all the political battles of the country which were fought out here, were embittered by the influence of the local atmosphere.

But this city, which had to struggle so much harder than any other in Germany, developed precisely on this account an elasticity of spirit which was to become unique. It was the true spirit of a great city, alien to sentimentality and over-emotionalism, to smugness and highfalutin romanticism. Its people looked facts in the face with an impudent grin, worked hard and skilfully, had a ready humour with a bite in it, were quick and adaptable, always ready to take the rough with the smooth, extremely critical but hard-headed, healthy, strong, hardy, thrifty. No one could get the best of the Berliner; but he was an honest fellow, whose candour, cheerfulness and cheek were refreshing and disarming. At heart, the spirit of this city was related to the best and most creative forces active in Germany at the time, with its determined criticism of hollow traditions and of the affected, hypocritical vampires of the State, the Church, and the upper classes.

The people of Berlin were not credulous and could see through empty oratory as quickly as the best; they did not like to be thought gullible and simple and were always ready to prove the contrary with good-tempered insolence. Their wit was sometimes so caustic that that warm heart behind it was effectively hidden. Only people with their wits about them and no finicking ways could hold their own in Berlin, and thus it happened that many who had been irresistibly drawn by its lure could find no good word for the capital. It was not an easy city to understand as it went on developing into the only world city of the German tongue, and it has retained this characteristic. It has remained a city of contrasts, combining the spirit of Frederick the Great and the eighteenth century with that of the modern revolutionary, at once dynastic and democratic, arrogant and liberal; the home of quiet research and shrieking sensationalism; a temple of art and a palace of shoddy; adoring the military, yet cosmopolitan, rural and pioneer; a compound of all German, and even all European possibilities; and thus for a wideawake child of his age, an inexhaustible forum of thought and action. The Berlin spirit was ironically critical of itself and therefore immune to criticism from outside. The best feature of its people was this touch of greatness; never to be irascible or easily insulted, always in good-humour, not hesitant, but not too rough; tackling opponents and problems with determination but without wrath.

Its contemporaries found something "Babylonian" about Berlin—it was a wild mixture of types and dialects; Berlin's own dialect became fixed in literature about this time through the medium of farces and humorous periodicals—which was just what it needed to secure its development into the speech of a world-city. The Berliner became a special breed of Prussian, modelled by the capital out of the Eastern European provincial immigrant. But as Berlin grew, so the difference increased between the nature of the Berliner and that of the other Prussians. The strong French element introduced by the settlers who had fled to Berlin because of their faith may have had a great part in its composition, so may the Jewish element. The Prussian in the mass was heavy, unimaginative, unintellectual; but the Berliner became lively, proud of being educated, rejoicing in his freedom; he found common ground with all that was best in the spirit of Breslau, Stettin, or Königsberg; and thus Berlin became the forcing-ground of the super-clever middle-class spirit of opposition which seemed so inconvenient, even annoying and dangerous to the tradition-bound Prussian State.

In their drawing-rooms these Berliners learned to handle philosophy, literature, and the theatre in paradoxical speech, playfully intellectual, springing lightly from these to them; but they were not only amusing, they cultivated independent judgments and delivered their criticisms of state and society. Bettina von Arnim began by adoring Goethe and ended as a student of pauperism—there was something symbolic in this development. The old ties, cemented by ancestry, class, fortune, were in process of dissolution. People sought new communities in order to discuss the political and social needs of the day. There was, as yet, no such thing as public opinion—it was represented by the semi-publicity of leagues and clubs, meetings in confectioners' and reading-rooms. If Kranzler was the haunt of society, Stehely and Spargnapani were the liberal café clubs, merchants met at Courtin's—but at Fuchs', which was *Unter den Linden*, there was already a kind of cabaret, performing little farcical sketches with political allusions.

An especially characteristic feature of the age was the *Zeitungshalle*, the Newspaper Reading Room founded in 1846 by Gustav Julius. Beginning as a reading-room it developed into a meeting-place of opposition spirits, especially during the sittings of the Federal Diet. People of all classes met there, to make acquaintances, discuss affairs of the day and deliver orations. There was real life in this, political passions ran high —all they needed was to get out into the open air.

No one in England thought for a moment of entering upon an entente with Austria and Russia; many political thinkers both on the English and German side thought better of the prospects of an entirely different combination—an Anglo-Prussian alliance. General von Canitz, Prussian Foreign

Minister, had raised the question of such an alliance as early as 1840, but afterwards became more sceptical about it and in the years immediately preceding the Revolution, he was among those who preferred to cling to the alliance of the three Eastern powers. Frederick William IV had an outspoken preference for the England of the High Church and the Tories. He wrote once to Canitz, "The Whigs are lousy rascals and always will be!!!"—thus demonstrating his absolute blindness to the growth of a modern England. He was enamoured of an England of aristocratic tradition, majestic ecclesiastical organization and ivy-covered ancestral seats, he knew scarcely anything of an England of world-wide mercantile speculation and of coal mines. As godfather to the Prince of Wales, later King Edward VII, he had enjoyed the comfortable splendour of English life, which, free from bureaucratic pedantry and barren militarism, flattered his instinct for art and luxury. The toasts heard at this christening had a political flavour: England and Prussia were to mean something to one another. Queen Victoria and the Prince Consort paid their return visit, to the Rhine, in 1845. A breach of etiquette seems to have spoilt everything. At a banquet at Stolzenfels Castle, the Austrian Archduke Friedrich was given precedence over Prince Albert. Queen Victoria, who was extremely sensitive on this point, actually did not visit the Prussian Court again for many years, in spite of the near relationship which was cemented later. It may well be that this trifle rendered a political rapprochement between England and Prussia more difficult. Of course the decisive factor lay elsewhere.

Two men had warmly espoused the cause of a Prussian-English alliance in pre-Revolution days—one in an important official position, the other a man whose position as a relative of the English reigning house gave him intimate opportunities of becoming an expert in international politics: the first was Bunsen, Prussian envoy to the English court, the other, Prince Karl Leiningen, the elder half-brother of Queen

60

Victoria and at once brother-in-law and cousin to the Prince Consort.

Bunsen, about whom there has been much dispute, was certainly no diplomatic business-man full of sly tricks and business routine; he was at once less and more than this, a rich personality of deep culture, his character drawn on broad lines. He was the representative of a noble, highly-strung Germanicism, a patriotic humanist, winning all hearts by his buoyant indefatigability; always concerned rather with great and last things than with petty matters of every day. He was at once a scholar and a prophet, an expert and an artist, in many ways the inspirer of ideas which were only to become practical possibilities years after his death, such as disarmament, reconciliation of peoples, and a league of nations. One can well understand that this man, so accomplished as writer and orator, a pietist who was also a popular society lion—who combined a certain sanctity which clung to him from his ecclesiastical ancestry with a knowledge of men and the world derived from the same source—had qualities precisely adequate to the English world in which he found himself. His marriage made him half an Englishman and enabled him to take a congenial part in everything English on an equal footing, to the disadvantage only of those who refused to profit by such stores of hoarded knowledge as were his to command. He was well posted in the only centre of the world which could seriously claim to be considered as such; in re-reading his dispatches and notes, we find an irresistible magic in the rich variety of his views, his well-considered purpose, his patriotic conscientiousness. He was probably the most genuine of all Frederick William's friends, freer, warmer, and more German than Radowitz, who mantled his sharper cleverness with so much mystery and so much calculation. In discussing the possibility of a rapprochement between Prussia and England Bunsen pointed out the striking fact that the principal concern for England was that the Prussian customs dues should remain moderate. The protective taxes raised by the *Zollverein* were still endurable to English industrialists, and enough goods came into Germany by way of the Hanseatic cities and the States bordering the North Sea, which did not belong to the Customs Federation.

We shall see why Prussia and Germany could not come together. "The measure of Prussia's political influence is more than ever her power in Germany, her leadership of German progress," Bunsen had written, with perfect truth. Prussia preferred to run after Nicholas I and Metternich who had turned away from her, instead of accepting an honest parting and stretching out a hand to Liberalism. The best English statesmen wished to see "Frederick William IV at the head of the movement of legitimate progress." Prussia's part should be to unite and strengthen Germany.

The fundamental ideas of Prince Karl Leiningen, that high-minded, thoughtful German aristocrat, were in agreement with this. He was a lively defendant of the ideas of the day among his fellow-princes. On February 6th, he wrote to Prince Albert from Waldleiningen:

"You know my hobby horse, a close alliance between England and Germany, so infinitely important to the well-being of both countries." On March 5th, he wrote: "The influence of Prussia, which has already attained to great power through the Customs Federation, will become gigantic through her conversion to constitutionalism, of which she will soon stand *bon gré mal gré* at the head in Germany." Leiningen foresaw that Prussia in growing strong would have to absorb the petty princes in one way or another. In July 1847, he wrote to Prince Albert: "Prussia can only attain to great power if Germany be united as a whole and with her. Prussia, i.e. Germany, will then be the most powerful Continental Great Power. Austria is therefore allying more closely with Russia and makes use of the King of Prussia's credulous gullibility to give him the most perfidious advice. . . . I cannot repeat often enough that only a strong and united Germany can be a true support to England in the great battle that cannot fail to come." Prince Leiningen deplored the mercantile-political conflict between the countries of the Customs Federation and England as a barrier to the desired political rapprochement. It was not the economic-political point of view which seemed to him decisive, but the home and foreign political aspect. Frederic List, who was a close friend of his, agreed with him in this. Through Bunsen's mediation his correspondence with Prince Albert and his notes came to the knowledge of Frederick William IV; but on Bunsen's advice, Leiningen refrained from an attempt to plead his views in person to the Prussian King. He would have had no success: the King was bent upon "producing the play without Hamlet," as Prince Albert wrote to his brother-in-law.

Frederick William IV did not understand the connection between league reform, foreign policy, and constitutionalism. Canitz, frosty, and self-possessed, said, on November 3, 1847, that Prussia's task was "to tread the right path with firm and quiet step."

A Prussian foreign minister to whom the Russian envoy read his dispatches, begging him for his judgment and advice, and who complained to this foreign diplomatist about the Prussian envoys abroad and grumbled about Metternich, the same Metternich with whom he was in deeply respectful correspondence—such a foreign minister would have been incapable of taking a new course in Prussian policy, even though the King had been other than he was. Meyendorff, the Russian envoy, treated the wavering, conceited Canitz as he deserved. He had him in his pocket when he flattered him by calling him "a statesman of the conservative principle." When that no longer served, he was so harsh that Canitz at once sang small. Meyendorff could write, conscious of his power: "I was very mild when it was a question of tariffs and cartels, but I was quite extraordinarily unpleasant if there was any sign of an attempt to do anything whatever without us and Austria. . . . These people should never attempt politics on the grand scale, for they know nothing about it." When, in the autumn of 1847, Frederick William IV sent out a hint that he would like to meet Nicholas I, who was then in Poland, Nicholas answered that he loved the King with all his heart and would delight in a conversation with him; "but our opinions on matters of State are so at variance that we could not possibly understand one another, and it is therefore better to avoid a meeting." Instead, the Prince of Prussia met the Russian Cesarevitch and his wife at Darmstadt; it was the first time that they had avoided the court of Berlin. The Prince of Prussia was the more eager to cement the tottering relationship to the Czar's court, since he particularly admired the Grand Duchess Caesarevna.

Prussia got the worst of it everywhere and strewed complaints in all directions; she thought the French cabinet perfidious and unreliable. Palmerston's violent, annoying policy confused and dismayed her, but he was the only one who had any success in the Swiss affair. Prussia ran the painful, ridiculous danger of breaking the peace with Switzerland, if not running an actual risk of war, in the matter of the neutrality of Neuenburg. The Prussian envoy, von Sydow, actually received orders to break off diplomatic relations with Switzerland in the event of the occupation of Neuenburg, and to retire to Constance: if General von Pfuel, the military commander, had to give way to force, he should issue a formal protest.

The State of Frederick the Great was torn internally by religious contentions, social division, political confusion; in Europe, isolated as it was, with its unfortunate frontiers, it could scarcely be reckoned any longer among the Great Powers.

## CHAPTER THREE

# BAVARIA

THE AUSTRIAN Imperial State and Prussia, as a Great
Power, were both part of Germany and at the same
time, outside it. Bavaria was very proud of being the
strongest of the purely Germanic powers. "On account of
her strength, Bavaria takes first place among the purely German
countries," wrote Count Luxburg, the Bavarian envoy, from
Vienna, on March 9, 1848. It is easy to perceive the fallacy
in this frequently proclaimed statement—for the main mass
of the Prussian State, which belonged to the German Confederation, greatly exceeded Bavaria both in size and population. Even the smaller western half of Prussia, consisting of
the Rhineland and Westphalia, counted for more than the
whole of Bavaria. There was another aspect of the matter to
which Bavaria was fond of drawing attention, which carried
more conviction. Count Luxburg wrote again on February 15,
1848, that he thanked heaven "that for the last thirty years
Bavaria has possessed a constitution *en vigeur* which guarantees
and preserves the authority of the monarch on the most solid
basis. Thus, when all the world around her is full of excitement
and disorder, Bavaria will remain erect and intact—*pour ainsi
dire hors de cause.*" This prophecy was fulfilled. After the stormy
proceedings which led to a change in the monarchy in March
1848, Bavaria went through the revolutionary period in
comparative calm, and in part this may actually be attributed

to the fact that, at least formally, Bavaria was already a constitutional State.

To be at once the largest and the most German constitutional State presented at that time considerable historical possibilities. Bavaria, which had preserved the name of the old ancestral duchy in its proper place since primeval times (with far greater right than the kingdom of Saxony) had far more significance than any other German petty state or even one of medium strength—she was, as it were, a Great Power which had been stunted in its development. The Wittelsbach family had been on the Rhine and on the Danube since the days of the Hohenstaufen. They were certainly a nobler house than the Hohenzollern or any other electoral house, the most serious, though luckless rivals of the Hapsburgs of Vienna. They, too, had often worn the imperial crown, even as late as the eighteenth century. They had often been weakened by family quarrels and the fortunes of war and had risen, mainly in consequence of the spirit of the counter-reformation and their friendships with many rulers of France, finally, through the favour of Emperor Napoleon. The Bavarian State thus had a double mission to fulfil: to prevent these Austrian cousins from penetrating too deeply into Germany by keeping them on leading strings; and, aided by Prussia, Bavaria prevented the Austrians from rounding off their influence and concentrating their power in South Germany, for she herself had expanded into a strong power and thus served all those who were interested in promoting German disunion, both the Electoral group and the Great Power, France. Frederick the Great's Prussia may have combined for the moment with France against Vienna—but this was merely an episode; Bavaria's understanding with France endured for centuries. But the spirit of the counter-reformation again bound France to Austria and furthered the growth of a common opposition to Protestant Northern Germany. Catholicism, awakening anew, was to achieve its greatest triumphs precisely in its super-national form through the Bavarian capital; the currents of sympathy ran to and fro, from Rome to Munich, from Munich to the Rhine and West-phalia. And Bavaria, a kingdom of the Rhenish Confederation, inspired by Napoleon, became a member of the German Con-federation, having preserved the full power of its sovereignty. It was a State resting on the oldest, richest, most German soil, where there was nothing shallow, threadbare, hybrid, pallid or colonial as in the Prussian North and East, but every-thing full of rude natural vigour, bursting with health. Next to the Bavarians on their mountains and plateaus flourished the Swabians and the folk of the Upper Palatinate, the Fran-conians from the Main and the Rhinelanders from the Rhine Palatinate—all the German tribes except the Saxons.

Some of them had belonged to cities of the realm, others had been subjects of bishops and abbots, of princes, counts and feudal lords—it was a glorious mixture of customs, beliefs, dialects, national costumes, trades and manner of living—a merry compound of the rough peasant and the lively towns-man, of humility and frankness, of rural caution and city cultivation. It was a mixture thoroughly and unmistakably German, both in its good and weak points. A splendid folk, well-fed and carefree, skilled in woodwork and carving and the weaver's art, richly dowered with a long inheritance of living artistic tradition.

This new Bavaria was a "realm"—and had a right to the title; but it should have gone on growing after this sudden accretion in order to exercise all the influence of a realm; the Inn district had been lost to neighbouring Austria even before the age of Napoleon; North Tyrol, ethnically and politically a most natural concomitant had only been held for a short time, after the heaviest fighting; the upper reaches of the Danube, including Ulm, an important Danubian fortress, had fallen to the lot of neighbouring Württemberg, so that the political frontier cut Swabia in two and, absurdly enough, Nördlingen belonged to Bavaria, but Ulm to Württemberg;

the West Rhenish Palatinate belonged to Bavaria, as a small West German frontier province, so that there was not only a "Rhenish Prussia," but also a "Rhenish Bavaria"—but the East Rhenish Palatinate, greatly to the sorrow of the Palatinate Wittelsbach line, which now reigned in Munich, had been assigned to Baden. Prussia continually endeavoured to connect her Eastern and Western halves, and in Bavaria must needs develop a similar desire, not without equal justification. Old Bavaria had been a Danubian province, but possessed only a section of the middle Danube, which left Bavarian territory the moment it became properly navigable. Bavarian Franconia was the country of the Main, stretching out towards the west, just as Old Bavaria's urge was towards the east. But here the gap was still more perceptible. Frankfort, capital of Franconia, dominant city of the Main, had remained outside Bavarian boundaries, to the extreme annoyance of those responsible for Bavarian politics, and so had Mainz, city and fortress, and the mouth of the Main. Thus Bavaria was thrust somewhat into the background on the Danube and on the Main; in spite of the Rhine Palatinate, she was forced away from the Rhine and therefore removed from the focal point of German culture and German economic policy. Bavaria was dowered with wealth of land and people—yet she became a backwoods State with a backwoods population. It is easy to imagine that a leader of great political energy might have created a South German Great Power out of this realm which had not had its fair share, just as Greater Prussia later came into existence in the north. But Bavaria was not granted any such leader and therefore she developed a certain sensitiveness with regard to the more violent and happier Prussia, which was entirely comprehensible from a historical point of view. The famous South German sense of humour deserted its owners at this point. The weaker the kingdom of Bavaria became, the more seriously did it take its importance. It increased Bavaria's difficulties that she held the Catholic Primacy for

Germany, and was at pains to retain it in the interests of her position apart from regional considerations. Even in the Bismarckian Empire, the King of Bavaria was still the secret Catholic Emperor. This position, guaranteed by the presence of the Papal Nuncio in Munich, had a most sensibly weakening effect upon Bavaria's relation to the movement for German unity. If the new German Empire were to be Greater Germany, if the new Emperor were to be Catholic, then Austria could not be ignored and Bavaria was the last to wish to ignore her, in spite of the old jealousy. But those who wished to set Austria aside must turn to the Prussian, that is to say, to the Protestant Emperor. Bavaria could do no more than feel annoyed, she might make hindrances and difficulties as long as possible, but she could not undertake serious rivalry—even if she had willed to do so: no true leader of the liberal and national movement in Germany could have endured the prospect of Bavarian supremacy. Was there not a third way out? Bavaria might ally herself with the smaller and petty states in Germany so as to attain some political significance by the side of the two real great powers; such a diplomatic combination was repeatedly attempted, but could not lead to any new form of State. However, Bavaria early discovered a splendid substitute for a leading political position in an all-embracing patronage of German cultural values. It was a very healthy instinct and its father was King Ludwig I.

This ruler was always a Count Palatine of the Rhine Palatinate rather than a King of Bavaria; he should have been ruling as Elector at the great Castle of Heidelberg in full-blooded Renaissance days. He fitted no better into out-of-the-world Munich than did the famous collection of paintings which had been brought from Dusseldorf. At the beginning of the nineteenth century—the Biedermeier period, corresponding to English early Victorian— Munich was still a little royal residence in Baroque style, with a semi-rural population of petty citizens: Jesuitical-

Romanesque seventeenth century without a trace of the eighteenth—little better than the residential cities of extinct Wittelsbach dynasties, Ingolstadt, Straubing, and Landshut, certainly far less of a city than Augsburg or Nuremberg. It had neither the charm of a great mediaeval tradition nor of modern elegance. No one in those days would have thought of comparing the humble crooked streets of little Munich with the monumental glories of Dresden, much less of Vienna. With a certain violent energy, King Ludwig set about making this Munich into a genuine capital; building began on a grand scale, classic, Byzantine, Romanesque; sometimes the architecture was a mere copy of a Florentine or Greek original; in any case it was a copy. Homes were built for the art collections from the Lower Rhine and from Greece, specious, in the heroic manner, pretentious rather than impressive or genuine, but expressions of a determined spirit, rather a frame for a greater future than a suitable vessel to contain an already existing present.

As Crown Prince, King Ludwig paid an exaggerated homage to Napoleon, kissing his hand and bending the knee before him. Later he welcomed the advent of Emperor Nicholas of Russia to the throne with equal enthusiasm—it took place almost simultaneously with his own accession and he therefore regarded it as an augury of the development of Bavarian-Russian relations. The King had been born at Strassburg; his longing for the Palatinate, cheated of the hotly contended city of Mannheim, sought to appease itself by the founding of Ludwigshafen, christened after himself. In 1841, he caused Nikolaus Becker, author of the song "Never shall they possess it, the free, the German Rhine" to be presented with a loving cup, bearing the inscription "The Count Palatine of the Rhine Palatinate to the Poet of the Song *The German Rhine*, 1840." The cup was designed by Schwanthaler; but the song of the free German Rhine was not permitted to be sung in Bavaria in the presence of the French Ambassador. It would have endangered French–Bavarian relations, which were particularly important on account of Greece. For King Ludwig's son, Otto, had become the first king of the liberated Hellenes. There was a Bavarian Orient policy and European questions were discussed in Munich, even though they were not decided there; in consequence of a number of misunderstandings, the degree of culture, normalized by the German classical period in literature, was to be kept up, proved and actuated by a mixture of humanistic grammar school, archaeology and philo-hellenism. King Ludwig no doubt considered all this "truly Teutonic."

Contemporaries drew many a comparison between the two royal brothers-in-law, Bavarian Ludwig and Prussian Frederick William. They were both erratic autocrats, full of moods, with a leaning to the intellectual. But Ludwig was the more earthly and healthy of the two; he was more of a man, had something of rude peasant strength about him. He loved the coarse simplicity of Bavarian fare, and liked to take a friendly glass with his artist-craftsmen. He was actually one of themselves in his flow of original ideas, temperamental jollity, volubility and *joie de vivre*. Frederick William had more cultivated tastes, he was truly brilliant. Ludwig's imagination was apt to run away with him, he was uncritical, gullible, his wit was not caustic, his pompous manner often irresistibly ludicrous; but he was a manly fellow without pretences, and his little oddities were forgiven and forgotten because he was such a genuine good sort. Although in his early days he had been overflowing with enthusiasm, burning as with the fire of genius, Frederick William's physical impotence gave him in later life a philistine air of self-satisfied puritanism which made his spiritual lack of harmony still more unendurable. Ludwig's heart was in the right place and his feelings perfectly normal, he was a joyous sinner and a good Catholic, and his people, in whose pleasures and jollities he participated so gladly, loved him as he deserved. When he strolled about his Munich with short, irregular steps, he was a most erratic pedestrian—his subjects looked with real affection on the stately figure, the intellectual head, the sparkling eye that looked every man in the face. The inhabitants of the royal town of Munich stared in astonishment at the endless lines of new streets, the pillared temples and triumphal arches with which their king presented them; but craftsmen and brewers found plenty to do and everyone was prosperous. The motto of the artists and students was, as ever, live and let live. Sentiment and the stomach had always been well served in old Munich; head work came afterwards, no one cared much for mental effort. Munich prospered and King Ludwig was a favourite. In his passion for building he was as crazy as in political matters; his poetry was crazier still; everything that Ludwig did had a touch of foolishness—but it was entertaining, hearty foolishness.

King Ludwig paid honour to Dürer and Goethe such as no German prince had ever paid to any artist, living or dead; it was very largely due to him that workers in the German arts were no longer considered as superior artisans and court servants, but as free creative spirits, free men. He loved his artists as he loved no one else.

He made short work of his artists' petty jealousies and envious rivalry, treating them with rough and ready sympathy, without fear or favour, he admitted to being tyrannical and impatient, since this was in his nature: he was full of his mission and he stood alone. The older Court society, predominantly French and rationalistic in its tendencies, watched the new-fangled doings with critical and mocking scepticism; the masses devouring their beer and sausage and letting their furnished rooms, went on munching with a broad Bavarian grin, but otherwise quite unaffected by the developments in the world of art. A higher class of citizen with an intelligent interest in cultural values and in the King's battle for the new German art was in process of development. Ludwig, though a boon companion to his artists, was a stern master, even violent when occasion arose; there was an unforgettable incident concerning Cornelius, who was royally forbidden to enter the Ludwig Church, because he had been lazy and could no longer paint properly! The King spent a great deal of money on his plans, no doubt too much. He did not wish to be cheated and liked to prove his ability to count the cost, even to the point of parsimony.

Thus King Ludwig reigned in Bavaria and toiled for Germania. He felt himself to be a very personification of the Teuton soul, and his Teutonic Valhalla stood on the banks of the Danube, near the Austrian frontier, where no German would have thought of looking for it. The cold, bare, correctly copied Greek temple would not in any way have reminded the visitor of the German Valhalla and of German intellectual achievement, even if it had been completely filled with "immortals" as was intended. Much more successful was Ludwig's Hall of Liberation at Kelheim, a central building of imposing grandeur, in spite of its derivative character, a heroic ballad in marble. King Ludwig endeavoured all his life long to serve the spirit of the Wars of Liberation, the traditions of German greatness; yet, unusual, even important as he was, he was destined to plunge his country and his people into a greater state of confusion than any German prince of the century, either before or after him.

"As long as we do not issue orders to the contrary"—was the customary conclusion of King Ludwig's decrees. This was the Royal conception of the Bavarian constitution: wherever the consent of the diets was not expressly required, the King believed that there were no limits to his monarchical rights. The text of the Bavarian Constitution was certainly full of contradictions and the election laws extremely faulty. But anyone with an honest desire to act in accordance with the Constitution could have achieved a great deal. It was Bavarian tactics to attempt by means of the mere existence of a constitution to win the favour of middle-class movements whose aim was the achievement of freedom. This constitution was to be interpreted in such a manner as to maintain harmonious relations with the reactionary forces in Austria and Prussia. The realm of Bavaria was in a class by itself, it was in Bavarian interests to preserve an independent existence in Europe between the pressure of the real great powers and that of the revolutionary movement which had looked so threatening in the Rhine Palatinate in 1832; the best ally that Bavaria could have was Neo-Roman Catholicism. The people of the Palatinate and the Franconians represented the "Revolution" in the Bavarian "Empire"—they were middle-class, liberal, many of them Protestants. The Old Bavarians could only retain their political preponderance by using the young strength of newly-awakened international Catholicism for their own purposes. In Bavaria itself there had been attempts ever since 1814 to create a Catholic organization with political aims. To perfect this was the historic task of the Abel Ministry, which had been in office since 1838. The leader of the battle-cry was a great man of an older generation, Görres, whose last and least happy years were devoted to a furious battle against the whole modern, and at the same time Protestant, world. The Görres circle was the primary cell of Bavarian party clericalism, at this time still tinged with conservatism. Publicistic opposition to the ruling press, such as the *Neue Münchener Zeitung*, the *Neue Würzburger Zeitung*, was rendered impossible by means of the censorship and if this did not suffice, by arbitrary police measures; non-Bavarian newspapers were forbidden entry into the kingdom.

Abel called the Press "a venal prostitute," and declared that he could not govern without a strict censorship. Papers were preferred which were as staid and innocuous as the Nuremberg *Peace and War Courier* or the *Correspondent About and for Germany*. Catholic Germany now made a move to defend its interests by means of publicity, operating from Bavaria on a broad and well-founded basis. Such was the outspoken purpose of the *Historical-Political Papers for Catholic Germany*, founded in 1838 by Görres and Philipps. The spirit of intolerance took hold of official life. Undesirable officials were ruthlessly retired, either temporarily or permanently, on a wretchedly inadequate pension, or at the very least plagued as much as possible as a disciplinary measure. The royal rescript of August 11, 1838, demanded that at the Catholic military services, all officers and men should bend the knee during the transubstantiation and at the blessing. The result was the notorious Bent Knee dispute, which lasted for many years. The Government gave the protesting Protestant soldiery permission to leave the service on payment of the sum due from those prevented by physical disability from serving.

Many took advantage of this remarkable outlet. Only in 1843, after Prince Leiningen, as member of the Bavarian Upper House, had made personal representations to the King, and also to Abel, was the order made that the two religions in the army should each hold their own services. The obligatory bending of the knee was at last abolished in 1844. This step did considerable damage to the King's political reputation.

The spirit of constriction also seized upon the Universities, especially upon Ludwig's spoilt darling, the Munich University. It was largely due to Görres that a certain course of lectures was imposed upon the students. There were to be control examinations every half-year; an aspirant who failed for the second or third time could not become an official of the State, and in Bavaria this also included physicians and lawyers, who were also assigned to positions by the State. There were numerous incursions into pedagogic freedom. In 1840, Professor von der Pfordten, who had been denounced to the King as ultra-liberal, was transferred from his Würzburg professorship to the Court of Appeal at Aschaffenburg—he preferred to go as a professor to Saxony, from whence he returned to Bavaria as Prime Minister in 1849. An order issued in 1838 forbade laymen to give theological lectures —which affected such men as Schelling and Baader. About twenty new monasteries were founded in the same year. In 1844 there were fifty-six monasteries and seventy-six nunneries. Besides the Benedictines there were monastic orders of every kind, Franciscans, Carmelites, Augustines, Redemptorists; individual members of the Society of Jesus appeared in Bavaria at various points and attempted to found colleges. The effect upon Protestantism was plainly apparent: orthodoxy got the upper hand. An uncompromising Old Lutheranism attempted to organize forces of resistance among the Protestant Church officials. The equality of religious beliefs, which was secured by law, was now endangered in many individual cases. Protestant churches and schools were openly neglected in favour of the Catholic institutions. There was a great increase in pilgrimages, petitionary and otherwise, and in the number of conversions. In the selection of bishops the elderly cathedral dignitaries of the proven German school were passed over in favour of zealous young College men who could be relied upon in the matter of propaganda. To be sure, when a priest of the Kajetan Church in Munich went so far as to preach a sermon lamenting the lost hopes of the Catholic Church because Crown Prince Maximilian had married the Prussian Princess Marie, who was a "non-Catholic," the Government deprived him of his benefice. Shortly before, in November 1841, the death of the Protestant Queen-Mother had for the first time revealed to the mass of the public the gulf between King Ludwig and the Neo-Catholics. The Munich clergy refused in the most offensive manner to participate in the funeral ceremonies. King Ludwig was properly wrathful.

Thus old Bavarian feeling could only maintain its supremacy

in the Kingdom of Bavaria by allying itself with international Catholicism, which was once more acutely combative. This alliance was very strong. It was represented at Court, although with certain eccentricities, by Ludwig's second son, Prince Luitpold, whose marriage to the Archduchess of Tuscany was fully in accordance with clerical expectations. The ecclesiastics little suspected that Luitpold's ambition was to succeed his brother Otto on the throne of Greece and that he was perfectly prepared to go over to the Orthodox Church in order to achieve this end. Had they known it they would have been greatly disappointed. But the masses of the people were also inflamed anew. There was something rough and ready about the Bavarian ecclesiastical spirit, it was democratic in its way, it emphasized the local spirit and local independence and this was one of the foundations of its great political strength. This primitive old Bavarian spirit could not easily be intimidated; when it became known that in Munich in 1839 there were far more illegitimate than legitimate births and that this condition of things had persisted in subsequent years, the outraged middle-class morality of the rest of Germany was confronted by a very determined defence. This state of things, said the Bavarians, was just a consequence of the fiery nature of a race which had preserved its natural strong passions; the people were not accustomed to reckon and consider as did the colder North German population, and a true Bavarian would rather marry a girl who had become a mother than not, he liked to be sure of securing plenty of progeny. When the assize courts were introduced into Bavaria in 1848 there were statistics to prove what had long been palpable—that in Upper and Lower Bavaria more crimes came before the courts than in all other parts of the country taken together. But the explanation came pat: this impulsive folk of shepherds and hunters did not trouble to call upon the courts with their endless scribblings when they quarrelled with one another, but took the law into their own hands as in the old heroic days. Unfortunately, however, cases of thievery and arson were far more common than those of wounding and manslaughter!

Old Bavaria was thus a strange patch of country, rich in many charms, rather barbaric in its manners and customs; its peculiarities both political and ecclesiastical, were a hindrance to the new Bavaria. Traffic developed more slowly in Bavaria than anywhere else; in 1848 there were only two stretches of railway. There were many complaints about the state of the roads, and the coaches drove slower in Bavaria than anywhere else. In 1841, over two hundred aspirants, after eleven years of training, were still waiting for positions in the service of the State. The petty and lower officials were worse paid than anywhere else in Germany, whereas those in higher positions received extra emoluments of all kinds. This had a bad effect on the spirit of the bureaucracy as a class. A professor extra-ordinary received a lower salary than a valet of the bedchamber. In 1840, the "French year," although 6–7 million gulden were set apart for armaments, startling deficiencies became apparent. The rifles were only breech-loaders, there was a shortage of weapons and of ammunition, improvements in the artillery were only made on paper. Very little was demanded of the officers in their examinations, they needed only to pass well in scripture and to make a great show of piety and morality. Positions remained unfilled for years, troops were mentioned in the lists that did not exist at all. According to the letter of the law, privates must serve with the colours for six years. In reality, however, they served but two or three. The soldiers were expressly permitted to pursue supplementary occupations —they worked with master craftsmen as occasional apprentices, cobbling at many a trade which they understood at best no more than half; they lounged in taverns, blacked boots and did a day's work here and there at brick-laying or on a farm. All this did nothing to increase the prestige of the army. There was a shortage of staff officers, regimental colonels and generals. "Even the captains are most of them so old and feeble that they

78

would scarcely be capable of enduring another campaign . . ."
wrote Baron von Brenner, Austrian envoy, to Metternich,
on March 6, 1848. Only a few batteries had their full complement of horses. Certainly King Ludwig was averse to all
forms of military expenditure, but the most necessary expenses
should have been seen to. The army lacked all confidence in
itself. King Ludwig was his own Minister of Finance and preferred to dispose of large sums rather than small ones. The
secret of his system was his so-called "Savings." Thus, the
budget of 1835–38 showed a saving of twenty million gulden.
The Diets were allowed no voice in the disposal of these
moneys and even had no control over them. The "Constitutional Understanding" of 1843 was supposed to do away with
these conditions, but no improvement followed. The national
real estate alone produced a millionfold surplus every year.
But the national debt did not grow any less, rather it increased.
The royal household and Court accounted for over three
million gulden in 1845–46. But the King had no idea of con-
fining himself even to this considerable sum. His Eastern policy,
his building schemes and all his other hobbies could only be
carried on if he retained complete control of all finances and
by a mixture of autocracy and mercantile cunning he contrived to establish this state of things. It was a matter of absolute
indifference to him whether his soldiery were properly shod
or a village schoolhouse received the new roof it needed.
Village teachers were forced to help as navvies in the digging
of a canal, because they could not exist on their salaries.

As for the parliament, the Diet and the First Chamber, the
assembly of the Councillors of the Crown of Bavaria—two
days after the "Knee-bending Edict"—the Abel government
issued an order which was just as characteristic: petitions were
no longer to be addressed to the Government as the highest
instance, but to His Majesty himself; instead of "citizen," the
expression "subject" was to be used; instead of "Ministry of
State," it was to be "Royal Ministry." King Ludwig had ex-

pressed wishes of this kind as far back as 1836. Constitutionalism in Bavaria was in process of being hollowed out from within. It was only a sort of screen, still inconvenient to the Abel Government and to the monarch, but no longer dangerous. Abel already dared to remark that the constitution was not representative, but merely represented the property-owners. Since a third of the 1838 Diet was composed of Protestants, it was dissolved and the numbers and disposition of the members regulated anew. Many of those elected were forced to ask the King's permission, which was refused to all persons who were considered undesirable. Many were also refused the necessary leave of absence to attend the sittings. This happened to all the lawyers elected save one; it happened to six of the eight property-owners elected to represent the Rhine Palatinate. As far as possible, independent intellectuals were excluded from the chamber. It was more convenient to deal with officials, clergy and those engaged in commercial pursuits.

To be sure, during these years, the upper house, the Chamber of Councillors of the Realm, came to represent an independent and long-sighted policy. Mixed motives, some fine, some petty, inspired this opposition of the *Reichsräte* to the Abel Government. The new Court Order of Precedence of 1841 set the immediate Princes and Counts below the throne officials, intermediate princes, officers of the Royal household and archbishops. This was a heavy blow to the justifiable pride of such great families as Thurn and Taxis of Regensburg, Pappenheim in the Altmühl valley, Leiningen of the Odenwald, and many another. These hereditary councillors could not be intimidated as easily as the more dependent Diet members, they treasured the new rights of the councillors' chamber as a continuation of and a compensation for old privileges that had lapsed, and they had the courage of their convictions. These high and mighty gentlemen saw in Karl von Abel (a man of hot-blooded, businesslike character who, like so many leading Bavarian statesmen of the nineteenth century, was not a Bavarian at all, but came from the good Imperial city of Wetzlar) only an impudent, bureaucratic busybody, an insidious parvenu, against whose artfulness and energy one must be on one's guard. Abel, being a renegade, was particularly eager and had to swallow many a snub from the councillors. When he hurled insults at his predecessors, the much discussed Prince Öttingen-Wallerstein, Munich was treated to the unusual spectacle of a duel between a reigning and a retired Prime Minister, in which both parties survived—not only physically, but, as far as Abel was concerned, even officially. In 1846, Prince Karl Theodor Wrede, eldest son of the field-marshal, who was a member of the Chamber of Councillors, began an open campaign against the Abel Government. He accused Abel of breaches of the constitution, of acting against the King's wishes and depriving Protestants of their proper rights. Unfortunately, he spoiled the effect of some of his most weighty accusations by concluding with a complaint about the one-sided lowering of the price of beer in the *Hofbräuhaus*.

To be sure, in Bavaria, especially in Old Bavaria, the price of beer was an important public matter, perhaps the most important of all. As early as 1843, an attempt had been made to raise the price of beer; the Government had already consented to the alteration—but the brewers were intimidated by threats, stones were thrown at brewery windows, inflammatory speeches were made in beer gardens, and the Government withdrew the rise in price "in order to prevent excitement." The same attempt was made in 1844. But on the evening of the publication of the amendment, all Munich beer-halls except two had been wrecked and plundered. The military had been called out and had not succeeded in preventing the excesses, in fact some of the soldiers had taken part in them. Munich was just celebrating the marriage of Princess Hildegarde to Archduke Albrecht; and Prince Luitpold had just returned from his wedding. The people were participating enthusiastically in both these events—yet the tumult went on for days. On May 3rd, the beer cellars, which had been restored after a fashion, were again attacked and baker's shops were also plundered. The Riot Acts were posted up. Nevertheless, corn dealers were attacked in the corn market. What was to be done? The brewers came to the rescue and aided the helpless Government to solve the problem by "voluntarily" relinquishing the extra halfpenny. The clerical press declared that the Opposition, especially the Protestants, were to blame for these May riots. Similar excesses were also committed in Augsburg and Nuremberg.

Bavaria, still almost wholly agrarian, found it easiest to survive the social crisis of the age, because it had remained stationary at a relatively healthy early stage of development. But the beer riots had shown the people of Munich that they could enforce their will; none the less, the clerical governing powers could always secure the people of Munich when they so desired. The Church bound them with bonds closer than anything which the Opposition, divided among itself, could ever succeed in spinning. It was not being out of touch with the lower classes which was the weakness of the Abel Government, but, in the main, its relations to the Councillors and to the King.

King Ludwig did not favour the "Ultramontanes"; he was too gruff and upright, and wished to be a Lord and a Teuton in his own Bavarian house. But he had still less in common with the Liberals. Jealously he scented criticism and control, a minimizing of royal power, an attempt to interfere, to influence, to put a check on his autocracy. It was a long time since the day when the censor had struck out a poem on account of its liberal opinions which had been taken from a printed collection of the King's poems. Now King Ludwig's insulted majesty was roused to wrath against the Liberals. Nothing else left such a stain on his memory as the Eisenmann Case. This Würzburg physician had already been accused of high treason before the July Revolution, on account

82

of his participation in secret societies. He had been acquitted, but was "banished" to a small town in Franconia. King Ludwig took an interest in him, favoured his paper, the *Bayrisches Volksblatt*, and even requested him to work out a plan for a Bavarian national newspaper. Eisenmann wanted to retain his independence and declined the editorship. This was fatal to him. The King, always sensitive, seems to have taken offence. Eisenmann's paper was suppressed. He was again accused of high treason on account of an article taken from a periodical which had already passed the censor. After a period of strict "investigatory imprisonment" he was condemned in 1836 to "hard labour for an uncertain term of years and to recant before the King's portrait." We would gladly endure even more of King Ludwig's poems—if only he had not given his consent to this. It is one of the crassest cases of the period. Eisenmann was not pardoned until 1847; in 1848 he was granted damages of fifteen thousand gulden as compensation for his unjust imprisonment, which had permanently ruined his health.

King Ludwig was one of those men whom one would rather defend than accuse. The Eisenmann case throws a darker shadow than the case of Lola Montez—yet it was this which decided the King's fate.


Donna Maria de Dolores de los Montes, known as Lola Montez, came to Munich in the autumn of 1846, intending to dance at the Royal theatre. The manager would not engage her, so she asked an audience of the King. The King's chamberlain refused to admit her, and there was a violent scene. The King ordered her to be admitted, so that he could give her a talking to. This first meeting decided everything. Rumour has it that Ludwig cast doubts upon the genuineness of her nobly curved bosom—whereupon Lola snatched up a pair of scissors from the table and ripped open her dress.

Lola Montez was born in 1820 in Montrose, Scotland. Her real name was Betsey Watson, and she was the love-child of a Scottish Captain of the name of Edward Gilbert; her mother was a Creole who later married an English colonel. Lola lived for a time in the East Indies, was the wife of an English officer named James, who had eloped with her to this remote spot. She soon ran away from him with an Irishman. Then she became the mistress of the Duke of Richmond and is said also to have had affairs with Lord Palmerston and the younger Peel. She appeared as a Spanish dancer for the first time at the Queen's Theatre, London. In 1843, she was expelled from Berlin and the same fate befell her in Warsaw, Baden-Baden, and Paris. In a great scandal of the day, the Dujarier Case in Paris, 1845, she appeared before the Court as the mistress of the man who had been shot. Dujarier had given her a fortune, especially shares in the Palais Royal theatre. Probably her interest in politics dated from this period. Most likely she was not a first-class artiste, although she had the tigerish vivacity that inspires the Andalusian dance. Her adventurous career was determined above all by her relations with men. She was more than beautiful—a mixture of Mary Queen of Scots and Josephine Beauharnais: she had glorious dark-blue eyes, raven-black hair, and olive complexion, proud lips, nobly-cut features which bore traces of her many experiences, and a fine and graceful figure.

Munich was astonished; the beery, village worthies who were its inhabitants shuddered agreeably at the unusual combination of a bad reputation and splendid looks; but the Señora's most remarkable feature was her more than masculine courage. She whipped the boots of the Golden Stag Inn, where she stayed when she first arrived in Munich, and boxed the landlord's ears. An Englishman named Murray, brother of Lord Elibank, who accompanied her and was probably her *souteneur*, calmly looked on when such scenes were in progress.

84

King Ludwig had just been learning Spanish, the true heroic language of the world of romance; and now he met a "Spanish Lady." She must read Calderon and Cervantes to him and could chatter charmingly of what she had read. There is no doubt that the passionate attachment of this man, already sixty-one years of age, had something noble and intellectual about it. King Ludwig solemnly assured the worried Prince-Bishop Diepenbrock that his love of Lola did not include the purely physical aspect. Those near to him confirm this. The Bavarian envoy in Berlin officially declared the same. One should not quibble over Ludwig's love of truth—on the contrary, we have here one of the most decisive points. Perhaps he made a virtue of necessity. The King was an old man and contact with an enchanting and vigorous young woman excited him erotically beyond all bounds. He had always been original, now his eccentricity exceeded all limits. Since natural passion was denied to him, he tried to substitute for it a perverse love of pleasure. It is easy to laugh at such a spectacle, but regarded from a purely human angle, it is both touching and moving. In him, too, "the old volcano flamed again," as the poet has it. He had never shown much knowledge of human nature, and the world turned for him upon the axis of his own sensitive, arrogant age. The senile artist-prince raised up a great courtesan to be the goddess of his declining years.

The old gentleman was completely transformed; he had eyes and thoughts only for Lola, and no expense was too great for him. Contrary to all usage, Major-General von Heideck, his Controller of Finance, now received a general's salary. Certainly he now had plenty to do. The dancer was fitted out with silverware and a fine equipage. As early as 1846, the King bought her a house in the hope of thus securing her full rights of citizenship—the plan miscarried owing to the opposition of the Munich magistracy and town council. The King now spent all his evenings at Heideck's house, where he could see

Lola—Count Seinsheim and Count Rechberg were also of the company. He also met her every day, called for her and took her home again, on foot. Business soon suffered, the King had no time for anything else; he seemed to be physically and mentally exhausted and caused his physicians great anxiety.

Lola had great taste. The King had a villa built for her in the Barer Strasse—Irlein the master-mason made sixty thousand gulden out of it. Lola filled it with beautiful examples of fine English arts and crafts of the period; she sang with spirit to her own accompaniment on guitar and piano. She could chatter with charm and intelligence. She knew her way about the great world anywhere in Western Europe and conjured up about her an atmosphere of wit and luxury which others beside the King found it difficult to resist.

She was proud of having reached an apex of her career and used to write "maitresse du Roi" under her signature. When she went shopping, she would say, "My Louis will pay." No one knows how close her relations were at first to English Liberalism; Liberalism and libertinage were for her related conceptions. She regarded herself as an important representative of a free, urbane, broadminded conception of life in opposition to puritans and philistines. One of her first political actions was to intercede successfully for the badly-paid school teachers who had appealed in vain to the King, the Diet, and the Government for an increase in salary. Soon she was openly fighting the "surplice cabinet." Among her adherents and political advisers were Professor Herrmann, and Ploetz, correspondent of the *Augsburg Allgemeine Zeitung*—who was excluded from his dining circle in consequence. Others of her group were Dr. Curtius, a military staff physician, Angioletta Maier, a dancer, and Lieutenant Nussbaumer of the artillery, who was Lola's lover by the King's express permission.

We can well understand that the Clerical Party was greatly concerned. In spite of the many differences of opinion which the Church had fought out with King Ludwig in course of time, he was now lauded in addresses and manifestos as the most pious of kings, protector of church and creed. Certainly all might have been expiated according to custom by a sufficiency of penitential donations; but in many respects the position was unprecedented. Like most German princes of the time, King Ludwig had already had a number of love affairs, usually with actresses and Bavarian girls such as mesdames Lizius, Dahn, Vespermann, Späth, and many another. Church, court, and country had tolerated these relationships as being in the normal order of things and public opinion had never concerned itself about them. The new position created by Lola was not only a personal but also a political problem. This platonic love affair with a foreign woman of loose reputation in which the poor old King cut a laughable figure, made his position as monarch untenable in the long run. Lola tried to strengthen her position by an alliance with the Liberals and the Protestants. The King himself was heartily tired of the Abel Government. The scandal was the beginning of a political reversal. It must needs be an important one, for it was a huge scandal and continually grew worse. The King wrote poems to Lola. He promised to make her a countess; but there were formal difficulties in the way. The Abel Government retired rather than consent. A much honoured professor was dismissed from the University for congratulating Abel. The students gathered before Lola's house and hooted insults. The militia was called out to restore order, but they failed to appear; their wives had hidden their uniforms.

After Lola had become Countess of Landsfeld, she took up what she and many others called the fight against the Jesuits. Those who were against the Ultramontanes in Bavaria were known simply as "Lolamontanes." She had her own party among the students. Her espousal of liberal opinions gained her adherents and the goodwill of agents all over Europe. In Bavaria her unpopularity grew. Her demand for the removal of the University from Munich woke up the Catholic Bavarian soul which saw its profits in danger. The King's own tyranny where any slight to Lola was concerned, fatally undermined his power. Demands were made of him that Lola should be banished. Finally, Queen Therese, who had been silent up to this point, added her word of warning to the King. On February 11th there was a rising. The people stormed Lola's villa; but she had been warned by her spies and had fled summarily, without waiting to secure either money or jewels.

Baron von Brenner, the Austrian Minister in Munich, said after the catastrophe:

"Though but little blood flowed in these three days, yet the movement and its result had all the value of a revolution. . . . The people grew twenty years riper in these few days."

## CHAPTER FOUR

# THE PETTY STATES

IN AUSTRIA lurked Europe, in Prussia, Germany—to be sure, it was only a fragment of Europe, a fragment of Germany, but just on this account political tension was at its highest here, and threads were woven in the web of political destiny. Bavaria was a great State and yet no great power; her strength was physical rather than spiritual, and peculiarly German in that she hindered more than she helped. Bavaria liked to take a hand in the great game the great ones played—but soon showed plainly that her real place was among the petty states.

The pettiness of petty states was Germany's real historical destiny in the nineteenth century—conditions cried aloud for revolution, and nothing but revolution could bring about any improvement. Kingdom, principality or free State—it made no difference, neither did a few extra square miles of territory, nor a couple of thousand head more or less of population; the condition of petty state was not only political, but also spiritual—a manner of life, a way of thinking, a system, and a style. There is no such thing as a middle state—the expression was once used, but it was dictated only by a mistaken politeness. The only State with any claim to such a title was Bavaria. The others were petty states, dwarf states, split-off bits of states, dukedoms promoted to be states. Petty states were the ruling form of existence in old Germany. It was natural for a

German to love his mill in the valley, the onion-shaped steeple of his village church, the fountain in the market-place, the little streets by the river, the humpbacked gable of his ancestral home; that had always been in the nature of things and should and would always be the same. That did not mean that a German must bow and scrape like a lackey before a hundred little Highnesses or be a country bumpkin in a thousand forgotten hamlets. Yet we know that the sovereignty of many petty lords poisoned the very sources of the old German freedom. In the old realm, however, there had at least been an Emperor who reigned over all the highnesses, serenities, and excellencies, and his majesty turned them all into dwarfs. Now majesty was going cheap, even the Grand Dukes ranked as royalties. As a solitary remnant of the solemn ceremonial of choosing an Emperor and crowning him at Frankfort, one Elector lingered like a ghost in the German Confederation, which otherwise claimed to be so international, so diplomatic, and so reasonable. What was life like in these petty states?—they were made up of insignificant lords with long titles, little residential capitals dominated by great castles, scraps of countries, patched together, divided by idiotic frontiers, bearing a huge burden of officialdom and soldiery, petty dignitaries with high and mighty manners, little wits and long tongues, small souls and glittering decorations. They were political chimeras, each demanding strength and sacrifice, veneration and confidence from credulous dependants, which thrust themselves between little native towns and the great fatherland. Farmers and townspeople had to find their feet in this maze. Most of them were good at it, under pressure of circumstance; for jobs, trade, acquisition of property—in short the whole business of making a living —depended upon patronage, favour and power. There was painfully little difference between a lackey and a State official, between a soldier and a policeman, between a beadle and a judge. The prevailing atmosphere was a kind of homely brutality. If you were careful with your curtsey, and swept off your hat low and frequently, you could live well enough, cultivate a paunch and keep a bottle in the cellar, as long as you never forgot to drink his Highness's health. You could grumble as much as you liked, as long as you were prepared to bow and scrape whenever matters looked serious. It was hard to rise and many went to ruin, but a man who gave what was wanted, who married into a well-connected family, who thought more of the Guild than of the handicraft, read nothing unnecessary and was never heard to doubt the divinity of his betters—such a man was in clover. And yet there were natures so ungrateful as to wish to make an end of all this swollen importance, this solemn farce of government, who were revolted by the decorative sugar-candy courts and the lecturing officials—who wanted to escape from the cliques and cabals, the gossiping and whispering, the intrigues and petty persecutions of clergy and police. No one longed so wearily, wrathfully and with tears for a free, strong, united Germany, for a new great fatherland in a new great world, as the German living in the Germany of the petty states.

William I, the new king of Württemberg after 1816, was one of the most remarkable figures among the German princes of the time. He had earned considerable laurels as a general, especially distinguishing himself against the great Emperor Napoleon at Montereau. His sister was married to King Jerome, and he never quite emerged from the atmosphere of the Napoleonic era. His second wife was the sister of Emperor Alexander I and Nicholas I; in accordance with his wishes, his son married Grand-duchess Olga, daughter of Nicholas I. How the good people of Stuttgart stared when the Russian dowry arrived, in nine dray-loads and five carriages packed high, everything garlanded with wreaths of flowers. These Russian relatives stiffened the King's backbone and put certain opportunities into his hand, of which he gladly took advantage. In 1814–15 he had been among those who demanded the return of Alsace; he loved to imagine himself as commander-in-chief of a united German army, for his favourite pose was that of the brave, blunt soldier. His geniality rang false, he was a busybody, always full of plots and intrigues, winning many a success by his personal momentary charm, yet never really achieving anything because he always bluntly and naïvely imagined that everything else was less acute than himself. He was so busy plotting and intriguing that he never noticed that people saw through him.

Politically his aims were usually diametrically opposed to his achievements; he would like to have been a very modern monarch and to live in an atmosphere of liberal thought; but as he was stubborn and obstinate, his actions more nearly resembled those of a determined despot. He loved to dream of confronting the Great Powers by a "pure" Germany; but he found it quite impossible to make friends with neighbouring Bavaria, even with this end in view. He did not think much of Austria and enjoyed annoying Metternich; but he would have thought it shameful to afford Prussia any genuine support. He sometimes spoke of Germanism and progress; but he was always sincere about one thing—the aggrandizement of Württemberg. What he did for agriculture and for people's schools, for a sound system of taxation and for the idea of the *Zollverein* was usually well done. It was done in a bureaucratically violent fashion, but it did get done. His beautiful kingdom was too small and simple to please him; he thought he was destined for greater things. He would gladly have accepted the staff of office and laurels of a German field-marshal, or the imperial crown.

This little Kingdom of Württemberg was the costliest of gems and would have sufficed to absorb the energies of a far more distinguished ruler. His subjects were true descendants of the most gifted German tribe—vintners and townsmen, courtiers and professors, peasants from mountain huts, fruit farmers and ploughmen from the Kocher, former subjects of dukes and barons, of prince-bishops and monasteries, but true Swabians from the Danube to the Neckar—except for a few Franks in the north and Alemans in the south. These Swabians were of a more serious temper than the Franks, with more stamina than the hybrid races of the Rhine plain, more refined and cleverer than the Bavarians, more brilliant than the people of Lower Saxony, more honest and tougher than those of Upper Saxony. A people of eccentrics and grumblers, fanatics and poets, cautiously, unremittingly energetic, exhausting themselves in destructive and wearying quarrels with their nearest neighbours, but at their best, united and surprising in their strength and inner riches. They have produced the most marvellously rough-hewn characters, originals, inventive, quarrelsome, creative, trampish, troublesome, but capable at once of highest poetic flights and deepest philosophic thought. Writers enjoyed writing more here, schoolmasters were prouder of their learning, preachers more eloquent, advocates more dogmatic, peasants more miserly, merchants greedier than elsewhere in Germany; no stranger ever felt quite at home with them or could get the best of them. But things were achieved here, creative things: carven and smelted, ploughed and planted, built and judged. There was a firmly-rooted pride in equitable dealing and honesty of purpose; here good work must be done for the State, and free German convictions must come to fruition.

The most artificial of all Napoleon's newly-created states was probably the Grand Duchy of Baden. The all too narrow strip of country which only attained to more reasonable proportions in its southern section, snuggled shyly between the Rhine, the Black Forest, and the Lake of Constance, and was obliged to put up with foreign neighbours to the west and south—neighbours whose pressure was felt the more because Alemannic cousins occupied the land beyond the frontier posts both in Switzerland and in France. Whether by accident or design the foreigners' possession of the same language and feelings caused their way of thinking and their form of state to react with strongly propagandist effect upon Baden. Württemberg lay relatively secure in the many folds of her mountainous territory, penetrated only by the upper courses of rivers; Stuttgart, the capital, had no difficulty in holding her own against such backward cities as Reutlingen, Heilbronn, or Ulm, to say nothing of still smaller townships. In the State of Baden there was no representative race like the Swabians of Württemberg. There were Alemans and folk from the Palatinate wondrously harnessed together in defiance of all historic development under the sceptre of a petty upstart dynasty, whose land of origin was the weakest element in this patchwork state.

How could a dull sober city like Karlsruhe, artificially constructed as a margravial residence of the plain, compete with Heidelberg, most German of universities; with Mannheim's cheeky burgess bustle; or with the power of Austrian tradition in Catholic Freiburg, capital of the Breisgau? The Rhine was anything but a frontier, much less a protection to Baden. A State was too small and weak a thing to have any effect upon this European waterway, with its will to traffic. The Rhine brought Baden's destiny rolling in from France and Switzerland—Baden must make the best of it. But the Rhine also joined Baden to the north, to her Hessian neighbours and above all, to Prussia. This South German State turned her back, so to speak, upon her South German neighbours and looked to west and north. The Baden dynasty, enjoying the fruits of the best inheritance of the electoral Palatinate, could expect no friendly feelings from Bavaria and was indeed regarded with open contempt. Her relations with Württemberg developed all too soon into a permanent condition of

94

jealous fault-finding. A dark shadow, cast by the moving and mysterious figure of Caspar Hauser, lay heavily upon the new Hochberg dynasty. The unsavoury scandal which so fatally connected the banker Moritz von Haber with the grand-ducal family, further weakened the position of the reigning house. Just before the March Revolution of 1848, the Bavarian envoy wrote that public spirit was much improved; "but what was totally lacking and vainly sought after, was any kind of hearty good-feeling for the reigning family."

Grand-Duke Leopold, first regent of the new line, wore his uniform well, like all the Hochbergs, but intellectually he was a nullity, naturally good-natured but incapable of speaking a word to a simple burgess, dependent upon empty-headed courtiers and obsequious toadies, shy and nervous by nature and therefore inclined to believe everything that was whispered in his ear and to adopt the pose of a severe and minatory ruler towards all popular leaders and such un-canny personalities. This insignificant prince evidently suffered under the curse that hung over his family, became gradually embittered and withdrew more and more completely from public life. The "Camarilla" looked after everything. Politi-cally, the Grand Duke was always painfully subject to inde-cision. When the Council of Ministers was unanimous, he found no difficulty in making up his mind. But if one member of the Cabinet raised a contradictory voice, he felt just as much or as little confidence in him as in all the others and fell into hopeless hesitation. How important to the building up of his country was the energy—even though all too meddle-some—shown by the King of Württemberg! Such a factor was entirely lacking in Baden. That Markgrave William, the second brother of the Grand Duke, should have come to the rescue, was anything but fortunate. The Markgrave conducted army affairs almost independently, as he thought best. He was a domi-nating general who had waxed mighty in Bonaparte's spirit, and was only too inclined to make use of his arrogant energy in other fields, particularly in the matter of appointments.

All these folk of the Palatinate, Rhenish Austrians, Mark-grave's subjects, Swabians from the Lake of Constance who had been turned by a whim of German history into Badensians, had truly deserved to fall into particularly good hands, to be particularly well protected. They were torn asunder by temperament and belief, customs and traditions, manner of speech and rhythm of living. What a contrast there was between the rough cheerfulness of a Neckar bargee and the dark, thoughtful seriousness of a peasant farmer from the heights of the Black Forest! There was a lighter-hearted strain that dwelt further on down the valley of the Rhine; these people were at once gentle and hot-headed, like their scirocco, the warm, rain-bringing "Föhn" wind, easily inflamed and impatient, comfortable, yet quick-witted, argumentative, but soon good friends again over clinking glasses. The whole land of Baden was a spoilt child of nature. It was Germany's golden garden, crowned by the refined, peaceful beauty of extensive pine-forests, a mild, warm tract of country, guarded by the blue hills, its people hospitable and friendly, perhaps a little too mild; full of amenities and humanities, with a feeling of kinship to all, eagerly absorbing culture and education, rather artistic than philosophical and inclined to overrate the value of the moment, the mood, themselves, and their own ways. The great stream of contemporary thought washed up to the land of Baden like the waters of the Rhine; she was exposed to its influence, wished to be and must be exposed to it, being western and European as she was. It was much later that Baden earned the honourable title of "a model country" bestowed in part in a not unjustifiable irony. Before and during the Revolution of 1848 it was anything but a model country and the contrasts of German life showed themselves here with especial crassness. This most artificial of all the states of the Rhine confederation had least of them all become a solid State, capable of resisting outside forces.

The reasons for this were far-reaching. Baden had an excellent constitution, but she was a frame without any picture. The proceedings of the Badensian Chamber deserved the attention they excited beyond the frontier of the little State. Yet the balance of political life was not in parliament, but in officialdom. The organization of administration was directly descended from the French prefecture system; the fundamental idea was that only a body of officials not native to the soil, responsible only to the central administration, could weld such various fragments of countries and populations into a unit. The weakness of the dynasty further increased the importance of the bureaucracy: the schematic wardenship of the ministerial officials of Karlsruhe thus took up the cudgels against all the native idiosyncracies of the folk of the Palatinate and of the Breisgau. Ministers still had no responsibility. The local government constitution of 1831 was not fully developed; the Press was suppressed. Courtiers and clergy supported the officials in their anti-constitutional efforts. The First Chamber lent itself only too eagerly to use as a tool against the elected Second Chamber. It was composed of the worst elements of the Court who were sensitively opposed to new demands, willing to make small alterations, but inclined to disregard the main matter at stake. The Second Chamber, thrust forward by a few lawyers in its midst, therefore developed a legal aspect, worked strictly according to the very thorough order of the day, and in its long-winded, often purely academical debates, endeavoured to proceed beyond the interests of individual strata to sober first principles and justifiable progress. It was just this ambition which annoyed the Government and irritated it into malicious acts of petty aggravation.

The first merchant who ever rose to honour in a German parliament, was Friedrich Bassermann of Mannheim; his business successes rendered him independent while still a young

97                                                      D

man, and he spoke and worked against the old system with an energetic simplicity, a solid understanding, a good will to construction which astonished his hearers. Naturally he soon became a leading representative of modern German citizenship. The *Landtags Zeitung* which he edited and published gave welcome publicity, far beyond Baden's frontiers, to the Chamber's proceedings. Many of the bills were intentionally programmatic in character, intended less to become law in Baden than to make propaganda in Germany, such as the petition to reduce the standing army and introduce a universal reserve force. Sharper and more critical in his thought than Bassermann, less prone to eloquence, was Karl Mathy, a very capable, quiet, severe, cool expert, long experienced in political battles, who had left the service of the State in the 'thirties in order to devote himself to journalism. That he had to earn his living as a school teacher in Switzerland had but strengthened his will. Feared by many, his knowledge of finance and his function as publisher of the *Rundschau*, as well as contributor to the *Landtags Zeitung* made him a power in the present and still more one to be reckoned with in the future. All these men, from Itzstein to Mathy, lived in the conviction that the creative world of the civilian was now about to come into its own, that the new conception of life and labour would build Germany over anew, and replace the dynastic-bureaucratic spirit. They hoped to attain these ends in Baden, as in the rest of Germany, by means of peaceful evolution; they saw the danger of impending revolution, but the nearer it approached, the less they desired it. They were inspired by the fresh young impulses that moved Germany at this time; they did what they could to bring about public consideration of political, religious and social questions, to awaken the fire of enthusiasm. Baden was in their minds, but Germany still more, their eyes were on Prussia and her struggles for a form of parliament, for they regarded this as an event which must materially affect the Fatherland as a whole. As an outcome of these ideas and feelings, the *Deutsche Zeitung* was founded at Heidelberg, the only paper which ever deserved this name. The very heart of Germany throbbed in its pages. The German spirit of the Middle Rhine is found here, pleading with South German warmth and West European intellectuality that German differences might be composed, that all strong and good forces in the Fatherland might be molten together to freedom and greatness. The object of the *Deutsche Zeitung*, said Gervinus in the prospectus, was to bridge over the "line of the Main" in constitutional life. A "free national governing body" must be created for Germany; Prussia must be the leader of Germany's constitutional history—this was clearly recognized and approved.

All who represented the policy of the *Deutsche Zeitung* must believe that the princes and officials could be amenable to instruction. There were already sceptics, and they wrenched unmercifully at the unity of liberal optimism. Was it not disturbing that the Prussian Government, on which such high hopes were set, amiably suffered the most poisonous attacks to be levelled by the socialistic *Trierer Zeitung* at the constitutional system? But when the attacked wished to rise in defence the censor's scissors were at once set clipping! In Baden, Gustav von Struve, a moody, eccentric man, embittered by these persecutions, thought social revolution the only means of achieving real progress. Struve was the son of an Imperial Russian Councillor of State, and was descended from an old German noble line whose members had been in Russian service only for two generations. "I have not a thread on me that is Russian," Struve used to say, when he was accused of being Russian, and he was right. His fanaticism was the only thing this diplomatic, cranky phrenologist and vegetarian, this learned lawyer, had in common with the dark passion of a Russian revolutionary. The dry pedant, *déclassé* and embittered, was only too German in many a bad sense without any strong good points to compensate for the evil. Outwardly unprepossessing, a stiff, unbending speaker, he could not win adherents by force of personality; his moralizing manner evoked boredom rather than admiration. His real strength appeared when he took a pen in hand; his style was sophistical, unmerciful, provocative, childishly intricate in idea, but in form full of the daring mordancy of the true revolutionary. Nothing could be more annoying to such a man than a conciliatory government and a moderate opposition, inwardly prepared to take over the reins of government. In his *Deutsche Zuschauer* Struve coined hard words for the "bourgeois parliamentarians: "Mandarins, parade-ground heroes, lip liberals," he called them.

The Badensian chamber had sixty-three members—Struve called them the sixty-three Rabbits; one lion was worth them all—and he evidently thought of himself as this one lion. Or did he mean the member Friedrich Hecker? Struve gained a growing influence over this young lawyer of Mannheim, imparted to him a knowledge of French and English socialistic theories, really made of him the "Social-Democrat" which Hecker was the first to call himself. His personality was certainly very different from Struve's, that gloomy man of the study, that grey phantast. Hecker was a splendid fellow, outwardly a fine masculine type, full of a great hunger for life, an eccentric person but a gay one, ready for any mad trick, long after his wild student's days were over. His gift of fascination had a great effect upon the crowds; he was full of self-confidence, full of desire for applause. He was a born leader, a born hero—in a world of comfortable philistines, his brilliant ideas, baroque manners and eloquent speech must be doubly impressive. He was certainly a man who could lead a storm upon the bureaucratic big-wigs, armed with wit and epigram and the clever arguments of a lawyer. Instinct showed him the essentials—he always found engrossing and fruitful themes —such as, in 1844, responsibility for ministers. No one could doubt his juristic talent; politically everything was rather in a muddle for him; he had read a good deal and could impress people with his reminiscences. He never had time to think things over quietly and clarify his own views. He did not want to; for battle meant more to him than reflection; he went storming forwards, believed in his inspiration and scarcely knew whence he had come, much less whither he was going. He entertained his grateful hearers with wit and rough humour and swayed them to his will. He had not much patience with preparation and consideration; he trusted the moment, feeling himself its darling. He was always to command, open as the day, a splendid companion and a faithful friend. Women and admirers ran after him, the more enthusiastically the more violently he threw them off. Since he was a spoiled child of happiness, he naturally had his moods; no one dare aggravate his obstinacy, and party discipline was burdensome enough to him. Old Itzstein, on account of his dialectic art and superior calm, was best able to contend with Hecker who, half jack-of-all-trades, half prima-donna, could easily be influenced through his vanity and who was bound to exercise a strong influence in unusual times by virtue of his charm, his heedless impetus, his childish joy in adventure and his belief in the miraculous. Struve seems to have been Hecker's destiny; in Hecker he found all the qualities which he lacked and perhaps painfully longed to possess. He was clever and more critical than Hecker, he goaded his ambition to ever greater heights; he convinced him that he, too, must will to achieve "the Whole" and not "the Half" with which the "bourgeois" Opposition were content. As early as March 1847, Hecker, estranged from his former colleagues, wished to resign from the Chamber, in order to seek new fields of action. At an expenditure of considerable effort, he was induced to remain. The Moderates also took pains to retain the strong and con-genial man. On the other hand, the moderate Liberals tried to prevent Struve's entry into the Chamber. His battle was already fully social-revolutionary. Consequently, the government

101

party had some significant successes in the supplementary elections of the autumn of 1847.

Heinrich von Gagern, who had fought at the Battle of Waterloo before he was sixteen, had been one of the founders and representatives of students' freedom leagues (Burschenschaften) in Heidelberg, Göttingen, and Jena. After completing his studies in Switzerland, he entered the civil service in Hesse-Darmstadt. He was heard of for the first time in the "stormy Diet" of 1832–33; he made a strong impression by his statement that he was first a German and then a Hessian. He was one of those to put a motion condemning abuses of office by ministers. After the dissolution of the Diet it was demanded of him that he surrender his key as a gentleman of the Bedchamber. He countered his enforced retirement on pension by sending in his resignation. He now devoted himself to agriculture, ceased from 1836 on to be a member of the Diet and took over his father's Rhenish estate. Close relations soon bound him to the leaders of the Badensian Opposition. He shared their views, but differed markedly from them on many points; for one thing he was never able to forget or set aside the aristocrat even in the weakest. He had no relations with the actual masses of the people and avoided, rather than sought them. There was in his nature something powerful and manly; much of his effectiveness depended upon his figure and his voice, his chivalrous bearing and power of expressive speech. But his speeches were too long, too abstract, too universal, too pompous—the effort not always commensurate with the cause. Thus from the beginning he made more impression through what he was than through what he did. His character surpassed his intellect; his best moments came when he obeyed his decent patriotic instincts; he was not equal to complicated situations or very important tasks—he lacked cool wit, critical acerbity.

As president of the Agricultural League in Rhenish Hesse, Heinrich von Gagern came into contact with all sorts and conditions of men. As he was quiet and yet cautious, he remained loyally within the lawful barriers and was driven forward by compelling ambition; he was considered in 1846 to be a man who would necessarily be heard of again. The Prussian envoy spoke of him as a personality "of parts as excellent as his principles are dangerous."

In the world of the German petty states we can distinguish a number of separate groups. We have had a look at the South German-Rhenish group; this also includes the territory of the Landgrave of Hesse-Homburg. The lord of this province appeared in Darmstadt from time to time to beg decorations for his favourites; but in every other respect he was particularly sensitive about emphasizing his sovereign rights. Frankfort, too, Free city and seat of the German Federation, belonged to this South-West German-Rhenish group, but at the same time to the special group of the four Free cities of Germany which still retained this character and must be treated separately. Geographically speaking, the North-West German group joined immediately on to the South-West group. Hanover, Electoral Hesse, Oldenburg, Brunswick, Waldeck, both the Lippes and Holstein belonged to this group; eastward of these came the Saxon-Thuringian group; finally the two Mecklenburgs comprised the East German group. The North-West German group —a compact and impressive mass—divided the two halves of Prussia from one another; the Saxon-Thuringian group was not so closely welded, but it was politically of equal importance and acted as a wall between Prussia, the Great Power, on the one hand and the Austrian Imperial State and Bavaria on the other. The only political importance of the East German group, consisting of the two Mecklenburgs, was that it served as an enclave inside Prussia. Thus the most Germanic lands of the south-west of Central Germany and Lower Saxony were completely in the grip of petty states. When the South-West Germans rallied to Württemberg, for instance, the North Germans to Hanover, the Central Germans to Saxony, it was possible of them either to cripple the policy of Prussia or Bavaria very effectively, or to afford it very considerable support. The jealous variance which reigned in this world of petty states usually prevented such possibilities from materializing. The lack of harmony was most perceptible round about Frankfort and in Thuringia; here the true patriots felt most strongly the painfulness and absurdity of the curse that lay upon Germany.

The position of the Grand Duchy of Hesse with regard to her neighbours in Central and North Germany might be compared to that of Württemberg in South Germany. Hesse's geographical position resembled that of Württemberg; it is a mountain country, pushed back from the Rhine by its hills; only in the country of Hanau does it touch the Main, otherwise it dominates only the upper courses of smaller rivers. With their excitable volubility, their tendency to political extremes, the Main Franconians of Hanau were a strange, almost an uncanny element in the Grand Duchy. The true Hessians, living between Fulda, Harburg, and Cassel, were akin in many ways to the Swabians; they drew real strength out of rich soil, had cautious minds of their own, loved custom and tradition, distrusted strangers' volatility, and had a strong sense of justice. Hesse did not produce as many brilliant and original sons as Swabia, but just as many who were capable, honourable, and reliable. Just as Württemberg stood between Bavaria and Baden, so Electoral Hesse stood between the stronger, more powerful Kingdom of Hanover and the weaker Grand Duchy of Hesse, which was influenced by Rhenish and liberal ideas. Electoral Hesse, like Württemberg, was mainly a country of peasants, craftsmen and officials, a country containing many small independent householders, still undisturbed, untroubled, by the industrial age. Numbers of young people wandered off every year into the more progressive neighbouring states to serve as harvest workers, day labourers, or domestic servants.

How contradictory it was, that such a loyal, patient, steady race as the Hessians should have received one of the very worst rulers among the many good and less good German princely houses! On the other hand, the tyranny of Hessian princes through generations did much to strengthen their subjects' feeling for order and ordered freedom. It is surely significant that in Hesse an independent system of law was instituted as early as the eighteenth century (Edict of 1743) and was further developed when in 1821, the processes of the law were separated from the administration. As early as 1765, the private Crown lands had been declared to be national property. The episode of the Kingdom of Westphalia brought much trouble upon the country, but also a whole series of reforms, which accustomed the population of Electoral Hesse to an existence as modern citizens—such as public, responsible justice, and Courts of Assize. When the Electoral House was restored the old Constitution was actually put out of commission up to the time of the July Revolution, because it was impossible to come to an agreement with the Diets. The new Hessian constitution of January 5, 1831, however, was rightly considered to be one of the freest in Germany. The pity of it was that the Electoral House did everything in its power to nullify the popular rights already established. According to the Constitution there was only one Chamber in Hesse: the electoral government was obstinately and distrustfully opposed to it. The ball flew to and fro. The princes, gentry, and nobles belonging to the Chamber, played a sorry part. They either supported the Government in perfect servility or else they were submerged in the great mass of the other deputies without any opportunity or ability to lead or to intercede. The nobility in Hesse may have been united as a class, but economically, as a consequence of the lack of a system of entail, they were weakened and divided. Except for the great estates of Malsburg, Waitz von Eschen, and Berlepsch, their lands were small, and were subdivided and burdened with debt. The Gilsas had three farms next to one another, each of them supporting a number of individual families. Two rich foundations at least provided for the unmarried daughters. Many of the nobles thought regretfully of the days of King Jerome; and the Corsican wealth of hair and the Buonaparte chin which appeared with a certain frequency among the county families of Hesse, kept the memory of Napoleon's brother alive and green. The restored Electoral House made it difficult precisely for those about the Court to remain as loyal as it was natural for them to feel. Thus the nobles with seats in the Chamber were often enough in doubt whether they should continue to make a stand against the middle-class liberal Opposition or not preferably join them against the Government. The liaison between Elector Wilhelm II and the Countess Reichenbach had deeply wounded the feelings of the nobility and the popular movement of 1831 therefore enjoyed considerable secret support in high places. At this time the Elector had given up living in Cassel and had retired with the Countess to Frankfort and appointed the Prince-Elector Friedrich Wilhelm to be co-Regent. The Regent looked after affairs quite on his own accord. Only the presentation of decorations was attended to by father and son alike. On February 10, 1846, Count Galen, Prussian envoy, wrote: "For the last ten months I have met no one, high or low, who did not feel either depressed or insulted and always by the ruler in person." Indeed, no rank, no degree was excepted. A volume of antagonism and hate had accumulated against the Regent. He was distrustful by nature and his clumsiness showed itself in his hesitating manner of speech. His gloomy disposition was probably proof against flattery, but also against any sensible criticism. It was astonishing that a prince whose nature was so arrogant should be so fond of gossip and tattle; but he sought the petty and despicable wherever it was to be found, discovered weaknesses and private interests everywhere, pedantically determined every step in advance, fulminated wrathfully against every disturbance, continually imagining threats and insults to his person. He purposely withdrew his favour suddenly and jeered at the disappointment that ensued. Growing continually narrower and pettier, he suffered only little minds about him. At first probably rather unhappy than evil, he became a real fatality for his unfortunate country. A brutal ruler, he horrified his poor people of Cassel by threatening to send artillery to destroy the Octagon in Wilhemshöhe Park unless it were at once put into repair—of course, at public expense! The prince had no good nature of any kind. Evidently he found it quite irresistible to insult every man jack of his subjects and injure their interests whenever it was in his power. And when he succeeded (which was almost invariably the case) his joy was so unabashed and openly displayed that people developed a feeling of absolute disgust for such a character. Worse than his tyranny, his incalculable whims, was this trait of maliciousness, sometimes amounting to absolute cruelty. The state of things grew worse from year to year and discontent waxed mightily in the land of Hesse—in this modest, decent, credulous country, where the least spark of good nature could kindle a flame of enthusiasm.

Countess Schaumburg, the prince's wife, was personally popular, as mother of several children, although she was known to favour those who served her interests. Prince Metternich showered attentions upon her. The Prince had purchased the lady in Bonn from her first husband, Lehmann, an officer of Hussars. In Electoral Hesse, people were thoroughly accustomed to loose living on the part of their rulers; there was the offspring Hessenstein and Haynau; and now there were also the lines Schaumburg and Hanau. The two sons of the Lehmann marriage were ennobled as Herren von Scholley.

This wild genealogy would not of itself have done the Regent any particular harm. His callousness, his obstinacy, his whims left deep wounds—and, of course, the shameless way in which he sought to found fortunes for his illegitimate descendants. That a serious control of outgoing expenses was desirable in a State "where for the last three princely generations millions had wandered into the pockets of illegitimate descendants—or at least, such as could not succeed to the title," as the Prussian envoy put it, was obvious.

Hanover, the largest of the German principalities, characteristically bore the name of the capital city, as was usual with the petty states. In consequence of the union with England, which lasted until 1837, the position of this State in Germany was a special one, of far-reaching importance. On Hanover's account, London State craft had been committed to a certain Continental policy which necessitated a defensive attitude towards France and a comradely feeling to the German States, especially to Prussia. Geographically and ethnically, the quiet and lovely Lower Saxon country formed a natural bridge to Anglo-Saxondom. The separation of Hanover from England which became necessary in consequence of Queen Victoria's accession was almost universally appreciated at the time as a piece of good luck for Hanover. Considered regionally, this may have been partly true. Speaking from the point of view of universal history, matters look rather different. The Franco-British Entente Cordiale became a living political combination only after this separation. It sometimes retired into the background, but never again disappeared completely from politics on the great scale. England turned aside from Central Europe. Hanover herself, the independent kingdom, was too large to be content with a position as a kind of Prussian enclave, like Anhalt or Mecklenburg; she was too small to be able to pursue a successful policy independent of the all-embracing Prussian State. If she worked together with Austria, the South Germans and Saxony, she must arouse the enmity of the mighty

Prussian neighbour, to which she eventually fell victim. If England and Hanover had remained together, Germany's unity would have needed to be consummated with more caution. The German Empire of 1871 would have been able to uphold the alliance of Waterloo without any difficulty; instead of which she slipped involuntarily into an opposition to England. Thus the history of nations was curiously and wondrously bound up with the accidents of dynastic succession.

The National Property Law (1833) had a calming effect upon the population of Hanover because the new regulation removed any appearance there had been that "the fat of the land" was being skimmed off and sent to London; it was rather the other way round. In the course of a century, the English Royal House had presented large sums to the ancestral land in that they renounced their dues and did not exact repayments.

Of course there was still an "old Hanover," composed of an old settled aristocracy who shared official positions with the better families among the well-to-do citizens. They were all held together by a quiet instinct for political order and probity; but this was just as much a vital force in the clear uprightness of the small citizenry and the calm pride of the farming population, which was widely distributed, many living like little lords on their farms in the midst of their wide and fruitful fields under the watery low-hung Low German skies. The language was clearer, more sharply accentuated and purer than in other parts of Germany, but easily became somewhat superior, on the strength of an inborn self-confidence. The people's manner of speaking was careful and could almost be called elegant, even among the simple folk, and a spirit of pertinacious criticism underlay their quiet sense of humour. Ever since ancient times there had been superior brains which evolved great thoughts about law and the State. Even in the modest average man there lurked a talent for recognizing what was practical and sensible. Here, too, as elsewhere in Germany, a violent longing for securing freedom began to awaken—here, it first became manifest in municipal administration. Old Osnabrück produced the finest fighter for political rights in the whole province of Hanover, in the person of its splendid Mayor Stüve. He was descended from an old official family, and son of that Osnabrück Mayor Stüve whose unselfish devotion to the general good in the stormy days of the Wars of Liberation had cost him his life at an early age. Johann Karl Bertram Stüve grew up in a proud tradition of upright public service. As a boy he had taken part in the Jahn gymnastic movement and the Students' Freedom Movement and, dissatisfied with the practice of law, had penetrated deep into the history of his native city and of Lower Saxony. Thus he ripened into a worthy successor of J. J. Möser, perfecting what Möser had begun, and he remained true to this preoccupation with history right into his old age—although or perhaps just because he took such a lively share in the political labours of his day. As a true friend of burgess and farmer, the mayor and member of parliament fought for the liberation of land and property, for order and clarity in communal life, for unity in State administration. The determined enthusiasm of this man, who appeared so unassuming, and was susceptible to no influence, defied all annoyance and unpleasantness and must needs be effective in achieving what was right and just—in accordance with Goethe's motto, which he adopted for his own: "Free in mind, but self-restrained—thinking of the next step gained."

The Hanoverian National Property Law of 1833 had made a beginning—many a necessary supplement could have been gradually and quietly developed from it. But it was now thrown out by the Duke of Cumberland, who ascended the throne of Hanover as King Ernst August, in 1837.

The character of this rabid sexagenarian was well-known all over Europe. Hanover had no good to expect from him. He had been a daring soldier, though he was never a general, or even a leader; in England he had fought for all Tory interests with iron obstinacy—his stubborn resistance to instruction was still greater than his military aplomb. As head of 300,000 Orangemen, he felt himself to be a power in England, and in the interests of young Queen Victoria, the turn of affairs that carried the wicked and incalculable disturber of the peace off to the Continent was blessed by the politically well-informed. He was poorly educated and understood nothing of the longings that stirred the Germany of his day. His inborn Guelph arrogance was heightened by insular snobbery. Such a despiser of his kind, surrounded by dark clouds of scandal, must needs find a certain delight in disturbing the peace, denying justice, stamping out happiness and mocking at the modest and weak. This man could work hard when he chose; his inborn wit saw through the weaknesses of his opponents and flayed them with sovereign sarcasm; his impudent plain-speaking rose superior in every practical way to honest German thoroughness, loyally grubbing over trifles and haggling over petty points. Artful as he was, he always spoke in plain terms of the most secret affairs of State, even before the lackeys. His iron nature was for a long time equal to anything, even to measureless unreason in the matter of diet. The only really sympathetic trait in his nature was his private charity and care for old faithful retainers.

Owing to a strange course of development, the name of the Saxon race was thrust out of its homeland in North-West Germany and planted by the royal families in Central Germany and even as far as Eastern Germany. Old Saxon, that is Lower Saxon territory, only embraced a part of the Prussian province of Saxony. But the Kingdom of Saxony had been hard pushed and much diminished by the rise of Prussia. The Albertinian line of electors and the many scions of the Ernestinian line, distinguishable only by their various places of residence, took up territory which was not really Saxon at all. The Thuringians had always been there, and next, beginning already in Thuringia, there came the Upper-German-Slavic mixture whose nature seems in many respects to be the complete contrary of Old Saxon and Lower Saxon; in Lower Saxony we find a people slow, silent, enduring, distrustful; in Thuringia, and still more in the Kingdom of Saxony, we find mobile adaptability, a companionable tendency to chatter, willingness to make friends. On the one hand, a tendency to brooding and fanciful imaginings, to eccentricity and obstinacy; on the other, untiring energy, business acumen, practical enterprise, ready adaptability. On the one hand men with a quiet, almost melancholy sense of humour and deep feeling for justice and decency, men who had themselves well in hand, but had little gift for art; on the other hand, men ready of tongue, witty, fond of teasing, easy-going and unceremonious, with much artistic talent, but more likely to be technicians or musicians than imaginative writers or painters—men fond of their own opinions and proud of their education.

Thuringia, heart of Germany, has always presented a microcosmic panorama of the destiny of the German organism. Up to our own time, Thuringia has given us a classic exhibition of the splitting into petty states, the worst legacy of the old empire, such as must excite the mournful amusement of all who were more or less concerned with it. The merry, industrious population was and remained all too freely supplied with princes and overlords; castles and monasteries were stormed and laid in ruins—new castles and lordly seats soon sprang up again in the pleasant valleys, among the rugged rocks, in the lonely forests and on the lush meadows of the plains. From the Wartburg to the fortress of Coburg, from the "Stone of Peace" at Gotha to the most sacred haunts of Weimar, there was many a building to bear witness to the veneration and protection afforded by German princes to the faith and spirit, science and genius of the regions. There were so many royalties in Thuringia and so few masculine Christian names in comparison, that the people and history were forced to give nicknames to most of them in order to distinguish one from another. Thus there was a Friedrich the Stern, Ernst the Pious, Albrecht the Naughty, Ludwig the Holy; for another Friedrich no more characteristic nickname could be found than Friedrich of the Bitten Cheek—his mother having given him this mark. Every possibility of division of inheritance and succession had been tried among these rulers of Thuringia, two brothers even once taking turns to reign at the same time. There had once been as many as twenty-four of these rulers; there were still ten. Oldenburg had two far-flung pieces of territory, Birkenfeld and the principality of Lübeck. Brunswick consisted of a number of scattered oddments; but there were far more curiosities of the kind in Thuringia, which put the rest of Germany in the shade. The Grand Duchy of Saxony-Weimar-Eisenach consisted of two principal parts and eleven islands; Coburg-Gotha had two principal parts and nine enclaves, Altenburg, one main section and five enclaves. The countries had been divided up as if they were estates—every one was to have a richer and a poorer portion, a bit of woodland and a bit of pasture.

The attempt to clear up the property muddle in Thuringia by a Partition Commission failed in 1826, on account of the special wishes of the individual rulers. There could be no political life, no real political history in such a country. By splitting up into the pettiest of petty states, the princes cultivated the spirit of the small town, the spirit of scandal-mongering cliques, cringing dependency, toadying, the false smile and crocodile tear of assiduous devotion; certainly there was such a thing as history and administration, of course there was economic development and growth of education—but less a Saxon-Weimarian development than Thuringian and German. Everything valuable and progressive in the bits of states must, even more than elsewhere, serve and belong to the Fatherland as a whole. The Thuringian petty states, managed after the fashion of private estates, might perhaps do well enough for a time, as they had done in olden days; but as soon as a modern State organization was demanded, such contradictions arose, that the decay and dissolution of tradition became inevitable. In the quiet valleys of the many-hollowed mountain country, there were still many peculiarities of speech, custom, and costume. What a contrast between the poverty-stricken woodland villages with their beginnings of home industries, their poaching habits, their strange atmosphere of doleful devil-may-care, and the broadly-planned, comfortable, flowery agricultural villages, where there was no lack of cakes and ale and dancing on the green! Nowhere were the farmers so proud as in Altenburg. The strangest costume in Germany was worn here with dignity, especially by the women with their high bibs and all-too-abbreviated, close-fitting skirts. Over a thousand farmers and their wives and daughters were present at the famous Altenburg Farmer's Wedding of 1843. Six hundred horses took part, brilliantly currycombed and gaily decorated. One hundred and fifty young men followed the best man, one hundred and thirty-three richly dressed girls were bridesmaids. In the village hall of Altenburg, the old loving cup made the rounds and even the Duke himself descended from his castle and celebrated with his peasants. Yet in the city of Altenburg, a strong radical movement, even a convinced republicanism were to develop.

The old Thuringian coaching villages owed much to the country's central position—but their golden age was definitely over when the railway between Berlin and Frankfort was finished at last in spite of all the difficulties put in its way by Electoral Hesse. The secret capital of Thuringia was still, as it had always been, Erfurt, the old seat of great mercantile houses, carriers, and agents; it was from here that Prussia took a hand in the economic and traffic policy of Thuringia and its petty-state ways, allying herself with the modern spirit of the citizens, whose intellect had always been stimulated by the presence of the university in opposition to the baroque spirit of petty princedom. Gera and Greiz, Zeulenroda and Apolda were already considerable manufacturing towns; Suhl, an old German arsenal, blossomed anew with its rifle factories in response to Prussia's considerable demand—whereas Ruhla had to take to making knives, finding that only a few connoisseurs still took pleasure in its famous meerschaum pipes since cigar smoking had come into fashion. On account of Prussia's Zollverein Sonneberg again rose to be a great centre of the toy industry—at starvation wages, to be sure, for a turner received only two Kreuzer for a dozen toy post-horns. Pitch and tar were the industry of Ilmenau, Elgersburg, and Gräfenroda. The forest, Thuringia's pride and fortune, had since olden times belonged for the most part to ruling houses. In Weimar 44 per cent of the forest belonged to the Grand Duke, in Meiningen 43 per cent, in Gotha as much as 75 per cent to their princes. Arboriculture was a well-nurtured science, hunting the deer and wild boar the favourite and most brilliant sport. But woe to the subject who should presume to take his share! The forest impoverished the people and enriched their princes. We may well say that it was only forest riches which enabled the Duke of Gotha to collect books and coins and the ruler of Coburg his famous copperplate engravings. Weimar could not have composed poetry and produced plays, Jena could not have furthered research and thought without the foundation of this forest wealth. Gotha and Hildburghausen were rivals of the printing press; each residency wished to excel the others in museums, pleasure gardens and stately architecture. After the great generation of poets was extinct, Weimar, feeling the unrest of the lesser successor, devoted attention to the graphic arts and to music. Naturally such munificence on the part of unduly moneyed princes encouraged a whole section of the middle-class as a kind of clientèle. The intellectual element was swamped by the purveyors to the Court, by mean inquisitiveness, and the pertinacity of parasites.

Martin Luther was nowhere so near and familiar a figure as he was in Thuringia and Electoral Saxony. He had grown to manhood here, suffered and laboured here, his strong courage and determined action had shown their first fruits here. People knew the places where he had lived, been persecuted and again and again marvellously snatched from danger. His Bible came from the Wartburg, his Lord was a fortress like Coburg. The churches in which he had preached loomed the more venerable through such mists of memory. The folk already had their legends of the Kyffhäuser with its Barbarossa and of Tannhäuser in the Venusberg, and now, more alive, warming the heart, came many a legend, saying, and story of Dr. Martin, the Man of God, the Man of the People—Luther churches and Luther oaks bore witness to his name. There were not many Catholics in Thuringia. In many places Jews were scarcely allowed, in others not at all. Luther's spirit was powerful; in Divine Service the oldest form still persisted in many cases. But tolerance was the rule. On the spot where Boniface had first preached, a three-armed candelabra was erected, a Catholic, a Lutheran, and a Calvinist minister consecrated it in common. In front of the lofty Cathedral of Erfurt, which together with the Church of St. Severin, dominates the market-place so gloriously, the Evangelical and Catholic school children sang in chorus on every St. Martin's Day, in honour of the good Saint and the great Reformer.

The March of Meissen and the March of Brandenburg had been rivals for centuries. Both had the dignity of electorates, both achieved royal honours through association with non-German powers. If the Electors of Brandenburg merely became regents for Prussia as fief holders of Poland they soon succeeded in assuming sovereignty as kings. But Electoral Saxony allied herself with Poland at first hand and thus rose in rank and prestige almost to the status of a European Great Power. Even today Warsaw has the Saxon Garden and the Saxon Palace to remind us of that East-German-West-Slavonic Union which strengthened both countries politically and enriched them in cultural aspects. The Electoral Saxon dynasty of the Wettins and their nobility now became Roman Catholic and baroque, grand seigneurs, patrons of art, artists in living. On account of Poland, the dynasty and the nobles thought themselves much superior to the Hohenzollerns and their land Junkers. Certainly they were more grandiose, greater lords in outlay and extravagance, in architecture and luxury, and the nobles could bear comparison with their Silesian, Bohemian, and Polish neighbours. Precisely on this account, the dynasty and nobles in Saxony were especially estranged from the people. The energy of the subjects was astonishingly developed at a very early stage. Their industry and ingratiating manners paved the way to success, their wants remained simple for a long time, and were cautiously rational. Only such barbaric neighbours as Brandenburgian Prussians and Bavarian Franks could have cast moral aspersions upon the polite tact that governed Saxon cultural intercourse. But the unmannerly Prussians had conducted their politics for a long time past at Saxony's expense. The Wettins took sides with Austria, later with Napoleon, and thus Prussia's rise and good fortune was Electoral Saxony's downfall. The Kingdom of Saxony was a very modest remnant of the old magnificent possessions— and the Prussians had even annexed the name of Saxony for a province which at that time was still styled a "dukedom." Leipzig, at any rate, had not become part of Prussia, and this at least was a blessing for the political and intellectual culture of all Germany. Thus the proud old merchant city could develop in relative freedom and remain the ruling centre of German literary production. The Prussian censorship would never have permitted her to assume such a lordly position.

Dresden remained the aesthetically cultivated and loyal residential city of a particularly ceremonial and dignified Court, which now sought to find in pious grandiloquence and cautious patronage of art and learning a substitute for lost political importance.

The German Catholic Movement brought several men of decided Liberal opinions to the fore: Franz Wigard, master of stenography, Rewitzer, a master-weaver, Heinrich Wuttke, a professor of history, who came from Silesia—and above all, Robert Blum, one of the most important figures of the age and perhaps the most remarkable.

For amongst all these bearers of deeply-founded university learning, among the well-meaning descendants of old official families, in the fairly large circle of freedom-loving aristocrats, among the paunchy masters of farms or factories, among the many brilliant, patriotic writers, schooled by drawing-room intercourse and foreign travel, by the study of world literature, as well as by the sterling simplicity of German middle-class culture—into the midst of this loyal, well-attuned circle of leaders of the Revolution of 1848, trod a man who had nothing of all this, who was nothing of all this, a man who had come from the depths—a rare thing enough in those days!—into the midst of this middle-class world, in spite of all barriers and blocks that might have kept him down—a man who could truly say that whatever he was, he had made of himself. Freiligrath later called him a Child of the People, a proletarian, using the fashionable word of the day; it was only half true. Bitter poverty dogged him from the cradle, a far worse thing in the privileged class society of 1800 than later proletarian scarcity. Blum went to a Jesuit school up to the fifth class; then he learnt many things, but he had neither time nor means to learn a real trade. He was pitched about from pillar to post, given a job, exploited—then off he went again, to clutch at something new and work his way up. He had the great physical strength of the true man of the people, a wideawake mind, always on the watch for new impressions, and he felt a healthy courage surging in him, an urge to turn himself and the rusty society about him, on which he was continually bruising himself, into something better. He worked for a lamp factory and wrote poems for Saphir's "Schnellpost." He sat for years at the cash-desk of the Leipzig theatre, after beginning there as porter; he not only kept the books, but turned wholly to literature. The city of booksellers made a bookseller of him; he read, he wrote many well-observed, well-written articles, he made fun, in good Rhenish fashion, in the pages of the *Sächsische Vaterlandsblätter* of the ways of the petty state, and he issued popular anthologies. The merchant sense had awakened in him. In his lean days he had learned to value every penny saved, he laid aside one thaler after another, became a happy husband and father, and prospered more and more as a result of untiring toil. He had the Rhenish gift of eloquence; he gave the sober Saxons something to which they were not accustomed—a quality rare in those climes—the warmth of true passion. On Schiller's Day, every year on November 10th, which was also his own birthday, he collected an evergrowing circle of listeners about him in the Schiller Society which he had founded; the poet of freedom and of the people gained a new prophetic grandeur, a figure set up for the people by a man out of their midst. His method of oratory was new; he did not teach, nor was he learned; but he talked "cultured" as was then demanded of him; making a clever use of poetical quotations. He was very clever in boldly summarizing historical and political developments, powerful because informed by a sound and honest humanity, carrying the hearers away by the driving power of political will behind the words. He also founded a society for practising oratory and thereby educated his followers. From the State he demanded not only political rights, but also possibilities of work for everyone. The new and continually growing class of mercantile and artisan employees, condemned to lack of independence and influence, saw in Robert Blum a fragment of themselves, in his thick-set figure with the irregular features and the shaggy beard, a simple, rough and very vital man of the people. He knew their language, their tastes, and their needs from his own experience. He need take no pains to understand and explain them to himself, and therefore these oppressed and yearning people understood him in their turn. He spread about him a magic sense of power. Serious and manly was Robert Blum's speech, often swelling to heights of solemnity; in the mastery of sonorous periods he had not his equal. Then again he would flatter his hearers and move them to the ready tears that flowed so easily in those days. There is an ugliness that fascinates: Blum might have stood model for some roughly carved Apostle Peter or James on an altar on the Lower Rhine; his irresistible prophetic quality was labelled demagogy by his opponents. His qualities as popular orator and agitator were equalled by scarcely another man of his age; but it would soon appear that in matters political he could also speculate cautiously and reckon like a clever tactician.

In the course of a stormy and arduous life of toil, Robert Blum had become estranged from the Roman Catholic faith of his childhood without openly breaking with it. He married according to the Evangelical rite, but joined the German Catholic Movement; it was welcome to him for the sake of the cause, for he felt as a free and liberty-loving Christian, but also because here he saw new possibilities of working effectively. He liked to fight against the mighty; he was always battling for emotional values; the State and society were as sacred to him as religion. And everywhere and always he was fighting for his most sacred goddess—Liberty.

The real old German nobility still remained for the most

120

part as securely entrenched as ever behind influence, fortune and prestige in their castles and towers. The citizen's castle was the city. The only country that could compete with Germany in the matter of princely and noble residences was Italy. In richness of variety of municipal development, Germany probably surpassed even Italy. Now, of all the many city republics of the old empire, only four remained—the two smaller, Lübeck, the old Queen of the Baltic, and Bremen, ruler of the North Sea, and the two larger: Hamburg, the first city on German soil that really developed the spirit of a great city, and, finally, Germany's most dignified city, Frankfort, proud of its Emperors and of Goethe, now a royal residency and capital of the German Federation.

Once the Emperors of the Holy Roman Empire had reigned remote and almost divine over the German city republics. Now this illusionary uppermost overlordship had also disappeared. The last four cities stood stately as republican equals of the principalities. But the republican spirit was not only alive in these four cities which had remained free. Everywhere the old imperial cities sought to maintain their civic individualities as against the royal residency towns.

We can distinguish three groups of German cities in which opposition first reared its head against the tyranny of the princes, against the remnants of absolutism and feudalism. The first group is that of the former ecclesiastical residencies, a small number of which were still seats of bishops and archbishops. The Neo-Roman movement, with which German Catholicism was also imbued, had a strong tinge of democracy. In spite of many obvious contradictions, this agreed pretty well in decisive points with the spirit which was awakening in the middle and lower classes. Cologne and Mainz, Trier and Hildesheim, Paderborn and Münster, Erfurt and Quedlinburg, Eichstädt and Osnabrück, Speyer and Würzburg, Bamberg and Regensburg—different as they were, they had an older or newer spiritual relationship and they all combined to develop this movement, the decisive moment of which was the loud or low-voiced opposition to the government of the moment and to the temporal ruling house. There was something radical in all these States, in many even a touch of republicanism.

The second group was made up of the smaller university towns. The old constitutions of the universities had sprung from the aristocratic city republics of the European Middle Ages; the universities had nearly all become representative of the spirit of independence towards governments, representatives of the great philosophical and literary culture of the German Revival, representatives, too, of the battle for the liberty proper to a free citizen. Graz and Innsbruck, Tübingen and Heidelberg, Freib˘rg and Bonn, Jena and Kiel, Göttingen and Giessen, Marburg and Halle—each had its martyrs among the professors and still more among the students; they were all German, far more than they were Austrian, Hanoverian, Württembergian, Badensian, Hessian, Thuringian or Prussian; they also had a decisive effect upon the spirit of the cities in which they lived; they made of these cities islands of culture, of intellect, of liberal ideas; and where ever there was a living, productive, civic spirit, as in Breslau and Leipzig, university and burgesses combined in a relation which was fruitful for both parties. If a public for a Catholic People's Party came into being in the former ecclesiastical sees, in the university cities there were leaders and followers for a German-Patriotic Progressive Party.

The former Imperial cities and the still remaining Free cities form the third group. Augsburg and Nuremberg fought against the royal capital, Munich. These two particularly dignified Imperial cities actually succeeded in surviving the Imperial Deputation's Main Closure, but finally fell victim to the new State of Bavaria. But in Kempten, too, in Memmingen, Lindau, Kaufbeuren, Nördlingen, Dinkelsbühl, Rothenburg, and Schweinfurt, there was an individual spirit, a consciousness of personal values and individual tradition, an aversion to being governed from above, after having governed oneself so long. Against the reign of princes in Stuttgart we find the former Imperial cities arrayed—Ulm and Ravensburg, Reutlingen and Esslingen, Rottweil and Aalen, Schwäbisch Gmünd, Biberach, and especially Heilbronn. It was no accident that precisely in Offenburg, which now belonged to Baden, there were such mighty liberal demonstrations—here, too, we find old Imperial city spirit. How proudly old Wimpfen, now become a Hesse-Darmstadt enclave, resented Darmstadt governmental wisdom —and the Prussian enclave Wetzlar was in a like position. In the midst of Nassau, on the River Lahn, she dreamed of the glorious days of the Imperial Courts of Chancery. Gelnhausen now belonged to Electoral Hesse, Friedberg to the Grand Duchy of Hesse; Prussia had taken over relatively few old Imperial cities, with the exception of Wetzlar; only Dortmund, Goslar, Mühlhausen, and Nordhausen; but they too were favourable centres for fomenting the spirit of middle-class opposition. To be sure, these Imperial cities had not become democratic republics; but they were filled with the spirit of middle-class toil, the spirit of progress and decay according to ability and effort, the spirit of co-operation in life and labour. Much had grown stunted and weazen in bad times; the elected city lords had stiffened in the arabesques of tradition; but the burgess was a law unto himself, distrusting the prince, the army, and the officials alike. The new principalities reciprocated this distrust and were careful to keep the old city republics on short commons—in order to have all the more surplus for their residencies. In the long run, these communities reaped all manner of advantages from belonging to a large national body, some of them blossomed afresh, but others gradually petrified and were re-discovered as interesting relics by a later and once more romantic age.


Lübeck was the smallest of the four remaining city republics.

Long before the history of the Buddenbrooks was written by one of her great sons, Lübeck herself had suffered the Buddenbrook fate. Once, as chief city of the Hanseatic League, she had waged war against Denmark, had reigned on Bornholm and owned counting houses in London, Bergen, Wisby, and Novgorod. This old Lübeck grandeur had long since disappeared; but the shield of Lübeck was still held high with republican pride. Her position on the "Lübeck stream" was incomparable—the much-winding Trave, emptying into the deep-cut bay, offered, as of old, the best harbour on the Baltic coast, comparable only with the favoured harbours of English coast towns. It was decided to regulate the Trave, when Kiel, with its railway to Altona, threatened to divert the shipping. Independent and self-confident, the merchants of Lübeck carried on their trade in timber, pitch, hemp, and wines; their splendidly developed commission and carrying trade brought in rich and easily-earned profits. For a long time Lübeck was the leading port of exchange for southern fruits and wines and western manufactured goods to Scandinavia and Russia. Until 1846, the steamship service of St. Petersburg was privileged by the Czar of Russia. It was the best travelling connection and meant big business for Lübeck, until Prussia developed Stettin into a dangerous rival. The old town was far enough removed from the new life that stirred in Germany; no great river bound it up with the heart of the Fatherland, as the Elbe bound Hamburg and the Weser, Bremen. Lübeck kept its place with dignity and comfort in its corner of Eastern Germany, a great figure to her Mecklenburg and Holstein neighbours, yet small compared to Hamburg or to Prussia.

Conditions in Bremen were less easy going. Here civic freedom was a relatively new thing; the key in the Bremen coat of arms proved that the city's first claim to importance had been as an ecclesiastical centre and the seat of archiepiscopal power. The burgess lords had to fight for their right of self-determination against the old ecclesiastical domination. The warlike Archbishop Albert II burnt the wooden figure of Roland, symbol of the city's independence—then Roland was set up again, this time in enduring stone. The constitution dated from the fifteenth century and was but little altered in 1813. Up to the year 1848, the Bremen citizen took the oath of "Eintracht," "Neue Eintracht," and the Bürgerbuch— Unity, New Unity and the Citizen's Code—a mixture of principles, traditions, laws, and judgments, things written, and things of hearsay, a hotch-potch which, taken altogether, formed a kind of fundamental law—and up to the beginning of the century, this oath was taken in broadest Lower Saxon dialect. It was not until 1648 that the Emperor acknowledged Bremen's immediate subordinacy to the Crown, and it was not until 1741 that jealous Hanover consented to recognize this. The Council reigned mightily over the city; at its side was the Citizens' Assembly; the members' term of office was also for life, but they were a convention of Notables, invited to stand for office by the Council, not elected; they cast their votes according to parishes and families, and managed all business as quietly as possible, through their trusted agents who knew every man in his home. Only citizens of the old town sat in this convention; the new town and the suburbs were not represented; the countryfolk were wholly under the city's thumb, they were in a league of owner-farmers and had no political rights of any kind. The commercial spirit which gave the city life and riches, never allowed caste and class privilege to gain an undue influence. Agrarian aristocracy can hold its own for centuries; among the merchant patricians of Bremen there was a relatively rapid rise and fall. Riches, prestige, dignity, influence among the burgesses must be preserved by toil and ability. Old families dwindled rapidly away, new ones rose still more rapidly.

Apart from wars and princes, in its corner of the North Sea coast, closer to East Friesland and Holland than to the Empire.

and long threatened by Sweden, Bremen carried on an upright and capable civic existence, cautious and decisive, filled with the stern concentration of the Calvinistic spirit, a Calvinist city, rejecting Lutherans almost as sternly as Catholics and quite without Jews. Ships from Bremen had sailed since olden times to Spain and Portugal, to Bordeaux and Rotterdam, to London and Riga. The young merchant usually went to England to learn his craft, and voyages to the United States, to the West Indies or Buenos Aires were an everyday matter since the 'twenties. Although much in the city itself was hide-bound, the mercantile element was inwardly at high tension and its members applied to their actions the measure of the great world, to which the Germany of that day did not belong.

This little Bremen with its ever-growing commerce had a rare piece of good fortune, especially rare in German petty states, but not only in these—she possessed a statesman. Johann Smidt, born in 1775, was the son of a clergyman of the Calvinist persuasion and himself studied theology; when he was only twenty-seven, he was chosen a member of the Senate. He soon became Mayor. He was a most intellectual man of simple nature, and perhaps the first to comprehend in full clarity the commercial and cultural mission of the Hanseatic League. As a good Bremensian and German patriot, he battled for this end, trying to create the best possibilities of free development for his native city. For many years he represented Bremen in the Frankfort Federal Diet: here he took care that the Grand Duke of Oldenburg should no longer burden traffic on the lower Weser by inflicting an excise duty at Elsfleth. Smith's most historic action, however, was to acquire a barren strip of heath on the Lower Weser near Hanover, almost in secret, much to the annoyance of many of his critical and short-sighted countrymen. Here was the cradle of Bremerhaven, the bridge to world traffic for the Free State, lying as it did, deep inland, as it were, in the background.

London is a world city, because it is a city on the sea; Paris has always had its "Le Havre," its sea and world harbour, a near neighbour to rescue it from continental narrowness. It is a part of German destiny that Germany is so deserted by the sea. The Baltic, once the scene of great historical events, sank, in consequence of the development of true overseas traffic, to a kind of inland water; and the German North Sea coast, with its tendency to silt up with sand and the wall of islands in front of it, has the most unfavourable configuration imaginable. Nowhere is there a great natural harbour which would render the growth and development of a mighty city possible. Bremen and Hamburg both lay deep inland; both must, as it were, run after the sea.

All German capitals have a decided continental character. Vienna is a suburb of the mountains; in order to reach the sea, she must cross mountains and traverse the lands of stranger peoples. No German city is further removed from the sea and the great world than Munich. Frankfort and Cologne are at least, like Vienna, connected with the sea by great rivers, but their nearest coast bears a foreign flag. Berlin's position is distinctly that of a city set upon a small river and its marine suburb, Stettin, also lies unfortunately on a Baltic blind alley. This explains why Hamburg became the first German great city, both in spirit and power; for although other cities surpassed her in extent and population, they retained their small-town character much longer.

Hamburg's trade, secured by numerous commercial treaties with all great foreign powers, rose in the 'twenties and 'thirties to even prouder heights. Even at that time, the European continent was Hamburg's customer, and the Anglo-Saxon and Spanish oversea world Hamburg's business friend. In these peaceful days money was much more quickly earned than a generation later. Lübeck remained cabined and confined, Bremen correctly professional; but in Hamburg there developed a comfortable feeling of superiority, a taste for the highest quality, a love of pleasure which was thorough and almost temperamental, an undismayed, never discouraged instinct for daring enterprise—all unique in the Germany of that day. Only in such a country as Germany, where generations of petty princes' subjects had never been able to get enough to eat, was it possible for the Hamburg citizen to acquire a reputation for undue enjoyment of the pleasures of the table; as a sterling Republican, good things to eat were as much a matter of course to him as a good stroke of business or a good play at the theatre. The Hamburg citizen was no narrow Puritan; he understood men and the world well enough to enjoy many a good laugh at both; but he balanced this worldly wisdom by using his knowledge to ensure a handsome annual balance on the credit side of his banking account. He had as good a judgment of the comfortable qualities of an armchair as of the trustworthiness of a ship; in spite of his occasional enjoyment of light entertainment, he had a contempt for disorderly living of any kind; that a respectable man should live in his own house seemed to him not only a matter of course, but almost a moral obligation. He understood most things in the world, but least of all that anybody could despise money.

The constitution was scarcely in accordance with such worldly-wise ripeness of civic enterprise. After the Liberation in 1819, the Senate clung to the method of supplementing from within which had been established by the reforms of 1710 and 1712. A modest step forward was the admission of Calvinists and Roman Catholics to the dignity of Councillor, which had until then been reserved for Lutherans. But the Jews were not given any further rights. Not until 1833 were the citizens of the suburbs admitted to the Citizens' Convention. The countryfolk continued to be deprived of all political rights.

Thus we have an aristocratic-class republic, living in pompous, arabesque style. On account of this cumbrous and opaque machinery, overburdened with weight of tradition, the legal, educational and police affairs of the great, flourishing city were not administered in accordance with actual civic needs. In Bremen and still more in Lübeck, the State remained much longer in harmonious adjustment with the city's real life; in Hamburg everything was more earnest and serious. The crooked little alleys of the old town, the wretched haunts of poverty and misery on the banks of stagnant canals were a horrible contrast to the rising prosperity of the commercial classes, and traditional patriarchal care could do but little to bridge such differences.

A terrible catastrophe which befell Hamburg in 1842—the great fire—eventually proved to be a great blessing. Patriotic sympathy went out to help the Hamburgers—her sister city, Frankfort, at its head—and once more brought Hamburg, which had been in closer connection with England and overseas than with Germany, back into a new community with the rest of the country. The best element in the Hamburg spirit came into its own; in rebuilding the city, of which a fifth had been destroyed, many had the courage to begin rebuilding the State. Publicists launched their proposals, patriotic society was aroused. The parishes began to wake up and the Senate actually determined to allow outsiders a glimpse of the budget. To the discomfort of the rich, there was a lively discussion as to the possibility of Hamburg joining the Customs Federation. The influential merchants remained supporters of Free Trade, and when Richard Cobden passed through Hamburg in 1847, they gave him a demonstratively enthusiastic reception. An unheard of event happened.

In rebuilding the destroyed quarters of the town, a number of abuses had come to light which could only serve to strengthen the spirit of opposition. The technicians presented a petition to the Senate, complaining with reason that from engineer to navvy, all the men employed were English, and that machines and material had been procured from England which could have been bought cheaper in Germany. Even the estimates were set forth in English measurements and prices and had been hung up in the Town Hall in English without any translation being provided.

The cult of everything English was a weakness to which the Hamburgers were to be subject for a long time to come; often it looked as though this German city were really an Anglo-Saxon harbour and wharf on the Continent, a kind of European Hong Kong. The half of all the ships that ran into Hamburg flew the Union Jack.

Lübeck, Bremen, and Hamburg always lay somewhat removed from Germany, their individual life was almost independent of the Empire and probably the Empire could do quite well without them. But Frankfort's destiny had always been historically bound up with that of the Empire. The free city, as a republic, now lay squeezed in between many principalities. The sea was for the three Hanseatic states the best portion of their sovereign territory and at the same time their guarantee of freedom. No one had attempted to interfere with this freedom after the Wars of Liberation. Frankfort, the city on the Main, was an object of many desires. Bavaria would like to have acquired Frankfort in order to gain a bridge to the Rhine and the Palatinate—quite justifiably from the point of view of her historical development. Frankfort had the warm partisanship of the Freiherr vom Stein to thank for the preservation of her freedom. Metternich was obviously won over by a munificent gift of money. It is strange to observe how Frankfort's fate is bound up with the individualities of the three great German statesmen of the nineteenth century. Stein's feeling for freedom and justice and Metternich's covetousness procured the city her republican independence, until Bismarck's Prussian greed for annexation made an end of it.

For those Germans and others who have the misfortune not to come from Frankfort, it is difficult to comprehend the measure and unique quality of Frankfortian self-confidence. Frankfort, to be sure, was the capital and seat of the German

Federation and therefore had reason to feel herself the most distinguished of German cities. Economically and intellectually she dominated a West German-South-West German district bounded approximately by the line Eisenach-Coblenz-Karlsruhe-Würzburg. Frankfort had developed herself into a centre on the Middle Rhine between the countries of the Upper and the Lower Rhine—on the strength of her position, famous for centuries and always victorious over all difficulties, at the remarkable corner where the Rhineland, South Germany, and Central Germany all find a meeting-point. A more healthy and straightforward course of older German history might have made of Frankfort a world city, which could have rivalled Paris. She now remained behind, but maintained herself bravely as a great city on the Rhenish backbone of Europe, equal to Zürich and Milan, Cologne, Brussels, and Amsterdam. Frankfort, as a Latin poet of the sixteenth century put it in his affected way, was Mercury's daughter. In connection with the two annual fairs, she became a great centre of exchange, market of middlemen, rising from trade in goods to transport and then to finance. The commercial class was made up of patrician landowners interested in commerce, foreign capitalists, especially religious refugees from France and merchants from Lombardy as well as smaller commission agents, warehouse managers, and money-brokers. The older types were related to the Hanseatic merchants, and industrious, calculating toil, quiet, secure methods were the rule of the day. But after the Wars of Liberation, the moneylending business developed especially by the side of the old trade in manufactured goods, wool, spices, and wines. All potentates great and small who found themselves short of ready cash turned to the market where Bethmann, Passavant, and Rothschild were domiciled. The bureaucratic-military administrative bodies of the German Federative states were financed in the republic of Frankfort; here an arrangement was always made to deal with State or princely debts and a good portion of loyal subjects' tax payments flowed as interest, simple or compound, into the pockets of the Frankfort bankers. Capital piled upon capital, one speculation grew out of another, stock exchange gambling drew many smaller speculators into its fascinating clutches. Joy in many-sided occasional trading with great risks and appropriately high profits, began to develop in Frankfort. This was known as "shooting the flying bird." Thus a new bustle, but also much daring enterprise, entered the commercial world of Frankfort. It was appropriate to the temperament of the city. People did not take life so easily nor were they so quick of speech, as on the Rhine, not so polite and adaptable as in Saxony, not so robust as in Suebia, nor so blunt as in Bavaria. They had a warm-hearted, quick-witted gruffness, a determined daring, an impudent joy in disrespectful mockery; punishing foolish snobbery and foppish affectation as severely as heavy-witted simplicity. As inhabitants of a great city, the Frankforters felt sceptical, versatile, vastly superior to the three divisions of Hesse or to their Frankish neighbours up and down the Main. In Frankfort, too, there naturally existed an old-fashioned type of ancient Philistine inhabitant; but the best of these good citizens was that they refused to be impressed by anything, or at any rate acted as if this were impossible. Delightfully eccentric characters flourished in such a soil, many of whose tricks and oddities have become immortal. In Frankfort people were sociable rather than sensitive, and extremely unceremonious, even to the uppermost strata of the rich; here, too, people spoke their minds without hesitation and only became polite when under the urgent necessity of coolly refusing anything. The genuine Frankforter took a pretty serious view of life, the inheritance of a stern old Protestantism; to waste money and vital energy was thought vulgar and still worse—stupid. The houses of the patrician families were outwardly simple enough—all the more costly was the art wealth of the interiors. There were many treasures of pictures and bronzes, especially from France and the Netherlands. Public display was contrary to sterling tradition, and the Frankforter knew no better ideal of life than what he called "quiet riches." Many North Germans, who always wanted to be "refined," found it difficult to comprehend this curious Frankfort genuineness. There was a wondrous mixture here of strength and weakness, breadth and narrowness, touchiness and good nature, sweetness and irascibility. This was apparent, too, in their treatment of the Jews. They were accounted a separate class which was not to rise unduly; people made fun of them, but nearly always in a good-natured way. In the long run, they too, were a bit of Frankfort life, they belonged to it, they took a lively part in the cultural life of their native town; they were respected for their artistic taste and love of family, for their loyal adaptability—all qualities held in high honour in the civic republic of Frankfort. A humane feeling for everything Franconian prevented race mania from developing here. It was unfortunately the nature of the Frankforters to say more than they were prepared to answer for; their tendency to grumble and quibble, to tattle and gossip certainly needed understanding, otherwise one might have attributed a false importance to it. Pedantically to take offence was hotly resented by the Frankforter; the only thing that annoyed him more was a conceited assumption of superior knowledge. Every true Frankforter thought his family the best and most truly Frankfortian; they presented a united front only against outsiders whom they pitied exceedingly. The republic was small, but extremely proud of its independence; people were touchy and distrustful, certainly not without cause. The neighbourhood of so many princes, the honourable presence in person of the high and mighty Federative Assembly oppressed the self-consciousness of the Frankforters, and it was no wonder if their sense of humour sometimes deserted the political leaders of the Free city when exposed to the many annoyances caused them by these powerful personages with their frequent attacks of ill-humour. In the less responsible lower classes this sense of humour bubbled up irresistibly against everything in its path, even against its own high authorities. There was no German city which knew the ways of German princes so intimately, and therefore there was none so republican in spirit. All the secrets of their financial difficulties were known, their desires in the matter of amusement, their little shifts and cheats behind the backs of their stilted bureaucrats and patient subjects. The Frankfort merchants did business with their princes, made as much out of them as possible and kept their thoughts to themselves. As true German republicans, they naturally took a special enjoyment in their social relations with princes and aristocrats. The spirit of Frankfort had always been more mobile and more joyous than that of the Hanseats. We see the being of the true Frankforter in the cheery strength of the Frau Rat, Goethe's mother, in the delicious bad behaviour of Bettina, Klinger's stormy naturalness, Savigny's preoccupation with historical law, Börne's finesse in writing, Clemens Brentano's brilliant phantasy—all these qualities went to make up the only German city in which Goethe could have been born, or Schopenhauer been content to die.

Respectfully, the much bowed Main, grown old, turned aside here, so that he might once more enjoy the prospect of the rosy shimmering towers of the city and the white brilliance of the new houses on the quay; the Gothic cupolas of the Cathedral of the Emperors, pompous with inner dignity, a pillar of the Empire, the Paulskirche, for which its historic destiny was waiting, the delicate spire of the Councillors' Chapel of St. Nicholas, and then all the others. The sovereign citizen of this city was a loving son and a respectful gentleman at the same time. He knew all the crooked gables thrust forward over ground floors in the maze of tiny alleys, the curious old names, signs, and landmarks, the mysterious flight of houses on the Schirn, the splashing of baroque fountains in merry, little squares, the curving darkness of the bridges, the dangling green bushes that proclaimed new wine in the inns of Sachsenhausen—and of course, the silvery patrician elegance of the villas outside the city gates. He was proud that so much German history had taken place between the five points of the Eschenheimer Tower and the proud steps in the gables of the Römer —German history which was also the history of Frankfort.

The Frankfort Constitution was the most modern in the four Free cities; but it, too, was old-fashioned enough. This Constitution of 1716 was called "Konstitutionsergänzungsakte" (Supplementary Constitutional Acts) and was therefore intended to alter the old city constitution according to the "needs of present conditions." Article 5 sounded very hopeful, since "all sovereign rights and the self-administration of the city rested upon the Christian citizens as a whole." This seemed to do away with old patrician privileges; the Calvinists and Roman Catholics would have equal rights with the Lutherans, as in Hamburg; but here, too, certain classes would be deliberately excluded from political rights; the so-called Israelite citizens, and certain citizens known as "Beisassen" and "Permissionists." In 1824, the Jews were granted the same rights as Christians at private law, but economically they were still bound; they were only allowed to celebrate fifteen marriages a year. Permissionists were strangers and also shop-assistants and servants who needed a "Permission card" to remain in Frankfort. "Beisassen" were small citizens who had not the means to purchase citizen rights; they bore the burdens of citizenship without reaping any of the privileges. The inhabitants of the villages belonging to Frankfort were also denied all political rights; still, in 1818, serfdom was abolished and then the countryfolks' tributes in kind were turned into pretty oppressive money taxes. In point of numbers, only rather more than half of the Frankfort city population enjoyed civic rights.

Germany's riches were also Germany's poverty. The world of the petty states was full of culture of art and well-meaning charity, full of well-protected folk and powerful individuality.

But it was stuffed fuller of ceremonial and court pomposity, the wisdom of officials, the narrowness of the nobility and the whims of princes. How cleverly and independently, how freely, with what proud consciousness of itself, civic spirit succeeded in developing in the Free cities, in spite of all inner weaknesses, not oppressed, not bowed down, not exploited, never suppressed. Austria, Prussia, Bavaria managed to give their subjects a number of possibilities of development within the conditions of the monarchy of the time. But prince-ridden petty states imposed far more restrictions; he who would be free and German must necessarily deny their spirit as a whole. Therefore in the petty states any attachment to the Fatherland as a whole was considered particularly revolutionary. A battle for the new German State was therefore also a life and death battle against the whole idea of the petty state.

CHAPTER FIVE

# GERMANY

√

THERE WERE German great powers and German dwarf states, potentates of every grade, republics, dominions of all kinds, secularized, won by agreement or merely annexed—but where was Germany?

There was a German language and culture, there were German customs and German art, German thought, and German faith; but there was no German State.

The German people had now grasped at all that was high and great and had made their own whatever an ancient and noble people can acquire and possess—but one thing was still missing—a political form that should be worthy of them. The German people longed to create their strong, free State; that is the true meaning of the German Revolution of 1848–49.

Germany was ripe—indeed, overripe to become a German State. In Wolfgang Goethe, Germanism had given to the world the most radiant being the century was to produce. Goethe's language embraced the literature of the world and gave it to the Germans. Shakespeare and the Spaniards, the Orient and India became their intellectual possessions. Hegel, with glorious violence, had formed life, art, and history into a final synthesis of thought; it could only be followed by revolutionary self-dissolution. In the theatre, in the literary magazines, in university lecture-halls, two generations disputed about the soul of the German and the meaning of the world, about the consciousness and value of a culture whose defenders believed with some justice that they had reached the height of German development. At this time the Germans were the most cultured people in Europe, but also proudest of their culture; educated to produce intellectually even when very little talent was available, borne aloft by knowledge, but also weighed down by it. This course of development was very welcome to the bearers of political and economic power in the Germany of the day. Could there be a better sphere of action for the powers of the young generation than literary quarrelling, polemics among professors, theatre scandals, and arguments of aesthetes? As long as the triumph of a great actress like Henriette Sontag, or the poetic duel between Heinrich Heine and Count August Platen could stir the country as events of deep moment —so long would Germany be easy to rule. Distance from everyday cares was certainly a preliminary condition of truly great intellectual and artistic creation. But the characteristic feature of the situation in Germany was that those in power deliberately fostered the separation of the broadly intellectual classes from political and economic activity, that they purposely cultivated the type of the impractical scholar, apparently in the interests of German culture, but actually in the interests of their own political supremacy. When the scholar was carefully tied down to the narrow conditions of life natural to his usually modest origin in the lower-middle classes; when he was cleverly handled and every advantage taken of his inborn respect for authority, of his unwillingness to make any claims, of his simple, honest nature, then these rulers had their perfect subject—the industrious, trustful, reverent German of the 'twenties and 'thirties, busy with and distracted by things of the intellect, a man who imagined his superiors to be just as decent fellows as he was himself.

But for a long time there had been other German types. German nationality came into being in the days of Napoleonic oppression and blossomed gloriously during the Wars of

Liberation; the Students' Freedom League, above all, kept this ideal alive until the Revolution of 1848. The one feeling which dominated the German Nationalist was as simple as it was strong and deeply felt. Instead of thirty-six Fatherlands he wanted one German Fatherland, instead of the old sunken empire a new, strong growth, instead of the dead theocratic imperial sovereignty a youthful, vigorous, popular Emperor; in a word, he wanted to see the German State on an equal footing with other European states; perhaps, since it was his own German State, a little superior to the others. Beside the German Nationalist stood the German political humanist. He, too, wanted an Emperor and an Empire—but he thought more of the home policy of the new Germany than of her foreign policy; above all things, he wanted liberty to reign in the State, he even expected it to come from the State, for he put right before might. To give a man of personality the opportunity to develop freely, secured by a just State, devoted to peaceful toil, master of free speech, at peace with his neighbours, respected by foreign lands—the German political humanist could think of nothing higher, he saw perfection in this ideal. Finally, the German Revolutionary stepped up to the Humanist's side, the newest political type in Germany, visible as early as 1815, but only awakened to fulness of life and activity by the July Revolution of 1830. The soul of his being was criticism. He no longer believed either in tradition or in the present. He did not believe in nationalism, for he saw the same nationalism everywhere and feared that these Nationalists would come into conflict. He was a good German all the same, perhaps precisely on this account, and demanded unity and the sovereign of the German nation as a preliminary to everything else. The German Revolutionary was also in favour of a lawful state, but he did not believe that the principalities already existing were able or inclined to develop it. He did not believe in the goodwill of rulers and officialdom, and therefore he wished to break down in order to build up, to destroy in order that he might create. He thought that the old Germany must pass away in order that a young Germany might arise. Finally, the German Revolutionary did not believe in conferences, in constitutional paragraphs, in State aid and economic guardianship, for behind the demand for a new German State he recognized the necessity that a new German—or even a new European, democratic society should come into being. The German Revolutionary wanted battle and must necessarily desire it. These three political types in the Germany of 1848 had their intellectual roots in Germany's great literary epoch and prepared the way for the immediate appearance of the first political parties. The German Nationalist derived from the Romantic movement in literature, the German Humanist from Classicism and the German Revolutionary from the *Sturm und Drang* poets. The German Nationalist developed into the Conservative, the Humanist into a Liberal, the Revolutionary into Democrat and Socialist.

The first half of the nineteenth century produced many brilliant men in Germany, far more than the second half. At the time of the Revolution, 1848–49, there were five men of real genius in Germany—but not one of them had any decisive influence upon the turn of events. Only one of them was a real politician—Otto von Bismarck, and he was too young to play any but a very minor rôle; Karl Marx, his opposite pole in world history, was already beginning to have a great effect, but it was not in the active part of a conspirator that he rose to his highest power, but through the revolutionary power of the scientific work which he wrote much later on. Arthur Schopenhauer stood grumpily aside from the battle for the German State, profoundly estranged from historic events, and it was only after the Revolution that the spirit of the age, resigned and in need of comfort, gave audience at last to his impatiently attendant genius. Richard Wagner's glowing temperament drove him to the barricades and into exile—he almost fell victim to the Revolution; but then it was he, more than anyone else, who, in his works of art, inspired by Schopenhauer, helped the Germans intellectually to overcome their sorrowful destiny and girded them into the new era. The fifth and last man of genius of the age, Heinrich Heine, was the boldest herald of the revolutionary idea; from Paris he rejoiced and trembled with the Germans at home in their hopes and in their collapse, but his faith in a new young social German State was to crumble away all too soon.

The battle for the German State found no man of genius to form and shape its course in 1848–49. This was one of the reasons for its failure.

German Nationalist, German Humanist, and German Revolutionary were united most amazingly in Heinrich Heine. Richard Wagner, too, had something of all three types. Karl Marx filled the German Revolutionary with new ideas, whereas Bismarck's Prussian particularism must first become German, and Schopenhauer's philosophy of will and suffering remained on a super-political plane. It is a strange dispensation that it was Heinrich Heine, the German-Jew from the Rhine, gloriously gifted as a poet, unstable, torn by indecision, over-sensitive, tortured by his own ever-changing moods, master and victim of the fascinating poison of his magic gift of words, who has given us the liveliest picture of the destiny of the Revolutionary age. As an exile and oppressed, he knew the struggle for freedom and justice in his own person, he was enthusiastic for an emperor with the old black, red, and gold standard, and ridiculed the petty princes; he prophesied that a truly civilized State would rise in the rejuvenated Europe of the democratic era; he called to the exploited to rebel, for he shuddered at the beggarly idea of equality entertained by some of the early socialists. Heinrich Heine, political poet and author, levelled the most bitter attacks against the Prussian King Frederick William IV, to whom he was nearly related in the character of his intellectual gifts; but he was full of the contempt which the genius must feel for the semi-genius, full, one might say, of cousinly hate—himself tortured by many of the same emotions which also worked upon the King; but he was far wiser, his poetical nature much stronger, the whole man as superior as only the citizen of a coming age can be in comparison with the monarch of an age in decay.

Poor King Ludwig of Bavaria! His laboriously turned verse was now massacred by one of the greatest masters of graceful verbal melody. The whole clumsy, tiresome world of the super-Teutons burst asunder on the clashing sword-point of a truly sovereign wit. Heinrich Heine the clown was a philosopher of the breed of Shakespeare's wise clowns, to whom only the highest and last things are worthy of being taken seriously, and these with a seriousness to which trivial hypocrites could never attain. Among the highest and last things, Heine set the immortal Germany which he bore within himself and which he must therefore love, in which he never ceased to believe and for which he longed so fervently to find a worthy and dignified form, longed with all the glow of a poet's fervent heart.

The group of German writers whom we have been used in accordance with their own and contemporary usage to call "Young Germany," had at once the good and ill luck to fill and even overfill their generation and to suffer themselves to be filled to overflowing by it. Their work often had the actuality of a leading article or a speech in Parliament, both of which could only exist at the time in a very limited measure, and they were usually still more ephemeral than these. Yet the beholder of today feels a particular magic proceeding from this generation of authors. They carried on what the *Sturm und Drang* generation had begun, the relentless criticism of State and society belonging to the period of the great French Revolution; they prepared the way for the aspirations of the naturalistic movement in art in the 'eighties and 'nineties; this, too, was the pioneer and herald of a new European upheaval. Few of the works of the "Young Germans" have anything to say to us today from an artistic point of view; but we are all the more moved by their battle spirit, their faith, their fate, and the force of their will to achieve a new vital form. The eldest of them, at least one who died before seeing 1848, was not a true artist, but after Lessing, the first occasional writer of high calibre in Germany and, with Görres and Gentz, the leader of the political publicists. His name was Ludwig Börne. In talent at least the equal of the other two, he was greatly their superior in character and nobility of purpose. Börne's prose, charged with glowing feeling, but cooled on ice, had, in its brevity, its shorn clarity, its ruthless and untiring logic, something of the Republican ethic with which this Frankfort Jew was inspired. Serious democratic demands had soon been turned by oppression into impatient bitterness. The whole age turned as he did from the drama of the boards to the exciting and frightful struggles of the political world-stage. Börne's masterly prose began as belles-lettres and ended in leading articles. After the July revolution, there was a revulsion to poetry in Germany; there had been enough lyrics about love and the moon, roses and nightingales; rhythms and verse-forms were exhausted. The age of prose had come, prose as a form and prose as a medium. Art was confused with romanticism and romanticism with reaction. The journalist made his appearance, sharper, colder, more daring than the wavy-haired poet, whose yielding unworldliness began to appear faintly ludicrous. The journalist-author, inspired by a high mission, was now to proclaim that Germany, too, was informed by a new will to action. Authority and society looked with distrust mingled with ignorance at this new generation of "scribblers." What had these people of no antecedents to do with public affairs? What meaning could be attached to the opinions of people with neither family, a steady income, a solid education, or a university degree? The battle of officialdom against "Young Germany" meant much more than an attempt to suppress inconvenient literary production—it was a fight, hopeless, but supported by all the authority of the State, against the modern spirit which was set up in arms to proclaim "a new age in the world" and to deliver a smashing blow at the traditions of the Biedermeier age.

This new age was to have a religion deeper than that to be found in the orthodoxy of the existing Christian churches. Goethe, the Greeks and Hegel had pointed the way to a joyous, optimistic pantheism; the new age of the world should have a new freer State than existed in the Germany of the day—it should be the people's State with justice for all Germans such as the great Revolution that boiled up again in July 1830 had demanded for France and for all Europe, as young Italy, young Poland, liberal England, indeed every people of the age sought to achieve for itself, in order to become an equal and recognized link in the chain of a young, united Europe; the new age was to realize a new social order. Most of these young German writers were the sons of artisans in the towns or small farmers; they were bound to hate the old German castes and cliques, inspired as they were by the spirit of a new free humanity. What pastors and schoolteachers preached was in all too perfect accordance with police supervision and bureaucratic snobbery which had cabined and confined their whole lives. What, after all, had been the practical outcome of Schiller's call to freedom? Because of it, he was a living presence to this generation, the poetic tribune of the rising German spirit.

The rulers of the many states found it convenient to stamp their subjects as early as possible into the mould of an honest calling and dampen the fiery student spirit by the prospect of a certain, if small pension on retirement. How strange, how alarming, that there should now be men who had the boldness —in fact, the impudence—to expect to live by their pens, and in defiance of the wisdom of schoolmaster and official, relying neither upon title nor dignity, but only upon their own names, to attempt to teach, inflame, and entertain the public, perhaps even to rouse them up against respectability and order! These writers were so bold that they did not stay properly at home in one of the six and thirty fatherlands, but went on journeys and described to all who were bound fast to house and field, workshop and family cares, the wonders of the great world, landscapes of picturesque charm; men full of power and impetuosity, strange happenings, singular customs, but above all healthier, freer, more humane conditions of life than those at home. New knowledge was disseminated, more exciting and compelling than had ever been served up by the older generation of writers with their endless verbosities—knowledge of the State, of the people, of economics—knowledge of the glorious, inexhaustible, eternally young reality of the present and the future of being, law and rhythm of human society. Wordy and leaden had been German learning, pompous with expert knowledge, full of self-confidence, infallible, soured, unpalatable. The leaders of knowledge certainly might have been renewed and enriched by the classical age of awakening. A theologian like Schleiermacher, a jurist like Savigny, a historian like Dahlmann spoke to the best of the nation—and they wrote German with a noble simplicity, comprehensible to any layman. But the young writers set up something new by the side of science—public opinion. Had not the Germans learned enough, toiled, explored enough, believed in "objectivity," laboured to find the final truth? Was there nothing else in Germany which demanded the intellect and the power of the whole man—the fruition of practical reality? Must it not at last be brought into agreement with this actual maturity of the German people? Did these princes and ministers deserve the trust and reverence which they exacted? Were these officials educated enough, conscientious enough? Why did a section of the middle classes suddenly grow very rich, another, greater proportion, ever poorer and poorer? Whence came the shortage of food? Finally, why were women suppressed, left in ignorance and dependence, chained by marriage, driven to want and the streets?

Wilhelm Weitling, a Magdeburg tailor's assistant, was the first pioneer of a real political socialistic-communistic purpose. He was a man with a certain knowledge of the world, son of a French officer and a poor Thuringian girl, much knocked about from pillar to post and often roughly handled. He was by no means an original thinker, but warm-hearted, receptive and gifted in popular declamation of other people's ideas. He was not easily discouraged and, defying mishaps and persecution, went on agitating and was always able to win over new followers by the exercise of his captivating personal qualities. In Paris, as a member of the League of the Just, Weitling filled himself with the ideas of Cabet and Fourier and became their apostle. Since 1839 he had been publishing pamphlets and magazines, founded societies in Switzerland and preached a convinced communism, referring its principles back to the Primitive Christians, full of hatred of the ruling classes, passionately serious, brilliant in form, yet unmeasured and crass. He did not even hesitate to recommend robbery and plunder as a means of combating ruling society. Then again he would soften and stroke children's heads, for he regarded their future as if it were his own.

For a time the Swiss authorities arrested Weitling, expelled him and attempted to suppress his agitation—but it continued to exist here and there. Since the arrest of Weitling and the Swiss Commissions Report, written and published by Bluntschli, the great public had become aware of the existence of practical German communism, the evidence of its effects being visible in Hamburg, Berlin, Elberfeld, and Silesia. It won adherents in the artisans' league, and was spread over the country

146

even into small communities by itinerant workmen. It is difficult to secure any figures. The Russian Government kept a
sharp eye on the Communist movement, had detailed reports
sent from Paris and used *agents provocateurs*, such as the former
officer A. von Bornstedt, who later issued the Deutsch-
Brüsseler Zeitung. In Berlin, the police discovered a Communist plot in 1846. In Königsberg, Breslau, and other places
there were arrests, interrogations, and confiscations. Nothing
much came of it all. Although there were already great numbers of workers in North Germany and Saxony—most of them
were thoroughly sceptical of the new teachings and inclined
more to political radicalism than to revolutionary class warfare. Things were different in the Rhineland and Westphalia.

The most gifted and effective personality in this Rhenish-
Westphalian group was Friedrich Engels—a warm-blooded
personality, life pulsing hotly through every vein. Son and
grandson of well-to-do manufacturers of Barmen and therefore armed with the best possible inside knowledge of the
"bourgeoisie," he was a polished, joyous fighter, a real man,
who acted and wrote out of the fulness of his nature, hammer-
ing every word in the fire of faith in the service of a great
and good cause. In 1845, after five years in England, he published the work *Position of the Working Classes in England*,
which made a deep impression in Germany. It was an absolute
contrast to L. Stein's book—not the work of a learned thinker
and sharp-sighted politician, but the accusation of an agitator,
to whom fate had given a pair of brilliant, wide-open eyes and
the gift of painting what he saw in words and moving the
hearts of men by his pictures. In the model country of liberal
faith, the paradise of parliamentary government and free trade,
Engels now showed that there were such things as filthy slum
dwellings, and brutal exploitation of the helpless, ragged
toilers by narrow-minded, highly-respectable business men,
and the most indifferent, degenerate lower classes, kept in their
place by class injustice. This was the price paid for the comfort

of a gentlemanly civilization. Engels may have generalized over many a regional abuse, may sometimes have taken too simple a view or described too monotonously—yet the spontaneously written book conveyed the effect of immediacy and was as rousing as a blare of trumpets. It woke the people and warned them. The Rhenish-Westphalian industrial middle classes also felt uncomfortable, as if they had been exposed. The book had not been aimed at them, but they had been hit, nevertheless. Their workmen were still unsuspicious and trustful—but since 1842 they felt the effects of the trade crises; the linen crisis had already taken the bread from the mouths of hundreds of workmen. The manufacturers had grown rich and wished to keep their riches, and therefore they hardened their hearts and transferred the burden of the crisis to the shoulders of their workmen. Communistic doctrines now gained ground in the Rhineland and began to spread—"one is always falling over Communists," wrote Engels to Karl Marx.

Engels had declared the Revolution to be unavoidable—a battle between sharply divided classes—this idea which Lorenz Stein had first made known in Germany, had meanwhile taken possession of young Karl Marx, who had gone to Paris—Marx and Engels were at one in this idea. In his capacity as editor of the *Rheinischen Zeitung*, Marx had been a social critic, but not yet a communistic revolutionary. His ideas developed thus during his stay in France. It was the development of an intellect of unmerciful superiority. Sharply and arrogantly, with the sovereignty of an honest and impatient spirit, he now thrust from him all that had previously been thought and striven for—however much it may formerly have influenced him. His friendship with Engels was in a way necessary, perhaps the most necessary link in the dialectic process which perfected the life-work of Karl Marx. Engels was his antithesis, his penetrating reason needed Engels's imagination, his ice-cold logic, Engels's warmth of outlook, his postulates, Engels's impressions. Marx was obstinate, sarcastic, self-confident, a high priest in cold infallibility, wounding people's feelings by his insistence on his own opinion, but a deeply original, creative nature, always at high tension. Engels adapted himself and gave way, his human qualities enriched Marx's intellectual gifts—he served respectfully and thus accomplished something decisive; he loosened up Marx's ponderous judaic revolutionary ethics and formed them into a flaming torch of faith, a super-national will to freedom, instinct with humanity. The earliest work by Marx and Engels in common appeared in the *Deutsch-französische Jahrbüchern* and the *Pariser Vorwärts*.

As a result of comprehensive studies and efforts in composition, they worked out a "Communistic Manifesto" which appeared just before the outbreak of the Revolution of 1848. What was really or apparently new about this, at any rate, most effective, was twofold; the political idea of revolution was claimed for use in class warfare and the national middle-class revolution was confronted by the international proletarian revolution with violent reversal of all previous orders of society as its aim. Considered from a purely scientific point of view, it was certainly an error to assume that all previous history of society was a history of class combat. But the history of the contemporary generation certainly began to be a class war, although it was not a struggle as it was claimed here, between two classes only. There were enough proletarians in Germany already, but there was not yet a proletariate. The middle classes were still the heart of the people and would remain so for a long time to come. For Germany, at any rate, the idea of a decisive battle between the working-classes and the "bourgeoisie" was a misguided notion of fateful and far-reaching import. Things were different in France and England; but here, too, the strength of the aristocratic, bourgeois and middle-class powers had been underestimated. The communistic manifesto utilized a good many of the ideas of pre-Marx socialism—such as the salary law of the Ricardo school.

But practical political aims were formulated here with a propagandic effectiveness, an unexampled brevity and clarity which was destined to occupy the thoughts of many future generations. The slogan—"Proletarians of all countries, Unite!" —was a bold, unparalleled negation of the State, including the free citizen State which had not yet come into existence in Germany. Nothing was said about the form to be taken by the State of the future, and this was certainly a hiatus. But the authors said all the more about the new organization of property. Nothing could have contributed more surely to render the hardworking middle-class citizen suspicious of the revolutionary idea supported and utilized by the Communists and prepare him to conclude an alliance with the old powers of society. The communistic manifesto—although to all practical purpose, it at first attracted no attention—thus did much to bring about the failure of the middle-class revolution, the success of which would have been the natural preliminary to the proletarian revolution—at least according to historical logic as understood by Marx and Engels.

Socialism and communism, which are so closely connected in idea, became more and more differentiated during the 'forties and have been completely separated since about 1846. Socialism was a philosophy, developed out of humanitarianism, pity, ethics, desire to improve the world; communism was action, party, criticism, class hatred, political strife, destruction of the opponent, reversal of the traditional; socialism was optimistic evolution; communism was a revolution born of contempt of humanity. Both movements had Utopian features —however hotly Marx and Engels reproached the others with their Utopianism. Both Marx and Engels were most unjust to those who were nearest to them—perhaps, as fighters, it was necessary. But he who does not understand their one-sidedness, conditioned by the age, precisely in their polemic, does not comprehend their true greatness.

The expressions "petty bourgeoisie" and "petty bourgeois"

have acquired such a contemptuous flavour owing to the great
Communists Marx and Engels, that one should no longer make
use of them in a historical study which seeks to represent the
nature of things. Even Proudhon was branded by Marx as
a petty bourgeois and Engels labelled such revolutionary
idealists as Freiligrath and Dronke as philistines. Everyone who
would not subscribe to their every word and particularly everyone who had been Socialist or Communist before them, was
an ideologist, a fool, a Utopian or a Philistine, usually all at
once. In order to appreciate properly the social conditions in
Germany at this time, we must realize that the largest class,
both in town and country, was the middle class. It had been
the largest for at least two generations, but this condition of
things did not last much longer. The final dissolution of the
German middle class was one of the consequences of the revolution of 1848-49. The middle class were the actual living
heart of the population—most of the great German artists and
thinkers came of them—here was the brimming storehouse of
German industry, German labour and German sentiment. Their
core was the German yeoman farmer, the skilled artisan, ship-
owner, manufacturer, innkeeper, and trader, as well as the small
pensioner living in the cities, the minor official, the parson,
the teacher, the solicitor, the doctor. These were worthy,
capable men who lived simply, needing but little in comparison to the needs of the Western European, their existence
busy, independent, and dignified, founded on mutual respect.
The main point about this middle-classs society was that its
members secured their honest living and wished to remain as
they were, perhaps rising a little within the limits of their own
decent sphere.

Over their heads the middle classes saw the feudal nobility
and, branching off from them, the court, the nobility of the
administration and of the sword, an unattainable, unshakeable
caste, deeply reverenced, sometimes sharply criticized, but
secretly much envied. Below them, the middle classes saw the

ranks of the economically dependent—in the country, the agricultural labourers, drovers, threshers, ploughboys—the common seamen, shop assistants, servants, lackeys, artisans with no hope of ever becoming master, and finally, the factory hands. The significant factor of the middle class is its combination of ability with a certain amount of property and a certain degree of culture. A man must own something, in order to use his knowledge and ability in an independent station of life. The important point that distinguished the lower classes was that they did not own anything, or at least, not enough. They were poor. They could not set up a shop or an independent trade. They were forced to serve. But they could rise by dint of great industry and a certain amount of good fortune. It was particularly common in the cities for persons of the lower classes to rise into the middle class; through their savings, on account of special talents, or by marriage—through some combination of one and another, many of them achieved a state of independence. On this account alone, these lower classes in the Germany of the day could not be called a proletariate. Individuals preached a fighting class consciousness in despair of ever being able to make anything of themselves in the existing condition of society, but it was only applicable to some of the actual factory workers and the worst paid country labourers, subject to the chances of a daily wage; all others lived loyally within the bounds of society as it was; they desired a greater measure of freedom, but not revolution; they wished to make their way. The apprentice hoped to become master, difficult as it was already beginning to be; the servant-girl married the artisan, the shop-assistant the huckster's widow.

This three strata system of society in Germany was thrown off its balance by the formation of a new social class between the aristocracy and the middle classes. We have been accustomed to label this class the "bourgeoisie," an expression derived from French literature which has become familiar in polemics, but does not exactly tally with German conditions, least of all with the pre-Revolutionary situation in 1848–49. On account of its tang of the city and of class struggle it is altogether a misleading term. What happened in Germany was the building up of a patrician class based on money and titles. The patriciate of titles came first. Holders of academic degrees successfully demanded especial respect from the rest of the middle-classes and were the first to find their way into the aristocracy, where their services were in request as pastors, legal advisers, doctors, and teachers. The university professors of the four faculties, usually sons of middle-class parents, some-times risen from the lower classes, were especially respected as representatives of outstanding dignity in an age when public opinion was chained hand and foot and education especially revered. Governments needed these men and often had to endure their critical opposition, courts and noble families patronized them; in the majority they were probably not so intellectually independent as their contemporaries believed—but their caste as a whole enjoyed patrician status, not without a certain self-satisfaction. The higher officialdom was also recruited for the most part from the middle classes; naturally the feudal aristocracy took the best and highest positions for their own descendants—but in a number of positions, espe-cially finance, economics, culture, law, it was impossible to do without the contribution of middle-class intelligence. This younger bureaucracy endeavoured successfully to emulate the old in its way of life and in its sentiments; it often fell with surprising alacrity into a certain antagonism to the middle classes from which it had sprung. The truly democratic spirit was more noticeable in the citizen who had risen to it than in officials of noble birth. The petty states needed relatively many officials—it was not always possible to fill every post satisfactorily with regional aspirants. Many a capable administrative official was imported—from Austria or more especially from Prussia, while Prussia, in return, was always receptive to exceptional talent. Thus the bureaucracy became estranged from the regional and provincial middle classes; its members became accustomed to regard the world from the standpoint of governmental superiority. Among the officers there was a similar state of things. So many were needed for Prussia that they would never have sufficed without the numerous aspirants from the middle classes, although these were mostly confined to the provincial infantry regiments, the artillery, and the sappers and miners. Similar conditions prevailed in the realm of the law. The German governments cultivated a neo-feudalism of uniforms and robes—a patrician caste according to titles, usually unsupported by appropriate means, but whose members were often more loyal than any other; but also, before and during the revolutionary period, frequently inspired by a moderate enthusiasm for reform. The feudal aristocrats looked down upon this new caste with their usual natural arrogance—but exercised considerable influence over them on account of their younger sons as well as all their poor relations; and on account of their ownership of land and their positions at court, they retained their actual influence upon economics and royal personages.

But it was just their economic influence which was disputed, to their great surprise, by a second stratum arising from the middle classes—the plutocrats. The wholesale merchant was the first in German mercantile cities to rise above the middle class as a power which amassed capital and speculated, working for profit instead of merely to earn a living. The old historical, usually feudal city patricians thus found themselves confronted by a new class of patricians. The principal difference was that although this new caste gladly and successfully adopted an aristocratic way of living, bought land and lived in castles, yet they never, when they remained true to themselves, aspired to quiet enjoyment of social and political power, but pushed on ruthlessly, greedy for work and still amassing capital. Even the leading manufacturers in Germany were types of the middle class—they had often begun their manufacturing as master artisans and rapidly grew from the modest satisfaction of customers' demands to the production of vast supplies in defiance of competition. Finally, since 1840, the carriers and agents of 1820 had become railway contractors; and it was not only ruling princes who needed money—traffic and industrial ventures also sought loans in the money market. The banker became the classic representative of capital, a separate power, no longer regional, impersonal, a mobilized force, with international connections, very sensitive and soon extremely powerful. The money patriciate went the same way as the title patriciate. Its members attempted to mix with the feudal aristocracy—the secret and glowing desire of both was to be ennobled. A title frequently accompanied the bestowal of a decoration in Austria and South Germany; in North Germany it was harder to get. But plutocracy needed a different state from that of the feudal aristocrats; its members tried to attract the governmental professors into a well-tempered liberalism. There were but few plutocrats in the 'forties—but they were restless and energetic. They wished to play a part, they longed for political influence. The "class war" took forms in the Germany of that day and later too, quite other than those dreamed of by the early Communists. Most of the battles were waged inside a particular class and not by one class against another. No one thought more of the citizen middle classes than the members of the wage-earning stratum which was dependent upon them, since their great ambition was to rise into this class. No one thought more of plutocrats and professors than the members of the middle classes—for they, too, wished to rise among them. And these men of degrees and gold dreamed of rising to the ranks of the feudal aristocracy. Thus the competition was fought out among members of the same class—

it was the plutocrats who first intellectually realized this battle, who put it into practice and infected all other strata with it. Above all, the plutocrats, in the interests of amassing capital, took pains to keep down the lower-class workmen and to prevent them from rising into the middle class and also sought as far as possible to keep the middle class in financial dependence, to split it up and discourage it, and finally draw the professors and feudal aristocracy into its own circle of interests and ideas. Society was in flux.

The great German personality who first realized the meaning of these interacting forces, was Friedrich List. Alexander Hamilton, Washington's assistant, had in his day carried the idea of American independence into the realm of economics simply by demanding that the United States should be independent of England in the sphere of commercial production. He said that America should produce what she required for herself, use the powers that she had, divide the labour to be done, and protect herself from competition. Then the population would increase and use up even the entire agricultural produce—the whole organism would become independent and healthy, whereas through free trade many values were drawn off. Friedrich List saw the realization of these principles during his journeyings in America and he now prepared a unique new scientific justification of them and drew the practical consequences for the Germany of his own day. Adam Müller had already subjected the classical doctrine of Adam Smith to severe criticism and demanded that the nation should be the bearer of economic production on a historical basis. We might also recall Fichte's idea of the business State sufficient unto itself, of the writings of Louis Say, the Frenchman, and of Fränzl, the Austrian. The decisive moment in List's work is perhaps less its learned than its political significance. In the end his desire was to achieve a peaceful universal union of peoples, but he very rightly believed that this could only be based upon the power and unity of each individual nation, which must also be expressed in terms of political economy. Therefore, as early as 1819, at the Federal Diet, he and Schnell demanded a customs line extending round the whole of Germany, that is, the abolition of internal customs duties; therefore he also demanded as a matter of principle that German manufacturing power should be developed—only through this could Germany secure her political and economic independence.

List taught that a protective customs system for all inland branches of manufacture would only temporarily raise the prices of goods; on the contrary, inland production would quickly revive again and make good the loss; the nation would be industrially educated, riches and power be gathered up and stored in the country, farmers be employed, all hands put to work, many having previously been superfluous, the nation, having arrived at the apex of this development, could once more return to the principles of free trade.

List had a fine feeling for historical associations, for the individual moment in national relationships—that must already have a beneficent effect upon the stiff formalism of classical national economy. But his instinct for the momentary condition of Germany amounted to genius. He, like others, demanded the development of a merchant marine sailing under the German flag, and with prophetic clarity he determined to build up the German railway system. If the Prusso-German Zollverein had followed List's advice at the time—the consequences would have been incalculable: Germany would have created for herself a national working-class and in connection with this would probably have arrived much sooner at the creation of a democratic national State. The political preponderance of the feudal aristocracy and their followers would soon have been broken.

Friedrich List met the fate which in the age of Frederick William IV and Metternich seemed almost inevitable for a German patriot of his rank and his prophetic power: he was misunderstood and badly treated, and ended, ill and in despair, by his own hand (1846).

List worked in the United States, France, Austria, and Hungary, and everywhere he left traces of his labours. He was perhaps the only truly cosmopolitan German of his age—a man without office and yet—or rather, just on this account—a man of national and international influence, a thinker and organizer, a publicist and propagandist, powerful in each, but incomparable in that he was a combination of them all. It is particularly rare in Germany for a thinker to have any sense of the practical. But here was a man possessed in equal measure by idea and action. And always, in everything, his beloved Germany came first.

In the year 1815, the German Federal Act was certainly a result of political compromise at a time of stress. Many of the states, especially the smaller ones, had undoubtedly wished to see the old empire restored; other patriots, especially Freiherr von Stein had demanded at least a modest degree of popular representation to supplement the assembly of diplomats. On the other hand, we must not forget that the German Federation was also an expression of strong and very positive ideas of the age and that further the Federal Act offered a goodly number of possibilities of development. The German Federation was clapped on to the Holy Alliance like the heart-shaped device on to the heraldic eagle, it was the main feature of the whole, a kind of Central European League of Nations, a guarantee of what already existed and of its further peaceful development. After the frightful Napoleonic war period, the peoples' most urgent demand was for peace. Further battles were now to take place in the form of negotiations, in exchange of opinions, in approximation of interests—but all arising from a community of Christian and humanitarian feelings. The Napoleonic universal State had perished of its own violence.

The principalities had conquered—the princes' holy alliance meant a renaissance of particularism, rulers' tyranny and at the same time, a new, peaceful universalism. The peoples, to be sure, must be modest in their demands. Napoleon knew well enough and expressly recognized that the nations, awakened and formed anew by the idea of liberty, had conquered him. The princes had let loose this spirit in their nations and were now faced by the difficult task of keeping it within bounds. When we consider the Federal Act of 1815, we feel plainly enough that its authors were endeavouring to meet in some way the demands for national liberty. Thus there is mention of the "prime principles of the Federation" which are to be set down, of "organic arrangements" in respect of its foreign military and internal relations. In cases of quarrels between members of the Federation, there was to be a military committee and then a "well-ordered instance of pacification" with a final judicial right of pronouncement. The famous Article 13 read: "In all federal states a constitution will be based on for Provincial Diets." Every differentiation in enjoyment of civic and political rights was to be abolished, not only for "Christian religious bodies"; the Jews were also to enjoy "civic improvement," and the possibility was to be discussed "how the enjoyment of civic rights in return for the assumption of all civic duties in the states of the Federation can be granted and secured to these persons" (Art. 16). They were to be allowed to purchase land; there was a promise of equality in the matter of military service, and equality of laws in the matter of freedom of the Press was announced, and discussion of the regulation of German shipping, commerce and traffic according to the principles of the Vienna Congress.

Considered as a whole, this Federal Act, with its twenty articles, was certainly a meagre and muddled piece of work—but practical goodwill could have made something out of it. Liberty-loving men set great hopes in the German Confederation during its early years. But its history up to 1848 shows the gradual death of all these once promising beginnings of development, of a budding fulfilment of national life.

Prince Karl Leiningen worked to clear up the misunderstanding between Bavaria and Prussia at the Diet, not only in the interests of the Confederation, but also in the interests of European politics. In May 1847, he passed through Frankfort, as he had often done before, and had a conference with the Prussian envoy to the Federation. He was on the way to London, where, on behalf of the Munich cabinet, he was to persuade the English government to take a benevolent attitude towards Greece. In federal politics, Leiningen worked for a Prusso-Bavarian understanding, in European politics for an Anglo-Prussian alliance. In subject matter, both were closely connected. Bavaria had broken with the ultramontane movement and had come into opposition with Austria. If Prussia were now to break away from Austria's tutelage and at last dared to conclude the alliance in contemplation of German freedom; if she thus determined to take the lead in federal reform, then her European prestige would soar and she would become a valuable ally for England, whose position was characterized by the old opposition to Russia and the newly-developed opposition to France. When Prince Leiningen passed through Frankfort again on his way back from England in June 1847, he was able to inform Count Dönhoff that England had a decided distrust of Austria, that excited feeling against France had only outwardly been assuaged and England wished to ally herself with Prussia. During these summer months, Leiningen's Coburg memorandum on federal reform came into being, which demanded that Austria should resign from all internal German questions, that Prussia should lead Germany, that there should be a decisively constitutional government in Prussia, this indicating that Prussia should ally herself with the liberal and national movement. Through Baron von Blittersdorf, Badensian envoy to the Federal Diet, who now showed himself to be a determined advocate of federal reform,

Leiningen was kept precisely informed as to the inner history of the Federal Diet and its almost hopeless infertility. His memoranda and his correspondence with his brother-in-law, the Prince Consort, are based to a great extent upon his exchange of ideas with Blittersdorf. Prince Albert took up Leiningen's ideas and as a result of these conversations, he wrote down his own, somewhat more cautious opinions, also in a memorandum, in the summer of 1847, when in the Highlands.

Ideas similar to those of Prince Leiningen appeared in similar form in various quarters; King Wilhelm of Württemberg, too, inclined to a similar conception of the position. Disappointment over Austria was too keen; on the other hand, no one knew what to make of Prussia's behaviour, since she continually deferred again to Austria. Canitz, to whom Count Dönhoff had forwarded Leiningen's memorandum, said: "It certainly contains very proper observations; as to his conclusions—that Austria should withdraw from Germany's affairs—I cannot suppress the judgment that the means proposed would be much worse than the existing evil. A German Confederation without Austria is a thoroughly impractical idea."

Canitz was incapable of penetrating the significance of the momentary position; neither was it given to Friedrich Wilhelm IV to grasp it when the memoranda of Leiningen and the Prince Consort were laid before him. He and his Radowitz had desired federal reform, but only in a pallid, half-hearted way. Radowitz expressed his ideas in the *Denkschrift über die vom Deutschen Bunde zu ergreifenden Massregeln*, of November 20, 1847.

He was a friend of the Prussian King and had been interested in the affairs of the Confederation for some time; at once officer and thinker, one of the strangest figures of the epoch, he was far from transparent, a fatalist, unfree, noble in sentiment, rich in much knowledge, almost suffering from the

burden of his learning, self-consciously instructive and yet
melancholy and estranged from the real world. Something
of ill-fortune clung to the homeless man who tried to be so
German and at the same time so Prussian; no one knew exactly
whence he came and he did not know himself exactly whither
he was going, in spite of all his clever importance, all his
doctrines of dignity. At the moment he made a great impression, but usually left behind a feeling of uncertainty. His was
a thoroughly Catholic nature—serious and full of faith, in the
ban of pious tradition and pious custom and therefore without
a real living relation to common things, to petty details, to
the everyday of politics—a man with no push, quite free from
cynicism, but unfortunately also lacking a good earthly sense
of humour, a magician, but rather a tiresome one. Thus he
floated in rather a saintly manner over the surface of things,
astonished when things did not turn out as he had anticipated,
but taking comfort in eternal values. He was not in the least
a practical politician; politics without ideas, without an intellectual humanitarianism, only for the sake of a tangible advantage, seizing the opportunity as it offered, would have seemed
to him a mean and worthless pursuit. But he was not a dreamer;
he was a cultivated member of the General Staff, and whatever
he said or wrote sparkled with logic. His intellect was awake,
he was a keen observer, with a compelling power of drawing
conclusions in a beautiful form. The richness of this personality
cannot be outlined in a few catchwords; it was too deep, too
strange, too fine. We may believe we understand him, but
we shall find that we do not. His features were pale and quiet,
his look keen and dark, his voice sharp and thin—he could set
forth his proofs in mathematical form, artfully turned, appearing carefully studied, even if, exceptionally, they were impromptu; all this was evidence of a nature which impressed
hearers but never carried them away, awakening interest,
curiosity, contradiction—but scarcely affection, a nature not
nearly so harmonious and complete as it appeared and wished

to appear. Radowitz, outwardly simple and correct, was inwardly a man who demanded much, who found the contiguous much too simple, the things of the present far too charged with emotion. The weakness of such ascetic, semi-ideologists is that they confuse the living reality with the trivial. It depends upon how one seizes hold and of what. Radowitz came from afar, and far-away things attracted him. If his temperament had had more fire, he could have seized and formed the most far-away things. It was not his gifts that failed him, but his blood. He liked to plunge deep into things and loved complications, but he seldom emerged, he lost himself—which he would never have acknowledged. He never cut a Gordian knot, but wearied himself out, untwisting it. When he spoke, he must have been more impressive than with his pen; and his writings are certainly of more significance than his actions.

Happiness is probably the only thing that one can confer without possessing it oneself; but Radowitz did not possess this talent either. His clever efforts failed not only because of the King's insufficiency, but partly because of his own. Both he and the King had an inner flaw in common; each had in excess what the other lacked.—

The term "radicalism" was a battle-cry of the time, which it would be better to delete from a scientific study of today. "Radical" is really a term for going to the roots of things, for unflinching, relentless logic; nationalism, clericalism, socialism can be radical just as well as liberalism. The great contrast in worlds of thought between the two revolutionary parties of 1848–49, would be best characterized as "autocracy" and "democracy." The régime of Czar Nicholas of Russia was autocratic and represented one pole of the political world of the day. The United States of America had a democratic form of government. They were the other pole. England and France, who at the time set such narrow limits to the right of franchize, were not yet perfect democracies; but they were in the midst of a development leading in that direction. In Spain, Portugal, and the South American republics, in several German small and medium states, in all European small and medium states, namely in Sweden and Norway, Denmark, Holland, Belgium, written constitutions were the fundamental fact of political life, however much or little liberal these constitutions might be. They all tended to repress royal autocracy, they signified a beginning of true democracy.

Just like feudalism and absolutism, democracy is a form of political life, belonging in origin and operation to the European-American circle of civilization. There is no purely national form of State constitution; and it was one of the greatest mistakes peculiar to German politics that the Germans believed that there was. Naturally the three reigning forms of statecraft since the Middle Ages, Feudal state, Royal absolutism, and Democracy, were adapted by each people in its own way and according to its own needs. Principles were the same everywhere. But it was one of the cleverest battle-cries of German Nationalist fighting groups to attempt to discredit the democratic form of state by decrying it as "un-German." Was absolutism, which German princes set up with so much enthusiasm after the Spanish and French pattern, a German form of state? Absolutism was also at one time in accord with Germany's needs and indispensable to her development. But whereas absolutism in Spain, France, and England established the nation as a whole against extraneous interests in national life, absolutism in Germany and Italy strengthened extraneous interests in opposition to the nation. Therefore the national idea in Spain, France, and England had from the very beginning the character of loyalty; it served development as a whole; in Germany it was forced into opposition. The national idea and the democratic State belong together. In England, where absolutism was an episode, the development towards democracy was never for a moment in opposition to the national idea; in France, absolutism furthered the growth of a productive bourgeoisie, which undertook the democratic organization of the whole nation.

In Germany, however, a nation could only be said to exist in such matters as speech, art, and creative thought; in Germany there were beginnings of a democratic development, but they served to strengthen particularism in individual states. Germany had neither a national nor a democratic State. One could not be achieved without the other. Germany, too, had a historical right to see all her children united in the form of state demanded by the development of the age—democracy.

This democracy was something entirely modern and had only the name in common with what might once have existed in days of antiquity, in a society and State which was built up on the broad basis of slavery. The roots of modern democracies were threefold: Christianity, natural science, and the philosophy of law. All men are equals before God and eternity —this primeval religious experience was renewed, as we know, through Protestantism and quickened, especially among the Calvinists, into unique practical action. Conditions of life are anthropologically, physically, chemically identical for every man; progress in knowledge of nature, in the new age established this natural equality with iron incontrovertability; before the law, in the eyes of the law, all men are equal—the great thinkers of the English, French, and German age of enlightenment unmercifully destroyed the old world of privilege, of subjection, of justice denied, restricted, unequally applied. All great European peoples laboured over this establishment of an idea, this experience of a new conscientiousness, represented by modern democracy. The United States' Declaration of Independence, their establishment of the rights of a man and citizen, was the first complete, victorious, truly efficacious revelation of the democratic idea. The real democrats never identified democracy with equality. This assumption of their opponents was an error, often an intentional misrepresentation and depreciation. True democracy precisely recognized the personal differentiations of mankind. The true democrat knew well enough that talent, health, property, education, temperament, energy, are fortunately differentiated a thousandfold in all humanity; he merely endeavoured to dethrone arrogance, prejudice, stupidity, and laziness as far as possible; he demanded neither equality of property nor equal political influence, nor even equal position in society for everyone; but he demanded a minimum of political rights, possibility of work and of achieving a certain social position for everyone; he wished to set the common basis of equal human values for all as high as possible, in order that the healthiest possible further development of the whole body might take place. In this development, those born to lead by virtue of talent and character, physical and spiritual qualities, should undertake the duties of leadership.

Optimism belongs to the being of democracy, a belief, if not in the inherent goodness of mankind, then at least in the insight, the aptitude, the goodwill of civilized man to give way to sensible opinion. Autocracy, on the contrary, lives by despising mankind; the autocrat works upon man's instincts and passions, using his good qualities, to be sure, but quite as ready to make use of his evil ones. Democracy sought to awaken in the subject the instinct to become a citizen of the State—democracy conferred liberty upon the lower classes. In the middle classes there was bound to be a strong following for these doctrines. The patriciate usually took to them unkindly; the feudal aristocracy saw in them a deadly enemy.

The democratic idea was the moving force of the epoch; its opponents might cast accusations of ideology, doctrinarism, at its exponents: of course democracy was based on an idea, of course it must develop a doctrine; of course this doctrine must be easy to understand, striking, and simple.

Democracy appealed to the politically impotent lower and middle strata, and promised them power in the State, that is, a share in political work, hitherto denied to them. It appealed

to all and would fain work for all. Democracy believed in itself
and inspired belief. People have contradicted the doctrine of
democracy—by other doctrines. The dogma could not be contradicted; it could only be combated by means of another
dogma. The democratic idea necessarily presented itself as
rationalistic, it appealed to reason, but naturally it also un-
chained instincts—ostensibly, humanity's best. Autocracy, too,
developed its doctrine, its ideology. It had an advantage in
that it need not begin with the idea, but with actual division
of power, tradition, custom, possessions, dignity with all
things of yesterday, the eternal yesterday, which was also to
be tomorrow, since it was "divinely willed." The fallacy was
naïve—for what reality does not appear "divinely willed?"
Things in themselves are necessarily conservative. Democracy
must first create its institutions, parties, press, societies, popular
representation—the whole organization of a people. Autocracy
was in possession of existing institutions . . . the autocrats got
their ideas afterwards and fitted them on to the existing
organizations—pitting them against the similar institutions
created by democracy. Thus Germany experienced a glorious
battle of wits, a battle, too, between classes and degrees of
society, a battle in which the dynasties, the army, and officialdom, that is, the mass of traditional authority, stood on one
side and on the other the leaders of the people, thinkers,
orators, authors, many professors and writers, scholars, the
politically talented among the middle and lower classes—the
true Germans of the German future.

Princes who believed in themselves have always remained
autocrats. They have instinctively felt that any concession
would lower their status, and historically speaking, they were
right. The medieval State had been dualistic—the modern
State could only be a unity. Either the prince or the people
must hold sovereign power. The constitutions invented in
Europe since the great French Revolution all made an attempt
to find a middle way between autocracy and democracy—

which could only exist as an intermediate stage. The unwritten British constitution, which remained dualistic and was only to develop into a unified democracy in the course of the nineteenth century by means of one reform law after another, soon became a model to be cited by all friends of a quiet, historically founded development, and as a panacea for all states seeking a practical form of political life between reaction and revolution, between authority and freedom, between autocracy and democracy, between the interests of dynasties and the will of the people. The French Charter of 1814, the Belgian Constitution of 1830, were attempts to create a new written version of the principles of British institutions according to continental needs. The South German constitutions also belong to this section. The strongest hindrance to the progress of the constitutional idea of popular representation was always the fallacy that "constitutions" and "parliaments" were non-German. The Prince-Consort was certainly in the right when he wrote to Frederick William IV on December 12, 1847: "The monarchist principle is not historically old German, but only an imitation of French absolutism. To demand the return of popular rights is not French and radical, but truly German and conservative." Between Provincial Diets and constitutional assemblies there is naturally only a difference of degree of development. At the beginning of that development stood the dualism of crowns and diets, at the end, unified democracy.

German liberals were particularly anxious to find a comforting compromise between autocracy and democracy. Liberalism and democracy bear much the same relation to one another as socialism and communism. Liberalism is a *Weltanschauung*, democracy a political programme; liberalism takes its rise from the person, from culture, from humanitarianism; democracy from the inhabitants of a State, from interests and power. Liberalism is predominantly idea and culture, democracy predominantly conviction and hard work, liberalism is strongest in negation, it denies the confinements of intellect, economy and lastly, it seeks to be free of something; democracy is positive, demands guarantees, control, ruthless realization of "freedom"; it demands the right to live, a new apportionment of actual power. The Liberal believes in benevolent rulers; wishes to reform the dynasty, officialdom, even the army and economic interests with his own spirit; he promises himself much from the harmonious interplay of all existing public authorities, he wishes to preserve and to develop; the democrat sees in the ruler, at the best, a useful functionary in the new State, but he considers the republic to be the best form of state, at any rate the most normal, peaceful and secure form; he rejects the superfluous ruling and commanding and would like to see officials and army supplied by the people; he would destroy what he cannot use and build up again on a firmly established plan. Liberalism is historic and therefore relative; democracy, dogmatic, categorical, and absolute. Liberalism can agree with political genius, and is willing to be used and even abused by one. Democracy only suffers genius when it is made perfect in itself. Liberalism leads all too easily to busybodying, policy of interests, speculation. Democracy congeals into an empty formula if it does not become popular experience, religiously determined popular will to popular leadership. Liberalism and democracy are on different planes, and therefore comparison between them runs in danger of going astray. Conservatism, liberalism and socialism must be grouped together: they are forms of political *Weltanschauung*.

On the other hand, autocracy, democracy, and communism must be grouped together; these are the corresponding political forms taken by these ideas in State and society. The first group is of predominantly contemplative character, the second group is active. A very great proportion of the types of German statesmen, thinkers, and party leaders can be explained by the contrast between autocracy and conservatism, democracy and liberalism, communism and socialism. We may add clericalism as an intellectual power of special origin, which was found ranged on the conservative side against liberalism, but also on the democratic side against autocracy, and thus was to secure for itself a unique position of power in Germany. It was fatal to German development before and during the Revolution of 1848–49 that socialistic and communistic tendencies combined with democratic ideas. Democracy fought against the existing State; Socialists and Communists were bound to recognize this as their own battle. The Democrat was also prepared, if necessary, to upset the existing state by force, but never thought of upsetting the existing state of society, or of a new dispensation to regulate the apportioning of property. Property was sacred to him; he demanded a change in the balance of political power, expecting thus to render the rise of the lower and middle classes possible; he was a sworn enemy of all dictators, also, of course, of the dictatorship of the proletariat. The Democrat welcomed the access of auxiliaries from the lowest classes in whom the communistic idea was already working—and the Communist leaders quite intentionally supported democracy's battle. Every opponent of the existing order was finally labelled "a Democrat."

This gave rise to a new position which a part of the middle classes, especially the money and title patriciate regarded as extremely threatening. They, too, wished to see an end of autocracy, or at least to control its powers by a liberal constitution. They wished to assume the reins of power; the storm from below was quite to their taste, as long as it remained within bounds. But when the Democrat also turned against them, when property, commerce, the whole organization of business were in question, when there was talk of upsetting the existing order of society and economics, these people began to feel really uncomfortable; they at once moderated their own liberal demands and hastily allied themselves with the threatened autocracy, which was only too glad to put the old means of power, the army and bureaucracy, at the service of "law and order."

The democratic idea had to bear the brunt of the damage.


The tragic side of this condition of things became more accentuated when the battle between autocracy and democracy took on an international character. There was an international European concert of princes, at its head, Czar Nicholas and Prince Metternich. This concern was most intimately bound together by ties of relationship and similarity of courts and ways of living. Its members considered themselves defenders of morals, prosperity, culture, and religion. They formed the first real international. Louis Philippe's July kingship also belonged unquestionably, since the breach with England, to the princes' concern. England, which could not forgive the French for their disgraceful intrigue in the matter of the Spanish marriage, was ready to support the movement of European democracy, in order to make difficulties for the concert of princes, and especially to put one of its leaders, Czar Nicholas, in an uncomfortable position. Considered from the point of view of foreign policy, the fall of the July kingdom was a severe blow to the concert of princes, a triumph of European democracy, and a great advantage to England. The three unsolved great national problems of the age, the German, the Polish, and the Italian, were remarkably intertwined with the battle of European democracy.

Certainly they were not the only ones. The success of the Greek struggle for independence showed the national movements in Servia and Roumania where their aim should lie. The Balkan peoples' struggle for freedom already began to increase the bitterness of Franco-British feeling, and even to sow dissension between the two vanguards of autocracy, Austria and Russia. But in the main, this was preparation for a later epoch. In foreign politics, the problems that counted in the revolutionary period of 1848–49 were the German, the Polish, and the Italian.

The German question was one of a democratic constitution for all Germany, but just on this account it was a question of frontiers, of the separation of German populations from stranger folk. The frontier between Pole and German was extraordinarily difficult to determine on account of ethnical assimilation, even from a purely national point of view, disregarding military and economic aspects. It was just as difficult in Styria and Karinthia to define the frontier against the South Slavs, or in South Tyrol against the Italians. If here, in the south and east, the national frontiers of Austria and Prussia extended beyond the bounds of purely German population, if in the two Silesias, in Bohemia, Moravia, and Hungary, any attempt to define a frontier line among the wildly-assorted national mixtures would have been nonsensical, yet in the west, towards France, the German frontier had retreated from the population. The purely German Alsatians and the German-speaking part of the Lothringians were French citizens. Since Luxemburg and Limburg were members of the German Confederation, the frontier in the north-west again protruded among non-German peoples.

Singular was the condition of the German northern frontier and it was from here that the national idea was to receive its strongest impetus in the year of revolution. Dynastic and democratic impulses, foreign, political, and economic, philosophic and ethnical, were all interlocked in the battle for the dukedoms of Schleswig and Holstein. We know that Holstein belonged to the German Confederation; her Duke, the King of Denmark, was, as such, a member of the German Confederation; but the King of Denmark was also sovereign duke of Schleswig. Amongst the conditions insisted upon by the King of Denmark when he was chosen Duke of Schleswig und Holstein in 1460, was the one that these countries should remain "inseparable" for "ever." To be sure, the inseparability was very soon interfered with, and in history there may be a desire for, but no fulfilment of "eternal" regulations. The division of the dukedoms into the Royal Danish and Gottorp ducal line only came to an end in 1773. Since then the King of Denmark was feudal lord of Schleswig, but held Holstein in fief from the Roman Emperor, he was regent of the royal share in both dukedoms, as well as of the ducal Gottorp portion and of that held in common by both.

In Denmark, the Lex regia of 1665 had done away with Salic law. In the dukedoms only the male line could succeed and this was expressly stated, according to German law.

Denmark had always been a small country with great ambitions; she had come badly out of the Napoleonic war years: Norway was joined by Sweden. Efforts to extend the Danish language over the dukedoms began as early as the end of the eighteenth century. They were now intensified. The idea of a united Danish State came into being; out of this came the idea of a pan-Scandinavian union. Danish self-confidence was at work in both ideas and Danish national interests made use of all modern maxims of government in handling the dukedoms. The old German-Danish cultural communion which had done so much for Klopstock, Schiller, and many another, was now to disappear.

The German court nobility had played out their political part in Copenhagen; they would like to have continued to constitute a Schleswig and Holstein republic of nobles. But the romantically awakened Danish popular feeling worked against them—and amongst them a German national feeling had arisen which prompted them to keep within bounds.

The most fanatic Danes could not deny that Holstein was a purely German land; the inhabitants were low Saxon, quiet and rather slow-going, inartistic, given to reserve in their own narrow circles, hard, tough, critical, and unyielding. Altona was an "all-too-near" neighbour of Hamburg; the knights of Wagrien, the East Holstein Slavonic District, were the proudest of the proud. But in Schleswig, too, the purely German element predominated. The men of Schleswig were somewhat quicker and bolder, smarter and more eager than those of Holstein, steeled by many a hard fight, and grown wise and keen in old yeoman freedom. A bare third of the population in Schleswig understood Danish, a bare quarter in North Schleswig spoke folk Danish in West Jute dialect.

The Danish and German broad dialects were heartily mixed. The gradual progress of Danish in the frontier territory was mainly due to the immigration of Danish serving folk—the intelligent population of the towns and the thriving citizens were German. The dialects were peasant speech. Cultivated people spoke good German, only far in the north, pure Danish. The Frisians on the West coast, whom the Danes claimed without any right as their own, were a Germanic tribe with their own Frisian language and culture, but hearing German in church and school and politically feeling themselves as Germans.

The lovely, "sea-surrounded" northland of Schleswig-Holstein does not display its natural contrasts in vain: on the East coast the mild pleasantness of wooded bays and fiords, the charmingly lively region of lakes and hills—on the West coast, the grand melancholy of the marshy flatlands, farther north the loneliness of the heath and the heroic battle of the islands with the land-devouring onset of the North Sea. Schleswig-Holstein unites both: homely devotion to the soil, and eyes looking out over the great world. This was a reason why it was at this time a land fraught with destiny.

Only through Schleswig-Holstein could a new Germany come into being, a North-Sea-Baltic State in the full sense of the term; naturally neither the chief Baltic power, Russia, nor the chief North Sea power, England, were in favour of it. It was unbearable to the newly-awakened national feeling that Danes should rule over Germans; but Germans' rule over Danes encountered the same difficulties. There were enough German dynasties; it was questionable whether another petty state would be much to Germany's advantage. But what was German did not belong to Greater Denmark, but to a greater Germany—only no one knew yet exactly what was meant by such a term. The aim was as simple as it was great and necessary. The way was dark. Schleswig-Holstein was a European problem, but so was Greater Germany. Both could only be solved by someone who understood both.

Germany could only become a national State if it became a democracy. A unified popular power abroad was equivalent to organized popular freedom at home.

At what precise moment did the German Revolution of 1848–49 begin? Everything was German Revolution—Herwegh's sweeping verse, Feuerbach's relentless thought, Uhland's moving words at the Frankfort Meeting of Germanic Philologues in 1846, Prince Leiningen's appeal to Prussia, Friedrich List's call for German national economy, the misery of artisan and peasant labourer, the crushing programme of the great Communist leaders, the idea of the war of liberty against Russia, the Lola scandal, the song and strife about Schleswig-Holstein. How embarrassed, how petty seemed the representatives of the old order in comparison! But there was one idea which in a way cemented all these ideas together, which arched itself above all these individual contradictions like a synthesis of opposites—the idea of a German parliament.

A true popular representation is an organ, a central function of the living being of a nation—as an expression of will, a place to make laws, to administrate, govern and control—that was the most sacred belief of the age.

On February 12, 1848, Friedrich Bassermann put a motion to the Baden Second Chamber to create a representative of the German chamber of estates at the German Federation. The idea was old; conditions at the moment lent to it a fiery force; Italy was already aflame. The German movement began spontaneously. Less than fourteen days later, revolution broke out in Paris, the one known as the February Revolution.

## CHAPTER SIX

# THE MARCH REVOLUTION

THE FRENCH February Revolution was both fortunate and unfortunate for events in Germany. It roused up a storm there that at first carried all before it. It was at once a national and a European movement, at once liberal and democratic, dictated by purpose, but still more by feeling and emotion. It not only overwhelmed its opponents much too quickly—but also its own exponents. Success came easily almost everywhere—it intoxicated and deceived—most of all, the momentary victors.

This spring of 1848 was a natural phenomenon, such as Germany's grudging climate seldom grants even to the more fortunate lands of the Rhine, Main, and Neckar, and scarcely ever to the northern and eastern valleys. The bewitching sunshine caused not only nature but also human beings to break into unsuspected blossom; they collected their thoughts and spoke, they demanded and achieved everything, they wreathed their brows, pledged one another deep, and celebrated feasts; enemies embraced one another, outcasts and heretics rose to joyous leadership, the guilty and the accursed vanished quietly, nobody raised a hand against them in this lyrical spring. German good nature and trustfulness triumphed over all caution, over all the hard, bad, harrowing experiences of other days. Only in 1813, 1870, and 1914 was anything like it seen in Germany. But these were all war periods, when the overwhelming feeling of belonging to "a band of brothers" was fanned by danger from without. In 1848, this motive was by no means absent—people unjustly imagined themselves threatened by France and, perhaps more justly, by Russia. But other impulses were far more powerful. Therefore the March experience of 1848 represents something which is unique in Germany's history. For the first time, all German states spoke the same political language and recognized the same political faith. When we compare the March demands and successes in the various states we are startled to find them often conforming almost literally with one another. Actual events happened with amazing similarity in many places, often simultaneously. The German nation had become a fact, something living, like a flower in its cup. The petals were springing open. Otherwise nothing was actually happening. But this was decisive. After March 1848, no one could doubt the existence of the German nation without incurring its curse. All these Austrians, Prussians, Bavarians, Württembergers and the rest, had been turned by this March whirlwind into what they had so long desired to become—free Germans. Now they wanted to assemble and vent their opinions, to pass judgments freely and in public, to govern themselves, by elections, by free speech, self-respecting, dignified, law-abiding, and peaceful.

This was an age that believed in the power of the word, as never before or after. Beautiful, genuine, great, true words were for these people deliverance and solution of all problems. They fought with words, won victories with them and were astonished that there could still be powers that refused to bow to words, despising and abusing them. The people of this age listened to the words of men of the people and put their trust in the words of princes. Words built up the new, longed-for world, pure and good. Words were deeds, became flesh and blood; noble, strong, clever, fascinating words revealed a political Germany, the magic of which will still preserve a charm in days long beyond our own. Soul was in the word, sentiment, truth, and the will of the age. But every *Logos* is certain to meet with its *Logos* destiny.

This March of the year 1848 was the great turning-point of German history in the nineteenth century. Since then there has been the distinction, pre-March and post-March. There was a sharp division of spirits, heads, and hearts. Everyone had to be on one side of the barricades or the other. Pre-March was certainly far from dead, post-March was certainly not yet quite alive. The battle was now between the two. Many attempts were made to reconcile them, which was as possible and necessary as all compromises, but, on the whole, unfruitful.

This new Germany of 1848 blossomed like the spring, which no contemporary ever forgot. Everywhere everyone was amazed at the miracle which had happened to these patient, good-hearted, decent Germans; it came a little late, to be sure —but they were thankful and happy. They might now have everything, and wanted everything at once: their princes and their freedom, their little states and the great Fatherland, a benevolent bureaucracy and elected representatives, a strong army and peace between nations, German unity and neighbourliness on every hand, prosperous business for big promotors and plenty of food for everyone—probably even a democratic State with a crowned Emperor at the head of it!

The Democratic Movement began in Baden. There were stormy meetings in Mannheim, Karlsruhe, Heidelberg. The demands made were for the abolition of all arbitrary laws, for equal rights for religious sects, for trial by jury, a militia, progressive income-tax, responsibility of ministers—a very mixed list of economic, national, and social reforms. In the Odenwald and the Black Forest, traditional regions of rural over-population, there were peasant revolts, which invariably began by attacks upon the Jews. The apex of all these events was the meeting at Offenburg on March 19th, a mass demonstration at which, under Hecker's leadership, a purely democratic programme was determined upon. Clubs dedicated to the carrying-out of the programme were to be founded in Baden and all over Germany. The proclamation of the Republic seemed to be the very next step. There were similar movements in Württemberg, Hesse-Darmstadt, and Nassau. New governments, formed by the leaders of the Opposition, were set up, the martyrs to the cause of freedom were liberated, Committees of Safety were organized, militia instituted. In Electoral Hesse, Hanau, which was completely radical, took the lead, and even threatened to cut loose from sleepy Cassel. The wicked old King of Hanover could not, to be sure, agree to the idea of a German Parliament, but kept his promises better than many another German prince who was supposed to incline to liberalism. In Thuringia the Song of the Robbers was heard once again: "A free life it is we lead"—and the idea of mediatization had a strongly social-revolutionary character here from the very beginning. In the Kingdom of Saxony, "the entire German Fatherland and the Dynasties," the individual governments were to be approached in the matter. Seven members of the Heidelberg Assembly were asked to prepare proposals and to get out the invitations to the larger assembly of representative men of Germany as swiftly as possible.

This Heidelberg declaration implied complete revolution in the question of reorganization of all Germany. The governments of Vienna and Berlin were still unshaken. In spite of this the Diet was thrust on one side; the people did not want to work against the governments, but with them, and above all, they did not want to wait any longer. That the leaders of the popular movement were not served by a German Parliament alone, can plainly be seen by the resolution which Heinrich von Gagern and his friends put to the Hessian Chamber of February 27th. This went much further than Bassermann's: an interim Federal leader was to be nominated simultaneously with the summoning of the National representatives, the conduct of foreign affairs, the army and national military training to be placed in the hands of a Cabinet, whose members were to be responsible only to the interim leader and to the nation.

Those promulgating these ideas in the south-west were the March ministers, Gagern at their head; the governments of Nassau, the Grand Duchy of Hesse and Baden sent the Legations Councillor of Nassau, Max von Gagern, Heinrich von Gagern's younger brother, and General Count Lehrbach to win over the governments of the German states to the Heidelberg principles. Gervinus was asked to work out a plan. We may say that the ideas represented by the *Deutsche Zeitung* undertook practically to reconstruct the Germany of their day.

Hecker and Struve had also taken part in the Heidelberg assembly and had voted for the published declaration. They were not the only supporters of the republican State, but the majority were monarchistic and desired a constitutional monarchy, or "parliamentarian" as it was then called. The Republicans at this time—before the outbreak of revolution in Vienna and Berlin—thought a slower development preferable. By the end of March their opinions had changed. At the Heidelberg meeting, the members from Rhenish Prussia had been particularly conspicuous—the faith in Prussia which still prevailed gave them a special position. At that time they represented the idea that the United Diet should meet at least every second year on the Rhine, just to cement the Rhineland to Prussia. There were serious people who again talked of separation and the formation of a Rhine State with a Catholic prince. The men from Heidelberg, discussing an elected imperial president for all Germany, received a message from the King of Württemberg: they should rather take the King of Prussia as Emperor; the small sovereign states must disappear. Unless they could decide to form only four or five large states, the republic was inevitable. Heinrich von Gagern told the Prussians in all form that a South German separate alliance was impossible. Geographically speaking, Prussia was "the necessary axis of German unity." The idea of a ministerial congress was unpopular. A congress over which Austria presided would be a misfortune for Germany. The governments of Nassau and Baden took up a similar standpoint; the south-west states were firmly on the side of the popular movement; in the first half of March, Prussia need only have stretched out a hand.

The position in the German Federal Diet at Frankfort was also most favourable for a Prussian initiative. Count Dönhoff wrote to Berlin on February 18th that the general desire was to see Prussia at the wheel; Austria's part was to be only nominal. Count Dönhoff was in charge, in the absence of the Austrian presidial envoy; he was full of patriotic energy and hoped to carry the hesitating Berlin government with him. But the King of Prussia thought everything must go by way of Vienna, and sent his Radowitz there. Berlin worked out a very modest programme including a Press law, publication of diet reports, federal consulates, and a regulation of German emigration. When the Paris February Revolution became known, Berlin again thought nothing more urgent than immediate consultation with the Austrian court. Radowitz talked in Vienna about military measures for German safety and the immediate assembly of all German governments. On March 1st, the Frankfort Diet issued an official proclamation which spoke another language.

This document appealed as "the legal organ of the national and political unity of Germany" to the German governments and people, exhorted them to work together harmoniously and loyally in the interests of upholding invulnerability abroad, and quiet and order, security and prosperity at home. The Diet promised "to care for Germany's security abroad as well as to further national interests at home." Germany "must be raised to the position which is hers of right among the nations of Europe."

Thus we see the Diet seeking to claim the national idea as its own sphere of labour and using the language of the very men whom it had persecuted for decades and who had retaliated by despising it. The Diet saw the Revolution at work and declared evolution to be necessary. The answer from all the well-informed was mockery, justifiably bitter. Count Dönhoff, to be sure, hoped for the best; he was the intellectual father of the appeal. He had acted without instructions and now attempted to justify his fault in Berlin. He pleaded with King Frederick William IV to use the great last moment "to constitute German nationality on a new basis and make Germany great, strong, and mighty."

In the intoxication of the March Revolution, rolling inexorably forward, the Diet members probably felt themselves somewhat out of date. They might have kept quite passive and awaited results—that would perhaps have been the proudest and most tactful thing to do. Count Dönhof attempted to whip them on, to put the Diet at the head of the movement—in German and Prussian interests. It was a despairing battle to uphold the last shreds of reputation, a fight for existence. The Diet, like an old, broken-winded nag, entered the race at the side of the youthful, plunging chargers of the German Freedom Movement.

Count Dönhoff developed the idea in a report of March 5th, destined for Berlin, of a shield and colours for the Confederation, which had already been agreed to long before by the King of Prussia. The very next day the Diet gave its decision, adopting the old German Imperial Eagle as the Federal arms, and the colours of the former German Imperial standard as colours of the German Confederation. Dönhoff meant this as a friendly gesture, but at this moment it made a painful impression without saving the Confederation's face in public opinion. People laughed at the idea that the good old "Bund" was now about to commit the very political offence which it had severely punished thousands of times and flaunt the forbidden colours.

But Austria and Prussia believed that they could placate this mighty popular movement by summoning a Congress of

Princes at Dresden, which was planned for March 25th. The two Great Powers sent circular letters of invitation to the other governments and the imperially privileged Wiener Zeitung even called public attention to this event (in No. 76). The task of the Princes' Congress was to be "to set up Norms and Principles," to be carried out by the Federal Assembly. The difference between Count Dönhoff and his Berlin government now found full expression. He had formed a committee which protested in the sharpest terms at the manner of Austria's presidency.

Canitz deeply resented these views of his envoy; he wrote angrily on the margin: "Are my communications of February 29th, March 3rd and 7th, regarded as non avenues?" He declared Dönhoff to be presumptuous and ambitious. In reality, the envoy was more far-sighted than the minister, for he was in the midst of the popular movement in West Germany and took a correct view of its importance.

Nevertheless, Prussia clung to the Dresden Congress. If not a Congress of Princes, she hoped at least to see a congress of envoys. Jordan, envoy in Dresden, warned his government that the Saxon authorities were well-intentioned but weak, and therefore in no position to shield illustrious guests from insult; there was no censorship and the Saxon Diet would be meeting on March 20th. The envoy, again expressing disapproval, undertook to deliver the invitation. The Prussian scheme plunged most of the governments into difficulties. Bavaria expressly declined to take any part. Vienna proposed to transplant the Federal Assembly to Potsdam—so that Prussia might take entire responsibility. The contradiction between the Federal resolve of March 10th and the Prussian congress was clear enough. If Prussia had known of it, said the Grand Duke of Hesse, she could never have thought of the Diplomatic Congress. In consequence of the Dresden invitation, the Federal Diet suspended the resolve of March 10th, only to take it up again when the Congress idea was finally abandoned.

The Prussian Foreign Minister, von Canitz, thought nothing of a German parliament; a parliament, he wrote to Bernstorff, "implies a united government to stand at its side or above it, as well as independence of other corporations representing interests."

"Where is the central government," he asked, "which one could wish to set beside a German Parliament?"

The answer was given before the question was put—but unfortunately, Berlin had no ears to hear it. In a conversation which Heinrich von Gagern had with von Bockelberg, Prussian envoy, on March 19th, he expressly referred to the motion which he had put when still a member of the Hessian chamber: the King of Prussia should be Federal Dictator and hold the central power in the Federation. Gagern desired no congress, either in Potsdam or in Dresden; the only solution he thought possible was to resolve the Federal Assembly into the proposed congress; the aim could only be attained through the Federation, Frankfort must remain the seat of assembly. A parliament without a counter-balance would be a republic; one must find a legal way of connection with the Federal Assembly. Gagern and his friends went so far in their loyalty that they now almost regretted the Heidelberg resolutions, which prepared the way for the "Preliminary Parliament." He and Gervinus took pains to prevent this "Vorparliament" from taking place in Frankfort, Gagern also declared that he had not signed the proclamation, his name had been added without his consent. It was not in accordance with his present position. Welcker declared that he would do everything possible to preserve the private character of the pre-Parliament. Thus it was the very leaders of the Heidelberg Movement who applied the brakes, because they feared that the Revolution would sweep over them and swallow them up. Everything waited for Prussia: Prussia need only stretch out a hand—Austria was paralysed, Prussia could have put through the Federal Reform. But only before the 18th of March!

184

Many later observers have thought that Bavaria at this time missed one of her greatest opportunities. At the moment when King Ludwig could have taken a leading part in the German chaos, he was himself obliged, on account of the Lola Montez affair, to resign his crown. The guardian angel of Bavaria in these troubled days was Prince Leiningen. It was due solely to his tact and candour that the King's abdication on March 20th, though accompanied by stormy episodes, yet caused no tremor in the foundations of the State. The banishment of Lola took place in a carnival spirit of good-humoured jest, for the Munich man-in-the-street had a certain weakness for her. The good citizens, as usual in such cases, had no notion of the political background of the scandal. The result was that King Ludwig fell because neither the nobility, nor the army, nor clerical circles had any more faith in him. But the new King Maximilian was very much more Bavarian and quite devoid of any Greater German feelings. Hearty coarseness was replaced by retiring pedantry. Bavarian blue and white were the colours now nailed to the mast. The German democratic movement could no longer base any hopes upon Bavaria.

Thus there existed simultaneously in Germany: first, a purely revolutionary movement—we may call it the Heidelberg Movement; its followers were working for a pre-parliament and a national assembly; secondly, a diplomatic action by the petty states (Lehrbach–Gagern Mission), with the aim of intercepting this revolutionary movement and putting it into a legalized form; thirdly, a reform movement of the Federal Diet under Dönhoff's leadership; fourthly, the diplomatic action of the Great Powers. Undoubtedly, the strongest of these was the purely revolutionary movement; the feeling against diplomacy, military force, reactionary policy, and the Diet was far more powerful than any other.

A revolution has always that measure of historical justification which is given to it by the failure of the governing powers. The German popular movement had risen against the spirit of Metternich; this man was more than a historic personality; he was a system, a principle; it was what he wished to be; he had always stood erect and standing, he fell. If his human dignity was in ratio to the historical greatness for which he had lived, it redounds to his honour; but one must also understand the hate which boiled up against him. Since Napoleon I, no man had been so hated in Germany as was Prince Metternich. Napoleon was after all a foreign fiend, a scourge of destiny, a natural phenomenon, destroying German life in order that German life might be awakened anew. But Metternich was himself a German, and sacrificed the best, the youngest, the noblest in the world of German liberty and culture for decades to the principle of autocracy, because the Imperial State was only held together by autocracy and only by its means could Austria with all its tributaries rise above and tyrannize over Germany, Italy, Poland, Hungary, South Slavonia—a prime power in Europe.

The news of the February Revolution completely broke up Prince Metternich. The measures which he summoned the energy to take had no effect. Czar Nicholas, remembering Cracow, was very cool, expressed distrust and preferred to treat with Prussia. His offer to Metternich to assist in keeping order by occupying Galicia with Russian troops, in order to leave the Austrian troops free for Italy, was unspeakably humiliating. In London, where Metternich made a cautious inquiry about help against Italy, he only reaped an acid denial, decorated with all-too-well deserved reproaches in Palmerston's rounded eloquence. The negotiations with Prussia, conducted in Vienna by Radowitz, had only the meagre result of which we have already heard, the idea of the Dresden Congress. Metternich was at his wit's end, depressed, incapable of action; he merely mooted the conference idea, which had been stale for decades; any concession that he was prepared to make to Prussian wishes for federal reform, was out of date before it was even formulated; doubtless the old prince was far from cherishing any diabolical plan against the territory of other members of the Federation, such as Bavaria. Since the Tobacco riots in Milan in January, Italy had been in a threatening state of crisis. At the end of February, the political movement set in the west and south of Germany. In Vienna the first result was a commercial panic. A storm on the banks began, paper money was changed into silver wherever possible and the silver stored up at home. The municipal savings banks could hardly deal with the despairing customers. Small business came to a standstill, big business was only transacted where absolutely necessary. The general pressure increased until it became unbearable. Everything that Dr. Karl Beidtel had prophesied in his pamphlet *Die Geldangelegenheiten Oesterreichs* (Austria's Money Affairs) now seemed to be coming true; he had also demanded the abolition of payment of interest on State loans and that an advisory popular representative body should be called together. In addition to this came in foreign affairs the tension with France. Count Flahaut, French ambassador to Vienna, refused to obey Lamartine's demand that he should continue to fulfil his functions; he declared that he had been accredited to King Louis Philippe and therefore handed affairs over to the chief ambassadorial secretary and departed to England.

Relations with France had reached a critical stage, but Prince Metternich lacked the energy to do anything to clarify them. On the one hand he endeavoured to get the great powers to declare themselves against France in a body; on the other hand, he avoided answering questions as to whether Austria recognized the French Republic or not; he said that he saw no reason to interrupt international intercourse; France did not recognize Austrian agreements, but acted as if they existed *de facto*—Austria would take exactly the same attitude towards the republic in France.

Germany, pronounced Metternich in his portentous fashion, must not be caught unawares by events, but France must not be given any cause for invasion. This was very wise, but somewhat theoretical. Events in Germany daily widened the gulf that yawned between the constitutional states of the south and west on the one hand and Austria on the other. People were asking themselves anxiously in Vienna whether a mutual struggle for Germany's independence would be possible if it came to that. The Diet of Lower Austria already began to raise critical voices against Metternich's system of foreign policy, the debt to Russia was especially resented and talk was heard of raising a loan of fifty million gulden in order to pay off these debts. The Lower Austrian Diet was to assemble on March 13th—this day had been regarded for a long time previous as a historical turning-point; far-reaching motions were expected. In the country house of Baron Doblhoff, a member of the Diet, all the energy and intellect of the opposition forces had been foregathering for months past. The Bohemian Diets were also arranging to convene. But the first great action happened in Hungary. On March 3rd, Kossuth made his powerful accusatory speech in the House of Estates against the Viennese policy of stagnation, bayonets, and family interests; he demanded the right of nations to a will of their own and that Hungary as well as the other countries of the Austrian Empire should now at last be granted true parliamentary institutions. No Austrian newspaper was allowed to make mention of this speech; but hundreds of reprints and extracts went to Vienna and into the provinces.

The Viennese government hereupon appointed an Upper Court of Censorship, a feeble imitation of a far from reputable Prussian original; at the Court Chancellery, the greatest enemy of the Diet's energies, a secretary for Diet questions was appointed; financial reforms were even planned with a Central Committee from the Diet executive organ; officials were forbidden in a circular letter to utter any opinions on "financial or Italian matters." There was, in fact, altogether too much grumbling and complaining. The reign of the "Swelled Heads," the State Conference, was over and done with. In the Imperial family conference, Archduchess Sophie, Archduke Johann and Count Kolowrat, spoke in favour of a new trend of things. Archduke Ludwig and Metternich withstood obstinately. It happened as it must—the various oppositional groups began to work together. The judicial-political Reading Society had relations with Kossuth. The Lower Austrian Trade League resolved in the sitting of March 8th, in the presence of Archduke Franz Karl and Count Kolowrat, to accept the chairman's proposal (it was Arthabern a well-known manufacturer), to send an address to the Emperor. The Archduke agreed and undertook to deliver it. In future, said the address, there should be a rapprochement with the common fatherland, future measures should, contrary to former practice, further the interests of all by wisdom and practicability.

These leagues, private and often non-political organizations of the awakened citizenry, were the natural vessels of the March movement in Vienna. They were bound to one another by influential members, they had in their ranks officials, professors, merchants, writers, and artists. Baron Doblhoff's was the most outspokenly political. They issued an address, edited by Bauernfeld and the ubiquitous Alexander Bach, which was presented to the Viennese public for signature from March 7th on. The police could not succeed in confiscating it. The address demanded solidarity of German and Austrian interests, listed constitutional guarantees and emphasized the dangers of further procrastination. Signatories were collected everywhere. Among the societies was the powerful Shakespeare Club and they were now joined by the old and influential military burghers. The whole movement really came from the educated and prosperous middle classes, it was the work of loyal men who were relatively easy to satisfy. The address went on March 11th to the Commission of the Diet, which undertook to deliver it to the Lower Austrian Diet. But it was the students whose temperament stirred Vienna's political will to the highest pitch of excitement. The idea of a students' petition was first mooted, half in jest, in the bar-parlour of a suburban inn. A few days later, the large hall of the university was crowded for a long discussion as to the final text. Freedom of the Press and of speech, liberty to teach and to study, religious equality, popular representation—all the March demands were summed up here in a particularly clear and summary form. More than two thousand students supported the petition; Professors Hye and Endlicher undertook to deliver it to the Emperor in person. In an audience with Archduke Ludwig, they spoke openly against Metternich and Count Seldnitzky, minister of police. He defended Metternich and dismissed them without an answer, but he shook hands with Endlicher. On the evening of March 12th, they were received by the Emperor, who promised that the matter should be "considered," but that was all. Thus the critical 13th of March drew near.

There were thus four stages of the movement in Vienna; the old Court opposition party of the Archdukes and Kolowrat, the Diet opposition, about whose views Archduke Johann and Archduchess Sophie were well informed, the moderate citizen movement and the livelier action of the young academicians. These groups were all united in demanding the fall of Metternich. Popular movements always tend to fasten the responsibility for unbearable abuses upon individuals and to build all their hopes for a newer and happier age upon their overthrow or even destruction; the removal of Metternich must imply the removal of the principle, the system—Metternich, the man was weak and old, he would fain have forbidden the Revolution as he staggered from power; but the idea of Austrian autocracy was destined to outlive both Metternich and the political movement of 1848.

What did the four groups demand? The Court opposition, led by Archduchess Sophie and Archduke Johann, wished to safeguard the dynasty and to make as many concessions to the demands of the time as might be necessary to that end; the aristocratic diets desired a regulated participation in government, control of bureaucratic domination by "popular representation," imperial Diets, but only in the spirit of their own organization, expanded by the admission of representations of the higher classes of burghers. The citizen movement demanded decided reforms, liberal and centralistic, and a modern constitution. The only revolutionary spirit blazed among the students in the great lecture-room.

The decisive day was the 13th of March. The decision taken in Vienna on this day can be summed up in one short phrase: Fall of Prince Metternich. Citizens, students, officials, all allied themselves with the Prince's old enemies at court, the Archduke Johann at their head. Metternich wished to crush the democratic rising by any possible means, Prince Alfred Windischgrätz was to undertake this task, the same man who conquered revolutionary Vienna six months later. The veteran statesman bowed only to the express wishes of the Imperial family, with that graceful dignity which was natural to him. Everyone was tremendously relieved; even the court lackeys applauded. But it was at once felt that it was this one name which had held the State together.

A wave of black, red, and gold flooded over the Imperial city; red cockades and ribbons were already to be seen in the working-class quarters. A wreath of blossoms was set upon the head of the statue of Joseph, the first democratic emperor.

But next to German demands, those of the Slavs and Hungarians now made themselves heard. Vienna was at the same time German and Greater Austrian, it depended upon its dynasty, which was a guarantee of its position in Europe. But the demand arose in Prague for a union of Bohemia, Moravia, and Silesia under a democratic representative. It was already clear that the Revolution would mean a national crisis for the Imperial State. Was it to be resolved into its component parts?

The thought of a constitution released all national aspirations, its democratic battering-ram shook the foundations of Imperial autocracy. Germanicism found itself on the defensive, it was easy to become reactionary, if there was alliance with dynastic interests. Could one rule simultaneously in a liberal and a centralistic spirit? Despotism was certainly simpler.

If we compare the European and German prospects of the two great powers, Prussia and Austria, at the beginning of the Revolution of 1848, we are surprised to note the preponderance of Prussia; it had perhaps never been so excessive before and scarcely ever after. Austria suffered severely from the burden of Metternich; in spite of all disappointments and lack of clarity, Prussia's King Frederick William IV seemed to belong to the future. He was more German than Prussian, more black, red, and gold, than black and white. The "old Prussian" circles had no love for him. His talents, station, and the general situation made him the man of destiny of his age. When Metternich had at last fallen, everyone breathed more freely, but his absence left a gap. Metternich had ruined Austria, but in order to rise again, Austria needed a couple more of his kidney. Prussia was a much healthier State and yet she suffered a crisis of great severity. In Austria, as everywhere in Germany, the Revolution had prevailed, but the battle had not been properly fought to a finish. The existing powers had come to an understanding with the popular movement just in time. Persons and principles were sacrificed in order that the holders might retain their power, or share it only with the rising citizen patriciates of money and title. The middle and lower classes were to accept this and make the best of it. The unique feature of the Revolution of 1848 was that autocracy nowhere felt completely vanquished, nor democracy that it was completely victorious. Extremes retired from the scene, the golden mean was the chosen way. Revolution had come to a halt before the throne, as the saying went. The people trusted the word of their princes, the rulers the decency and love of order of their people. Feeling all over Germany was therefore optimistic. Only in Prussia things were different. Only in Berlin was there serious fighting; here only was there much bloodshed and great bitterness; here only were there victors and victims. In this fact reposes the historical significance of the 18th of March.

The 18th of March, which was a Saturday, dawned, and nothing decisive had happened as yet. The party of compromise at court had actually thrust the military party aside; the public knew nothing and could know nothing of this. Everywhere on the morning of this day there were large assemblies of citizens; the plan of a procession to the palace, in order to present the people's demands direct to the King in a mass petition, was again discussed. Canitz said a day later that he had known of a plot to capture the palace by apparently friendly means and enforce further concessions from the King, possibly even his abdication and that of the Prince of Prussia. No doubt someone gave utterance to such a likely idea, but it is difficult to believe in the existence of any such "plot."

In the morning, the King received the Rhine deputation, from Cologne, the Prince of Prussia also being present; the deputation spoke of the threatening situation and demanded an "instantaneous great-hearted decision" from the King. The King replied that these wishes were in accordance with his plans; he would put himself at Germany's head, grant all necessary liberties; in a few hours a proclamation would appear to this effect.

The tension had reached its highest point. The municipal authorities were in constant consultation and sent a deputation to the palace, demanding the dissolution of the existing ministry, a modern constitution, the right of the citizens to bear arms and the withdrawal of the troops. This deputation was also received amiably by the King and dismissed with gracious promises. He gave them the draft edict to read. The authorities announced that the King had already passed a law granting freedom of the Press and guaranteed the truth of this —an act remarkably in excess of their competencies, but proving all the more certainly how necessary a pacification of the populace was thought by those who really understood the prevailing feeling.

About two o'clock in the afternoon, both proclamations actually appeared. The one abolished the censorship, but imposed no inconsiderable restrictions on the newspaper Press; the second called up the United Diet at an earlier date, April 2nd, but laid the principal stress upon a re-organization of the German federal constitution; that a modern constitution was to be granted to Prussia was hidden away in an auxiliary sentence; representation in the Federation "necessarily entailed a constitutional government for all German territories"— therefore, also for Prussia. In spite of this, both proclamations were thankfully received, they purported to be voluntary actions, although in fact there was little that was voluntary about them. The King could appear twice on the balcony to receive popular acclaim.

This success brought the other, still unfulfilled demands, all the more clearly to the fore. The most important and decisive of these was for the withdrawal of the troops. In Vienna, too, they had been sent outside the city bounds; the citizens of Berlin had for days been far more irritated than ever the Viennese had been by troops whose spirit and bearing were justly felt to be alien to the people and wholly inimical to them. If the King were to become a popular king of a people's State, he should trust himself to his people and do without the protection of his guards. But Prussia was a military State— there was greatness in this, an essential factor of her existence. Yet the city of Berlin was a modern city, grown up over the head of the old Prussia and ready to create a new one. The cry "Withdraw the troops!" was full of historical symbolism. Berlin wanted clarity, Berlin wanted a victory.

It would not in the least have diminished the reputation

of the Government to have decreased the number of troops in Berlin; it would have been a sign of confidence and would not have meant running any risk, for the overwhelming majority of the Berlin populace were content with the con-cessions. A change of ministers was immediately impending. Bodelschwingh, the Minister of the Interior, had declared that he would have nothing to do with the new era. Canitz was completely exhausted and so was Thile. Count Arnim-Boitzenburg, as Prime Minister elect, was already at the palace. The edicts were signed by the Prince of Prussia—thus the heir-apparent and leader of the military party had acceded, however unwillingly, to the citizens' demands. But no resolve was made to stop the overflowing of troops into Berlin. The normal Berlin garrison was at least twelve thousand, rela-tively more than any other German capital, but the city of over four hundred thousand inhabitants had only two hundred and four policemen. On account of the partial mobilization and the access of troops from other regions, the garrison had swollen to over twenty thousand by the morning of March 19th. There was a great contrast between General von Pfuel and General von Prittwitz. Pfuel, the freshly nominated Governor of Berlin, was a man of deep culture and ideas touched with genius, the exact opposite of a martinet; he did not wish to treat people harshly, he wished to divert passions, to display the troops as little as possible and do nothing unless actually attacked. The Prince of Prussia did not in the least agree with Pfuel. Prittwitz, commander of the guards, was much more to the taste of such an outright militarist.

Between one and two o'clock it became known that the King would summon a new cabinet—the names of Schwerin, Auerswald, Camphausen, Beckerath, seemed to invite confi-dence. But about the same time the high command over all the troops in and around Berlin was put into the hands of General von Prittwitz. General von Pfuel had gone to pay a brief visit to his family, from whom his duties had separated him for several days. This moment was seized upon by his enemies, the leaders of the reactionary party, especially Count Alvensleben, to induce the King to allow Prittwitz to be insinuated into the command. It was later declared that Pfuel could not be found or had been "cut off by the rebels." When he returned to the palace an hour later, he found the situation completely changed. The martinets were at the wheel.

Crowds collected in front of the palace. Nobody was armed, nobody jeered or booed. The better-dressed were decidedly in the majority. The atmosphere was one of joyous expectation. But there were loud demands for the withdrawal of the troops, as had been determined in the mass petition of the morning. Possibly the King's entourage expected an attack; in any case Prittwitz received from Frederick William IV, who now wished to do something to please the army, an order to cause cavalry to "clean up" the Palace square. A squadron of dragoon guards undertook the task. They rode out of the palace towards the Kurfürsten bridge at a slow trot. Prittwitz himself accompanied them, and as his word of command was unheard in the noise, he drew his sword. Many dragoons followed his example. The riders therefore trotted towards the crowd with drawn swords and not with sheathed weapons, as the King, falsely informed, afterwards declared. They trotted into the crowd—it had all the appearance of an attack. Without the knowledge or desire of the General, Major von Falkenstein now sent the first company of the Kaiser Franz regiment to the Breite Strasse, the second towards the Lange Brücke—he seems to have imagined that the General, surrounded by the crowd, was in danger. Although Prittwitz gave a contrary command, the infantry movement was carried out—at whose higher command was never discovered. As the riflemen of the first company also marched forward from the corner of the Breite Strasse towards the Lange Brücke, suddenly two rifle shots rang out. At the interrogation later, Corporal

196

Hettgen said that a civilian had struck the hammer of his musket with a stick, causing a shot to be discharged. Grenadier Kulm said that he had, without waiting for orders, moved his rifle into his right hand ready for attack, and in so doing had let off a shot.

Both pieces of evidence are full of internal and external improbabilities. A muzzle-loading rifle can only be fired by the blow of a stick on the trigger if the trigger be already cocked; and is it credible that a corporal would allow a civilian to strike his weapon? It is far more likely that the civilian aimed a blow at the corporal, that the corporal fended it off and thereby discharged a shot. Still, we may allow that the first shot may have been purely accidental, but what about the second? Another accident directly after the first seems scarcely probable. It is out of the question that at such a serious moment a grenadier should bring his rifle to the attack of his own accord and in performing an action so often practised should "accidentally" discharge a shot! Entries in the diary of the late Kaiser Friedrich point to a possible solution of the mystery; his tutor, Count Königsmarck, read to the young prince a letter from his father, the Prince of Prussia, on the afternoon of March 18th, in which the first shot was described as above; the second, it was said, was also accidental; "and when a grenadier in the foremost rank heard the two shots, he thought a command to 'Fire!' had been given, and he presented and fired, without hitting anyone." Nowhere else is there any mention of three shots; indeed, there were only two. But the second "accident" may really have happened in this way—that the grenadier thought a command had been given, and therefore fired. But if a command to fire had really been uttered, there would have been a large number of shots. Neither the corporal nor the grenadier were punished— nothing much can be learned from this fact. But we must not fail to notice that in the immediately issued diplomatic reports, there is nothing about an "accident."

Prittwitz had the confidence of the party of reaction; he had become commander-in-chief because, "as it appears, the reactionary party wished to provoke a conflict," says Nobiling in his notes. The conflict had now begun. The action of the military in attacking was provocative in the highest degree and completely contradictory to official orders. There had been no order to the crowd to disperse. The cry "Betrayed!" was heard everywhere, and not without inner justification. The special constables, who had entreated the military to retire, now also tore off their badges, broke their wands of office and shouted of betrayal. The cries of rage and embitterment spread from one to another through all the streets. People cried "assassins," although no one had been wounded by the two first shots. Only immediate eye-witnesses knew this, and the contrary was at once noised abroad. The impression upon the populace was that, in spite of all concessions, the military had been let loose upon the people, just as on previous days. Malicious purpose seemed clearly proven. If the King had mounted a horse and shown himself to the people, with a word of explanation and pacification, perhaps quiet would have been restored and bloodshed avoided. But he remained in his palace and let things go as they would. Only the Prime Minister, Count Arnim-Boitzenburg, appeared on the balcony of the *Schloss* with a white flag. He came down in the street with it, but all in vain. In the afternoon, a banner bearing the one word "Misunderstanding!" was still hanging out of one of the palace windows. Various city councillors went at once to the palace in an attempt at mediation, but the standpoint of military honour would now allow of no further possibilities of parley. It was said to be impossible to withdraw the troops—the battle had begun. Many on both sides had wished for conflict, a great many on the military side thought it a welcome opportunity to withdraw all the concessions already granted. The Prince of Prussia spoke to this effect the same evening.

All grades of the population in Berlin took part in the memorable battles which now ensued. It was, as nowhere else in Germany, plainly a deliberate battle of the civilian against the military, of the free and democratic spirit against brute force. At the time there was only a small group of determined republicans and convinced socialists in Berlin. The people of Berlin did not fight against the King's person, however much they considered him to blame, nor against the institution of monarchy. The majority did not in the least wish to bring about a collapse of the present state of things, the end of the existing order of the State. All they wanted was the security of a constitutional development and no interference by reactionary military circles. Therefore they built hundreds of barricades in a few hours, and thousands took their lives in their hands, unconcernedly heroic.

Many regrettable incidents happened, and on the other hand, the military went to work with especial brutality. The troops, fully equipped as for active service, even provided with entrenching material, had been in a state of irritation for days past. Their quarters had been unsatisfactory, they had been overworked. Most of them were young soldiers with only half a year's service, raw recruits from country districts, physically fit, but exceedingly raw material from an intellectual and military point of view, and (having had matters explained to them in a highly primitive fashion by arrogant and excited officers), ready to strike in blind fury at the "rebels," "rioters," and "mob." Very little skill in leadership was displayed. There was a lot of promiscuous shooting into windows and doors. The infantry usually attempted to storm the barricades from the front, thus exposing themselves to shots and stone-throwing from the houses, and also greatly retarded their progress by entering houses and following up real or imaginary marksmen. It was not until the June battles of 1848 that Cavaignac in Paris carried out the new method of carrying the barricades; that is, to break through the houses and so take the defenders of the barricade in the rear. The cavalry were of little use on the torn-up roads; progress was made only after the artillery had been brought up. They fired heavily, not only upon the barricades, but into the houses. The people's defenders had only two guns, small brass cannon which were loaded with marbles. A stocking, filled with forty or fifty marbles, was the lading of such a cannon. Two men who had served their military term in the artillery, Gustav Hesse, a turner, and Fitchner, a locksmith, served these cannon. Hesse, especially, was so daring that he became the hero of the day, and later, on every festive occasion during the whole revolutionary period, he was accustomed to wear the wreath of victory with which his comrades presented him as a souvenir of March 18th.

Barricades had sprung up so quickly in the centre of Berlin that the government party at once said and ever afterwards repeated that there must have been a concerted plan. The Russian General Count Benckendorff, who was then military attaché in Berlin and probably the only foreign officer who witnessed the street fighting, also said in his report to Czar Nicholas on March 24th, that the revolt must have been in preparation for a long time through Communistic propaganda in Switzerland, France, and South Germany, without the Prussian Government being aware of the threads or the men who were weaving them, or understanding how to choke the movement in the bud or bring the conflict, once it had broken out, to a speedy conclusion. Count Trautmannsdorff, the Austrian envoy, writes in a similar vein. The only explanation that diplomat could find for the fact that a popular rising could meet with such success in opposition to the apparently firmly rooted power of the Prussian State, was that the government had failed in the face of a mysterious, internationally organized, revolutionary power.

The failure of the government had certainly made the catastrophe of March 18th possible, not only in a general political sense; the technical helplessness, so to speak, with which the machinery of the State, particularly the police president, von Minutoli, confronted the movement, was indeed remarkable. On the one hand, Minutoli had tried to placate the popular movement, on the other hand he had unwittingly brought grist to the mill of the reactionary party at the palace by his exaggerated reports, and thus had a share of guilt in the excessively violent behaviour of the soldiery. Yet it is certain that no deliberate preparation for the struggle had been made by the people (for instance, under the influence of international "emmissaries.")

We cannot assume that there were more than a hundred Poles among them and there were only two Frenchmen, as far as is known, one a hairdresser's assistant, the other a merchant from Mühlhausen, Alsace. The barricades were erected spontaneously, mostly at street corners, and there was no necessity for any particular plan. At the most important points, such as the corner of Friedrich Strasse and Behren Strasse, there were no barricades at all! All the inhabitants, including women and children, helped to build the barricades, and they varied entirely according to local conditions. The first finished barricade at the corner of Oberwall and Jäger Strasse was made up of two hackney coaches, a carriage, the sentry-box from the front of the Bank, pavement curbing, and some barrels. Hackney coaches were held up several times and the coachmen had to leave them and lead their nags home. Carts which happened to pass, laden with bricks or timber, were particularly welcome. Omnibuses were also requisitioned. The barricade in the Friedrich Strasse opposite the Polish chemist's was eked out by Mother Schmiddecke's fruit stall, well-known to every Berliner.

"Give us the stall, Ma, save the apples, quick," cried the amateur warriors, and they packed away as much of the fruit as possible in safety, helped by the street urchins. The biggest barricade was at the corner of the New König Strasse looking on Alexander Platz; here a really strong breastwork had been built up by piling granite blocks from the pavement round an upturned cart. A number of oil-barrels were piled on each other to form the barricade in the Tauben Strasse. On top of these came stones, earth, and lamp posts. At the Rosenthal Gate, all the streets leading to the square were shut off by five barricades, making a veritable fortress. It may be that one or another courageous man had spoken to his neighbours during the days of high tension preceding the 18th of March, discussing where and how a barricade should be erected if the worst came to the worst; but there is no sign of a strategic plan. Neither did the fighting folk attempt to create any system of communication between the main centres of the struggle. Nor can there be any question of a prepared supply of weapons. The people were sorely in need of arms. The armourers' shops were emptied, with the promise to return the weapons after the battle, a promise which was kept in nearly every case. Weapons were requisitioned from the properties of the theatres. Planks, cudgels, dung forks, old rusty sabres had to serve, because there was a lack of pistols and muskets. Hammers were also used in hand-to-hand fighting. Lead bullets were cast in the streets, boys and youths helping eagerly. In other places they forged lances. Someone had the brilliant idea of noting all the addresses of officers out of the directory and taking their weapons away from their wives. Other houses were also searched for weapons, for example, Alexander von Humboldt's house, to the great indignation of that learned man. The only really successful fighters were the members of the Berlin Rifle Guilds, who kept up a well-aimed fire from the roofs with their excellent rifles on the Alexander Platz and on the old Town Hall. Count Benckendorff also wrote: "The Guild of Riflemen did the most harm to the troops." In the Kommandanten Strasse, wires had been stretched across the streets, in the Leipziger Strasse, the street was strewn with broken glass. Stones and granite blocks from the pavements were thrown from the roofs. The battle, which had begun at three in the afternoon, went on until the next morning, and hour by hour developed more of the horrible features of an embittered civil war. Various persons who had nothing to do with the fighting accidentally met the brunt of it. Here a confectioner was hit inside his shop, there a servant girl as she looked out of window. Children also fell victims. Here and there houses burst into flames. August, director of the Köllnisch Grammar School, a veteran of the Wars of Liberation, who, out of humanity, had taken in wounded barricade fighters and cared for them, was severely maltreated by Potsdam Grenadiers who broke into his house. His nephew, Hermann von Holtzendorf, who had taken no part, was struck dead in the street by the soldiers, who thought his flowing beard looked democratic.

It is difficult to tell how many students took part in the fighting. There may have been about a hundred. Several students, such as Aegidi, the Swiss von Salis, Feenburg-Tongorski, the Russian, who was later caught after the storm on the Armoury and extradited to Russia, became leaders during the critical days. Relatively well-dressed young men were often taken for students, although they were really tradesmen or professional men. It was students who galloped on horseback to the Oranienburg Gate in order to summon the workers from the machine shops to the battle. The workmen answered the call, especially those from the great Borsig works; about nine hundred marched into the city, swinging heavy iron bars in their powerful fists, valiant auxiliaries in the struggle, with their power of endurance and trained strength. Armed artisans' apprentices rang an alarm peal on the church bells and kept on ringing all night long; there was a dark red glow of flame, drums rolled, rifles cracked, there was a rattling, rolling, clattering, roaring, screaming of women, smell of warm gunpowder—then bright moonlight and mild air—such was the night of Revolution in Berlin.

Who were the leaders of the people? Dr. Rutenberg, afterwards editor of the *Staatszeitung*, Dr. Löwenberg, who stood at the head of the radical students, Dr. Woeniger who had originated the idea of the mass petition, Urban, the veterinary surgeon, whose tremendous growth of hair and beard made him one of the best-known street figures, Levin Weiss, the "philosopher," who was fatally hit by a case-shot in the König Strasse; not one of these people was a real leader, who saw the proceedings as a whole and followed a definite plan. The Berlin people had only petty officers, but no field-marshal. It is scarcely possible to state even approximately the number of combatants; we must distinguish between a very large body of helpers and a much smaller body of actual fighters. The numbers of helpers, persons who assisted in building the barricades, who searched for weapons, provided food and drink, gave shelter and aid, amounted to many tens of thousands, for the barricades extended right out into the suburbs, the mass of the people were in movement, active, excited, at work. The numbers of real fighters were limited by lack of weapons and probably did not exceed three or four thousand. The number of troops scarcely equalled the total number of revolutionaries in action; but the military were naturally superior to the actual fighters in numbers, equipment, and reserves. Many barricades were held for hours by only a few defenders, because the streets themselves were occupied by fighters.

The March days were a severe trial for Frederick William IV. It was evident that the storm of events had a physically exhausting effect upon him. The Russian envoy, von Meyendorff, wrote on March 17th: "The King neither sleeps nor eats—it excites him and weakens him." However, Frederick William pulled himself together again and again, held himself well and made a strong impression upon his entourage and visitors. On the morning of March 18th, he spoke in his old touching style to the deputation from the Rhine. Afterwards, when he appeared on the balcony, he was too much moved to be capable of speaking to the rejoicing crowds. The King experienced the greatest emotional crises—a complete reversal of his policy! Even his consent to the periodicity of the United Diet was the contrary of convictions which he had often enough proclaimed in all solemnity—and now these two edicts, with their improvised constitutional tendency! For nearly fourteen days he had obstinately resisted all advice to put himself at the head of the German movement—and now he was suddenly going to do it because the fall of Metternich had lamed Austria and put her out of the running. There can be no question of consistency in Friedrich Wilhelm's attitude during the March troubles. He was only consistent inasmuch as he always did exactly the opposite of what he had said before, and when things did not move quickly enough, went back to his first idea or started up a third one—and in spite of all his contradictory actions he constantly emphasized to all his advisers the superiority of his royal insight and position. Now, against his will, he had made what he considered to be far-reaching concessions to the demands of the time—and in spite of these his troops were engaged in embittered street fighting with the people of Berlin. The people felt that the King had betrayed them; this really was not the case. The King felt that the people had betrayed him; this was no less untrue. The small reactionary party of the Old Prussians had desired the battle and now declared that it must be fought out on purely military lines. The small revolutionary party had also desired the battle and prepared for it; they took up arms gladly and believed the outbreak of the struggle to be the best proof of the dishonesty of the King and his promises. The reactionary party saw a solution only in the victory of the military, the revolutionary party saw a solution only in the victory of the fighting people. But the King saw in the battles a misunderstanding and a misfortune—and he was right to the core. The moderate section of the population, in a numerical majority, were of the same opinion.

At the beginning of the street fighting, many well-meant attempts were made in the very streets to calm the conflicting passions—one, for instance, by Police-President von Minutoli, one by Town Councillor Nobiling. But they had only a momentary success.

The Hessian Chargé d'Affaires, Major-General von Schaeffer-Bernstein, reported as an eyewitness: "I saw myself how citizens and members of the Rifle Guilds wearing their badges went about as special constables among the individual groups of rebels and endeavoured in every way to pacify them; they were roughly handled and driven off with jeers." The general's carriage was also stopped in the evening by well-meaning burghers—they turned him back that he might avoid unpleasantness. From three o'clock in the afternoon, the most various deputations appeared one after another at the palace, attempting to persuade the King to withdraw the troops; the rector and deans of the university in their official robes, Mayor Krausnick with a number of councillors, Bishop Neander, etc.

The King declared at first that there could be no question of the troops retreating. If the inhabitants of Berlin were rebels, they must be treated as such. But in speaking to Bishop Neander, he already made the concession that the attack on the barricade by the Kölln Town Hall should be put off for three hours if by that time the barricade had been taken down and the black, red, and gold flag on the d'Heureuse pastry-cook's shop, which was visible from the palace, had been removed. Bishop Neander and his deputation, however, evidently did nothing to get this idea put into practice. The beginning of artillery gun fire had a great effect upon the King's nerves; he found it difficult to endure, even physically, it paralysed him; he hid his face in his hands, sat sunk in an apathy, now and then falling into a fit of sobbing. Then he forced himself to become calm again, and such enforced bravery is worth more than the robust courage of coarser natures. In the evening he received Baron Georg von Vincke, leader of the opposition and, since he was already spiritually and physically shattered, he was susceptible to argument, all the more so as it agreed with his own innermost feelings. Vincke emphasized two points; the military situation was decidedly serious, the weary and badly-nourished troops were no longer attacking so strongly, they were indifferent. It was useless to attempt night attacks on the barricades. The troops should be withdrawn and concentrated round the Palace. The whole struggle could not be judged from a purely military point of view, but from a political standpoint, and therefore it was desirable to end the battle on a basis of good understanding as soon as possible. To Vincke, as a politician, a clear victory of either the military and the party of reaction or of the people and the revolutionary idea must be equally detrimental; we cannot doubt, in a man of his character, that his advice was sincere. But how an understanding was ever to be brought about—there lay the great difficulty. It must be done in a strong and dignified fashion.

The assertion that the troops were indifferent was, as a generalization, exaggerated. A company had hesitated to attack, and Prittwitz had been obliged to lead the attack himself. Other symptoms were visible only later. Prittwitz, like every other officer, wished to win quickly and completely—but unfortunately he did not find it possible!

It remained a fact that the military was at first scarcely to be restrained, the soldiers threw themselves furiously into the battle; but they made little progress because the difficulties were so great. General von Prittwitz's plan was to capture a part of the city and then await further developments. He had not troops enough to capture the whole town. The King had approved this plan. If the revolutionary rising still continued during the following days, the General proposed to withdraw the troops from the city, invest it and open fire upon it at various points. From a purely military point of view, this was no doubt perfectly correct. Count Benckendorff says in his report that the possibilities were threefold; first, to continue the battle in the city, to clean it up and subdue it—that would have been the boldest plan; secondly, the troops might be withdrawn and the city blockaded; this would have been the most sensible plan from a military point of view; thirdly, to remain in the positions already won and await further developments—that was only excusable if it were a subterfuge to gain time. The military party wanted the battle carried on in purely military fashion: they thought—war is war—and from their point of view they were quite right. But it was no less true that this matter could not be treated thus. War is not civil war. Was the King to see a part of his capital go up in flames? Count Lerchenfeld wrote on March 27th: "Half Berlin would have gone up in flames. The King had the choice between giving up his guard and seeing his capital destroyed."

The American consul, Donelson, went still further when he wrote on March 20th: "The determination of the King therefore to change his ministry and throw himself upon the loyalty of his subjects was the only course he could pursue to save the crown." No further troops could be obtained from Stettin; Wrangel had already been obliged to permit militia there. Suppose the Rhineland fell away, suppose East Prussia rose, and Silesia? The Revolution had conquered all over Germany! Was Prussia, was Germany to be recaptured and overthrown by Russian troops? War with Denmark was imminent, rebellion in Poland, Austria was about to fall apart. Prussia could be mighty hand in hand with the popular movement—and now the movement was to be violently crushed, precisely in Berlin! Politically speaking, the Berlin street fighting was an absurdity, humanly speaking it was a crime, from a Christian standpoint it was a sin—the King felt it as such and could not feel otherwise.

His nature was not in the least militaristic. His brother, the

Prince of Prussia, flung his sword on the table when there was talk of withdrawing the troops. Frederick William believed it would be truly Christian, German and royal to extend a forgiving hand. He had often captivated by eloquence and personal charm. Why not again? At midnight, he ordered General von Prittwitz to hold what he had won, but advance no further—and, his good humour restored, sat down to compose his famous appeal "To my dear Berliners." He spoke to them like a father to his prodigal son. He put the blame for the misunderstandings on malicious strangers. The barricades must be removed, men full of the "true old Berlin spirit" should come to speak with him. Then everywhere except a few important buildings, on his royal word, should be cleared of troops. Finally, he spoke of forgetting and forgiving, of the Queen's tears and invoked God's blessing upon Germany and Prussia.

Never was Frederick William so true to himself as in this proclamation; tender and noble, rather pompous, a little insincere, very gracious and rather sly, pious and somewhat cowardly—and in any case, totally lacking in political sense! The revolutionaries and soldiers, fighters in the streets on both sides, could only laugh in bitter mockery at such ingenuous arrogance. The proclamation appeared in the early morning and the effect was positively painful. Yet the idea was right enough—only its form and tone were completely impossible.

From a military point of view the battle was entirely undecided. Things stood still at the Alexander Platz, the artillery sheds at the Oranienburger Tor and the iron foundry had been on fire since midnight, the people had burned all the customs houses, and Hesse, leading the storm, had taken the reservist arsenal in the Linden Strasse. In the night Prittwitz had ordered the cavalry out of the city to combine with the cavalry from Potsdam; thus the investiture of Berlin was prepared—he reserved only two regiments. At seven in the morning, he told the troops that there might be a peaceful settlement; there

should be no more aggressive measures, and peaceful and unarmed inhabitants should be allowed to go about the streets.
Several parties of troops had shown unwillingness to fight.

In the suburbs and more distant streets the people stood
ready to carry on the fight, embittered over the happenings
of the day before and both irritated and encouraged by the
King's proclamation. They respected churchgoing hours—
for March 19th was a Sunday—and prepared to resume the
fighting later. It was an armistice, negotiations began between
the two parties. This was already a triumph for the revolution.
Fighting had begun because the people desired the withdrawal
of the troops—the King had promised this on conditions, and
these conditions must now be debated.

Negotiations began at the Palace at half-past seven. Rellstab,
Nobiling, Krausnick, citizens of all degrees appeared. They
demanded withdrawal of the troops and arms for the citizens.
The King, in the spirit of his proclamation, demanded the
destruction of the barricades. Nobiling went with two others
and a military observer to the Alexander Platz to persuade
the revolutionaries to tear down the barricades there. They
succeeded in stopping the fighting in this quarter, which shows
that this method was the right one. It is hard to see why it
should not, with a little goodwill, have been successful everywhere. But the military party had no goodwill. They did not
want an understanding. The King did not trust his own military judgment and when he heard that the barricade in the
König Strasse had been removed, he departed from his correct
standpoint that the troops should withdraw bit by bit as the
barricades were removed, and promised a deputation under
Major Naunyn that since the barricades were being destroyed,
the troops should all be withdrawn. He forgot to add that
certain buildings would still remain occupied. Prittwitz and
the Prince of Prussia enforced this demand, Bodelschwingh
replied excitedly that the King's order for withdrawal of all
troops had been quite definite. Prittwitz withdrew the troops

from the barricades to the palace. They looked weary, and he ordered them to their barracks. Count Stolberg went to find out whether he had understood the King correctly, the Prince of Prussia had a brief, lively argument with his brother. The King declared belatedly that the palace, arsenal, and palace square should remain under occupation as stated in the proclamation. But considering the discipline and condition of the troops, Prittwitz completed the withdrawal and there was no one to gainsay him.

It is difficult to understand how this state of things came about. It was the combined result of the King's lack of decision and clarity, the sensitiveness and incapability of the high military command, the tension between army and civilians, lack of vision, and ill will. The troops, who had not conquered, but were still unconquered, withdrew. The barricade fighters, who also had not conquered, were certainly the moral and political victors. The only one who was really conquered was the unhappy King, whose continual physical and spiritual weakness had transformed a political situation which had at the beginning of March been excellent, into its exact opposite. Count Trautmannsdorff has preserved a "clever utterance" on the command to the troops to withdraw: "The King reminds me of someone who can see a number of stairways leading down from the house, but prefers to spring out of the window."

A good deal of blame must be laid at the door of leading personages, both ministers and military officials. The King was remarkably badly served. Bodelschwingh no longer considered himself in office, but he had no right to let the proclamation be printed and published without comment or correction—for its good and correct intention was fully annulled by its incorrect form. He also passed on the fateful order to the troops with complete carelessness—he knew the King well enough to realize that he should not have acted thus. Count Arnim passively stood by at the argument between the King and

Bodelschwingh, displaying a singular lack of clear thinking and energy. The Prince of Prussia also played an unhappy part in the affair. According to the strict orders of the late King Frederick William III, no royal prince was ever to take any part in street fighting—a wise edict that should have been strictly obeyed. The Prince of Prussia did not take any command, but he continually interfered in a conspicuous and unrestrained manner. Thus he incited a natural hatred in the people and did considerable damage to his own cause. Prittwitz was a man of quiet energy—but he certainly did not make the best use of the powers reposed in him. The achievements of the troops did not answer his expectations. He hated the King's conciliatory attitude, like all the other military men, but it is probably wronging him to assume that he deliberately exaggerated the King's orders when executing them, out of spite. Prittwitz thought that to continue fighting on the morning of the 19th would have no military value; when the masses of troops were concentrated before the palace, he really had no choice but to withdraw them or resume the battle under still more unfavourable conditions. It was not his purpose, but an inexcusable error, to leave so few troops in the palace. Prittwitz rightly feared the weakening of military discipline, above all that the troops would fraternize with the irregulars. Not only were the soldiery tired out, but there was a lack of provisions. If they had not withdrawn, the people would simply have starved them out. Even during the battle, refreshment of any kind was almost invariably refused to officers and soldiers. The troops marched off with bands playing, as on the parade ground—a victorious gesture which accorded ill with their appearance and the frightful experiences of the night of revolution. "Unter den Linden" the Sunday strollers were already about; but the people were incensed by the military music and demanded that the lively march be replaced by a hymn tune. It was natural that insults should be flung at the troops after such a night of battle. On the 20th, retreating artillery had to be accompanied by militia for their protection.

The prisoners taken from among the citizens were now set free. When a hundred prisoners had been taken in the afternoon of March 18th in the old city and brought into the palace yard, the King and his entourage assumed from their appearance that all the barricade fighters were "vagabonds." They were poor fellows whose humble working clothes did not stand the stress of battle as well as a soldier's uniform. It throws a revealing light upon the mentality of the reigning personages and also of the more prosperous citizens that during the whole revolutionary period they chose to regard the people's warriors as financial and moral riff-raff. The King's joke: "When you get the prisoners back, have a look at them and see whether you want to keep them"—therefore made a painful impression. Some laughed, others cursed. Naturally, in a great city such as Berlin, doubtful figures from the dark underworld were drawn into the popular movement—an unavoidable and inevitable aspect of civil war. It was certainly a mistake of the revolutionaries to set free the prisoners from the gaols. But not a single crime against property was committed in the night of revolution. Various public buildings were marked with the words "Property of the Citizens" in order to protect them. Men of all ranks took part in the barricade fighting, it was undoubtedly a proof of courage and considered an honour to fight for the people's cause. All the more disgraceful was the treatment to which the prisoners, whose numbers increased to nearly a thousand in the course of the night, were subjected. They were roughly handled and thrust into the castle cellars, where they were kept in low-ceilinged vaults filled with foul air, without food or drink, until four o'clock next morning. Then they were removed to Spandau under guard of the battalion which had been taken out of the fighting as untrustworthy. Evidently these troops wished to save their reputation, for they knocked the bound and helpless prisoners about in the most brutal fashion with the butt-end of their rifles, hurling insults at them. They remained in the dungeons of the fortress on bread and water until their liberation in the afternoon of March 19th. The magistracy, citizens, and city councillors opened a collection on behalf of these maltreated victims.

A mighty demonstration of the victorious revolution took place on March 22nd. The March Heroes, the "Märzgefallenen" were buried at the city's expense in the romantic Friedrichshain. There were one hundred and eighty-three coffins. Black banners flew from the city gates and from the palace, everyone was in mourning. At the Gendarmen Markt there was a solemn ceremony. Three clergy, one Evangelical, one Roman Catholic, and one Jewish, performed the funeral services. Then the vast procession began to move. The militia lined the streets, they presented arms as Gustav Hesse marched by in his blue smock, wearing his wreath of honour. At the head of the procession marched the artisans' guilds with their emblems and banners, women and girls carried wreaths, burghers were the coffin-bearers. All the clergy followed, then representatives of the government, the police president, the professors of the university in their gowns, headed by their rector, among them Alexander von Humboldt. Then came a great number of armed students, the mayor and council in robes of office, with the exception of the servile Mayor Krausnick, who had been forced to resign. Then came the factory workers, the valiant mechanics, led by Borsig in person, the Poles with their red and white flag, the Italians, some of them singers from the Opera House, with their green, white, and red national flag, then upper school boys, deputations, guilds and societies of all kinds with their flags and banners. There were also deputies from various towns, such as Hamburg, Halle, Frankfort on the Oder, and Brunswick. The music played over and over the favourite old hymn, "Jesus, in Whom I Trust"—since the scene in the palace yard, when the King had perforce saluted the revolutionary dead, this had become the hymn of the Revolution. The Riflemen's Guild fired salvos of honour over the graves. There were about twenty thousand people in the funeral procession. As it passed the palace, the King and his ministers on the balcony bared their heads until all the coffins had passed. Friedrich Wilhelm was wearing full general's uniform.

The victory of the Berlin Revolution meant to those who had experienced it a guarantee of the idea of democracy and freedom. A proposal to bury the army in Friedrichshain at the same time as a sign of reconciliation had no success. But a milder atmosphere very soon began to prevail. In a workmen's petition of March 23rd to police headquarters, from twelve factories, headed by Borsig's, the words occur: "The grave which has closed above our beloved heroes has for ever buried all hatred and fraternal strife. We demand that a brotherly hand of forgiveness should also be extended to our army. Honour also to those soldiers who fell in obedience to their oath. We demand that they should also receive honourable burial, followed by the people. . . ." When the police president put the question to the leaders of the militia, he was told that there was no objection to the return of the regiments of the line to Berlin; a certain bitterness that still prevailed was directed only against the guards. As a matter of fact, the military returned as early as March 30th. The Brockhausen appeal to all Berliners contained a defence of the officers, who had fought only because they were pledged by oath. "Many, like Lieutenant Tüpke, who was killed, were Liberals, or even Republicans, and yet they fought."

Thus popular feeling in Berlin after the unhappy days of revolution was thoroughly loyal and hopeful of the future. A great deal might be done in Prussia by men of goodwill. But where was this goodwill to be found?

## CHAPTER SEVEN

# THE APRIL REVOLUTION

THE BERLIN March Revolution implied the moral and political victory of the citizens of a great city over the military forces, the victory of democracy over autocracy, and finally the victory of the idea of liberty and the German nation over reactionary Prussian particularism. In a military sense the people's warriors had not conquered; they would most likely have been defeated in Berlin if the old State authorities had dared to make ruthless use of all troops. They did not dare, and this already signified a victory for the revolutionary idea. It had conquered the whole of Germany, almost everywhere without difficulty. In Vienna the difficulties had been great; but Berlin was the first German city in which bloodshed and battles on the barricades had been honoured afterwards as a justifiable and honourable means of effecting a political purpose. The King had done honour to the March Heroes, the authorities had buried them in all solemnity as sacrificed heroes, pioneer fighters for a new State. This meant much to Prussia; the whole basis of the State had changed at a blow. The Revolution was legalized here; it now had the right to insist on building up the Prussian State for the people. But it meant just as much to all Germany. Prussia had been a land of promise to the best minds in Germany for a long time past. A decidedly revolutionary Prussia encouraged the claims of the decided Revolution all over Germany. And it also meant much to Europe. Berlin could now stand by the side of Paris. In Berlin "the people" also held the reigns of power. Berlin's old arrogance had new stuff to feed on. Its bourgeois self-importance was inflated and almost threatened by the social-revolutionary urge of the working-classes. Berlin was ripe to over-ripeness, Germany was astounded and proud at the same time. Europe, too, was astonished. The 18th of March gave Berlin a claim to be considered as a free German capital in a liberated Europe. No dynasty had been so proud of its military forces as the Hohenzollerns. They were now defeated, politically and morally, by the Revolution. The Hohenzollern dynasty never quite got over this. The ghost of the 18th of March always stood behind them. The King's troops had just been fighting against the black, red, and gold flag of the German Revolution, and already a Prussian king had seized the flag and waved it in the street. That could not be forgotten. This is the true significance of March 18th to the world. Berlin and the eternal right of revolution, Berlin and the dream of an immortal free Germany allied themselves for ever on this day.

But here lay the problem. Before March 18th, it was almost easy for Prussia and Germany to come together. Prussia, committed to revolution and with her King's authority shattered, was suddenly once more sundered from the rest of Germany. Prussia went her difficult way to become a free constitutional State. Germany was trying to found a national State. These ways led in different directions. There was not yet a Prussian "nation"—it was perhaps just about to develop. What was Germany to do with a Prussia, democratic to be sure, but freezing into particularism. What meaning could a Prussia hold that was so entirely concerned with her own affairs?

Friedrich Wilhelm's position in Germany was now completely ruined, whereas in Prussia it seemed to be salvaged to some extent. After March 18th, his plans for Germany were rejected on all sides. In Vienna they were regarded as a hostile act. The new cabinet informed Berlin that all negotiations with Radowitz would now be regarded as *non avenus*. The Viennese asked one another "whether the Prussian monarchy would survive the cannonade in Berlin."

The "Vorparlament" bears a historical label which correctly describes neither its nature nor its significance. It was in no way a legal instrument of popular representation, neither was its task completed when it prepared the way for a genuine German parliament. It was an assembly of notables, revolutionary in character and historically speaking the final stage of the almost annual meetings of German patriots since 1839. Now it was called together by the fifty-one Heidelbergers to prepare in collaboration with the governments a realization of the idea of a German parliament which was also to be a powerful central organ of national life. The revolutionary events in Vienna and Berlin had created an entirely new situation: the great powers were shaken, all purely governmental procedure condemned to infertility. The old leaders of the opposition had now become government officers—Römer in Wittenberg, Heinrich von Gagern in Hesse-Darmstadt. In Frankfort, the people now reigned sovereign by the side of the Federal Diet, conscious of their power and ready to use it, since there was no other unbroken power to set beside theirs. When events in Vienna and especially in Berlin became known in the south-west, Struve began to agitate quite openly in Freiburg and Heidelberg for the republic.

Invitations to Frankfort had been issued to "all previous or present members of the diets and participants in assemblies of lawgivers all over Germany." Individual invitations were also sent out. In various places, ordinary popular meetings elected members whom they trusted as representatives. Itzstein invited numerous publicists. This resulted in an assembly which was as mixed as possible. There were only two deputies from

Austria, but one hundred and fourteen from Prussia, fifty-two from Württemberg, actually seventy-two from Baden, and eighty-four from Hesse-Darmstadt, whereas Bavaria sent only forty-four, Saxony twenty-six, and Hanover nine. The Frankfort Assembly was regarded with great distrust by the governments even before it met. The Badensians, who not unreasonably feared that a great blow would be struck for the republic, were particularly suspicious. The Prussian envoy in Karlsruhe was admonished by various parties, even by liberals, to use his influence to persuade as many Prussian politicians as possible, popular with the people, but of a conservative turn of mind, to go to Frankfort, so that the Radicals should not obtain a majority. Herr von Wächter, Prime Minister of Württemberg, had the same idea. Berlin would have preferred to prevent the Frankfort assembly, and both the decree of March 18th and the calling up of the *Vereinigte Landtag* had been attempts to this end. But von Wächter considered its attainment quite impossible. Heinrich von Gagern, as Hessian Prime minister in Darmstadt, took energetic and effective measures to prevent the entry of armed forces, to the lively satisfaction of Count Dönhoff, Prussian envoy to the Diet. At times the idea was mooted to move the Pre-Parliament at least to Aachen, as the old Imperial city, and thus to keep it in Prussian hands, and perhaps succeed in swiftly bringing about a German kingdom or Prussian Empire to the annoyance of the Republicans.

Frankfort was gaily decorated; enthusiasm and belief in Germany's future pervaded the streets; hangings and wreaths changed the squares into halls of festival. There was a scent of spring, the Taunus hills shone azure in the distance. Fragrant pine boughs wreathed the triumphal arches, there was shouting and salutes of cannon, black, red, and gold floated from every roof. Even in the narrowest alleyway, this brightest of tri-colours flamed, as a cockade, a bow, a sash. Sylvester Jordan's entry resembled that of a triumphal popular monarch: next to him, the martyr of electoral Hesse, came Eisenmann, the martyr of Bavaria. The main street was filled with torchbearers in his honour. The Frankforters were delighted to receive so many distinguished guests and were brimming with the warm hospitality for which Frankfort was famous. "It is a festival of freedom of the most touching kind," said Johann Gustav Droysen.

But the sittings of the Pre-Parliament took place under the burden of serious trouble. The German Democratic Club in Paris had determined upon the invasion of the Rhineland and the proclamation of the German Republic. These and other alarming pieces of news gave rise to a terrible panic, memorable to all who experienced it for many a year as the French Alarm of March 25th–26th. This alone must have obliged the Pre-Parliament to put an end to the serious internal and external political crisis, if not by dictatorial measures, then at least by some decisive action. But what happened was only of a very mild nature. Struve presented a comprehensive Social-Revolutionary programme. But the majority were monarchistically inclined and wanted nothing to do with such ideas. A proposal to declare the Pre-Parliament in permanency was also rejected; as a substitute, the Committee of Fifty was set up, yet another compromise, and not the longed-for and liberating Parliament. At least a beginning was now made with the cleansing of the Federal Diet from reactionary elements.

When the Pre-Parliament had closed its last sitting, on April 2nd, the supporters of the old powers heaved a sigh of relief. No committee of public safety had been set up, no dictatorship declared, no republic proclaimed. No deeds of violence had been committed or contemplated; the decent, orderly, political Revolution had prevailed everywhere over the idea of social-revolutionary upheaval. The Pre-Parliament had been satisfied to prepare the way for a future National Assembly; it had made many suggestions, communicated many wishes—and also prepared a political foundation for its existence. This was accomplished by the adoption of the strange motion put by Alexander von Soiron; at first intended only to put the closure on what the majority considered the unnecessary discussions of the out-of-date Siebener programme, it then grew into a deliberate affirmation of the sovereignty of the people. The majority of the assembly declared "that the decision on the future constitution of Germany should rest solely and entirely with the National Assembly, to be elected by the people." Solely and entirely! So there was to be no consultation with the princes. Belief in a parliament could not have found more convinced or powerful expression. Anyone who desired collaboration with the princes was a conservative; the Soiron motion revealed that the majority was also split according to party. We might call these gentlemen of the Right Wing, the conservative constitutionalists; they turned up again later in reinforced numbers in the Paulskirche. The supporters of the Soiron motion were the revolutionary evolutionists, the victors of the March Revolution, the powers of the April Revolution, borne aloft by the events of the day, and swallowed up again by time; their leader, though not their brain, was Heinrich von Gagern. The thinker at their head was Mathy. In his biography of Friedrich von Gagern Heinrich calls his party the "Reform Party," later the "monarcistic-parliamentary Federal State party." Then came the democratic republicans, led by Robert Blum and on the extreme left wing, the republican social revolutionaries. Heinrich von Gagern calls them the "democratic-socialistic party," or the "republican, or rather the social-revolutionary party."

Thus four parties showed definite characteristics in the Pre-Parliament. All four groups derived in some way from liberalism—it was their spiritual inheritance, guaranteed most logically by the democratic republicans. Contemporary custom labelled as "democrats" all who were determined opponents of absolutism, bureaucracy, plutocracy, and the title patriciate, whether they were liberal men of compromise or red revolutionaries. "Democracy" was regarded as an international power, often, contrary to common sense, as a league of conspirators. The ideas which were derived from the English, American, and French revolutions, were international cultural treasure, whereas the movements themselves were national and grew in local soil.

There is no doubt that after the success of the revolutions in Vienna and Berlin the revolutionary idea received a notable impetus. During the sittings of the Pre-Parliament, feeling in the gallery was threatening enough at times. Von Bockelberg, Prussian envoy, characterized it as follows: "We thousands up here represent the people just as much and with more justice than you few hundreds up there, and if you will not give up the old tutorial system, then you force us into revolution, to bloody revolution in the streets—and you shall have it." When the Pre-Parliament came to an end, old Itzstein said to a man from Darmstadt: "But not one of you in Darmstadt wants a republic—well, you will have one, for they will give you one, whether you like it or not." At this time Zitz prophesied the coming of the Republic within fourteen days, and bitterly attacked the Gagern ministry in his paper, the *Mainzer Zeitung*.

The "National Committee of Germans in Switzerland" sent a declaration to the Pre-Parliament in the name of twenty thousand Germans living in Switzerland, demanding the immediate creation of a German republic. The declaration, in which it was said that no prince possessed either the talent, character, or antecendents to offer the people any guarantee of freedom and independence, closed with the words: "Deutschland über alles! Es lebe die deutsche Republik!" and was signed by the well-known communist Johann Philipp Becker, who was president of the Central Committee.

The radical-socialist committee in Lausanne also sent an appeal to the Pre-Parliament, demanding "the social republic which Christ founded and preached eighteen centuries ago."

After the Pre-Parliament had concluded its deliberations, the *Comité der Republikanischen Gesellschaft* in Wiesbaden gave out a pamphlet dated April 4th, bearing the title: "The Most Important Problems of the Present Day." Here, too, the Republic was again recommended as the best form of state—for it was "simplest, most practical and least expensive." "We save one hundred and thirty million gulden on courts, princes, ministers, etc., and another two hundred and twenty million on unnecessary soldiers." The happiness of fifty million people was more important than the apparent prosperity of thirty-three princely families.

Even in New York a "Deutscher Revolutionsverein" had been formed among resident Germans with the object of bringing about a republic in Germany, founding a publication to assist its ends, and collecting members and money. A general assembly was held on April 17th, at which a concerted plan for the inauguration of German-American revolutionary propaganda was presented.

The age was saturated with a belief in parliaments and constitutions. Everyone was possessed by the conviction that true national representation must necessarily lead to the best state constitution and thus to healthy public life. Those who looked deeper into the problem, from the point of view of society as a whole, also laid stress upon the constitutional question for tactical and propagandistic reasons. This was the case with Friedrich Hecker.

He had long ceased to be a Democrat in the true sense of the word. He was a popular leader by nature and his tendency to violence and terrorism had grown to a perfect passion in the last few weeks of the revolutionary period. His successes spoiled him, but also spurred him on. People expected great things of him, and in the south-west his power was great. Von Arnim, Prussian envoy in Karlsruhe, wrote of him that he was capable of recruiting at a word an army of more than twenty thousand despairing and fanatical unemployed working men. Hecker himself had a tendency to boast; in the last days of March he bragged loudly that he would march from place to place, with blazing torch, robbing and plundering, gathering all the ruined inhabitants into his band, through Poland into Russia, carrying the revolution to the shores of the Ural. Half a hero and half a highwayman, Friedrich Hecker was the man of the hour, wielding almost as much influence as a dictator, subduing everyone, most of all the government of Baden, by the sheer force of his reputation for decision and will power.

The symptoms of degeneration in the State of Baden increased to an alarming degree. A Mannheim regiment liberated the military prisoners and when the general march was ordered three hundred men did not appear, but stayed on in the ale-houses.

Much unrest was caused by the German factory workers dismissed in Thann, Mühlhausen, and Schlettstadt, who were now pouring across the Rhine and making for the north. The French Government was glad to be rid of these unemployed, and the Badensian government had to make the best of them. A decree of the Badensian ministry of home affairs of March 23rd, provided that only individuals and not whole troops should be allowed to enter the province, and they must carry no weapons and must be of good character. But it was evidently already too late. In Karlsruhe a society was formed to support and shelter these people. Daily such half-starved workmen came into the town and many committed offences. Numbers of them demonstrated in Karslruhe and demanded weapons. The militia therefore decided to make their rounds unarmed, so that they might not be deprived of their weapons! Fresh unrest arose among the peasants. They, too, were very much in favour of arms for the people—for they hoped thus to put up a successful defence of the properties they had seized. They, also, were enthusiastically in favour of the freedom of the Press—they called the bailiff the "presser," and thought Press freedom meant that there would be no more distraining!

In the Black Forest, the peasants said that their good Grand Duke, who had absolved them from paying taxes, would certainly grant them a republic.

From Switzerland and Alsace, republican propaganda flowed over the whole of Baden. An appeal signed by Ludwig Seeger appeared in the Berne newspapers of March 29th, in which universal arming of the German people was said to be of first importance. Next a great deal of money must be forthcoming. "Let us therefore unite to provide weapons and military organizations at once for all, including our penniless citizens."

Energetic preparations were made, especially in Berne, Biel, and Basle. On April 5th, Berne issued a decree forbidding the formation of armed societies for the purpose of interference in the affairs of neighbouring states, and declaring that any such societies already in existence must be dissolved. But this did little good. The frontier cantons mobilized contingents to prevent the violation of neutrality.

On March 25th, the *Basler National Zeitung* was the first paper on the Continent to print Ferdinand Freiligrath's song of black, red, and gold, reprinted from a London revolutionary paper. The rolling glory of these verses was intended as a summons to revolutionary battle, and actually had this effect. "The final battle's still to win"—sang the poet. "True freedom is still far removed"—passionately rising in fervour from verse to verse. His glowing spirit certainly did not "halt before the throne."

> Liberty is the nation
>   And rights for all to reap!
> Liberty holds an auction
>   And thirty crowns go cheap!
> Liberty is republican!

And once again—republican!
Powder is black,
Blood is red,
Golden flickers the flame!

"The great last combat"—proclaimed Freiligrath, should be for the republic and all that the free popular State could mean to a new generation. No living man was so deeply related to the spirit of this song as Friedrich Hecker.

There were twenty seven thousand Germans in Basle at this time; no wonder their assemblies made an impression. They performed military exercises in secret and founded a German Legion in Switzerland. A soldier from Baden demanded an insurrection and the invasion of Baden; his comrades would never fire on the people. Such an invasion was actually contemplated. A Swiss pamphlet circulated among Karlsruhe working men said that it would begin on April 3rd. But it was postponed to wait for the proclamation of the German Republic in Frankfort and Baden. At the first news of the provisional government, the march into Germany was to begin. This would also be the simplest method with regard to the Swiss authorities. The leaders were Johann Philipp Becker of Biel, and Schüler. Becker's secretary was Hattemer. Their agitation deserves a little consideration. Becker had connections with representatives of the Germans in Berne, Murten, Freiburg, Neuenburg, Vivis, Solothurn, Chaux-de-Fonds, Interlaken. Agents and letters with programmes and instructions went to and fro. Every hundred signatories formed a company, every five companies a battalion; the chief command of the "German Legion in Switzerland" was in the hands of the committee or council of war of seven members, tested officers and members of German workmen's societies in Switzerland. There were two kinds of members—those who bore arms and those who participated in administration and organization and collected subscriptions. . . . Meetings, resolutions, and proclamations of the German republicans took place in a full blaze of publicity. The *Schweizerische Nationalzeitung* of Tuesday, March 28th had a full report of the Biel assembly of the "German deputies" on March 26th. At this assembly, whose members separated with a cheer for the German Republic, the song *Revenge* was recited by its author, "S":

> A black train pacing solemnly,
> The long streets of Berlin shall see,
> Two hundred heroes dead must fall,
> It was a King who slew them all.
> Revenge!

> Till the last folk wear victory's crown,
> And the last throne be tumbled down,
> And the last dynasty run dry,
> Still shall this be the people's cry:
> Revenge!

What did the Swiss authorities make of all these proceedings? The governments of the cantons suffered what they could not or would not prevent.

Since the end of March all authorities of South-West Germany knew that they had to reckon with an invasion of German republicans from Alsace. In Paris, as we have seen, there had been a "German Democratic Society" since the middle of March, a group of about eight hundred German workmen; the editor of the *Brüsseler Deutschen Zeitung*, the well-known Adalbert von Bernstedt, took part in its founding. Georg Herwegh then undertook the leadership and Jakob Venedey, partly from wounded vanity, worked against him. But Herwegh was really ill-fitted for a post of leadership. He was a dreamer, egocentric and over-sensitive, bored by practical details, always at high tension, alternately dreaming and silent; and then violent and inclined to be despotic about trifles, a timid speaker, open to influence by anyone of strong will, unstable and yet obstinate; finally, completely dominated by his splendid, intelligent wife, all whose admiration could not make him into a great revolutionary leader. Herwegh himself, in spite of all spiritually aristocratic reservations, inclined to communism; Börnstein, Doll, Löwenfels were all more or less connected with communism. So was young Wilhelm Liebknecht.

The German workmen of these divisions were naturally well acquainted with socialistic and communistic ideas. All oppositional, anti-monarchical elements came together here. According to French law, every unemployed foreigner had a claim to monetary assistance as far as the frontier. The German legionaries wished to make use of this. Herwegh, however, had great scruples about accepting any support from the French Government. Otto von Corvin, former Prussian officer, was less scrupulous. The sum paid to both in the form of a loan was extremely modest, so that the legionaries were soon in want. The French Government's main object was to be rid of the burden of foreign unemployed—no responsible person connected the German Legion with any serious political plans. The French Government assisted all the Germans, Karl Marx also received money for his Communists. The German Legion was also joined by several Swiss, Poles, Italians, Hungarians, and Russians, one American, and a Turk. A number of French also smuggled themselves in. Corvin said there were about thirty. There was also a Polish Legion of about one thousand five hundred in Strasburg, they were officially encouraged by the French provisional Government. There had been a number of Polish emigrés in Strasburg for years; they nearly all received a small grant and contrived to live on these scanty alms from the French, which were humanitarian rather than political.

Counting the Poles, Herwegh reckoned on a corps of four to five thousand men. He thought of Cologne, Frankfort, Mannheim, Constance as main points of attack. The Strasburg authorities would not allow an attack on Baden and negotiated with the Karlsruhe ministry about the removal of the refugees. The idea was to confiscate the weapons of both Poles and Germans; the Poles were to be taken to Mannheim in divisions of forty men apiece, then by water to Cologne and by way of Danzig to Posen and Galicia, while the Germans were to be transported as quickly as possible through Baden to their various native states. Naturally the republican leaders in Baden, Eichler at their head, worked against such a solution. Eichler went himself to Strasburg to make sure of these auxiliaries. He had just come from Aachen, where on April 2nd he had introduced representatives of the German Republican Legion from France and had first proclaimed the Republic. It is scarcely comprehensible that the Baden government did not succeed in working with the French, and they prevented the revolt of which all the world was talking. The Baden commissioners offered Herwegh's volunteers free railway transport and sufficient funds for the journey if they would at once make individually and peaceably for their homes, each authenticated by his birth certificate. They all refused defiantly and said they had not made the long journey from Paris in order to give up all their plans in cowardly fashion just when they were on the point of being realized. Lichtenberger, the prefect of Strasburg, refused to provide them with arms, supposed to have been promised them by the French authorities in Paris, and declared that he would not allow them to remain any longer and if necessary would move them on by force. Herwegh made a very sensible demand to be sent to Schleswig-Holstein with his one thousand volunteers. Unfortunately the provisional government there had scruples and von Arnim told the Baden minister, von Dusch, that the Prussian and other German auxiliaries were ample for the purpose. "We neither need nor wish for such auxiliaries," it was said; there were enough combatants in the country (which was a notorious untruth)— and the duchies already had enough to support.

Herwegh and his men would probably have shown in the

war against Denmark that the greater part of their republican enthusiasm was honest German patriotism. Herwegh then negotiated in Basle, but the Swiss authorities would not admit his men, and thus, harried and driven, he was forced to attempt to get from Alsace over the Rhine to Baden.

Von Arnim said on April 19th: "Hecker's understanding is not so mad as it seems. The boundless cowardice and weakness of the grand-ducal government is forcing many well-meaning men, who are attached to the Grand Duke, to take sides with Hecker's republicans."

And yet the *coup d'état* failed.

Hecker left Mannheim on April 9th, never to return to his native town. That he had never dared to strike out from the centre of his power, was already the beginning of defeat. His closest collaborator, Ficker, was arrested. Warnings came from all sides. But Hecker was obstinate and would not give way. On April 12th, the proclamation of the two leaders, Hecker and Struve, appeared in the name of the Provisional Government. It met with but a feeble response. When Hecker marched out of Constance, on the morning of April 13th, less than sixty men followed his drums. He wore his large, flapping hat with its cock's feather, high boots, pistols in his belt, and a blue blouse. Such a costume had already been seen in the streets of Paris and during the Swiss Federal War. In spite of the whisperings of the pusillanimous, the troop gradually increased to eight hundred men.

Struve now appeared in Donaueschingen and a couple of hundred irregulars collected round him. Hecker arrived with his men. The situation had been fully transformed—the princely family of Fürstenberg had flown and the citizens of Donaueschingen saw red revolution in the face. Municipal delegates appeared again before General von Miller, but this time with an urgent plea that the city might be set free from the plague of the irregulars. The citizens formed up for the march, a man drove rapidly up by the post and energetically requested that the march be delayed, in order to prevent bloodshed. This was Struve, and he actually succeeded in so bluffing the Württembergians that they allowed the irregulars to march off in peace. Thus Hecker and Struve marched unhindered through the Black Forest. In Bernau, Hecker met Venedey and Spatz, the commissioners of the Fifty Committee; they offered a full amnesty if he would lay down his arms. Hecker felt that compared to these men of ink and paper he was a fighter and a liberating hero; he played rough jokes on them and felt more confidence in himself than ever. They had sought him in vain in Constance and Donaueschingen and composed a letter to him, the gist of which has been preserved. No doubt, they said much the same to him in person. The Democrats could not have appealed more impressively to the Social-Revolutionary. "Our aim," they said, "is a united free Germany on the broadest basis of popular freedom and happiness. The Pre-Parliament has left it to the constituting assembly to carry out this work. It will meet on May 1st. It will be a good meeting, if all friends of the people and the Fatherland are represented. We look forward with confidence to the assembly's decisions and prove our respect for the free opinions of the people by submitting our personal views and wishes to their decisions."

This was honest and to the point, but could scarcely kindle enthusiasm. As their conference with Hecker led to no result, they later exhorted the citizens of Baden to have nothing to do with Hecker; civil war would jeopardize the meeting of the National Assembly on May 1st.

Hecker's troop consisted mainly of young people, artisans, factory workers, peasants; but Sigel, as a professional officer, had persuaded the Constance militia to march with him. With additions by the way, his force amounted to three thousand men and they had two cannon. The third, the Rhine column, drummed up by the post-innkeeper Weishaar of Lottstetten, was distinctly a country troop. Weishaar, elected in Offenburg to the Diet Committee, was a splendid figure, a respected and prosperous citizen and a model to many of his class. Thus these three companies represented respectively the proletariat, the middle class, and the countrymen. It is hard to calculate the number of irregulars, there can scarcely have been more than six thousand. If they could all have been concentrated in one spot, they would have made a strong impression and probably had a success. But at this point their leadership failed completely. Hecker's messages, ordering them to assemble, did not arrive; he could not think of any forcible measures. His orders to blow up the bridges were not carried out. None of the leaders had enough vision or was cold-blooded enough to make of the mob a real revolutionary army. Sigel, the only man who could have done it, had not sufficient influence. Hecker and Struve often quarrelled, Weishaar soon lost interest. Everyone finally did as he thought fit. The most incredible fact is that Hecker twice rejected Herwegh's offer to bring him his German legion from Alsace. Herwegh's courageous wife Emma brought the message. But Hecker also believed the legend that Herwegh's volunteers mostly consisted of French and Poles, and he naturally did not wish to summon them over the Rhine.

In Constance and various other lake towns the Republic had now been proclaimed; the Badensian government had sent as governmental director an official named Peter, formerly a persecuted member of the opposition, thinking that his personality would produce great results; but Peter, more or less willingly, allowed himself to be chosen as chancellor of Hecker's republic, only to flee to Switzerland the very next day. In Offenburg, the revolutionary town council declared itself in sympathy with the revolt, because the members thought that Herwegh would cross the Rhine in the night. As he did not come, they denied the Republic again. But, fearing bloodshed, they refused to admit any troops, so that their attitude might be described as neutral.

The Badensian government hurried on the mobilization of the 8th German Federal army corps; Hessian troops marched in on April 5th. Württemberg and Bavaria also showed willingness to help. This was rather too much for the Badensians, who would rather have suppressed the revolt by themselves with as little bloodshed as possible. When the Württembergers appeared, their reception was cool; the Badensians had neglected to inform officials and parishes of their coming. Their assistance did not seem worth much when some of the Hessian troops mutinied at Rastatt and refused obedience to their officers at the bayonet point. Afterwards things were better. The Dutch ministry was badly disappointed by the French government, which promised rifles and then withdrew the promise. Baden bought thirty thousand in England. The impression prevailed that France rather enjoyed her neighbour's difficulties.

Baden could not decide who should lead the troops. A prince was out of the question; one could not expect him to fight against his own countrymen. It happened that the Dutch general Friedrich von Gagern, elder brother of Heinrich and Max, was on leave in Germany. He was the most gifted of the family, a personality of really comprehensive and deep culture. During the revolutionary weeks the name of Gagern had taken on a magic to which everyone was susceptible. Could not one subdue the magic of Hecker's name by the magic of Gagern's? Friedrich von Gagern was also considered a great strategist—the task of subduing the revolution seemed at first more difficult than it really was. On April 13th, Gagern was put at the head of the Badensian divisions, representing Markgrave Maximilian of Baden, with the rank of a Lieutenant-General. The effect was better upon the mass of the public than upon the circles to whom it was especially directed. Many officers of Baden threatened to quit the service—and it was indeed a poor testimony to the Baden military that no officer qualified for leadership could be found among them. The Württemberg officers declared that their King would never put his troops under Gagern's supreme command. The Republicans protested against the bringing in of a foreigner to suppress them. The position was peculiarly difficult for Gagern himself; he took over the Baden division without having enjoyed a spell of leave, put the letter from the King of the Netherlands, recalling him, on one side unopened, convinced that he must not refuse anything to his old Fatherland, and began his really extremely difficult task without any previous knowledge of the officers of the territory. The Frankfort Diet, in which the Netherlands envoy also had a seat, issued a kind of certificate to say that they considered General von Gagern's appointment desirable in the interests of protection for South-Western Germany. This created a certain legal basis. Friedrich was to command in civilian dress, as a kind of "civilian general." In the field he actually wore civilian dress with a sword and light military cap. In accordance with his extraordinary position, he felt it incumbent upon him to take all risks and secure a decisive success as soon as possible.

After Hecker's defeat it soon became customary to represent his whole enterprise as a farce. People shook with mocking laughter as they had shaken before with fear. We take a different view. Hecker was a popular leader, but no strategist, an inspired speaker, but no political tactician; his strongest point was his belief in himself. He was an illusionist, but very brave, a social-revolutionary dreamer, averse to terrorism of any kind. He was not a robber captain, but a humane revolutionary—not very much more than an attorney with a heart of gold and a flowing beard.

Hecker was quite right in believing the Badensian soldiery to be untrustworthy. General von Gagern put the Hessians in the front line. The Badensians were repeatedly passive; at Kandern they intentionally fired into the air.

Gagern's troops met Hecker's volunteers on the Scheidegg hill near Kandern on April 20th. Hecker had been wishing for days past that this conflict might take place. He hoped to do much more than win a victory over the troops—to win them over to his cause through the power of his personality and eloquence. Friedrich von Gagern had exactly the same idea. Thus there developed the remarkable situation that two armed bodies faced one another for hours, each in the hope that the other might be persuaded to join its ranks. Gagern invited Hecker to a personal interview on the little bridge at Kandern. Two bearers of powerful names and powerful ideas encountered one another in a brief battle of words.

"You are a clever man, a fine man, but a fanatic," said the General. The people's leader returned the aristocrat's accusation of fanaticism. They could not agree, but their behaviour was chivalrous and perfectly correct. A strange picture—the General in patrician civilian dress confronting the civilian in the uniform of a Social-Revolutionary, the worldly-wise, much travelled political thinker opposed to the dreamer to whom a distant future meant more than the rhythm of his own day—but both of them men of strong individuality who might have debated for hours in parliament and finally have found a path that they could tread in common. They only met this once in an out of the way corner of the Black Forest and could come to no understanding.

A ten minutes' pause had been agreed upon before the outbreak of hostilities; Willich—not Hecker—used the interval to withdraw the volunteers to more favourable ground up the hillside. The troops took this to be a retreat and advanced with confidence. Hecker made a last appeal to them. They wavered, even the Hessians. Gagern, having appealed in vain to the revolutionaries to discard their arms, now feared the issue and gave the order to attack. Conspicuous in his green cap and brown coat, he was one of the first to fall. Now the Hessians were embittered and fought fiercely; but the encounter was brief. During the lull, the revolutionaries exchanged the General's body for a flag they had lost, and withdrew. When the battle was resumed, the superiority of the troops was soon apparent. The men with the scythes could not stand up to modern weapons, they scattered in all directions. Hecker only escaped by chance, fled, completely exhausted, to Switzerland, attempted in vain to reach Sigel's column from Alsace and when the universal collapse was obvious, went to Muttenz in Canton Basle.

It was plain to all those with knowledge that the volunteers could never stand up to a well-led troop of regulars. But Hecker had hoped to persuade the troops to come over. Perhaps it was only through Gagern that this catastrophe was prevented; probably no Badensian officer could have asserted his authority. The legend that Gagern had been assassinated arose directly after the battle and was believed and spread by the Gagern family. An exact examination of the facts proves the falsity. Gagern's death was a sacrifice in quite another and deeper sense. His proven and considered advice was to be sorely missed by his brothers Heinrich and Max in times of the most serious political tension.

The battle of Kandern destroyed the magic power of Hecker's name. Hinkeldey met Weishaar's and Struve's columns near Steinen; the men fled, the leaders were able to save themselves; Struve was at first put under arrest in Säckingen, but he succeeded in so terrorizing the officials that they set him free and he was able to join Sigel. Just at this moment, Becker came to help with German workmen from Switzerland; the most numerous column, led by Sigel, was still advancing. But there was a lack of munition. Frau Struve tried to buy powder in Strasburg. Freiburg helped the rebels. Farmers from the neighbourhood, artisans, and gymnasts collected under the leadership of Langsdorff, himself a student and one of Jahn's gymnasts.

They terrorized the officials and the comfort-loving citizens so that they dared not take any measure against them. But Sigel was not equal to the task of leadership. Struve continually interfered with him. Government troops advanced from the plains of the Rhine. At Günterstal there was a tussle, in which Sigel's front line was forced to retreat. Here, too, Sigel, waving a white handkerchief, had first attempted to achieve an understanding. On April 24th, which was Easter Monday, Freiburg was attacked on three sides at once, by Hessians, Nassauers, and Badensians. The attack was successful, the defenders ran out of munition and the Badensians fought better, since the battle was not waged against Hecker himself. General Hoffmann of Baden was chiefly responsible for the success—he led the charge himself, six paces ahead of his men. Such an example was naturally a great help.


The popular movement was fed with democratic-socialistic ideas, which opponents tried to put into ill-repute by attributing to them a French origin. But these ideas dominated or influenced political life all over Western Europe, they were super-national and underwent modifications in every nation that adopted them. Hecker was, in his virtues and weaknesses, a thoroughly German personality—the hard-headed Alemannic peasants, workmen, and a couple of soldiers who marched with him, did so in a German urge to justice, lust of combat and because they believed in a better world which they were making for the future. Neither did the few French who marched with Herwegh make of his venture a "French" enterprise—he was a German and a poet, who believed he would soon have set up a new Germany in a new Europe. The Republic was for him a matter of conscience, of religion. It is odd that the Baden Government, proud to be marching in the van of German liberalism, now began to complain of foreign emissaries, foreign ideas, and foreign money, as soon as it was a question of democratic-socialistic ideas. The interests and ideas of the French Government were quite another matter. At last, Prussia was about to conclude the alliance with the German national idea which alone could secure for her hegemony in Germany. In the small states of West and South Germany, especially in Bavaria, there was opposition to this alliance. Republic, socialism and such uncanny matters were rejected, but civic parliamentarianism was in the midst of such things, and the states therefore felt more kinship with the French than with the Prussians who were only at the beginning of the development. Prussia opposed it violently. Only a few far-seeing men understood the misguided patriotism that inspired Hecker's revolt. It was just as false to leave the participants, especially the leaders, absolutely free, as it was to fill the prisons to overflowing with them and take long and complicated proceedings against them. Three thousand five hundred such cases were proceeded with in Baden. This alone serves to prove that the first Baden revolt was neither an idyll nor a joke. It was an attack of fever. It cost a couple of dozen lives and ruined a great many more. A political and social crisis had arisen in this State; it was for her responsible heads to see that she recovered.

The Fifty Committee was a moral authority; this meant much in and around Frankfort; when it attempted to extend its influence to a large State such as Prussia, or a small one like Electoral Hesse, its limitations soon became patent. Behind the Fifty Committee stood the Revolution, giving it impetus and energy. The Committee was already beginning to legalize the Revolution. The members would like to have governed, but they only took counsel in a great number of public and private meetings, altered their views, dispatched commissioners, who admonished everyone to keep order, and took a great delight in proclamations. It is significant that even outwardly, the Fifty Committee had no visible foundation. The matter of the members' dues was not regulated until August 31st.

The composition of the Committee was not altogether happy. As we have seen, the leader of the Social-Revolutionary party, Hecker and Struve, were not included—contemporaries, not only their followers, already recognized that this omission had literally driven the two into the streets. Still, the demo-cratic-republican school was represented by such men as Blum, Raveaux, Johann Jacoby of Königsberg, and Adam von Itzstein. A great weakness of the Pre-Parliament was the almost com-plete lack of Austrians; there were eight places reserved for them among the Fifty, but few responded to the invitation. Besides Wiesner and Count Bissingen, Schuselka, Kuranda, Endlicher, Hornbostl, Mühlfeld, and Schilling arrived. Hüb-ner later replaced Endlicher. Important was the express refusal of Palacky, the Bohemian; he would have nothing to do with Germany and its rebuilding. Bohemia came first with him, and then the Imperial State, dominated, or at least helped in the Government by West and South Slavs, the league of peoples in the Danube valley, a necessary bulwark against Russia.

"Verily, if the Imperial State of Austria did not already exist, it must be hastily created, in the interests of Europe, nay, in the interests of humanity." "Germany," said Palacky, "should calmly make up her mind to proclaim a Republic, the Austrian Imperial State must remain complete, along with the Germans belonging to it" (April 17th).

The Fifty Committee's answer, even before this intelligence arrived, was to give an especially solemn reception to the Austrian members in the German Reformed Church; repre-sentatives of the Viennese students accompanied the Austrian contingent, and in their picturesque semi-medieval costume, made a great impression and were enthusiastically received as heroes of the Viennese Revolution. Kuranda and Wächter were sent to Prague, but there were passionate differences of opinion. Palacky and his men thought it impossible to place Austria under the dominion of a German Empire, everything depended upon the future Bohemian Diet. Schilling, who had come direct from Vienna, answered that he was convinced that the Germans in Austria "would not be willing to be absorbed into a Czech-Illyrian Imperialism and that they must rather give up the dynasty than this Teutonism."

The Pre-Parliament and the Fifty Committee desired a Germany which would include Austria; the Viennese Government also displayed a tendency at this time to persist in their own path. Four days before the elections for the National Assembly on April 21st, the otherwise weak and hesitating Pillersdorf Ministry issued a plain-spoken official declaration in the *Wiener Zeitung*: Austria was filled with desire for an intimate connection with Germany, would take any opportunity of showing her devotion to the German cause—but could never reconcile her peculiar position and her special interests with unconditional submission to the Federal Assembly or consent to resign her right to independent internal administration. She would have to reserve a right to consider each resolution passed by the Federal Assembly on its merits. Otherwise she could not join the Confederation (afterwards officially corrected to "Federal State").

The declaration was tortuous, polite, anxious not to offend. But the spirit was that of Metternich. "Connection," "Anschluss"—this remarkable and scarcely fortunate word is used here probably for the first time to describe Austria's relationship to the rest of Germany. Behind all its cautious expressions of special interests, reserved rights and so on, its ignoring of Pre-Parliament and the Fifty Committee, was the negative of the Imperial State which even after the Viennese Revolution still considered itself a great power and was willing to live with Germany, but also in spite of Germany. Was this language understood in Frankfort? The Fifty Committee appointed a commission, declared the regulation of German relations to be a matter for the National Assembly, but demanded that all special interests should be subordinated to the aim of establishing a united Germany—with the assurance of Germany's aid should the Italians menace South Tyrol. It was all well-meant paper-talk. The Imperial State, painfully surprised at any attempt at interference, stood aside, a historical-political reality.

The relation of the Fifty Committee to the Federal Diet and to Prussia was the core of its existence. The old Federal Diet was now a thoroughly modernized body; but in this revolutionary Frankfort world, it represented the principle of legitimacy and always attempted to bend and guide everything that occurred towards legitimacy, often at the expense of its own dignity. As far as the Diet was concerned, the Revolution need make no further progress, the aim now was to secure and legitimize the victory, by means of alliances with still prevailing powers—dynasties, bureaucracy, the army. The first dispute between the Fifty Committee and the Diet arose on the question of electoral lists. The Diet had decided, on March 30th, upon a member to every seventy thousand population, the Pre-Parliament upon one to fifty thousand. The Diet's arrangements were antiquated—altered but little in 1842, they really dated from 1819—and common sense was entirely on the side of the Pre-Parliament. In spite of the advice of the seventeen confidential advisers, the Diet would not give way. At last the Committee threatened to recall the Pre-Parliament, whereupon the Diet gave its consent. News was coming in from all sides that there was resistance upon the broader basis.

Count Dönhoff wrote to Berlin on April 10th that the Fifty Committee "was behaving like a provisional government." Dönhoff felt that his period of usefulness in Frankfort was at an end and repeatedly asked to be recalled. But since Dahlmann refused to take over, Dönhoff carried on, although his recall had been decided—a most unfavourable state of things under such difficult political circumstances. Dahlmann gave as reason for his refusal that his work as one of the Seventeen took all his time; he was working with Albrecht on the concept of a new federal constitution and carried his point against Uhlands obstinate opposition. The Seventeen preserved a strict silence as to their often lively discussions; none of them spoke about them with their envoys, they were determined to let the Federal Assembly take no part, so as to be free of the taint that clung to it. When the concept was ready on April 26th it was immediately published, and the Diet thus confronted with something already in being. No objection was then raised to the publication of the Seventeen.

Dahlmann's plan for a constitution stands upright with iron dignity in the whirlwind of these revolutionary weeks. It is complement to the Austrian ministerial declaration; but unlike it, was not a gesture, but a programme, not an elaborate and carefully framed official document, but the manly expression of a true patriotic purpose. Here for the first time was an official proposal, a German political reality, we find the idea of a hereditary Emperor; also of an upper house, in which the princes should have seats, which Dahlmann himself later characterized as an unfortunate idea, next the plan for the lower house; he began by outlining the fundamental laws, touched on war diplomacy, commerce and customs, proposed a very authoritative Imperial court of justice, to serve also as national court of justice—in all a concept full of moderation and dignity, convincing in spite of certain weaknesses, to men of high character and settled culture, but unsatisfactory to consistent revolutionaries, and irritating and open to criticism to all powers of yesterday. Dahlmann's plan went under in a Diet Commission; it was subjected to a deal of quibbling and bungling; it was never laid before the National Assembly, which was its actual reason for existence. At the beginning of May, Heinrich von Gagern said to Gervinus, who had warmly advocated the constitutional plan of the Seventeen in the *Deutsche Zeitung*: "I hope Bockelberg (Prussian envoy in Darmstadt) finds the plan sufficiently good Prussian and conservative." But King Maximilian of Bavaria wrote to the Grand Duke of Hesse that the plan "annulled all ruling princes." Count Bray, Bavarian foreign minister said to Count Bernstorff, the Prussian envoy: "People would rather submit to a republican form than a hereditary monarchy." "A nation of five million people wants a king of its own," wrote Bray to Luxburg, Bavarian envoy to Vienna. Luxburg criticized the plan with equal acerbity. He feared that the idea behind it was to set up Prussia at the head of all Germany. Most of the Bavarian deputies would vote for Bavaria's independence.

Hanover, Saxony and Electoral Hesse agreed with Bavaria in their doubts about the most important points, so did Mecklenburg-Schwerin, whereas Weimar was in favour of the plan, on principle. In the Prussian Government, Baron Heinrich von Arnim would like to have used the Dahlmann plan to form a positive determinate little-German policy—but the King would not permit this. Frederick William IV now regretted nothing more fervently than his German programme of March 21st. He was now full of quite other plans. No regent, no corporation thus ventured to take up the Seventeen Plan with energy and do their best for it. For this hereditary empire in Germany would in the end mean a Prussian hereditary Emperor—and the King of Prussia was still Frederick William IV. Haste was an urgent necessity of the German Revolution; but it was just the advocates of a hereditary empire who needed time, a great deal of time, long enough to forget the 18th of March. If the new Austria turned away from Prussia, the Fifty Committee as bearer of the revolutionary principles, must naturally turn towards her. But Prussia also held back; the King, because he hated revolution and merely desired to become Arch Field-Marshal of the Empire, and the new democratic Prussia because its own new constitutional robes must first be cut to pattern.


Hecker's volunteers, Herwegh's legion—the whole social revolutionary movement would have been impossible without the working men. The political-military form of the volunteers and legions goes back to the time of the European wars of liberation against Napoleon; there were such bands of insurgent fighters drawn from the people, in Spain, the Alpine countries, Germany, Poland, Italy. The first German insurgent volunteers were Lützow's corps. But national ends could be more readily attained by this means, than revolutionary. Karl Marx in Paris spoke with bitter mockery of the Herwegh legion; it would only become an all too easy victim of the military-bourgeois reaction. He had quite other ideas for the revolutionary workers. Marx was now constituting the Communist League anew in Paris, a central committee was chosen, to which Wolff, Schapper, Baur, and Moll belonged, besides Marx and Engels; on April 1st it proclaimed a revolutionary programme for Germany, consisting of seventeen demands of the Communist party in Germany. Its main aims were: one indivisible German republic, payment for the people's representatives, arms for every man (the workers' armies are at the same time productive labour organizations), free administration of justice, abolition of all feudal burdens, transformation of princely and other feudal lands into national property, agriculture to be carried out on a grand scale according to scientific principles, mortgages on farms to become national property, rents and ground rents to be paid to the State, a national bank to replace the private banks, ending the mastery of the great financiers and creating credit for the whole people, all traffic facilities to be nationalized, salaries to be graded only according to the number of persons in the family, not according to rank, complete separation of Church and State, limitation of the right of inheritance, progressive taxation, no more taxes on consumption, erection of national workshops, guarantee of existence for all workers, care for unemployables, universal free education.

This communistic programme for Germany is a considerably watered version of the Communist Manifesto. Instead of the main demand for expropriation of landed property, we find more cautious individual provisions; smaller private property was not to be molested. This programme had much in common with Hecker's, Struve's, and other social-revolutionaries' principles. Even democratic bourgeois republicans could have agreed with much of it. In spite of this, the seventeen demands had scarcely any effect, public opinion took almost no notice of them. The first reprint was in the Berlin *Zeitungshalle* on April 5, 1848, afterwards they appeared in two other places. They were also distributed as a broadsheet. But the concessions which Karl Marx had made to the German political present-day had not gone nearly far enough: these "communistic" demands were not in the spirit of the time and they fell flat. The Communist League was not to play any important part as a complete organization in the German Revolution of 1848–49. Its members were everywhere, where class consciousness had been aroused in the German working-class of the time, but the German workers' movement of 1848–49 was not Marxist, nor Communist; it had strong pre-Marx socialistic impulses and was at once democratic and social in a new sense. The protagonist of this new spirit was a printer named Stephan Born, a man of Posen, who at the age of twenty had fought in a broadsheet for the idea that the workers should band themselves into a federation to battle against brutality and lack of education in the working-classes; justice should be attained, not by violence, but by intellectual weapons. "We want to build up a league to become human." Born then went to Paris and Brussels, where he gained strong impressions of the great Communist leaders; but except for a few blunders such as the pamphlet against Heinzen, he retained his own simple, objective nature, adapted to his day. When he arrived in Berlin at the end of March, entrusted by Karl Marx with the task of taking the Workers' Movement in Germany in hand, he saw at once that there was nothing to be done here with communism and that he himself no longer felt as a Communist. However, he was a disciple of Marx, and spoke at the workmen's meeting in Berlin against rioting, destruction of machines and "strong tactics." His burning idea was always: "We must organize *ourselves*."

Prussia's policy during the revolutionary period is only comprehensible when we remember the constant pressure from Russia. The retreat in April 1848 was only the first, but unfortunately not the last. German unity could be won by Prussia, even at that time only by fighting for it; at that moment it could have been achieved by alliance with England, with France a benevolent neutral, against Russia and the Imperial State of Austria which was breaking up. Bismarck would have taken the opposite front.

"J'ai le sang russe pour souffrir que les ouvriers gouvernent l'Europe," Czar Nicholas is supposed to have said in March 1848. This sentence is still today striking in its illumination of the deep gulf which existed between the greatest extremes of the century. Under the influence of the impression made by the Paris February Revolution, Prince Gortchakow wrote: "All eyes, all desires are turned upon the Emperor. He bears the fate of Europe visibly within his hand." After the Berlin March Revolution, Count Benckendorff said: "The shame which has come upon Europe will only raise our Emperor's position still higher. He is not only the Emperor de toutes les Russies, but all decent people will collect under his banner."

There were enough people at the Prussian court and in the Prussian officers' corps who shared these views. The coming

European war, which broke out seven years later over the Oriental question, was anticipated, even desired, by many. Prussia was then to stand at Russia's side. An anonymous pamphlet which appeared at the end of April in Berlin opposed popular enthusiasm for Poland and claimed that the restoration of Poland would only be in the interests of France, and therefore against the interests of Prussia and Germany; it was not a war with Russia that threatened, but a war with France. The pamphlet was a sensation, and could hardly increase Germany's confidence in Prussia. But it represented the real opinions of people who had always been powerful and had just regained their old power. Baron Heinrich von Arnim, foreign minister, with his eccentric ways of doing business and odd inspirations could not, in spite of all his original talents, hope to compete with them.

The troubles in Poland, the war in Schleswig, the Russian pressure, the difficult relations with the Frankfort unity movement—these were all burdens and complications for the Prussian great power. She certainly did not play a brilliant part— but she was not shaken to the depths. Berlin celebrated her revolutionary victory and practised living democratically. Similar events were happening in Breslau and Königsberg. We have seen the unrest and the popular movement on the Rhine. But there was also an Old Prussian province. The Camphausen Ministry did practically nothing to put the administration in the hands of liberal-minded men. The whole administration was absolutistic up to March 18th—how, indeed, could it be otherwise? Many now discovered a constitutional heart. But most did not think it necessary, they calmly remained at their posts. Berlin became estranged from the provinces. There were stormy doings in the capital, one popular meeting after another. But the need for quiet and order preponderated over everything else, the granting of arms to the people resulted in a completely bourgeois militia —the workers were passed over. The middle classes were afraid of them. The government left the militia to itself, along with the extra troops provided by the artists and students. This bashfulness in respect to the released spirits of revolution was quite characteristic of the leaders of the old liberal opposition who were now in prominent positions. Camphausen always feared that the Republic might be proclaimed in Berlin. But the dynasty was considered unshakeable by the majority in Berlin and still more so in the provinces, to be sure on the understanding that an honest constitutional policy would be pursued. The passivity of the Camphausen Ministry encouraged the growth of extremes; in Berlin, decided democracy, in the provinces, military-bureaucratic reaction. Things did not look well in Prussia—but in spite of everything, the State stood firm. Contrasted with this the condition of the Austrian Imperial State might well give rise to anxiety. There was still an Emperor—but whether the Imperial State was still a political reality was a matter of considerable doubt.

Hungary went its own way; the Archduke Palatine had his own independent ministry with Count Louis Batthyaany as Prime Minister—but without Kossuth. There were stormy protests, as against high treason, against any interference from Vienna. At times there was danger of complete separation under the red flag of the republic. But soon the Serbs and still more effectively, the Croats, turned against the independence of the Magyars. On March 25th, the National Assembly in Agram resolved to set the self-elected Banus Jellacic at the head of the three united kingdoms of Croatia, Slavonia, and Dalmatia. The South Slav nation thus entered the political battlefield; Jellacic was promoted in a few days from Major-General to Field-Marshal. Vienna was not at all concerned to further the Agram National Assembly—but the value of an opponent to Magyarism was at once perceived. The Hungarians still did honour to the Emperor—but the link was very weak. It was defection glossed over with a show of loyalty.

But the Italians hated Vienna and began a fight to the death.

Free Vienna could not well suppress freedom in Lombardy and Venice. It was fortunate for Austria that the rebellion turned into a war. When King Karl Albert of Sardinia declared war on Austria, the Vienna Revolution became patriotic. When Counts Arese and Bellenio arrived in Munich as deputies of the provisional Milan government they saw to their regret that the inroads of the Italians in Tyrol had shaken German sympathy for Italy.

For many reasons the Polish freedom movement was less dangerous to Austria than the Italian. The Polish aristocracy was at odds with the Polish farming classes for economic reasons. The peasants distrusted aristocratic leaders who talked much of the liberation of the farmers. But Count Franz Stadion made use of another oppositional force—nationalism. Later on he was charged with deliberate exaggeration, of having invented Ruthenian nationality in 1848. Everyone had always been aware of the existence of a Little Russian peasantry in Eastern Galicia, and the clever governor now successfully made use of the fact in order to steal a march on the Polish landowning aristocracy. In April Stadion abolished forced labour of the peasantry and promised that the State should recoup those who had the right to demand this labour. By this means he secured the allegiance of the peasants but at the same time caused a division among the nobles, for many a landowner found the promise of ready money very tempting in those days of scarcity. Nevertheless there was trouble in Lemberg and especially in Cracow. A provincial deputation went to Vienna to demand measures of freedom. There was incitement and protest, revolutionary passion broke loose in many a deed of violence. A revolt in the grand style, such as took place in Prussian Poland, was at first prevented, largely because of the prevailing fear of Russian intervention. Congress Poland resounded with the clang of weapons from the great Russian military camp—it was impossible to bring the Polish movement into play there. The Pan-Slavic idea found its way barred, then and later, by the relations between Russia and Poland. There was ill feeling between Austria and Prussia because the Prussian movement held up the refugees who wanted to get through to Posen, but let through those who wanted to get to Cracow. When the Cracow movement collapsed, refugees again collected in Breslau and were not sent back to France by Prussia. Count Trauttmansdorff lodged a serious protest on this account.

Thus the Austrian Imperial State managed Polish affairs better than the other partitionary powers, perhaps because of her plentiful experience with the West Slavs. Just at this time the most gifted West Slavs, the Czechs, began to press their claims. They were naturally antagonistic to Germany and Teutonism, but not to Austria, though their sympathies were with the new Austria. Palacky had told the Fifty Committee that only through partition and weakening of Austria could the centre of Austro-German power be transferred to Frankfort. Austria was to remain Austria, but the central state must become a federative state of free German and non-German countries. Their numerical superiority in population must give the Slavic countries the upper hand; thus German dominance must vanish from Austria, not the German language as a medium of government, but German cultural influence as a decisive factor. Austro-Slavism began its historic career. The Czechs had prepared their political work with their typical passionate devotion and clever, untiringly adaptive technique. The Wenzel committee, or civic committee in Prague was a popular council with unlimited authority. Beside it as armed power in Prague was the St. Wenzels Brotherhood, decorated at first with the scarlet cross, but afterwards as Svornost (Corps of Unity) in a costume less trying to respectable citizens' nerves, but still as determined as ever to represent fervent nationalism. The Vienna Government answered the Prague petition evasively, sent the young Archduke Franz Josef as Governor to Prague and granted independent central

officials and a new election Statute which was very favourable
to the Czechs. The Wenzels Committee endured, expanded,
changed its name to National Committee and remained the
real centre of all political and local happenings and an obedient
tool of Czech feeling, in spite of all protests of the German
inhabitants. Bohemia was about to become what Hungary
was already. The leading names in the country supported the
movement—Lobkowitz, Schwarzenberg, Auersperg, Harrach,
Czernin; by their means, Austro-Slavism soon became a power
at the Viennese court, a greater power than the German-
centralistic ministry and the black-red-gold Revolution in the
Imperial capital. The old Imperial State was breaking up—
Austro-Slavs alone could perhaps build up a new one. The
Czechs were the first to declare the black, red, and gold to be
a political symbol, directed against Austria, and to threaten
wearers of the German colours with ill treatment. The Bohemian National Committee thereupon recognized the right of
the Germans to wear these colours, but advised them not to
do so openly, in the interests of public peace. In Prague the
Austrian black and yellow flags were flown as well as the
Bohemian national colours, red and white.


But had not checkmate already been put to the Revolution?
The main stream was already diverted into a bed which made
of it a quiet, well-regulated stream. The oppressed, who had
now arisen, believed many things—their most sacred faith was
their hope in the great German parliament. In this idea the
thousandfold will-power of the age fused to an agglomerate,
as in the central dome of Renaissance architecture. Prussia, the
great power, Austria, the Imperial State created modern popular representative bodies, although both acted much too late,
enforced and yet hastily. Their national will to endure felt the
need of these institutions—who would resist the urge? Yet all
men of vision saw that there was danger in this competitive

creation of parliaments. The great German Parliament came into being slowly, far too slowly. At the beginning of April, even in the middle of April, it could have captured the malleable, flowing stream of events and compelled it to take form. When it at last assembled in Frankfort towards the end of May, the best element of revolution, the happy hour of action, was really already over.

Everything still seemed young and new in Germany. The healthy, patient, good-hearted people were awakened and enjoying their freedom. Printed paper flew about the streets, once so quiet and respectable; the street-corner men, once so apathetic, were now full of gossip and shouted the news from one alley to another; a crowd streamed up and down, gaping at huge posters, devouring the words of popular speakers, throwing stones through the windows of reactionaries, cheering the new men and totally refraining from slaughtering the old. No people is so sorry for fallen greatness or so good-natured to it as the German; they accepted it quite calmly that a malicious old reactionary like v. Kamptz should attempt to make himself agreeable by wearing the black, red, and gold cockade. Equipages, liveried servants, barrack-room manners and the bored arrogance of a few uniformed nincompoops who went by the name of lieutenants of the guard, had vanished from Berlin at one blow. The sober-sided city took on an easterly and proletarian character once military and court society had been wiped out. In the twisted old streets of baroque Vienna, in elegant old German Frankfort, the revolutionary picture was brighter. But everywhere irony and mockery was ready to heap upon the artificial, cleanshaven, affected, supercilious people who could not forget their exalted position. The Revolution brought changes in dress and manners. The blue or green blouse did not succeed in establishing itself as democratic costume. It remained a working-man's apparel, and was logically adopted by the volunteers. But the round grey hat, turned up at the side and worn of course with

a cockade of black, red, and gold, was adopted, and so was
the large black wideawake of the Italian revolutionaries such
as Robert Blum wore, and both of these soon replaced the
respectable top-hat of the loyal philistine, just as the citizen
frock-coat was now adopted as a matter of course by the lower
middle classes and replaced the former master-artisan's smock.
Since the upper classes delighted to discard the uniform and
wear the simple black coat, a plain civic manner of clothes
for all men alike was seen for the first time in Germany. Spots
of bright colour in street and inn-parlour came from the new
uniforms of civic guards and legionaries, blue, red, and grey,
but they had rather the air of being in costume with their
scarves, swords and braids, than of wearing uniform, especially
as these were purposely worn with a careless, unceremonious
air. People enjoyed being free of the word of command, of
surveillance, of prohibitions—wanted comforts, pleasure, freedom—therefore everyone shouted and disputed to his heart's
content, ate and drank in company, grew a long beard, and
paddled agreeably in the stream of circumstance. The inn was
the home of clubs and their new heroes. Mighty disputes and
discussions had always arisen over the mugs of light beer, the
little decanters of red or white wine, in the fume of tobacco-
filled inn parlours. Now the whole political life spread from
the back room into the big main hall and infected everybody,
even the most indifferent. In Frankfort the parties were soon
to be nicknamed after the inns their members frequented. It
was a great time for landlords. In the big cities, political salons
came into being—such as that of Frau Koch-Gontard in
Frankfort. People became acquainted more easily than ever
before, and were friendly and trusting; everyone who could
afford it offered hospitality to the apostles of freedom. When
they drove out, their horses and carriages were wreathed with
flowers; black, red, and golden streamers stretched across the
streets. Most of the scarves were embroidered by tender hands.
There was a new masculine ideal—the man with the courage

of his opinions, the orator, the hero of the pen, the man with convictions who could convince others, organizer, pressman, parliamentarian. The presses thundered feverishly, verses scribbled quickly in pencil were being sold in the streets an hour or two later; writers and artists competed for all they were worth; the papers sold hot from the press, market-women, 'prentices cheerfully paid their ha'pence, it was possible to print huge editions.

Such young, yeasty enthusiasm and excitement foamed all over Germany, over all Central and Western Europe. Many learned to know their beautiful country for the first time because they were obliged to journey to the capital on the nation's affairs. Many a liberal-minded Baron had never before spoken a word to an artisan on politics; the professor was a stranger to the merchant, the yeoman to the journalist, the lawyer to the working man. But now they all felt themselves Prussians together, or Austrians, but above all, Germans, citizens of a new and better world—they wanted to be one, to speak the same speech, they believed in their common destiny and were full of confidence. Poor, noble-hearted, trustful generation! The majority of the people desired no meaningless destruction of life and property, either then or later, no violence—but respect, the chance to rise, a share in public life, work to do and a bit of happiness. They were modest wishes, perhaps too modest, for he who is modest in politics usually gets nothing at all. Just as in olden days a smith had hammered into a country landowner's consciousness the warning: "Landgraf, be hard!" so the German people of 1848 should have been warned to be hard—hard and suspicious. They were fighting bureaucracy—yet they elected so many well-meaning officials into parliament, brimming over with carefully-worded promises; they were fighting aristocracy, but nobles found it particularly easy to become leaders in this new age, not only because many were really capable, but also because many were treated by the citizens with the old obsequious reverence. They were fighting the militarism of standing armies—but the new German national patriotism entangled Germany in conflicts on all sides.

Inexperienced in home politics, the Germans plunged with a certain joyous abandon into foreign quarrels and then called despairingly for generals, soldiers, and munitions, for no war with Denmark, Italy, or Poland could be fought by the militia. Rulers and courts were attacked and certain rulers were actually deposed or deprived of power, such as Ludwig of Bavaria and the old Grand Duke of Hesse—but the most dangerous and unreliable of all, Frederick William IV, was not forced to abdicate, and in the "liberal" Archduke Johann, the people secured, with a singular talent for miscasting, the very man who was to become the gravedigger of the Austrian and German revolution.

How optimistic they were! They thought that all that was necessary to effect reforms was to recognize what was wrong in public life, to recommend what was good and to pass a resolution about it. They were accustomed to expect history to have a logical meaning. The proclamations often speak, in the true spirit of Hegel, of a "world spirit" which was now to penetrate all State affairs, and now to be prevented from "rushing too violently" into republicanism.

The language of the time was lofty and overstrained, often in danger of dropping from the sublime to the ridiculous. Words flowed easily, the Germans were well schooled in eloquence. They felt solemn and reverent, tremendously serious, in the presence of their longed-for peoples' State. They attacked and avowed, were full of enthusiasm and hatred; indeed it was hatred that fired the enthusiasm of the barricade fighters. Berlin street poetry reflects plenty of hatred even after the victory, and the quick-witted Berliner also attacked with the keen weapons of satire all the loud-mouthed vauntings and last-minute convictions that were whirled to the top by the March events. It was in Berlin, where the old had been most fiercely attacked, that the first critical and sceptical voices were heard.

Now the parliament was to become a fact—but excitement was already being followed by reaction. Gervinus complains of this in his *Deutsche Zeitung*, the leading organ of Diet Reform, and warns the people not to let their energies slacken. Building-up had not ended; in fact it had been scarcely begun.

Heinrich von Gagern also spoke very pessimistially a few days before the convention of the Frankfort Parliament which was to bring him his greatest personal success.

People and systems, he complained, were so quickly used up in times of revolution; perhaps Germany would take a whole generation to calm down; republican and communistic ideas were spreading, the finest spirits were paralysed and intimidated.

The freedom movement of 1848 was the first great popular movement of the entire German peoples and constituted their country as a living member of a European movement; Germany was perhaps the most astonishing phenomenon of the age, for Europe had long since given up expecting Germany ever to show any will to unity and power, or that this ever could develop in the Central European complex of states and statelets. German freedom threatened the world of the German princes, even if at first only timidly and respectfully. German unity seemed likely to prove a threat to all Germany's neighbours. The National Movement of Liberation in 1813–15 had not spread over the whole of Germany; many West and South Germans stood aside and apart from it. German great powers and petty princes sacrificed the blood of the young German people with the ruthlessness of threatened egotism, upon the altars of their own power. The Students' League of Freedom, the Revolution of 1830 carried further a great deal of thought and awakened a great many; there were storms and martyrdoms, but no universal tremor, no shaking of the foundations of the old world. Only in 1848 was the outbreak universal. The

German political figure had arrived. A thousandfold created as literature, this figure now became flesh and blood, strong-willed, ready to risk everything, with all the good and evil qualities of revolutionary passion. The Germans had been such model subjects; now they were disrespectful, even insolent; there was libertinage of speech, manner, and way of life, usually deeply wounding to the older generation. They at once began to complain, as the elderly always do, of moral degeneration. With clearer vision than these reputables of the old school, we see boldness, strength, and individuality where they saw dare-devilry and impudence. No one would put in a defence of cruelty; but we can very well understand the spirit of these excesses. Pressure had been too strong. Youth in that pedagogic and pedantic fatherland had been obliged, above everything else, to hold its tongue. The authors were the first to rebel. Now the young men had their politics, and had every right to them. All the young spirits of Germany were in flux, animated as never before; students, young tradesmen, younger sons of the yeomanry, artisans, and workmen, even the serving-men organized themselves, formulated demands and chose their leaders; the new periodicals, clubs, and associations gave youth not only employment, but a meaning in life. Many had suddenly become important, many more were swollen with self-importance. It was easy to repeat catch phrases and spiritual independence is particularly rare during revolutions. Up to now in Germany everyone who had anything to do with government had usually been elderly, petrified, super-respectable. No one was more looked down upon than the poor devil who had no secure position. Now it was just these poor devils who made their voices heard; most of them were volunteers or on the barricades, they were not only prepared to shed their blood, they also wanted to speak and be heard, they wanted to count for something. Self-help by means of organization was one of the strongest driving forces of the age—many a mickle makes a muckle.

I

There were continued popular meetings, the people were taking shape and striving for experience. The people adopted the students' expressive "Philistine" and used it to decry a whole decrepit world which was being thrown out with an extra kick, lest it should once more return. "Down with the Aristocrats, down with the bureaucrats, down with the Philistines!" was the significant cry in Vienna. Political youth saw the Philistine everywhere, but especially in the solid citizen, the middle-class man who had accommodated himself willingly and respectfully to the aristocratic-bureaucratic system.

Political discussion, up to this time had been full of dignity, especially in its official and semi-official aspects. Now the people showed that they possessed quite another eloquence. Dialect seasoned speech, as it had long since enlivened the stage. Nobles may have thought it vulgar; the money and title patriciate trembled for prestige and purse; but nothing could be altered. The mass was in movement in Germany for the first time. Long peace, censorship, material prosperity in the upper and part of the middle classes had lulled all German governments into such security that nobody had believed a simultaneous expression of unrest and the urge to freedom could be possible. Count Dönhoff, who was wise, said it was a rare thing in history to find the masses possessed so simultaneously, so deeply, and so violently by the same ideas. They were certainly ideas, the Fatherland was always choked to repletion with ideas; but a closer examination must reveal that many said—reaction—and meant hunger, said—Parliament—and meant rise of the oppressed, said—constitution—and meant decent work and a decent wage. A Darmstadt broadsheet, dated the day before the opening of the National Assembly on May 18th, spoke of the growing security, which was breaking down many a strong bulwark, since the majority of the people had no work and no belongings. The author, Dr. Knispel, proposed to institute a money collection, partly to be used in immediate relief, partly to create work, but principally to support emigration. This was the voice of truth behind all the mountains of paper, the excited shouts, the rejoicing and the processions. Men were cheap and money dear. Whoever could pay for a banner had only to plant it somewhere to be sure of adherents. As long as the Revolution gave the people something to eat, it was popular. When most of the new men merely began giving the old institutions a new coat of paint, people began to ask what all the fuss had been about. A real new Germany could not be built up thus. The new masses in Germany demanded something further. They were the power, the future. These masses could be led, they could be welded into unity. They could be beaten down, starved out, by means of all the superior military-political, and economic potencies of which the Revolution had left the old powers in possession; but even the mightiest individual could not again destroy the entity of these masses as a social and political power.

PART II

PART II

## CHAPTER EIGHT

# THE BEGINNING OF THE FRANKFORT PARLIAMENT

THE GERMAN people acclaimed and reverenced their National Assembly of 1848 as a Goddess of Liberty, only to let this goddess die a year later "like a street woman in the gutter"—the expression used by Donoso Cortes, Spanish diplomatist, in a speech on the European situation on January 30, 1850. It was a bitter word for a bitter truth.

Since medieval days, England has strung her history on a chain of parliaments; some of them were weaker, some stronger; people, parties, and the institutions themselves were transformed—but the idea of the parliament was something sacred and remained impregnable in the changing flux of history. France's great National Assembly of 1789 stood at the head of a chain of representative assemblies of the French people which were in turn stormy, sanguinary, fettered, and intimidated, violated, disrupted, admired, and respected; for here the French people's greatest passion was unleashed, here only their final political destiny fulfilled. A politician must become a parliamentarian in order to become a statesman.

Germany has only had one German parliament worthy of the name. Only once, right up to the present day, did freely chosen representatives of *all* the German peoples come together in one chamber; only once did this people, ripened in spirit to a political communal will, find a parliamentary form; they found it only to burst it apart, and themselves be broken anew upon the ruins.

This alone serves to make of the Frankfort National Assembly a thing unique in history. It was as though the Germans must be unfortunate in their parliamentarism. We know that the German parliament had been the highest goal of political hopes for a generation past; this one comprehensive representative body of the whole nation was to bring release from the particularism of the diets of the separate states, comparable in dignity, authority, historical power only with the idea of the Emperor of all Germans which was now to be realized—perhaps—indeed, quite certainly—by its means. The nation, having attained its political majority only needed, so people thought, to make its voice heard, in order to create a constitution, elect its head and perfect Germany's history—the nation alone could compel even the unwilling, for she would be more sovereign than the sovereign—the flock should have the shepherd again, as Max von Schenkendorf had once sung.

This great hour had now come—through the majority of the nation. But at the very moment when the German parliamentary idea was realized in the Frankfort National Assembly, parliamentarism was chosen in Austria and Prussia as the medium for building up the new State; the already existing diets of the petty states received a new impetus and new tasks. Here, too, a new form was demanded for a new people with new aims; here too it was expected that there would be development or perhaps something new created by constitutional bodies. The whole country fell into an intoxication of elections; there were not so many parliamentarians in existence as were suddenly demanded. Things had gone slowly enough, now they were suddenly to go quickly. The parliament idea split itself up through too much application. Germany had suffered scarcity for decades—now she had a glut overnight. In former times the German people had produced too many princes, too many nobles, too many cities; this richness of production always meant confusion. Now again next to the Frankfort Parliament came the Austrian Reichstag, the Prussian National Assembly and the manyheaded parliaments of the petty states. There was talk now, discussions, party politics, constitutions designed, paragraphs disputed, tradition sharply criticized; and the new things must first be put on paper with much exercise of common sense, culture, patriotism, arrogance, ambition, and the momentary class interest. The old authorities seemed to be dead and the new were not quite alive.

The greatness and the weakness of the time is nowhere more tangibly expressed than in the Frankfort Parliament. As an ideal it stood alone and supreme, all-embracing, imbued with power, its members borne aloft by an overwhelming popular feeling, filled with their incomparable mission, inspired by the sacredness of the nation's hour of birth—yet the Parliament was from that very hour an object of dispute and doubt, its work stultified by the jealousy and competition of the individual states, itself forced to accumulate power and thus restless and irritable, residing in the most German part of Germany, and just on that account somewhat estranged from the centres where real decisions were taken; therefore this proud and courageous body suffered the truly German fate of having been strongest as an idea, and of growing ever feebler as its work and being came nearer to realization.

It belongs to the being of a revolution that many of the most reactionary are apt to discover that there is a progressive side to their nature; and just as much does it belong to the being of the counter-revolution that many rebels discover a conservative element in themselves. Herein lies one of the charms, but also the limitations, of all party history. The revolutionary possibilities had been so great in March and April that the conservative masses, which were now in movement, trembled before a possible repetition. They had to make up their minds to take active repulsive measures, but they could only ensure success by adapting themselves to the prevailing taste. An example of this was the leader of the Electoral Hessian Reaction, Vilmar, a Marburg schoolmaster, popularly known, with true folk wit, as "Muckerpapst" (Pope Stiggins). Now that the democratic stream was in full flood, he became very accommodating in his paper, the *Hessische Volksfreund* and declared that he had always wanted what was best in liberalism and the German national idea. The old student leaguer's piety was no doubt sincere; his fanaticism as coarse as it was sly, his way of casting suspicion on everyone whose opinions differed from his own, and trying to injure them in public opinion, certainly had a very earthly tinge. None the less, Vilmar had the courage of his opinions, whereas the Hessian nobility kept remarkably quiet in their country seats and waited for better times. The most influential Liberal in Electoral Hesse was Friedrich Oetker, lawyer and publicist, a lively, irrepressible fighter, full of the optimism of his day and borne up by it. His battles with Winkelblech during the elections to the Frankfort National Assembly, in the People's Committee, in the German Free Thought League and in the Workmen's League are a very characteristic struggle between the reform constitutionalism and the social-revolutionary idea, a conflict which had in it the very being of the German Revolutionary movement from the point of view of party history.

Liberalism before the Revolution had been in Germany largely a matter of education without any declared class character. The world of the academicians was, apart from most of the theologians of both churches, overwhelmingly "liberal," that is, humanitarian, rationalistic, yet bound to the existing scheme of things, however avowedly devoted to "Progress." A titled officer and gentleman farmer in East Prussia, an export merchant on the Rhine, a Silesian manufacturer—a ministerial counsellor in Vienna—they could all count themselves Liberals. Liberals of this kind had been preaching reform for decades before the Revolution—but now in the face of the popular movement which had broken out with such power, they seemed a little old-fashioned, clumsy, and pathetic. The mass of the Saxon middle classes, the rising lower orders, had quite other ideas. They found the much-praised historical development far too slow, they would not wait any longer. They had learned a different creed from the liberals, from the minority professors who had given them their education; determined free thinking, equality of political rights, the chance to rise and develop themselves—in other words, democracy, such as the English, American, French Revolutions had ostensibly or really produced, a free popular state. This demand everywhere permeated the election movement of April and May 1848— particularly defined in Saxony and very impressively in the Prussian cities.

In Prussia elections took place simultaneously for the Frankfort National Assembly and in Berlin for the Prussian National Assembly. This imparted a great liveliness to election activity, brought about a division of forces which did much harm. Most of the famous figures in the United Diets wanted to go to Frankfort—they were well known, they understood how to cope with the spirit of the time, and therefore appeared politically more definite than they were, and in Frankfort they appeared Prussian and particularistic and therefore more conservative than was desirable. Party organization was hardly developed and there was therefore no thought for successors. Men did not vote for parties, but for personalities. Usually there was a great shortage and thus men who already had some authority such as officials, judges, clergy, teachers of every kind, had the best chances. Anyone who was unknown must call attention to himself by the violence of his language.

Thus we have the remarkable result that the famous men, experienced, moderate, cautious, fettered to this and that, were sent to Frankfort—to Berlin the younger men, whose time now seemed to have come, the radicals, the hotspurs. It was plain that there were two Prussias—a Prussia consisting of provinces with historic, in part good German, traditions, and a Prussia bent on building up an energetic, modern, logical state for itself.

The task for the party leaders was to set the masses in movement and therefore to exert political influence; this was relatively easy in the cities. The clubs in Prussia were at first nothing more than workshops for turning out obedient candidates. The candidate, the respected local worthy, with family and social influence, and often naïve self-importance, became an important phenomenon of the time. Working men and lower middle class determined club and journalistic life during the election period, setting it at the level of their own taste and education. The notabilities, professional men, and more especially the nobles, kept well in the background.

In Austria the election battle was waged on the question of the "Anschluss," of the relation of Austria as a State to the Germany of the future. Only the Viennese democrats supported the idea of a strong central power in Frankfort. Moderate circles, especially in the provinces, could not imagine a Germany which was not under Vienna's leadership. Unconditional submission to the will of the Frankfort Parliament would have been considered political suicide. Young Giskra, for example, passionately combated the idea of the Staatenbund. The hearers rejoiced, but the majority then elected "good Austrians," people with black and yellow hearts under their black-red-and-golden scarves. In Bohemia voting either did not take place at all or incompletely. The Catholic people were told that Frankfort's aim was to evangelize them. In Moravia the peasants said that in Frankfort they were going to depose the Austrian Emperor and set up another in his stead. Palacky and Hawlicek were working for their federalistic, slavonic Austria; they felt that this was Austria's mission. In the Frankfort election they saw the welcome opportunity to complete their denial of old Austria.

How violently Count Auersperg (Anastasius Grün) was opposed by the Slovenes! "Slowenja," the society of Slovenian students in Vienna issued a call to the Krain Slovenes: they should refuse to vote for the German National Assembly and protest against official orders to do so. Auersperg tried to make things clear in a pamphlet "To My Slovenian Brothers."

The Prague Slav Congress was also intended as a counter-weight to the Frankfort Parliament—the Czech national radicals wanted to use it as the organ of their Austro-Slavism, naturally together with the Viennese dynasty. Their plans harmonized quite well with those of the Gagern-Dahlmann reform party. It was the "good Austrians" who were the losers. One of them, Helfert, complained: "In Vienna's Teutonian circles Frankfortianism reigns and the thoughtless crowd gabbles it after them. Has it ever happened in all history that the capital of a great realm should move heaven and earth to become the provincial capital of another country?"

The elections for the Frankfort Parliament reveal a good part of its history. When at last it assembled on May 18th, doubts, contradictions, problems were forgotten for a moment. Frankfort and the best elements of Germany rejoiced: they believed that they could now bring home the harvest of the Revolution. This educated generation had read enough historical descriptions of the English and French revolutions and thought they had learned something from them. Too much learning, as so often in Germany, was accompanied by lack of fire. The old laws were unbroken; states and princes were still alive, the achievements of March were reforms, concessions —borne on the shoulders of a body of men who used the traditional power of army and officialdom to protect public peace and order against a social-revolutionary will to further progress. When the Frankfort Parliament met, the counter-Revolution had already begun, almost unnoticed. This turning of the tables filled the life of the first German National Assembly with a contradiction which it was never able to overcome. The parliament was the proud daughter of the people, the national will, the sovereign of sovereigns. For the first time in centuries there was a purely German organ of opinion; should not everything bow to its voice? It was the voice of the free German future. Forty German princes, forty German bureaucracies, the whole mixture of self-possessed, touchy provincialism, would it all melt away at the will of the German parliament? Could it be welded into one folk, one State, with one national body of representatives? The Frankfort Parliament must be revolutionary, if it were to reach its goal, but it must make use of all counter-revolutionary means, if it were to complete its work in peace; it must demand obedience from the German royal states, whose powers secured its existence. The idea of terrorism was foreign to the German nature. The Revolution's intellectual leaders wanted everything to be legitimate; they were too timid to want to intimidate others. They abhorred bloodshed. They wanted nothing more than to direct the lust of battle into publicistic discussion, into parliamentary debate. This was a very advanced frame of mind, but it ran far ahead of existing institutions and the way of life of the great masses. Princes, nobility, and country folk still had a certain respect for revolutionaries who burnt castles and struck down opponents, but they had no understanding and no serious fear of revolutionaries who made speeches and fought their battles on paper.

The expectations which many Germans set upon the Frankfort Parliament were so general and so completely comprehensive that they could not be fulfilled either completely or quickly. The enthusiasm with which the National Assembly was greeted did not at first allow any doubts to become loud; the newness of the Parliament and the manner in which it was put together gave—it was felt—the best guarantee for the solution of the German problem. Most of the members expected the sittings to last for some months. If the situation had been more favourable for the Parliament in April, it was still not unfavourable: Austria was breaking up, Prussia forced into a national and liberal policy, foreign countries quite taken up with their own affairs—the authority of the National Assembly overshadowed everything.

Three hundred and thirty members walked solemnly in procession from the Kaisersaal of the Römer over the Römer hill and the Neue Kräme to the northern door of St. Paul's church, bare-headed, radiating hope and joy, reverence streaming out of them from within, in accordance with the nature of this worthy and credulous generation. There was a trace in the air of this golden Frankfort May morning of the sacred breath of the Wars of Liberation, of the dark incense of Roman Imperialism; but stronger was the storm-wind of the German future.

Not even half of the members who belonged to the National Assembly marched to the Paulskirche on that day. But the eight hundred and thirty-one men, members and later summoned substitutes who were elected, of course never all sat simultaneously in Parliament. The average attendance during the first months was between four hundred and five hundred; in winter a number of Austrians arrived, whom no one had seen before, from the semi-German districts, and increased the figures.

The Frankfort Parliament was an assembly of notabilities in which the lower classes of the public were most inadequately represented. Minkus, colonist, and dealer from Silesia, was the only real peasant; a remarkable man, communist agitator with Polish mother-tongue whose propaganda in his election district of Rosenberg and Kreuzburg was later to stir up tumults and refusals to pay taxes. No working-man sat in St. Paul's church; the small citizen class were represented by four master-craftsmen, eleven lower officers of the port and customs administration, inspectors, estate stewards; both among farmers and merchants (forty-six), the upper classes were greatly in the majority. There were a number of wholesale traders from Hamburg and Bremen, several bankers, various manufacturers, and owners of printing shops and breweries. Among the sixty representatives of agriculture there was only one tenant farmer; all the others were owners of large and middling estates. There were owners of vineyards and mines, North German and Silesian gentlemen farmers, a count from Tyrol, and numbers of titled landowners from all parts of Germany. The total number of representatives of commercial professions may not have exceeded one hundred and forty; the group of academicians was far more imposing; there were forty-nine university professors and doctors, fifty-seven professors and other teachers of higher schools, one hundred and fifty-seven judges and procurators, sixty-six lawyers, twenty mayors, one hundred and eighteen members of the higher administration, three diplomats, five librarians, eighteen physicians, sixteen Evangelical, sixteen Catholic, and one German-Catholic clergymen, forty-three writers, editors, and publicists—all in all, five hundred and sixty-nine academicians! If we reckon the booksellers (six) and officers (sixteen) among them, and when we remember that among those without a profession (one hundred and sixteen), a number certainly had enjoyed a higher education, then there must have been over six hundred.

The Frankfort Parliament was too much of a university and too little of a political stock exchange. It was no true reflection of the social strata in Germany at the time, but shows that the representatives were not elected according to their rank or profession, or party grouping, but according to their personal individual reputation. Thus we have the remarkable fact that this Parliament, chosen according to the principle of universal representation, greatly resembled in its consistency the French Chamber of Deputies of the July Monarchy, chosen according to census election.

Heinrich von Gagern has gone down to history as the classic

president of the Frankfort Parliament; his successor, Eduard Simson was certainly his superior in practical leadership; no one ever mastered the mass of members with such polished mildness, clarity, and calmness as he could command. But in Heinrich von Gagern the National Assembly beheld the best of itself, humanly and politically. His dignity was their dignity, his eloquence was theirs, he was the most imposing fulfilment of the time, and therefore unable to lead it on beyond itself. His presidency of the National Assembly certainly was the actual apex of his political life. As a truly political president, elevated by a programme and in the eyes of the public, himself the incorporation of that programme, only a small part of which was his own, Gagern naturally attracted the enmity, objective, and also personal, of all opponents of this programme; the radical element very quickly discovered what was lacking in this personality, his want of real originality, his dependence upon others, which he concealed by sensitive self-reliance and superior solemnity, his immovable manner, but ill-suited to comprehend anything alien; these insufficiencies only became plainly visible when he had become president of the Reichsministerium. As President of the Parliament he had the best personal opportunity of displaying these winning qualities to which he owed so much: the bewitching modesty with which he would beg the assembly's pardon for minute offences, thus satisfying his tremendous pride, the genuineness and purity of his feelings displayed so movingly in his condemnation of the excesses of the September Revolution; the warmth and depth of patriotism in him which found mighty expression in the boom of his deep and powerful voice.

The first great debates in the Chamber were to perfect a development towards the political middle-way, the way of the liberal-parliamentary reform party. The election tests caused Franz Raveaux to open up a question on May 19th, in the formalistic shell of which the greatest political problem of the day was encased. We know what it was: Prussia had at the same time held elections for the Frankfort Parliament and for its own National Assembly. Several members had been elected to both bodies: the Prussian government demanded a decision as to which of the two they intended to belong. Raveaux now took the standpoint that the Frankfort Parliament should declare that these members should have the right to both assemblies. Frankfort was thus to turn against Berlin, was to establish a superiority of position from the very beginning. Raveaux felt that the Frankfort Assembly should create a general constitution for the whole country. The individual German parliaments were to await the result and put off constitutional questions for the present. Seventeen amendments were put in on May 22nd; the plenitude of brains produced a plenitude of ideas; the minority demanded immediate discussion and the passing of a resolution; but unfortunately the majority succeeded in securing the appointment of a specially elected committee to deal with the matter. Parliament had a tendency to over-thoroughness and tediousness which it was difficult to correct. There was a great division of opinion on the Raveaux motion. The men of the Right, led by G. von Vincke, wished to set it aside, trusting, as they said, that all the German states would alter any point in their constitution which was later found to be in contradiction to the German constitution. This was certainly extremely trusting. The men of the Left, Schaffrath, Kolb, Moritz Hartmann, Robert Blum, wanted clarity; the mere fact that so many individual parliaments were concerned did not look like goodwill on the part of the other governments. They wished to see the "one and only" authority of the Pre-Parliament once more expressly confirmed. Finally, Werner of Coblenz framed a motion which put the will of the Left in a more cautious and agreeable form. "The National Assembly, as organ proceeding from the will and election of the German people, to found the unity and political liberty of Germany, declares that all resolutions passed by isolated German constitutions, which do not tally with the

Constitution now to be founded, may only be considered valid in so far as they do tally, having no regard to their previous validity."

There were few men in the Parliament with so much political instinct as Franz Raveaux; his French descent was palpable, not only in his slight, dark-eyed figure; he had inborn parliamentary tact, was at once fine and keen, open-hearted, and discreet. He saw which way feeling was tending and with all the power of his will to statesmanship preferred a useful victory to a defeat for the sake of obstinate defence of a principle. He supported the Werner motion, and sacrificed the literal "one and only." Both Right and Left now found that their point of view had won the victory; only a few still fought; the overwhelming majority now united in an enthusiastic declaration: the National Assembly declared itself to be sovereign above sovereigns; it must create the constitution, and all separate constitutions were to be revised in accordance with it. In the face of this impotence of the governments there were two courses open to the National Assembly: either to take the power so energetically into its own hands by way of revolution that the governments would bow to its will and accept its constitution, or to ally itself with one or more of the larger governments. It did both, one after another, then both at once. Thus it cemented its own unhappy fate.

Robert Blum made the first attempt to collect the men of the Left, first in the "Holländische Hof," then in the "Deutsche Hof;" the men of the Right soon met in the "Steinerne Haus." The Centre, numerically the strongest, but in their opinion least clear and uniform, met for their deliberations in the "Mainlust." The Left felt a special need to confer and this came to the tactical situation. Democratic and social-revolutionary ideas were only represented by a minority in the Frankfort Parliament, the most numerous party was that of liberal reform. The Left's only chance to gain respect and influence was by unity and a strong fighting front. The acceptance of the Werner Motion was celebrated at the "Deutsche Hof" inn as a victory; but some of the Left divined the defeat that lay concealed in this victory. This group fell away from Robert Blum whom they thought too much a man of compromise; the extreme Left strayed back to the "Holländische Hof" and soon to the "Donnersberg"; they called themselves the Democratic Party and represented the decided progressive movement along the revolutionary path already trodden; thus an accumulation of power in the Parliament, concentration of the political executive and military powers in Frankfort, universal arming of the people, an oath to be taken ratifying the March victories, a German republic. Zitz and von Trützschler, Brentano, Ludwig Simon, Fröbel, Professor Zimmermann and Arnold Ruge were leaders and chief speakers at the "Donnersberg." The "Deutscher Hof" remained rather amorphous in the early months; it was a permanent popular meeting rather than a limited club; its broadly conceived democratic and social-political programme still left open a possibility of "democratic monarchy." It was not actually organized as an institution until October. Next to Blum, Karl Vogt, Eisenstuck, Rösler of Öls, Kolb and Schüler, Löwe of Calbe, Nauwerck and Rossmässler were the leading spirits of the "Deutscher Hof." Old Adam von Itzstein no longer took an active part.

Austria was passing through a bad period during these months; but her old art of government was still being put to lively use. Von Schmerling, the new member and envoy, took a lease of the "Socrates" lodge, charging the rent to the Austrian State, and so created a centre for the Austrian group, a formation which came into being exactly like that of the Left, in recognition of the fact that a minority must stick together and be cautious. Other conservative elements joined them; the evangelical Pastor Jürgens from Brunswick was probably the first who in a kind of pastoral officiousness tried to form a party of right thinking men in opposition to the

Left. Even at the presidential election he had opposed Robert Blum's views. The meetings in "Socrates" soon lost their national character, the Austrians of the Left no longer came. Prussians and other particularists appeared, clericals and the orthodox. This party demanded that the National Assembly should be agreed upon with the other governments; they opposed its every attempt to pass laws of its own and every incursion into executive powers. Their scepticism against the central majority was in fact just as justified as the opposition from the Left. The Left themselves mistrusted the loyalty of the governments and the Right put its trust in the powers actually in the hands of the governments and on the enduring strength of their particularization. The Prussians von Radowitz and Vincke were fully at one on this point with Detmold of Hanover and von Beisler and von Lassaulx from Bavaria. What really separated them from the Austrians would not become clear until later. These men also sought satisfactory reform, but they stood the whole time with one foot and half a heart outside the National Assembly.

Thus the real victory of the March Revolution sat in the Centre of the Frankfort Parliament—upstart men of the day, old veterans of the battle for unity and freedom who had now at last achieved office, younger fighters and admirers, ambitious, moderate by nature, of a practical turn of mind, willing to undertake positive tasks and eager to grasp at rapid success; both important and personally and politically insignificant men came together in the Centre party. They were a broad and optimistic party, containing future ministers of the realm and nameless camp followers—a great number of the latter, who are a burden to every parliamentary body and yet have influence upon it in its actual work, as the mass of listeners whose voices count when the vote is taken. Between the decided Right and the declared Left there was a clear oppositional of mutually exclusive ideals of state censorship and philosophy. Between the Centre and the wing parties and within the centre itself there were the intimate oppositions of individual views and tactical differences; here, then, the exchange of ideas must broaden and become objective, and just on that account it could become energetic, embittered, and endless. The clearest line of cleavage in the whole National Assembly was that through the Centre; the Right Centre did not acknowledge unreservedly the principle of the sovereignty of the people, and the principle of the exclusive right of the Frankfort Parliament to create the German Constitution; but the Left Centre had no doubts on these points. The Right Centre deliberately postponed as long as possible a definite statement of policy, in order to unite as many members as possible under the pressure of its leading names. Dahlmann and Droysen were among them, Bassermann and Mathy, Georg Beseler and von Beckerath, Heckscher and Hergenhahn, Lette and Jürgens, Welcker and Simson, Waitz and Zachariä—a great many professors, many big names and clever heads, but no real leader —Heinrich von Gagern, as president, belonged to no party. Mevissen, working with Droysen, gave the first impulse to the union of this central body, this community of workers in the spirit of the old liberal reform movement, respecting the "sound territorial rights" and filled with a purpose, not only to create the constitution, but also to make at once a beginning of practical government "in agreement with the goodwill of princes and people." In the Right Centre, which, in accordance with its place of assembly, soon came to be known as the Casino party, the particular characteristics were represented which were to create the fame and seal the fate of the Frankfort Parliament, the urge to build up in faith and confidence, an urge born of learning and thought, a confidence at once self-confident and childishly trusting, certain that everything would turn out for the best, even though it were the final synthesis. Germans are not very good at destruction; even in revolution, they prefer to form connections with the old and develop from it, they would rather add an annexe and a new story than rebuild from the ground up. Even when their common sense applauds the new, they cling, instinctively and with reverence, to something old; their creative work must be bound up in some way with tradition. If no tradition exists, it must be dug up from somewhere or other. Energetic rejection of the tradition wounds the German's sense of propriety, he is warmed and won by clever leadership based on the old familiar usages. Here was the foundation of the Casino Party's power and significance; it was the group of the Conservative Revolutionaries; here, at least in idea, authority was reconciled to freedom. Schmerling, Gagern's clever opponent, also belonged to it; here there was time to wait, one could be a tribal particularist among patriots of the realm and a believer in the government among exponents of freedom, without at once acquiring an evil reputation as a reactionary.

The Left Centre became sharply divided from the Right Centre during the battles for central power; they took their name from the "Württemberger Hof" and in the accident of this name there lay something of a deeper meaning. For in the Right Centre, North German quietude and common sense had the upper hand, in the Left Centre, temperament and individual opinion, especially among the Franks and Swabians; there was much talent here, much adaptability, it was a young man's party, its members felt that they were the coming men and were ready to make mock of the caution urged by the Casino party. Their fundamental claims were for unreserved sovereignty of the people, but monarchy in the constitutional form (called, according to the language of the day, the parliamentary form)—the power of the individual states was to be limited in the interests of the existence of the Federal State. The idea of parliamentary monarchy separated them from the Left, the idea of sovereignty of the people from the Right.

The men of the "Württemberger Hof" were the least united, their meetings the stormiest. Among them were the most divisions and separate cliques, for here the convinced republican met the common-sense monarchist, those of the Right and of the Left whose world had crumbled, the immortal parliamentarians who sought to turn the necessity of conscience into the virtue of tactics. It was also the right place for the moderate, those bound ethically and rationally to the republican idea, such as Gabriel Riesser or Friedrich Theodor Vischer. The Left Centre had a good deal of arrogance of thought, ambition, and parliamentary activity. Here party compulsion was attempted for the first time, here the small chieftains reigned as well as the chosen leaders, here political views were filed and polished, and in so doing the real contact with the popular movement was lost. The turn for quiet historical culture of a professional origin which dominated the Right Centre, corresponded in the Left to a tendency to many-sided intellectuality. The men of the Left Centre made the most brilliant speeches in the debates, but they were so uncertain in their resolutions that Parliament's work was rendered more difficult. We shall later have more to do with the further development of parties in the National Assembly; it is an essential part of its history and the preliminary to an understanding of its political activity.

It must not be thought that this fundamental division of the Frankfort Parliament into Right Centre and Left had already crystallized clearly in these first weeks. There were types of members; those who held it absolutely necessary to form parties, those who condemned them on principle and those who were sometimes here, sometimes there, who joined the party of a strong speaker on a certain question but left it again on another occasion. The actual political figures of the assembly worked for enforced party unity as preliminary condition of any practical work—but they were a minority. Most of them felt better when they were more at liberty, voted as they happened to feel and were momentarily impressed, took part in the numerous ephemeral group formations and then found their way back to the great Casino mass party. Parliamentary discipline only developed gradually. In its first few weeks the National Assembly gave itself to the sheer happiness of being in existence, basked in the greatness of its task and was joyous and carefree as befitted the atmosphere of Frankfort and the bright idealistic optimism of the revolutionary summer.

The flood of speeches and motions which soon set in was a characteristic of this careless rapture as of the "doctrinal" tendency, the "pedantry" of the Germans once deplored by Jacob Grimm in a speech in the Paulskirche as a degeneration of their businesslike and orderly basic virtues. But such a warning, also repeated by others, had no lasting effect. To be sure the final business report was accepted as it stood on May 29th with the reserve that proposals for alterations should be discussed as soon as at least thirty members supported them. The order of business, a fair piece of work, built up on a knowledge of South German and foreign parliamentary usages, did not however render a rapid and undisturbed business procedure possible. Often enough the members failed to agree on fundamental conceptions, such as on the difference between the simple order of the day and one devoted to a special end. The decisive factor was that no business procedure, no business leadership could ever have been equal to dealing with the mass of proposals offered. The urge to express opinion in public, so long suppressed in the nation, now broke loose in full force. Only a few held back and were distinguished by their very silence—such as Gervinus and Rümelin.

The humiliating events of the Danish War, the flight of the German merchant ships before the Danish warships in German and Russian harbours, led to a movement in Germany for the creation of a fleet, which was one of the strongest emotions of the day. Fleet or Marine committees were formed all along the coast, but also inland; the Press was full of articles—and Diet, Seventeen Committee and Fifty Committee rivalled one another in manifestations for a German War Navy. The "Commission for Germany's Maritime Affairs," set up by the

Fifty Committee, announced a Marine Congress at Hamburg on May 31st. Here a Ministry of Marine was demanded. Projects and false hopes trod on each other's heels. There was talk of help from America, from Holland against Denmark; of plans to blow up the blockading Danish warships with barrels of gunpowder; to purchase warships in England and the United States. The Hamburg wholesale merchant Godeffroy and Captain Gutschow appeared in London on behalf of the Hamburg Committee for the Foundation of a German Marine, to buy ships for the German fleet. All they could find good enough were three large new warships—each costing between £35,000 and £50,000. They also enquired about cannon. In Hamburg a first German warship was on the stocks, in Bremen and Lübeck merchant ships were being turned into substitute ships of war. The young German national feeling nowhere showed such a peculiar mixture of strength and weakness as in the fleet question. Anyone who wanted to make a quick reputation for himself and become popular, took up this question—he could achieve fame overnight, as Wilhelm Jordan was to discover.

At the discussion on June 14th, there was a feeling of unity in Parliament such as was not demonstrated again at any later date. Only Wiesner criticized the preliminary work of the committee as insufficient for such a far-reaching proposal and Schlöffel, the Silesian, found that the people, sunk to proletarian level, could not have such burdens laid upon them. It was also pointed out that all German State funds were exhausted. Eisenstuck called attention to an important point: the National Assembly was prepared to grant moneys; but where was the Central Executive that would manage them in expert and responsible fashion? Thus the fleet question was politically bound up with the problem of the central power; in its double character as political matter and technical financial problem it made the rapid and clear development of these State matters doubly urgent. The National Assembly resolved almost unanimously that the sum of six million gulden should be granted, with the reserve that its spending be in the hands of the future central power. It was good that not only more or less expert speeches were heard upon this point, but that such a popular matter of armaments should become a spur to national activity.

Heinrich von Gagern was one of those men who believe what they say; he could more readily be charged with lack of acuteness than lack of openness. Gagern, as we know, wished, like Dahlmann and the others, to found the new Federal constitution on Prussia, not on Austria; he wished to demand much of Prussia in order to receive much; and he now resolved to yield to the feeling of the moment and secure the position of Vicar of the Empire for the Austrian Archduke. He did not perceive that in so doing he was building up the worst barrier possible in the way of himself and his friends. A directorate, even if royal or partly royal, was always easy to dominate, to over-ride; one could dissolve it in part and thus dissolve it wholly; but an archduke of the house of Habsburg-Lorraine, the popular youngest brother of the last Germanic Emperor, who had been crowned in this very Frankfort? Heinrich von Gagern, as president, knew his National Assembly: the Left wanted *one* man who should have the Executive in his hands, the Right wanted several princes, the Left wanted an election; through the Assembly itself, the Right wished an appointment by way of the governments. Only one possibility remained, that the Parliament should elect a Royal personage whose personality was so strong that the governments must be ready to give assent before they were asked. It was this position which drove Heinrich von Gagern to his memorable "bold stroke." The expression was coined by Mathy. Gagern's appearance on June 24th in the National Assembly was an event, the most important in his and the Assembly's career.

His seriousness, his authority, his slow manner of speaking, seeming always to be searching for adequate expression, never held his audience as they did at this hour; he seemed the truest, most genuine, most authoritative administrator of the nation. He represented the "practical," as the best solution, and thus uttered two sentences which, also in their form, impressed themselves upon his contemporaries. "I am about to play a bold stroke and I tell you we must ourselves create the provisional central power." Hereby von Gagern set himself apart from the motion put by the majority of the committee, also from the Schoder proposal, and took the Left standpoint. The storm of enthusiasm which filled the St. Paul's Church after these words showed how willingly Parliament followed him.

Here their president, aristocrat, minister, one of the most highly-placed leaders of the movement, spoke as a tribune for the right of the people's organ to create the executive for itself. Gagern had not demanded the setting aside of the governments as a principle; he saw no other way to make practical progress. Popular sovereignty should have its own way—but to choose a Prince! Gagern showed that the majority wished for only one man, but that no private personality could take office under such circumstances, and that a man of high position had been found who would be worthy of this highest place. "Not because he is a prince, but in spite of his being a prince." This was the other word of weight—applause came from all sides. After this day many people in Germany believed in the statesman Heinrich von Gagern. What Gagern stood for and accomplished was however, only the clever solution of a tactically difficult task, not the mastership of the greatest problem in German history. The governorship of Archduke Johann was satisfactory only in the moment of its accomplishment. Heinrich von Gagern's political life-work was to be broken precisely by this governorship. It was not Gagern, treading so unreservedly to the fore who was the victor, but Schmerling, who was always at work in the background. For him there could only be a Germany *with* Austria, and therefore the Vicar of the Empire must be none other than an Austrian archduke. Although he really was no lover of the sovereignty of the people he was of the opinion that this Vicar should be elected by Parliament; his position as Vicar would be untenable, he told the Prussian envoy, if the governments were to force him upon the Assembly. Precisely *because* he was a prince, he needed this authorization. Governments, he rightly held, who had set up an institution, could allow to disappear again, a Vicar of the Realm, elected by the National Assembly and recognized by the governments could call upon either of these political factors to assist him against the other. Now, said Schmerling to Usedom, the governments, Prussia at their head, their statesmen and generals, must enter the service of the new Federal executive and thus give it their bitter comment: "Even the Gagern brothers did not feel the difference that lies between the mediation of a little state and that of the Prussian Great Power."

## CHAPTER NINE

# THE GERMAN GREAT POWERS AND THE GOVERNMENT OF THE REALM

IN THE speech from the throne, with which Friedrich Wilhelm IV opened the Prussian National Assembly on May 22nd, he expressed regret that the internal affairs of Prussia had not permitted her to wait for the result of the Frankfort Parliament; the unity of Germany nevertheless remained his immovable goal.

Nothing in reality endangered the unity of Germany more than this rivalry of parliaments; Prussia and quite a number of Federal States, especially those dependent on Prussia, hastened in most marked fashion to create a counterweight to the Frankfort Parliament and so to hinder its character and influence, by summoning diet assemblies of their own. Robert Blum spoke publicly of these matters in Frankfort on May 27th, basing the speech on information provided by Römer, the Württemberg minister.

On May 23, 1815, Friedrich Wilhelm III had by cabinet order given out the most important of his various promises of a constitution; the opening of the Prussian National Assembly was therefore set for this day, for Friedrich Wilhelm IV was fond of commemoration days. But such a significant beginning did not bring the Berlin Parliament any good fortune. If the Frankfort National Assembly at any rate was able to leave its constitution as a legacy to a better German future and thus set itself the monument that was for ever to outlast its own mournful decline—the Berlin Parliament crashed on the rock of Old Prussia without leaving any such tangible and productive heritage. In Frankfort a homunculus of a State power must first be created in the hope that it might give birth to a living Realm in being. In Berlin, however, there was just that plenitude of earth-born, self-willed, self-sufficient political energy which was so sorely lacking in Frankfort. The Frankfort Assembly had far too much likeness to a political academy, the Berlin one to a political club. The German Parliament did not represent all Germany, nor the Prussian the complete Prussia. The lower classes were almost entirely lacking in Frankfort, the upper classes in Berlin. Both together would perhaps have made a good workable Upper and Lower House. As it was, similar and opposed, each worked for itself, they sought one another, suffered one another, were dependent upon one another and no love was wasted between them.

In the Frankfort Parliament there was something of the spirit of the Wars of Liberation and the great epoch of classic literature; thus in its majority it had a touch of the patrician. In all its verbosity and falsely-applied thoroughness this assembly had the rhythm of high German, or even universal tension. Beside it the Prussian Parliament seemed more trivial and provincial; it was not as if it had nothing of the spirit of the Prussian capital—indeed it may rather be said to have had too much; but circumstances had made it a bit second-class. In order to prove its right to existence, it laid undue stress on its purely Prussian aspect, so that Germany was almost forgotten and this Prussianism was informed with a spirit of progress not at all in accordance with the actual conditions of power. In the battle of the Prussian National Assembly there already lived something of the "Konflikt" period (1862–66), something of Prussian transformations which were not to be consummated until many years later. To have turned this royalist State into its very opposite was the hardest bit of political work accomplished in all Germany.

The actual composition of the Prussian National Assembly astonished all contemporary observers and the government most of all. It was an exact opposite to the United Provincial Diet. Aristocratic landowners, the chivalry of the Vereinigte Landtag, Prussia's characteristic estate, were only represented by three members; this was a plain answer to the refusal of the knights in the previous year to allow a few more members to the city and provincial boroughs. The majority of the nobles in the National Assembly were liberal and democratic, Count Reichenbach of Silesia an open Republican. But there were a large number of citizen landowners, and a still more real farmers. Among the sixty-eight farmers Silesia had sent nearly half, among them day labourers and cottagers, who could neither read nor write. It sometimes happened that when the second tests of voting in the house were taken, these people voted en masse contrary to their first vote. When the first maintenance moneys were paid out, several of them kissed the commissary's hand and declared without reserve that they earned far more here than at home—might the Landtag's life be long. There were about forty merchants and manufacturers in the National Assembly; but there were nearly as many artisans—twenty-eight. Small shopkeepers and assistants were also represented. There was no working man in the Assembly; the goldsmith Bisky was elected but never took his seat. The number of teachers—twenty-seven—far exceeded the number of learned men. Strikingly large was the number of clergy— fifty—many of them Catholics from the Rhineland, and among the Evangelicals they were mostly leaders of sects and enemies of orthodoxy. Lawyers also formed the main body of this parliament. One hundred officials of justice, fifty administrative officers, twenty-eight municipal officials, principally young men, the type of district judge, public prosecutor and syndic, a class which had always been oppressed by the antiquated bureaucracy and the nobles and which now came into its own; many of these men were gifted, with the talents of a publicist, a lawyer's readiness to plead, the self-possession conferred by superior knowledge, keen thinking, and ruthless political purpose. From the very beginning this National Assembly was regarded as a grave threat to the one already existing; in such a chamber, thought the Bavarian envoy, there could be no question of constitution of monarchy, aristocracy, etc. In any case, the National Assembly proved that a new Prussia was in existence which now confronted old Prussia. With dogged energy, a Prussia of the postulated State of Law, a democratic Prussia of the intellectuals, the Catholics and the Freethinkers, the middle and lower middle classes, men without family or influence, not at all a purely city folks' Prussia in opposition, but a movement of the whole folk of the hitherto oppressed, in which all classes were represented except the working men.

As in Frankfort, the Berlin Assembly at once divided into a Left, a Centre, and a Right. But whereas in Frankfort the personal influence and intellectual powers of the members were pretty evenly divided, increasing a little towards the moderate Centre, the Prussian Assembly showed a definite superiority in strength and originality in the Centre inclining to Left and in the Left. Even more than in Frankfort where cultural and social-philosophical points of view determined the formation of parties, division in Berlin was entirely according to views on the question of the Constitution. The decided Left wished to see a one-chamber system according to strict parliamentary doctrines on the basis of the sovereignty of the people whereby the only possible place left for a monarch would be the republican presidential chair. The majority of these men were in fact republicans, at any rate, in principle. Their strongest leader was Waldeck: he was a personality of rare power and most genuine integrity of mind, the finest type of German Higher Court judge, stern and warm-hearted, serious and upright, a Catholic Westphalian and not to be shaken in either respect, in faith or in local patriotism, once known as the peasant king on account of his great understanding of the earth-born class, from which he had himself so obviously sprung. He was well-schooled in communal self-administration and therefore more experienced in practical things than many of his party. Waldeck was in no way a frosty pedant: he had worked his way to democracy, doggedly and determinedly, as must a man of his origin and his pious attachments; he believed in the free peoples' State as fulfilment of the possibilities of mortal life with just the same certainty as he accepted his Church's doctrines of salvation. A pure fire burned in this already elderly man which was to kindle many others; it plunged him into defeats and politically impossible situations, for his pride was greater than his instinct for the common realities of high and almighty politics. It was the more tasteless for the leaders of Prussian reaction to attempt to charge this thoroughly reputable man with being a secret Ultramontane or, later, a conspirator in favour of the Red terror, and thus to attempt to discredit him and ruin his career.

If Waldeck was the representative orator of the decided Left, Johann Jacoby preferred and did well his work as organizer, influencing opinion and representing Parliament's purpose in the commissions; when he was beaten by a few votes by Eduard Simson, when standing as Königsberg's candidate for Frankfort, he threw himself with the vigour of wounded ambition into work for Prussia: he was a man of principles, whose word cut sharp as a knife, a cold logician, whose ruthlessly analytical mind reduced the rich variety of State life to the poverty and rigidity of a Spinoza-like mathematical formula. He had great significance as inspirer and keeper of the truths, but, for a leader and creator he was too inelastic and too isolated. The third leader of the decided Left was the highly-gifted public prosecutor Temme, a tough, hearty fellow, not so dignified as Waldeck, not so hard as Jacoby, much more a type of the times than these two, courageous, well-informed, full of enjoyment of his power to irritate the mighty and uprightly, ready to take all evil personal consequences. The much-admired popular orator Jung, one of the strongest demagogic talents in Berlin, Berends, owner of a printing office, Stein, school teacher from Silesia, d'Ester from the Rhineland—these also belonged to the influential men of the Hotel Mylius circle, where the Decided Left assembled.

Contrasted with so much talent and temperament, the decided Right in the National Assembly seemed quite small and poor. Vincke and Lichnowsky were in Frankfort; for a man like Bismarck-Schönhausen there was no such thing as a seat in Parliament after the March Revolution. The good Greifswald professor and director of the agricultural college at Eldena, Eduard Baumstark, bored the Assembly with his dull lecture-like speeches, livened up by all-too-modest jokes, as infallibly as August Reichensperger bored them with his dry lawyer-like pleadings; such men were of no use to the actual reactionary powers in Prussia and they were of no advantage to Camphausen's March ministry since their influence, whether used in support or in opposition, was nil. The weakening of the Right was one of the reasons for the split in the Centre. The Centre was truly the party of the day, the party of the March achievements. Its members were ready to work honestly at the realization of a Prussian constitutional State and believed nothing more was necessary for achieving this purpose than a loyal and homogeneous government. But this was not the only promise that was not fulfilled. The Centre was not united as to the goal; just as in Frankfort the decisive frontier cut through the midst of this party which as a closed block might have been able to enforce a course of quiet development. The Left Centre was honestly parliamentary, as much opposed to hidden absolutism as to a Republican form of state; the Right Centre also agreed to these general aims but after the fashion of the Old Liberals they claimed the right to exercise a moderating, soothing influence. This right section, consisting of thirty to forty members, was in a position, owing to the accident of the partition of mandates, to throw its weight upon one side or another and determine the most important decisions of an assembly of four hundred and two members either in a more authoritative or a more democratic sense. Their intellectual head, the later president of the National Assembly, Hans Victor von Unruh, was certainly an honest and courageous man; he was to have enough opportunity to display his bold convictions. But for the destiny of the Assembly, these "ifs" and "buts," this manysided, liberal, yet inwardly conservative manner, this supposed appeal only to reason and decency from case to case as need arose, without the invaluable party stencil, was fatal. The Right Centre, also called the Centre proper, the party of the Hotel de Russie was in this point the prerunner of the later National Liberals. The personal opposition between Unruh and Rodbertus, the Leader of the Left Centre evidently did much to further this development. The way Unruh speaks in his reminiscences goes to prove this. Unruh was a trained lawyer, sober and objective as a bureaucrat, dry and steady as a politician. But Rodbertus, the remarkable economic thinker, heir to old possessions, but self-possessed creator of new agricultural ways, a never satisfied, always battling fighter for social justice, had a personality full of colour and temperament, with diplomatic tact and always newly-proven power of mobile intellect, a man who attracted many strongly and naturally repelled others, but in whom that magic was at work without which no party can be formed. That the Left Centre, which in the main was his own creation, should bear him up to a position of responsibility or even obtain a ministerial post for him, seemed to him no more than natural. Ambition and talent distinguished many other members of the Left Centre; like the "Württemberger Hof" in Frankfort, it was the faction of the coming men; Gierke, later minister of agriculture, Schultze-Delitzsch, who first became known in it, the lively and temperamental Catholic chaplain von Berg, and finally, von Kirchmann, State attorney, belonged to them, the one a man of many talents, equally sharp-sighted as a critic of finance and critical philosopher, a man eager for liberty, as politician much too cautious, whom the Reaction was later to persecute so bitterly, without ever succeeding in subduing him. The Left Centre met Unter den Linden, in the Mielentz rooms.

The venerable Chief President von Schoen, as senior president (he was the oldest member) could no longer master the National Assembly; its first elected president was Milde of Breslau, son of a rich cotton-mill owner and himself a very successful cotton-spinner, the agreeable type of well-instructed manufacturer of the day, a lively, energetic man, full of goodwill, still able to speak the language of the rising middle-class without pompousness, too well-balanced to find ambition necessary. This excellent man, who enjoyed the confidence of the most varied circles, and kept it by assiduous correspondence, then became the first Prussian Minister of Commerce—though only for a few months. As president, his successor Grabow excelled him in full-throated oratory and energy—he had for decades been Mayor of Prenzlau, a tactful Old Liberal, keen and far-seeing, the pride of his native Uckermark, a type of the useful satellite of capable communal-politic origin, with whose well-balanced talent many of his contemporaries might be well content—whereas posterity had not been able to find much use for it.

In the face of all this wakening of many-sided popular opinion, the King's position was pitiful. He appeared completely altered; his ideas, his volatility, his elastic many-sided activities—all now seemed purposeless and unnecessary. "Everything has crashed as if touched by a magic wand," wrote General von Schäffer-Bernstein, Hessian envoy, "The King has almost disappeared—he lives almost unnoticed in the Potsdam town Palace, which he has always avoided; he comes to Berlin only for a few hours at a time—drives almost unnoticed from the Palace to see his ministers and back again. Faith in his brilliance and courage has been badly shaken. Shame and self-reproach lie heavy upon him. His weariness is actually visible." In May Frederick William then left for Sans Souci and here, as often as possible, the group of men collected about him who were soon to develop into a reactionary counter-government—Leopold von Gerlach, his adjutant-general, at their head. He thought of the July Revolution as the beginning of a hideous revolutionizing of Germany— or even worse: through the Stein-Hardenberg agrarian laws, Prussia had become "Communistically revolutionary," respect for property had ceased to be. The unfortunate monarch was now belaboured with pasted scrapbook history of this kind; it was under such impressions that he wrote his letters to the former Prime Minister, Camphausen, letters which seem so hearty and genuine, but in reality represent the King's opposition, at once naïve and artful, to his own ministers. This King, beaten by the March Revolution, had once more become a man of many words, he was going to keep order, he intoxicated himself with the thought of his power and royal dignity, he was the Defender of All Things Holy, which were being attacked. He had never desired honest parliamentarianism, it was impossible that he should desire it.

Von Aretin, Bavarian *chargé d'affaires*, wrote: "When you hear the King speak, you would think that he was prepared any day to mount a horse and defend his kingdom in the saddle, and meanwhile one government act after another destroys the auxiliary means which might serve such a purpose." In reality, not even the royalists had any confidence in the King. Gerlach and his people therefore continually urged him on to resistance; he "should not deviate by a hair's breadth"; "one must not only be morally, but also physically armed," the King wrote, an obedient echo, on May 15th. He complained loudly and volubly about the "injustice" done to him, he had a thousand transparent reasons to complain of his

ministers, he left everything to their responsibility and sub-
sequently took them to account. He issued orders, pleaded,
sulked, scolded alternately; he complained that he found himself in an unkingly and undignified position—through the
Ministry of State, whose work he himself, with his incalculable,
often plainly treacherous, certainly dubious attitude, had made
almost impossible. Frederick William could not and would
not accept the consequences of the March Revolution; he
could not keep the word he had pledged so unwillingly, he
quibbled, awaiting a moment when he could throw off all
responsibility for it. There was already a touch of falsity when
Frederick William refused to see his ministers in Potsdam, in
order not to take up their time, as he averred. In reality they
would have been in his way—in Potsdam he had other men.
How often he tried to alarm Camphausen by flaunting the
possibility of abdication; his honour as man, Prussian, and
King might demand it. In reality he had, under the influence
of the camarilla, fully abandoned this idea; the strengthening
of the consciousness of royal power could be plainly felt
in him.

Frederick William IV regarded the revolution as a sin; his
pious friends in Potsdam told him every evening that the King,
as a second St. George, must slay this dragon. There was a
whispering and flutter of rumour about this monarch, a making
of plans and writing of letters, arranging of audiences and
receptions—a web spun out of loyalty, arrogance, narrowness,
clique, and privilege: the King's wounded soul was comforted
by so much zeal, correct humility, vassal care of him and
nobility of feeling. He felt himself grow strong and well in
faith in himself and in his royal mission. But he did not observe
that he was getting farther and farther away from reality and
becoming estranged from a people that were supposed to love
him. The camarilla allowed only its trusted henchmen to
approach the King; with well-meant cruelty he was handed
"truths" about the March Revolution, about the popular move-

ment, about events in Posen, Schleswig, and Frankfort. Thus his confidence in the March Ministry, never very strong, was steadily undermined. He could not accommodate himself to them, he hesitated and frittered everything away, things had to be done over his head and then he had nothing to do, there was no more money to spend on building and making pictures and this infuriated him.

Frederick William enjoyed feeling himself a martyr and the chosen defender of sacred things. His taste had been cultivated on Dante and Raphael; in olden days he had covered invitation cards and minutes of conferences with designs made with his sharp-pointed pencil and expressing his fantastic imagination: basilicas of Ravenna, the cathedral of Aachen, Italian villas, Gothic and antique, Teutonism and Christianity eclectically combined to a dreamy universality. Added to all his arrogance, this prince had the arrogance of Christian-universal-historic culture in him; the coarseness of Berlin's political popular humour wounded not only his royal feelings of power, his nerves also vibrated in physical nausea. He felt himself besmirched in the most royal faith that he possessed. Because he was in the wrong and had been defeated, he could not forgive; because he was weak he took refuge in deceit and playing false on two or three fronts at once. He always took pleasure in playing with men and words; now he showed how far he could go in this respect. Here he was superior from the beginning to the good Gerlach and his friends. Among all the sweetly gossiping court generals, the respectful agitators with piously rolling eyeballs, whose Christianity was a subaltern misunderstanding, there was, to be sure, a single man: Bismarck-Schönhausen was still too young to do anything more during these months than serve the camarilla as adjutant-general—he was also politically too compromised to be able to show himself in the foreground. With the sharp, high tone in his voice, with his sly but honest eloquence, his inventive and perfectly ruthless power of decisiveness he exacted from

Gerlach's men and from the monarch an attention made up of respect and dislike.

The men of the Reaction, just beginning in the summer of 1848, had to live from hand to mouth, hoping for a *Deus ex machina*, and carefully preparing for the better time they hoped for. There was no real political leadership; from without one therefore saw more of the dissolution than of the inner cohesion in Prussia. The King was only a factor of uncertainty. He orated explanations to the officers, was warmly patriotic to the militia and dry and stiff to the members of the National Assembly. He, the born orator, became lame, uncertain, unclear. Many were sorry for him; when his star was low, the softness of his nature was disarming; no one could fully see through him.

We know that the Czechs refused to have anything to do with the Frankfort Parliament. They even went a step further: they confronted the German National Assembly with a Slavonian National Assembly. A general congress of Austrian Slavs was to meet in Prague on May 31st; it was in fact opened on June 3rd, after farseeing, careful preparation. For the first time West Slavs, East Slavs, and South Slavs of the Imperial State met in a city which could be claimed as Slavonic and applied the national and liberty-loving ideas of the age to their folkish unity.

Old, mad, queer Prague was full of picturesque national costumes; even the native citizen, long since a normal townsman, went about dressed in Czech national costume; youthful passion, shouting, pert self-assurance, jealous competitive spirit and the rude strength of true peasantry were all stirred together and made up a bewitching outbreak of will-power. It was all so unacademic, so spontaneous, so unrestrained, so glowing! Politically, these united Slavs meant a challenge to immediate battle issued to the coming German Empire, the old Austrian

Imperial State and Russian Czarism. If in Prague they had been satisfied with proclaiming adherence to Austro-Slavonicism—that is with the programme of an Austrian Federal State with co-operation of the Slavs, their national rights recognized —then a creative national influence might have emanated from the Prague Slav Congress. But the Congress stretched out a hand beyond Austro-Slavism; even the programme spoke of the reconciliation of Russians and Poles and expressed a hope that the Russian folk might soon see the light of freedom at home. Only one Russian took part in the meetings—but his name was Michael Bakunin. He and many Poles from Posen brought a touch of revolutionary passion to the Congress which was sharply differentiated from the manner of the quieter Czechs, who were greatly in the majority. The Congress demanded in a manifesto to the European people a universal European People's Congress to settle all international problems in the name of Liberty, Equality, and Fraternity. Free people, it was said, would understand each other better than paid diplomats; in the address to the Austrian Emperor it was demanded that Austria be transformed into a Federative State, that the principle of Nationality be applied to Hungary also, a Kingdom of Slovenia be instituted, and a mutual guarantee of nationality for Poles and Ruthenians be given. The Italian and German idea of unity had always threatened the old Imperial State; the rising of the Slavs threatened it with destruction or—gave it a foundation for building up a new structure. The Hungarians had thrown up allegiance to Vienna; the Prusso-German hereditary Emperor party did the same. Jellačič, the coming lord of Croats, Dalmatians, and Slovenes, offered a hand to the Czechs. Vienna was a republican-democratic island, the peasants of the German ancestral land did honour to their Emperor. The last supporters of the Imperial State could make no peace with Pan-Slavic-revolutionary tendencies—for they were directed against Russia, and Russia was the last hope. But Austro-Slavdom might be useful: two princes of Schwarzenberg, three Counts of Harrach, Count Mathias Thun—all took part in the Slav Congress. High aristocracy, army, countryfolk, bureaucracy, and Catholic Church were still in the Imperial State.

The half-witted Emperor Ferdinand lived at Innsbruck. Tyrolese peasants kept watch over the interior of the palace; they came together from all parts of the country, thrust aside the gold-braided Austrian and Hungarian guards and looked after the Imperial household with a kind of jealous loyalty. Their dignified and stubborn figures gave a picturesque aspect to the Innsbruck court castle. The court was very simple— there was as little etiquette as possible—the Court was supposed to be on its travels, the courtiers appeared in civil dress and booted. Many members of the aristocracy had left Vienna. Duchess Ferdinand of Württemberg, sister of Prince Metternich, and very like him both in feature, deep voice and tall figure, was taken for her brother and suffered indignities by students on the Linz steamboat, and the Baden envoy Baron Andlaw had to make peace. Countess Montecuccoli fled from Vienna disguised as a nursemaid; many of the Austrian aristocracy foregathered again at Bad Ischl. All the diplomatists followed the court to Innsbruck. The city was soon overcrowded, the inhabitants demanded exorbitant prices.

Empress Marianne had, in accordance with her natural character, adopted a perfectly passive attitude. The strong outward impulse of the extraordinary situation now awakened in her a power of action which surprised every one. Archduchess Sophie, the most energetic personality in Innsbruck, allied herself with the Empress; her son Franz Josef would be eighteen years old on August 18th, would then have attained his majority and could ascend the throne. She pursued this aim with motherly persistence, in spite of considerable obstacles. Her opponent was Archduke Johann. Of all the archdukes he was considered the most capable, but as sly as he was able. His personal ambition was great; plans to carve a Kingdom of Rhaetia (1812) for himself now lay far behind him; but his connections with the pioneers of the liberty movement remained alive. Now the revolution had thrust him, as an old enemy of Metternich, into the foreground and he expected to reap his harvest. Every one who knew him was aware that behind his winning simplicity and friendly, well-contrived words there was hidden a strong urge to power and popularity. The Empress and the Archduchess Sophie had not the least confidence in him; they feared that he would work to become Emperor himself. The Archduke, who always said he could never tear himself away from his Tyrolese mountains, did in fact aspire to the highest influence. He prevented a ministry with Count Franz Stadion at its head, the energetic Governor of Galicia, from whose enterprise the princesses had hoped good things for Vienna. Archduke Johann wished to go as far as possible with the Viennese popular movement. Therefore, with the aid of his old confidant, Baron von Wessenberg, whom he had contrived to have appointed Foreign Minister in the Pillersdorf cabinet, he put through a resolution that he should go to Vienna as Administrator of the Austrian Empire, Alter Ego of the Emperor. Even before his departure from Innsbruck, Johann succeeded in winning over Banus Jellačič to Austrian interests and thus in binding Hungary to remain a loyal dependent of the Imperial idea.

In Hungary all rights of a sovereign were deputed to Archduke Palatine Stephan; it was hoped that so the country might be fettered to the crumbling fabric of the dynastic leadership, in spite of Kossuth's agitation for a break with Austria. What Archduke Stephan was to Hungary, Archduke Johann hoped to be to Austria. Banus Jellačič might then be used with Prince Windischgrätz against the Hungarian idea of liberty as well as against the German. But why should all this be for the benefit of a young prince who was not yet of age and whose future was uncertain? The liberal Archdukes, Johann and Stephan had the present to themselves. Was not a dualistic solution the best for the Imperial State? The Prince Palatine could achieve the Hungarian crown; why should not Archduke Johann achieve the Imperial crown, the old German crown, the symbol of the true Greater Germany? Archduke Johann, just appointed Alter Ego of the Emperor, was elected a few days afterwards in Frankfort as Vicar of the Empire. Neither did he hesitate for a moment to accept this choice; he grasped almost greedily at this fruit, like someone who had planted the tree long ago and waited almost too long for the harvest. Now he believed that his time had come. It was a matter of course to him that he should unite the vice-regencies of Austria and Germany. He spoke of it quite openly in his proclamation of July 6th: "I therefore believe that I do nothing contrary to the duties reposed in me by the Emperor during his absence, on the contrary I believe that I can fulfil them with far better prospects of success, in that I accept both these important missions, so closely bound up with one another." He did not think he needed either the consent of the governments nor of Emperor Ferdinand before accepting the Frankfort election. In vain the Prussian envoy endeavoured to persuade the Archduke to accept only on condition of the Governments' consent. He wished to remove the National Assembly from Frankfort to Vienna, or perhaps Linz or Regensburg. It was Archduke Johann, too, who had been particularly agitated over King Frederick William IV's appeal, who had fought strenuously against the Imperial plans of the Prussian hereditary Emperor party, who had therefore approved and abetted the hoisting of black, red, and gold banners in Vienna. Now he thought he could regard himself as the man of the day and the popular Emperor of tomorrow.

When Archduke Johann left Innsbruck, his nephew, Franz Karl, charged him to dissolve the Committee of Safety, the democratic clubs, and the Aula in Vienna. Johann had no idea of doing anything of the kind. It was among the Archduke's most characteristic qualities that he always took the side of those to whom he was speaking. His mission was much applauded in Vienna; there had at first been talk of Archduke Franz Karl, who would not have been nearly so popular. Archduke Johann now extolled the popular vote as the single fount of his authority, in his proclamations to the Austrian and German people—but he assured the Federal Assembly that he had received his mandate by consent of the Governments. When he spoke to the students and to the men of the Committee of Safety, he used the language of the Revolution and spoke of the sovereign rights of the people; but when he received the Prussian envoy Count Bernstorff or other German diplomats, he was of opinion that the whole matter of the vicarship was really quite "illegal." Bernstorff answered only by a shrug of the shoulders.

Vienna greatly resented Archduke Johann's immediate acceptance of the Frankfort Vicarship of the Empire and the sudden journey to Frankfort. In the few days of his activity he would have had enough to do in working for a reconciliation between the Committee of Safety and the Pillersdorf Ministry. Now, during his absence, many powers were turned against him. The royal ladies and Franz Karl thought a combination of the Viennese and Frankfort positions quite impossible; the same view was held in Frankfort where nobody would consider the idea of moving the seat of the Assembly. It had been feared in Innsbruck that Archduke Johann would think the Frankfort experiment too dangerous and would not engage on it. He had written to Franz Karl that conditions in Frankfort drove him to despair. Now everyone was happy to be free of the ambitious man. Young Franz Josef was carefully held aloof from Johann. In spite of Johann's express desire, Franz Josef was not allowed to welcome him in Linz on his return from Frankfort—no wonder that the Imperial Vicar's wrath was kindled against the court at Innsbruck. There was to be nothing that could compromise the hope of the future. Johann returned once more to Vienna; but what many

people expected, a practical attempt to set him independently
at the head of the monarchy as Emperor, was not made. We
may say: Certainly the Vienna mandate helped the Archduke
to win the German Vicarship of the Empire, but this post, in
its turn, prevented the Vienna mandate from developing, as
in his inmost heart, he had hoped it would do. And because
he was forced to abandon Vienna, the Frankfort Vicarship
never became an Imperial crown. The Archduke had fallen
between two thrones.

The institution of the first Imperial ministry in Frankfort
had the outward appearance of fulfilling everything that had
been hoped for the new future Germany since the Bassermann
motions in February. In reality its pre-history and its whole
being were full of compromise, weakness, and contradiction.
The Austria of Windischgrätz and Archduchess Sophie turned
away from the imaginary realm of the Paulskirche; Prussia,
not only of the court camarilla, but also Hansemann's Prussia,
stood ill-temperedly aside, wishing to take her own path;
Bavaria was cool and thought she could and act like one of
the great powers. But that was not yet all. Had not Prince
Leiningen begged his cousin and brother-in-law, Prince Albert,
to see that an English envoy was dispatched to help the provisional Central power to attain the international position
which it needed? England had no idea of doing any such
thing. On the contrary, Prince Albert was horrified that Prince
Leiningen, as half-brother of an English queen, should harbour
such extreme unitarian ideas; did not Leiningen owe his position
to some extent to this very family relationship?—and it was
not working out as had been hoped. The Vicar of the Empire
and the Imperial ministry were already forced by the question
of Schleswig-Holstein to engage on foreign policy—grave
disappointments awaited them here. They were strong in the
circle of power represented by the Frankfort Parliament—but

this circle soon impinged upon other and more powerful circles. Parliamentary particularism was to combine with dynastic and bureaucratic particularism. And even in the Rhenish-South-West German corner, where the Frankfort Parliament was greatest, the social-revolutionary popular movement now also turned against the German National Assembly because it had, through the dynastic Vicariate, struck a pact with the old Powers.

CHAPTER TEN

# THE SEPTEMBER CRISIS

THERE WERE now many new Parliaments in Germany, many new ministers, and even a Vicar Imperial—the Revolution was tamed, the popular movement satisfied by so many new arrangements. All that was necessary now was to consult together, come to decisions and put the resolutions into practice. Who would withstand the will of the majority? The political rationalization process had begun; its logical course led to a clearly defined objective, a free and united Germany in a free, united Europe. But the self-possessed reasonableness of the philosophically trained spirit of the age was destined to be shattered by the power of something destructive and dynamic.

The optimists of the many German Parliaments of 1848 had faith in their own cause, as founders of sects and pedagogues are apt to have; they thought they held the key-word of liberation; they thought they could impart their political virtues and their knowledge to others; decent and dignified as they were, they desired the good of all—but they also wanted to be themselves. They felt themselves as free citizens of the coming popular State—and therefore the State must resemble them and those who were to belong to it must be formed after their image. They were both right and wrong in this: right, inasmuch as the future really belonged to them; wrong, inasmuch as they completely undervalued their opponents and therefore usually made use of the wrong weapons.

Threefold dynamics were ranged against them: the dynamics of dynastic particularism, the dynamics of power as expressed in foreign policy and the dynamics of the social-revolutionary and communistic idea. In Cologne, Karl Marx had been publishing the *Neue Rheinische Zeitung* since June 1st. Here was the seat of the committee of the Communist League; Friedrich Engels, Schapper, Moll were agitating in the Rhineland and in Westphalia. Everywhere workmen's unions were springing into existence: the Revolution should not pacify, thought these men, should not rationalize and lead to tangible reforms in the shape of new constitutions and statutes, but should be continued as a class war. Marx and Engels soon ridiculed the Frankfort Parliament as a mere learned council chamber, a place of chatter and gossip, whose members would never summon up the strength to break ruthlessly with the past and gather all revolutionary powers to the battle against the individual governments; they were sharp enough to scent the coming military-bureaucratic reaction in Prussia and hoped for a fresh revolt of the farmer-peasants against the feudalists; they demanded that the German people, once awakened to freedom, should support all ideas of freedom in all neighbouring nations, instead of allowing themselves to be wrongly used in attempting to suppress them; they demanded a German people's war against Russia as a means of self-liberation from the dynasties, from the economic pressure of the bourgeoisie, from the threatening barbarity of Czarism. The *Neue Rheinische Zeitung* uttered a good many erroneous individual opinions and could not unravel the tangled relationships in struggling Germany, with the sharp stilettos of its formulas of violence; the great effect which these articles made was by reason of their continually repeated profession of faith in the Republic, which nothing could shatter, their determined will to force on the disruption of society by appealing to the economic

interests of the lower classes. When Karl Marx stigmatized the
June battle in Paris as the end of all the dreams of the February
Revolution, and lauded the French proletariat, the new Frankfort Ministry of Justice demanded that the Public Prosecutor
should proceed against him.

The communistic agitation of Karl Marx and those who
agreed with him, the social-revolutionary work of Hecker and
Struve, the attempts to organize the workmen into trades
unions, as initiated by Stephan Born, and finally the democratic evolutionism of a Robert Blum, all ran together in the
minds of their contemporaries of the age of revolution. This
lay not only in the optical perspective or lack of perspective
with which we must always reckon in those who stand too
close to events; in the democratic clubs, practical convinced
communists met pre-Marx socialists and citizen revolutionaries; the working-classes of the few German great cities
were usually still too undeveloped for political organizations
of their own; they also often felt their status to be that of
the lower middle classes. Their leaders expressly desired that
their people should join in all oppositional leagues, in order
to gain influence, increase their striking power and prevent
compromises.

Communist agents were busy in very many different places
—always with the same idea: to make differences sharper and
more bitter, to sow dissension in the citizen movement which
in March had been almost a uniform body, to cast doubt and
suspicion upon the newly-arisen leaders, and so to increase
mistrust, unrest and criticism, and strengthen terroristic
instincts.

The Frankfort National Assembly was to give the German
people a new constitution; at the most various points they
trespassed upon the executive power; was the constituent body
to become a convention? The men of 1848 knew all about
the great French Revolution and liked to express their hopes
and fears in language based upon the phrases of that day. The

dynamic factor was the deepest danger for the Frankfort Parliament; less, perhaps the power complexes which threatened far outside its sphere, for at least the more far-sighted of its leaders soon began to reckon with these—but far more the demon of power which arose within itself. Parliament and central power took foreign policy in hand, national German foreign policy, decisive and self-possessed as no policy has been followed in Germany for many a year; but where were the powers of State to enforce that policy? The National Assembly took the Fleet Question firmly in hand; their Marine Committee did not trouble at all as to what the Marine Committee of the Federal Assembly might already have begun; the fleet was a national and very popular matter —therefore the Frankfort Parliament would see to it. If in Frankfort they had demanded a Prussian Imperial Minister of War, they were not thinking of an organizer for an office, but of a chieftain, who would serve the practical needs of preserving German safety at home and abroad; in these hottest days of Frankfort Imperial terrorism, the suggestion was to have military commands proceed direct from the Vicar; even the Prussian fortresses on West and East frontiers were to be declared Federal fortresses. It cannot be said that these ideas were fostered by Austria—Austria, nationally speaking, was a very problematical conception at this period; Austrian politicians, Schmerling at their head, were, however, working in this sense together with South German conservative national patriots and the men of Gagern's party; thus declared defenders of Prussian hegemony acquired a reputation of being enemies of Prussia; the idea was that Berlin in its momentary condition, would not be able to refuse Frankfort anything. But could Prussia, should Prussia, really give up its diplomats and its command of the army? In the Defence committee of the Frankfort Parliament, the Austrian Colonel von Mayern put a motion to change the Prussian oath of loyalty to the flag into an oath of loyalty to the Vicar, "since in this way reac-

tionary ideas of the royal government can best be prevented."
Even Prussian officers assented: General von Auerswald succeeded in foiling the plan.

The National Assembly thus desired a national army; if it
was to be created, it must be on the Prussian model and built
upon Prussia's foundations. As in the Polish and the Schleswig-
Holstein questions, the Parliament attempted to work both
with Prussia and against her; objectively, curiously enough,
a defensive policy, but tactically injurious, presuming a larger
understanding in the Prussian party to the pact than actually
existed. The Defence Committee of the National Assembly
demanded on July 7th that the governments of the separate
states should increase their troops to 1 per cent of the actual
number of inhabitants; 910,000 men should be available in
case of war. This meant, however, a considerable increase in
federal armaments and it was natural that in the debate the
foreign policy aspect of the matter came to the fore and that the
possibilities of war were discussed. The speakers of the Left
denied that there was any danger of war, inasmuch as France
was in question, they suspected that the increase of troops was
designed to strengthen reactionary resources and pointed to
the high costs, particularly oppressive at such a time of economic crisis. It was determined, by a considerable majority, to
empower the central executive to increase the German Army
to 2 per cent of the *momentary* inhabitants (previously the
federal figures of 1819—had served) and thus to lay the foundation for universal conscription without exception; there
should be no display about the accoutrements, thus preparing
the way for a future people's defence force. It was thus proposed to democratize and enrich the forces; plainly enough
the idea of the old Prussian Landwehr had been taken up and
was to be used in German interests to counterbalance the
preponderance of the active Prussian army.

The ill will towards dynastic militarism, particularly the
Prussian, repeatedly found expression in the National Assembly.

Men like Nauwerck and Ruge demanded disarmament, Raveaux spoke of the Prussian "soldateska," the wild soldiery, and aroused lively contradiction. But even the mild-mannered Beckerath thought that the military system had grown up on absolutistic principles and was in need of reorganization: there must be no more Austrian, no Prussian soldiers—only German citizens who carried German weapons—German warriors. Friedrich Theodor Vischer developed into a military specialist; no one comprehended so keenly as he the unhappiness and undesirability of a citizen army, forced to stand by the side of a standing army; he, like many others, wished for a true popular army, which would combine the spirit of liberty with true military discipline. Such a popular army—this idea always underlies the rest and sometimes comes to the fore—would be a powerful weapon in the hand of a popular central power, in order to carry out the resolutions passed by the National Assembly. Venedey of Cologne directly demanded a "Parliamentary army."

The Marine Committee, which could scarcely find enough work for its overflowing energies, also issued a report on the question of the German colours when the statute as to the German war and merchant-flag was laid before the National Assembly on July 31st. Black, red, and gold had conquered the whole of Germany since the March days. It had become the intoxicating symbol of the national, free popular movement. But criticism was now heard from the heraldic experts; Professor von Hefner wrote to von Peucker, Minister of War, that the metal (that is the gold) must be placed between the red and black, since every colour must impinge upon the metal. The report of the committee treated this objection with great seriousness, but established the fact that a black, red, and gold tricolour had never existed in the old German Empire; nevertheless, in view of the overwhelming prevalence of the black, red, and gold, they recommended that the colours be kept in this order; they also recommended that not the single-headed, but the double-headed eagle be adopted as a sign of the renaissance of the old empire and because it had already been used as a German symbol by the Federal Assembly. The majority of the National Assembly therefore determined upon tricolour and eagle. The law as to the German war and merchant-flag was proclaimed by the Vicar on November 13, 1848. It was officially communicated to the four states with which the central authority had official relations. The law did not apply to the war and merchant ships of the separate states; they hoisted only one flag, that of the individual state in accordance with marine custom. But the ships of the new German war fleet hoisted the German war-flag and were saluted by the states that had recognized it.

Archduke Johann gathered an Imperial ministry about him, his first prime minister being Prince Leiningen, the half-brother of Queen Victoria. Von Schmerling, an Austrian, was minister for home affairs, Heckscher, of Hamburg, for foreign affairs, General von Peucker, the Prussian, Imperial Minister of War. After the September Crisis, the cabinet was newly organized and enlarged. Robert Mohl, a Swabian, became Imperial Minister of Justice, Duckwitz from Bremen, Minister for Commerce and Trade. All these ministers built up a staff of officials and instituted a regular business procedure. The Provisional Central Executive also exercised the right to receive envoys, in succession to the "Bundestag," but received official recognition only from Belgium, Holland, Naples, and Switzerland, whereas the two most important Great Powers, Great Britain and France, confined themselves to semi-official relations.

The Frankfort empire had arms and colours, ministers and envoys, army and navy, Parliament and a head—much was temporary, provisional, conditional, half recognized; much existed only on paper, not yet a tangible effective influence: these beginnings were purposeful and decisive, supported by the will to fill up gaps, and to give a form for the future to the new Germany of the popular movement and the popular will. The weeks that lay between the issuing of these laws respecting the provisional central power and the September Revolution were probably the happiest in the history of the Frankfort Parliament. On July 3rd began the discussions as to basic rights—in dignity and with academic leisure in spite of warning and impatient voices. The Constitution Committee had deliberately set "Fundamental Rights" at the head of the plan for the new constitution; they wanted to conclude the Revolution, limit it, nail it down, and in so doing, justify and overcome it; they wished to prepare a friendly field of battle for common principles for the members from all corners of Germany who were still strangers to one another. It was high summer before these basic rights were ripe for discussion; so much had happened, there had been so much active accomplishment. There were enough members already who were eager to break away from the temporary and the theoretical; powers were plainly rising beside and behind the Paulskirche. Yet the majority decided upon a twofold discussion and on taking the vote, and all this went on until well into the winter; it was all very honest and very German to begin at the beginning of beginnings, and if not to agree about the underlying philosophy of the new German popular state, at least to become a little clearer about it. Most men of the National Assembly were particularly attached to the basic rights; this was clearly shown by the flood of proposals for amendments and sub-amendments, and the learned fashion in which the discussions on philosophical and juristic conceptions were enjoyed to the full. Even the very first words of the Constitution—"Every German"—aroused a discussion lasting for hours as to the meaning of the word "German." The economic committee came out with forty proposals of amendments, to which individual members added motions of their own. Old Grävell became a perfect terror to the Assembly, an academical jurist of an already old-fashioned type, a grey man with a grey voice, dry, wordy, and monotonous, but not to be turned from his track by any call to order. Giskra calculated that at the present rate of progress the end of the first discussion of the basic rights might be expected about April 1850. A motion of Venedey's to allow no discussion of motions not supported by at least twenty delegates, was rejected.

And yet—in all this breadth and tortuous pomposity there still lived the great longing of the age; out of these complaints could be felt the attachment to soil and parish, traditional food, and ancestral class in old Germany, and the cruel ruthlessness with which the court officials of the various provinces had treated Germans as "foreigners"—the whole burden of social prejudice and privilege. How often before the Revolution had the rights of individuals, their homes, their correspondence been violated, in how many thousands of instances! Enough men who had felt these abuses in their own persons now sat in the Paulskirche and could speak with personal knowledge of the measures necessary to give protection—men like Schlöffel and Sylvester Jordan. How well such men understood how the Press had been throttled! Not only the censorship was now forbidden, but also concessions, securities, State editions, restrictions upon printing offices and book publishers, and postal bans—all fetters upon the freedom of the Press. We know that they had experienced the tyranny of all these things. The apex of this first section of discussion was probably the debate on religious liberty and the relation between State and Church. The great subject demanded a wide perspective—their education, temperament, and the tenseness of the moment empowered the men of the Paulskirche to show how capable they were of rising to the occasion. The historic conceptions of State and Church hung together and were dependent upon one another like the ivy and the wall; splitting and holding together in one, obstinate, bound together by nature and destiny; the convinced churchmen of both faiths wanted to set the Church free of the State, and the freethinkers wanted to deliver the

State from the Church; von Beisler, Bavarian Minister of Culture, turned against a church which strove for temporal power, he demanded a new reform of the Church in all its members, in the democratic spirit of its original form: the unflinching speech cost him his official post. Karl Vogt spoke from the standpoint of the decided Agnostics for freedom of the Church, but also freedom of the schools. Döllinger did not advocate the separation of Church and State, but independence, and thus proclaimed the actual future; Nauwerck prophesied a new democratic period for the Catholic Church and condemned the fear of the Jesuits as foolishness, while Radowitz, speaking in the name of the Catholic members, declared himself against the introduction of the Jesuits; the Catholic Church in Germany had no need of the Order. The whole polyphony of the deeply moved Germania sacra, split into many churches, strong in conscience, sounded through the barren columnar round of the St. Paul's Church: pietists, Josephines, Knights of the Spirit, enthusiasts, and intellectuals, romantic Old-Christians and keen, cold Neo-Romanists, Protestant-Prussian patriots, liberal Catholics from the Rhine—there were many convictions in the Germany of that day, many with an urge to express their inward beliefs, many with courage to do so; but the best of it was that even in the greatest extremists, there was a will to co-operation, to union, to reconciliation at least in the form of the future State. This whittling down to a fine and warm tolerance may appear to the fanatic as weakness; historically speaking it is an inheritance from the intellectual renaissance and must be transmitted as a golden legacy to later German ages.

German passion for obstinate opiniatedness had completely obsessed the political questions of the day. But even this battle preserved the canons of dignity and good taste in Frankfort until the September Revolution. People thought they were laying foundations for later German generations and therefore hard work was done, in spite of the growing signs of parliamentary weariness. Was not the imaginary realm of the Paulskirche becoming a tangible presence? Who did not believe this, especially in Frankfort? Everyone was very certain, joyous, full of plans. Since one was convinced that one was making world history, one could afford to have a good, carefree laugh in one's spare time. Berlin's satire had a bitter taste, not only on account of regional intellectuality. In Frankfort they could afford to have more warmth of heart.

Now came the trouble over Schleswig-Holstein and the pitiful end of the war with Denmark dealt the Frankfort Assembly a mortal blow. Prussia, taking matters into her own hands, had given way on every point. Indignation in Germany was intense; the agreement of Malmö humiliated the old Great Power Prussia; but it had a crushing effect upon the just-emerging German Empire. Prussia had thus sacrificed the Revolution and the National idea at once.

September 16th was the black day of the Frankfort Parliament. This proud assembly, which thought to build up the new Germany out of its own sovereign powers, had within a few days given both assent and denial to the self-same matter of the duchies of Schleswig and Holstein. It was an illusion, that anything essential had been altered. Prussia had retreated at Malmö before the European Great Powers, she had sacrificed "the honour and dignity of Germany"; the majority of the National Assembly recognized this to the full and even agreed with it, because they had more need of Prussia than Prussia of them. Prussia's repute in Germany had suffered severely; now the National Assembly sacrificed a large proportion of its own fair fame, the maltreated Central Executive, the maltreated Ministry, were forced by opportunism to take the part of the very government, the very policy, from which they had received the hardest blows. Camphausen wrote to Berlin: "The victory belongs to those for whom one cannot conquer much without bleeding to death. Let us hope that we do not again encounter a case of so doubtful and hesitant a nature."

It would have been thought natural if Dahlmann had resigned from Parliament after the rejection of his motion demanding continuance of war with Denmark, but that he should have voted immediately afterwards for the Francke motion to accept the peace terms was fully incomprehensible. Waitz' behaviour was equally strange. The fitness of German professors for politics now seemed to many rather doubtful. The defection of the four members from Schleswig-Holstein aroused embitterment and disgust. Many honest patriots felt that they were being led by the nose. The lack of political vision seemed as obvious as the lack of political courage. The personal oppositions in Parliament were much sharpened by such experiences and thus its further work was greatly impeded. The parliamentary system as a means of forming a government and working executive seemed to have failed at this first serious test; even if the particular conditions were taken into consideration, something of this bad impression remained. Faith in Parliament and its powers had received a severe blow. The majority in Parliament had always been very national; it was just the loudest Nationalists who now retired with statesman-like gestures to the line of hasty compromise. And the parties of the Left, who had always been accused of internationalism, had preserved their patriotic feelings of steadfast loyalty. In the excitement of these September days, many began to doubt whether Parliament's work would come to a good end; a misfortune had happened, people somehow felt wounded and wretched. The passion of battle entered into the popular masses of the parliamentary city. Heckscher, Imperial Minister of Foreign Affairs, whose injured pride had led to such excesses in Parliament that he had been called to order, and his life threatened; in front of the palace of the Duke of Augustenbŭrg, to whom Frederick William IV had expressed his personal gratefulness for his support in Frankfort in the Danish affair, there were wild demonstrations. In the factions of the Left there was talk of seceding as one man, of constituting a Rump Parliament, or of dissolving the National Assembly and holding fresh elections. In the great assembly, over four thousand strong, on the meadow where the fair was held at Whitsuntide, wild and angry speeches were heard; the two hundred and fifty-seven who had given assent to the Danish peace were condemned as traitors; the Left were to constitute an independent government. German flags hung with crape were borne before the procession of protest as it marched into the city. The people demanded plain-speaking and—action. The national and democratic idea was up in arms against dynasticism and particularism, the moment seemed particularly favourable for a new outbreak of the revolutionary popular movement.

The position in the west and south-west of Germany was now most critical. Social-revolutionary connections ran from Cologne to Frankfort, from Frankfort to Hesse, to Thuringia, the Palatinate and Strasburg, and from there and from Switzerland into Baden. The great popular assembly on the Frankenplatz in Cologne, led by Heinrich Bürgers on September 13th, unanimously voted to send a sharp address to the Berlin National Assembly and decided to form a Committee of Safety. Four days later thousands met on a meadow at Worringen on the Rhine. The red flag had replaced black, red, and gold; the leader of the Düsseldorf delegation was the twenty-three-year-old Ferdinand Lassalle. The speakers supported the democratic-social republic. An address to the Frankfort National Assembly exhorted them to take a firm stand against Prussia. On September 25th barricades were erected in Cologne and martial law was proclaimed. In the south of Baden, Struve was ready to strike. His idea and Sigel's was to connect with the leaders of the Left in the Paulskirche and set up a provisional government for "all Republicans on both banks of the Rhine." The second Badensian revolt was a part of the great West German movement, which turned against the National Assembly and its dynastic central power, but frittered away its strength in a series of local and regional revolts.

Struve was no Communist and would have been bitterly mocked at by Karl Marx if his success had been greater. But he had a good share of pre-Marxian socialism; he had no conception of international battle organization; he wanted to set up a social-republican Germany by force. He was certainly no robber captain, as he was painted by the cheap wits of petty philistines. He never had any idea of enriching himself; he sought to attain a great and distant goal for Germany by any means that he thought necessary; it was not so much the means that were at fault, though many an excess may have aroused anger and made a painful impression, but the completely false judgment of the whole situation, the wrong-headedness of his whole political conception. Struve's strength was his lively and polemic grasp of momentary situations— he could reason and find proofs, rouse his readers and fill them with all the bitterness which had collected in those who were dispossessed. But he was a dry pedant, with no power of real political action, and so he who had none of Hecker's fire became the fool of the men of the eternal yesterday. Struve was a terrorist by conviction, but he could not bring himself to set up a guillotine as his assistants Löwenfels and Neff demanded. He was a Jacobin, moralistic, filled with an urge to improve the world, and no greater curse could descend upon him than the companionship of all kinds of joyous tramps, good-for-nothings, adventurers, and rascally opportunists who thought to make use of a Revolution to carve out new fortunes for themselves. These vagabonds, only outwardly good-natured, hung on the heels of Struve and his men, were with difficulty restrained from the worst excesses and did succeed in committing many a misdeed unperceived.

The after-effects of the Struve rising were far more important than that abortive enterprise itself. Nothing could have been more compromising to the Revolution than these threats to life and property. Now the attack was returned. The Revolution turned about, counter-revolution had its inception. It was the most significant consequence of the September crisis that the gulf between Right and Left now became so impassable. This was bitter for the revolutionary Right, for the liberal reform party, for the progressive nationalists. All these central groups had taken their driving force from their connection with the popular movement; they had made use of revolutionary means and drawn their consequences from the Revolution. Now the Revolution was going further, it threatened order, property, authority of every kind; the Social-Revolutionaries were just a small minority, the Communists still smaller; but their explosive power shook the entire moderate Centre.

The Counter-Revolution was on the march.

## CHAPTER ELEVEN

# THE COUNTER-REVOLUTION IN AUSTRIA

EMPEROR NICHOLAS I of Russia received a memorandum, in the summer of 1848 from a man by the name of A. Richter, of whom he had never heard. It made such an impression upon him that he sent it to the Czarevitch Alexander, annotated in his own hand. In this memorandum it was declared that revolutionary propaganda was no phantom, but a mighty organization which had declared war to the death upon the principle of authority. The governments had up to now been powerless against this invisible enemy; police did not suffice; this propaganda was superior to the work of paid spies; everywhere it had spun the nets of its permanent conspiracies; the only way to fight it was to make use of its own means; a monarchistic propaganda was necessary to counteract the anarchist propaganda; all good elements must be organized against the spirit of evil; revolutionary propaganda had developed on the Jesuit pattern; the "loyalists" must educate themselves in the same fashion and observe the same discipline. They must be ready to lead on the fight for authority, morality, and God, even though it might lead them to martyrdom.

Such ideas touched the innermost thoughts of the Russian Emperor; he too saw the battles of the day as a part of the eternal conflict between good and evil; to him Revolution

was a sin and he felt himself to be a sanctuary of good principles. How gladly, in summer, 1848, did he consider the plan
of a propaganda war upon—Prussia! It was hardly necessary,
for Prussia was ready to respond to diplomatic pressure. It
was also scarcely possible, for the Russian striking power was
crippled by disease in the army; only a proclamation of the
republic in Berlin would probably have precipitated an immediate intervention of the Emperor. Events in the Imperial
State of Austria and in the Balkans must needs awaken perturbation in Russia. The Italian and German freedom movements only had an indirect influence upon Russia; but if the
conflagration were to spread to the Slavic world, then Czarism
might also begin to totter. It was possible to adopt a waiting
policy towards revolutionary propaganda in Central Europe;
but if "anarchy" took the offensive in Eastern Europe then
she must attack in her turn, according to the principles of the
memorandum.

The Slav Congress at Prague had come to an end, without
achieving definite results. There was no Slavic unity as to the
aim to be pursued; the Slav Freedom and National Movement
was many-branched, contradictory and a representative of the
awakening of strong young national feeling against the Austrian Imperial State and dynastic Prussia, it also turned against
Czarism. Polish revolutionaries worked with Czechs and South
Slavs; the three great centres of propaganda were Prague,
Cracow, and Semlin. Bakunin transferred the idea and practical political form of Carbonarism to the Slavic world.
Wolhynia, the Ukraine and Podolia, Moldavia and Wallachia
were to be influenced; weapons were sent from Fiume to
Odessa. Everywhere there were trusty supporters; manifestos
in all the Slavic languages were printed by the publishing
houses of Brockhaus and Avenarius, in the form of prayers.
Emperor Nicholas had strong suspicions of his Slavophiles, even
when they declared that their aim was the union of all Slavs
under the sacred sceptre of the Czar. But Bakunin, whose task

was to rouse the Russian peasant, Bakunin, anarchistic Russian revolutionary by way of Hegel's doctrines—was the Emperor's mortal enemy. At that time, the attempt to create a Slavic popular movement with sufficient driving force against the old princely powers, failed; none other than the Slavs were fated to be the agents of suppressing national feeling in Germany, Austria, and Hungary. Czech regiments marched into Frankfort and against Vienna, Jellačičs Croats fought here and against the Hungarians, and finally the Russians trampled down Hungarian independence. The Central European civil war became a battle of nationalities in the near East; the bitterness with which it was fought, finally choked the Revolution in the name of the counter-revolution, in the sacred names of autocracy and order.

Archduke Johann no longer had any direct relations with the Imperial family. He had asked for and obtained thirty thousand gulden in June and July as Vice-Regent for the Emperor. As German Vicar of the Empire he set up a barrier between himself and Austria with a very obvious purpose in mind. He talked of "My former master, the Emperor." To be sure, this did not prevent him from drawing a pension of twelve thousand gulden as Austrian field-marshal and eight thousand gulden as chief of the engineers' corps, as well as his royal perquisites. In vain Johann also attempted to enforce a partition of the Imperial private fortune, in order to secure his share for his son, who had no claim to it.

Archduke Johann and his closest adviser, Schmerling, wished to make use of the increased authority which had accrued to the Vicarship through the successful quashing of the Frankfort September Revolution, in a decided stroke against Austria. The idea was to awaken a consciousness of the German allegiance in these provinces, inhabited by Germans, which had always shown a preference for Johann, and to use them as pawns against the Imperial house which had the support of the Slav party. Johann and Schmerling wanted a greater

Germany; the natural background of power for the future popular Emperor of Frankfort was a German Austria. The plans of the Frankfort central power therefore had in mind nothing less than the total destruction of the Austrian monarchy in the existing form; Schmerling spoke openly of this plan among his intimates; Hungary with its dependencies was to be an independent empire under Archduke Stephan with the title of King, the German provinces were to fall to Archduke Johann "and thus their closest connection with Germany would be secured and the future German Emperor would have his private power. France, England, and Italy were to be satisfied by the surrender of a large part of the Italian provinces, as well as the liberation of Poland. The rights and interests of the legitimate Imperial dynasty were to be bargained away cheaply, for which reason Herr von Schmerling found it expedient not to support too explicitly the claim of Archduke Franz Josef to the throne." (Report of Colonel Fischer, Frankfort, October 12, 1848.)

This historical perspective is most important! The Imperial State was to be dissolved, Franz Josef perhaps to be bought off with Bohemia and Moravia, Archduke Rainer with the remnants of Italy, the principle of nationalities was to be definitely extended to the monarchy, a true Greater Germany to be created! All Prussian observers agreed in their doubts and even fears of such plans. The central executive was expecting to create order of its own accord out of the Austrian chaos and, possibly to enforce peace by the use of Bavarian and other troops. To be sure, no Prussian troops could have been obtained. The position of the Frankforters was indeed difficult enough. They did not want to abandon the Germans in Austria, they had hopes of an Austro-German province; but the mainspring of energy was in Vienna; the capital was in favour of Greater Germany, but her tendency was too radical to please the taste of the central executive. The "anarchy" which the Frankforters had just suppressed at home, now seemed to be rearing its head in Vienna. The government fell into hesitation; they could not well support the German movement and put brakes on the "anarchic" tendency; for in Austria, both were one. Thus it came about that any interference from outside was powerless in Austria. The Archduke's plans went up in smoke. Archduke Stephan as Palatinate of Hungary had long been trying to maintain his power in the difficult struggle between the democratic patriots' party and the Imperial house. Again and again he had offered his resignation to the Kaiser in order to squeeze out fresh concessions; he left Hungary in September, in order not to become entirely a tool of Kossuth —certainly in the hope of returning. He felt a glowing hatred of Archduchess Sophie and it was returned in like measure; each thought they completely saw through the other. Archduke Stephan now appeared in Frankfort and had a consultation with Archduke Johann, then he went to England; everywhere he spoke of the impossibility of the prevailing Imperial rule, but without advocating the accession of the legitimate heir. He, who had played such a sorry part that he was despised by all parties alike, now declared in London that Lombardy must be given up; in this way he hoped to win Lord Palmerston over to his plans, for the Imperial house thought of him as the bitterest enemy of the black and yellow Imperial State. Thus the oppositions grew to great proportions. Kossuth's Hungary was at war with her South Slav and Slovakian subjects. The Hungarian Serbs delivered their blow as early as May, for the Emperor, against the revolutionaries in Budapest; Banus Jellačič, at first exiled, was reinstated in September without the knowledge of the Wessenberg ministry and led his Croats over the Drau. Between him and Windischgrätz there was a Slav understanding directed against Germans and Hungarians.

A great social impetus was imparted to the work of the Austrian Reichstag by the attempt made at last to liberate the peasants. The economic scarcity in the Imperial State furthered such endeavours. The anti-clerical note was especially perceptible in Vienna. The slogan "Away from Rome!" was coined at this time. Such an atmosphere widened the breach between old and new powers. The outbreak in Vienna occurred at the beginning of October. The popular movement was stained by the murder of Count Latour, Minister of War, who was hated, to be sure with some cause; a little more show of courage would probably have saved his wretched life.

The victory of the Vienna Revolution was decided by the conquest of the arsenal—the Reichstag had tried in vain to prevent it. The masses now had weapons enough; the number of armed students, citizens and working-men was estimated at one hundred thousand. The order was now issued that everyone should be armed. Count Auersperg now gave up his fixed position at Belvedere and went into camp at Feyersdorf. He had carried on curious negotiations with the Viennese; his demand that "the proletariate" should be deprived of arms, was rejected and met by the counter-demand that he should prevent Banus Jellačič's incursion into Austrian territory and force him to retreat. Auersperg then justified his march by the daily, even hourly, proofs afforded of the "hostility" of "the ill-intentioned section of the population." Provisions and traffic were delayed in every way, said he, but he would do nothing against the capital. His retreat was hasty, almost a flight, and much of his equipment was abandoned. The National Guard occupied his positions. A few days later, Auersperg had joined up to Jellačič.

Revolution reigned in Vienna; its leading organ of government was the very radical Municipal Council which had been newly constituted on October 7th; the Student Committee and the new committee of safety had far less influence. Tausenau's central committee tried in vain to carry out his idea of a convention with unlimited powers. Tausenau soon went to Budapest in order to try and get Hungarian help for Vienna; Chaizes, the focus of an overwhelmingly proletarian group which called itself "radical-liberal" and met in an inn in the working-class suburb of Wieden, took his place and played a part neither agreeable nor savoury. An attempt to transplant the revolutionary movement into the country, met with only slight success. The Reichstag refused to call up the reserves; the peasant-farmers turned a deaf ear to direct appeals in this direction. As a first step they raised all the prices of food for Vienna. Serious rebel movements only occurred in Styria, the native province of Archduke Johann. Here there was sympathy with Viennese ideas and this was more or less patiently endured by Count Wickenburg, the governor. Styrian national guards were summoned by telegraph to Vienna in order, as they were told, to lighten the hours of service for the Viennese national guard; thus the revolutionary element received considerable reinforcements.

The legal organs and the new revolutionary organs in Vienna avoided the word "republic," they spoke with deliberate emphasis of democratic monarchy as their true aim; only thus could they hope to penetrate to ancestral provinces, perhaps by means of their adherents. Who knows what might have happened if Archduke Johann had been able to come to Vienna at that hour! Austro-German, Greater German patriotism was the main pillar of the Viennese October Revolutionary programme; therefore the battle awoke such moving echoes all over Germany. But to this the social-revolutionary components were now added. The National Guard and the citizen militia had an extremely bourgeois character; the town council now guaranteed them part-pay and provision for widows; beside them came that new body, the mobile guard, with regular pay, part of it in kind—the proletariate in arms, an exceedingly mixed troop in improvised uniforms, which was divided into four battalions. They wore their red device as cockade, plume, ribbon or nosegay. This mobile guard soon became the axis of revolutionary action, it was the instrument of a declared political and social terrorism. Yet there were hardly any excesses against property; martial law was in force against plunderers. Such stern discipline prevailed that one of the mobile guard was shot out of hand for rape. This strong manifestation of armed proletarianism brought about an awakening of socialistic and communistic ideas. Various ideas, impulses, experimental reforms, appeared on the scene; nothing of the kind had as yet occurred in Germany. Many features of the Viennese October Revolution remind us of the events of the Paris Commune, of 1871, and later events in Russia. According to the purely democratic majority principle, the citizen element which had so often displayed black-and-yellow sympathies, must have had the upper hand. But it was completely intimidated by the revolutionary terror; the plainer it became that a fight to the death was imminent, the higher the excitement rose; the more unbridled was the expression of vital force, the more necessary it became to oppose dictatorial power to such conditions of intoxicated enthusiasm. Students and working men were brothers, the women were frantically admiring and devoted. The crackling, boiling, roar of a new age swept through the venerable city. Coquettish grace and coloured pomp seemed to have been carried away; a passion for life and work was kindled. Demands were made for the institution of social provisions for everyone, the abolition of classes, a social state founded upon law; the scholars gave a keen dialectic point to the instinctive wordless will of the working classes; there was talk of a fixed limit of working hours, of trades unions, communal accounts, minimum wages, insurance against sickness and death, profit-sharing for the workmen, reform of the taxes.

The most singular press organ of the Viennese revolutionary period was *Der Radikale*, which came completely to the fore during these October weeks. The editor was A. J. Becher, a musical critic by profession, but acquainted with extreme views through long residence in England. Himself a mild man, but in his views surprisingly and destructively logical, he was unshakable, passionate and therefore tremendously effective; his most eager collaborator was Hermann Jellinek, in origin a Moravian Jew, by education a young Hegelian and Talmudist; a sincere prophet of a better humanity, dark, tortuous, subtle in his phraseology, determined and merciless in his rejection of the outworn, misunderstood or only half comprehended by most people, but in his final aims one of the most progressive spirits of the day. Talented, fantastic, difficult to appraise in its effects, as was everything in revolutionary Vienna, was the new Press of the revolutionary summer; numbers of new papers arose, full of polemics and fiery speech, crude and witty popular sheets, others more crude than witty, satire, broad folk-humour, constructive and destructive, libellous or seriously political.

Wenzel Messenhauser was also a writer, author of the working-class drama "Gold weighs heavy." Becher, after an energetic campaign, had succeeded in having his friend and comrade appointed commander-in-chief for Vienna and environs by the Reichstag and the city council on October 12th. Messenhauser was a strange personality: son of a battalion drummer, he succeeded in the unusual rise from private to officer, studied world history, adopted "Caesar" as his second name as a symbol of his highest ideals, joined the staff of Saphir's *Humorist*, wrote short stories, poems, articles on art subjects—unripe, lacking in clarity, but not without brilliant ideas; he had connections with Laube and Freytag. Finally, his novel *The Gravedigger* which appeared under a pseudonym, brought him a literary success; in garrison in Galicia in 1848, he took over the organization of the national guard in Lemberg and was therefore obliged to leave the army. Free at last, he threw himself into the contemporary movement, issued a paper, wrote politics and poetry—always charming and amiable, enthusiastically championing liberty, but without real driving power; his little pamphlet, *How to Drill a National Guard* ran rapidly into six editions and made him famous. Personally he remained in the background, a good, modest, friendly fellow, burdened with literary narrowness which certainly tended to smother his pretty talents. Then came the great moment. Child at heart as he was, the man of thirty-six grasped eagerly at the high position offered him. Had not "Caesar's" hour struck at last? An officer, an exponent of liberty on the English model, a Greater-German, a friend of the working-class, an intellectual European—could there be a better leader in the fight for democracy, for the social revolution? As High Commander, he was still writing character studies of lower-class figures in the *Radical*; the proofs of his working-class play accompanied him into the dark nights of the decisive battles; the day before his execution he was consulting with the director of the Hofberg theatre about the production. He was more of a Wenzel than a Caesar; even a man of iron would have found it hard to defend Vienna; how could this artist with his dreamy eyes, be equal to it? Messenhauser organized a general staff and headquarters, looked after provisioning and uniforms, held, parades and inspected fortifications—all in the spirit of a well-meaning and rather simple captain, to which rank he had almost risen in the normal course of his military career. But he had no talents for maintaining himself as a dictator against the various revolutionary instances which were all so remarkably at daggers drawn; at least he secured the Polish General Bem, a trusted freebooter of Napoleonic days, a much battered revolutionary, to look after the strategic aspect of his task, the defence of the outer lines. Whereas Messenhauser exercised his elegant style every day in endless proclamations, only one such of Bem's is in existence; but it sparkles with the same curt decisiveness with which he used to rouse his men to enthusiasm. Bem, who could speak only broken German, would have been impossible as Commander-in-Chief; but Messenhauser was a calamity. How different would

Messenhauser's first adjutant, the fiery Fenner von Fennerberg, with his Italian blood, have been as a leader! He was the author of several of the more determined moves.

The Italians and Poles formed volunteer battalions of their own; there were also a number of other special bodies; Robert Blum and Julius Fröbel later joined the *corps d'élite*. The artillery was greatly augmented; many an old soldier volunteered, they had over seventy-two cannon, but soon ran short of ammunition; the cavalry were only a modest force; the richest citizens had belonged to the mounted national guard and most of them stayed at home.

Vienna was thus prepared to fight for freedom, at first very tangibly for Hungarian freedom, then for German and European freedom. This was battle for an idea, inspired by a generalized enthusiasm, simpler than in contemplation of the actual political powers in relation to one another. Here there were contradictions between the black-red-and-gold patriotism of the Greater-Germans and the red internationalism of the social-revolutionaries, contradictions which were felt very strongly in their individual aspects in the Reichstag, committee of safety, the city council, the lecture hall of the university, the high command, and the individual corps. The October Revolution had neither a compelling leader nor a uniform programme. It was a hindrance to its German-patriotic character that Poles such as Smolka and Bem exercised responsible influence; it went still more against the grain that for months M. Bernes, attaché to the French embassy had been playing a conspicuous part through his connections with the academicians, the Hungarians, the Italians, and also being extremely free with his money; after October 6th he went to Paris, reappeared, and vanished again from Vienna in the second half of the month, when the position became hopeless. Gentlemen of the Press such as Häfner and Tuvora did the same. It was Häfner, too, who asked de la Cour, the French chargé d'affaires, whether the diplomatic corps had taken any steps to protect the city from bombardment; de la Cour replied in the negative and received from the city council a request to prepare a protest against the threatened bombardment of Vienna. The Frenchman sent a verbal answer by his secretary that foreign representatives did not concern themselves in such affairs. It made a peculiar impression that the French chargé d'affaires should have been approached, although on account of his modest status he was the least suited as a go-between. Häfner ended his days in Paris as an agent of Napoleon III.

Thus many an impure element was mixed in the high and heady draught of the Viennese October battles. The best that the Vienna revolutionaries could claim for themselves was that they wanted to continue the popular movement of March and May; that the Imperial State should hold together was a matter of indifference to them in comparison with parliamentarism and social services: they wanted to perfect the meaning of the Revolution from within. From the point of view of the Imperial State idea this was nothing less than rebellion, revolution, crime.

Vienna was surrounded, besieged, conquered. On November 1st the black and yellow flag once more floated from St. Stephan's tower. The intoxication of revolution was over. The soldiers committed many excesses in the outlying parts of the town. How many innocent citizens were massacred no one can say. Robert Blum, too, was shot, his pardon arrived after his summary expectation had already taken place. The Counter-Revolution proceeded with true old-Austrian arbitrary muddle-headedness. Powerless to do anything in the matter, the Parliament in Frankfort protested in vain against the violation of the immunity of one of its most prominent members. Blum had taken part in the fighting on the barricades—and so he fell as a pioneer of Greater Germany, in Vienna, as a victim to the idea of a Greater Austria.

The military counter-revolution in Austria was anti-parliamentary in its inmost being. If things had gone according to the feudal aristocracy, the Reichstag would never have come together again at all, not even in Kremsier, and the parliamentarians who had remained behind in Vienna would have been proceeded against; but it was certainly cleverer to preserve the appearance of constitutional legitimacy. The adherents of parliamentarism must be deprived of Austrian-German Greater-German "democracy"—only thus could parliamentarism be completely destroyed. In reality a determined reign of the sword had now set in in the Imperial State. When at the beginning of October, the unfortunate Count Latour begged only four battalions for the Banus from Windischgrätz, the prince answered in a private letter: "Je vous réponds par un refus formel, car l'Armée de Bohème est destinée a rétablir l'ordre à Vienne." It had come about thus. The army, said Windischgrätz to the Bavarian envoy, was the last bulwark; democracy had proved incapable of creating anything. Windischgrätz had aged greatly in these last few months; he spoke very quietly, very moderately, fully convinced of himself and his mission. His mild, restrained, monosyllabic manner of a military grand seigneur fitted curiously well with his actions. He had taken an initiative. He had appeared in the Imperial camp without having been summoned, he told the Prussian envoy in a confidential conversation that the prince referred with acerbity to the intriguing ambition of the Archdukes. In consequence he was pursuing the preservation of the monarchy as a whole, the legitimate rights of his Imperial lord: "True German interests do not demand the lopping off of the German-Austrian provinces, but the preservation of German influence in the monarchy as a whole."

Thus Vienna's Greater-German patriotism was fought and beaten—in alliance with the Slavs—in the name of the "German idea." Windischgrätz was no hypocrite, nor was he fond of figurative speech; he took a very simple view of the intricate Austrian question and made use of simple means. He believed in Providence and believed himself to be its instrument; it may be that sometimes it was personally a hard thing for him to do what he conceived to be necessary. Welcker, with his classical culture, compared him to Wallenstein; but it was neither this dark spirit nor the fire of personal ambition that possessed him; the prince served the Emperor and the Imperial State in the battle against "Evil."

Prince Felix Schwarzenberg was not a prattler, not full of old man's vanity, no outworn oracle like Prince Metternich in his last stage: he was also far more Austrian. The counter-revolution of Emperor Ferdinand, the rococo of Maria Theresia rustled, flamed and smiled in the great South-German-Bohemian name of Schwarzenberg. A mediatised family like Fürstenberg, Hohenlohe or Leiningen, compensated by Bohemian properties of truly princely extent, brought forth even in its later descendants, such as Prince Felix, types of such European polish, such finished men of the world, that even the most cautious attempt to compare them with Prussian country knights must appear absurd on the face of it. Schwarzenberg was only fifteen years older than Bismarck; if these two had been the combatants for domination in German lands, Prussia's victory would have been more difficult of achievement. Destiny removed Schwarzenberg prematurely from the scene and granted Austria no substitute of equal value. He was a tall, thin figure, delicately built, moving gracefully and without effort, a narrow, smooth head, his glance dull and melancholy, grey before his time, and not only from the effects of typhoid fever, his slender aristocratic figure accentuated by the white uniform of an Austrian general: thus Schwarzenberg steps upon the great page of history, every inch a nobleman of purest breed, no man of iron, but tough and dry, no blusterer, but full of quiet arrogance, quiet lust of power.

"If only I had worked harder," Schwarzenberg said once, shortly before his death. No one had ever taught him to work. He was an amateur of medicine, studied animal magnetism, liked to titillate his nerves, racked to ruin in his early youth, at the hospitals and in the dissecting-rooms, enjoyed reading the classics and practised stealthy cruelty by going trout-fishing. His caustic tongue had already distinguished him as a young man and embittered many who suffered from it. Yet he always remained an exceedingly polite prince, carrying his arrogance with a friendly air. As nephew of the hesitating field-marshal of the Wars of Liberation, Schwarzenberg first became an officer, then turned to diplomacy, was obliged to leave St. Petersburg, having made himself impossible by a friendship with a Decabrist leader, compromised himself in Lisbon by his sympathies for Dom Miguel, went to Rio de Janeiro for a week on a special mission, then to London. Here he became convinced that parliamentarism was quite unsuitable for Austria. Until then a playful Don Juan, he met in England the great passion of his life. Lady Ellenborough left her husband, followed the Prince to Paris and presented him with a daughter. A pompous divorce case blazed the story to the world. Outwardly, Schwarzenberg remained an unmarried admirer of many women, but only outwardly was he a frivolous free-thinker. In the evenings he read Thomas à Kempis, developed ascetic leanings and was soon weary and somewhat bored by everything. The passion for knowledge died in him; he represented something and wished to remain as he was. He now became envoy to one Italian court after another, an easygoing, lenient master, yet sternly meticulous about matters of real importance, never excitable but with a sure wisdom in leadership. Musical to the core and with an expert knowledge of art, he enjoyed the years in Italy as a new but natural luxury; in Rome his beloved world of antiquity came alive for him. But all this, too, was soon over and done with. The year of revolution roused him from the slackness and emptiness of an evil scepticism; he fought on the Italian front, was wounded, put up as a candidate for the Reichstag in his Bohemian home village, his arm still in a sling, but was not elected—which cannot have improved his opinion of parliamentarism; between Radetzky and the Imperial court he served as a well-proved middleman. When a man of energy was needed, the wise Hübner could think of none better; in him was combined everything that the counter-revolution in Austria needed—a feudal lord, of one of the really great and truly Austrian families, a general and a diplomat, a man who knew the world and despised mankind. Schwarzenberg had awakened to danger and the lust of combat, he was a daring gambler, to whom only high stakes were worth playing for; he understood nothing of popular rights, and did not think it necessary to concern himself with them; but his instinct guided him as to the vital needs of an Imperial State. He was himself a fragment of this Imperial Austria and therefore his personal pride was accentuated as soon as it was called into question. So he went on his way, holding a loose rein, bolder and freer than was agreeable to Windischgrätz and many a malcontent of the army, somewhat visionary, almost a genius, calm, ice-cold. Freiherr von Linden, Württemberg's envoy, said of him: "Prince Schwarzenberg is a man of cold and dry understanding with an Austrian heart; he is no Teutomaniac, no Russophile; he knows where to set limits to his will and can pursue those ends with unfaltering firmness." Schwarzenberg was now capable of something which he had never done before. He could work from morning till far into the night, driven on and devoured by his will, and was master in his choice of assistants.

The victory of the counter-revolution in Austria, the decision to carry out the idea of the State as a unity in despite of popular passions, found a particularly happy and strong expression in the change of monarchy on December 2nd. Emperor Ferdinand, who had long become impossible as a ruler, now allowed himself to be pursuaded, greatly against his will and much out of favour with the idea of counter-revolution, to abdicate. After some hesitation, his brother, Archduke Franz Karl, also resigned his claims; and thus the way was free for Archduke Franz (who had just attained his eighteenth year and been declared of age in all Hapsburg-Lorraine lands, including Hungary) to ascend the throne. Archduchess Sophie had won the victory; all the older Archdukes could bury their dreams. The Imperial State of Austria had acquired a young ruler and was itself to regain its youth. The proclamation of the new Emperor revealed the position with perfect clarity: centralism, constitutionalism, the authority of the State: the point against Hungary could be plainly felt; this new, still uncrowned Hungarian king did not need to feel himself bound by all the concessions wrung from his predecessors during the revolutionary summer. For him Hungary was a conquered country, as soon as it should be really conquered; he was conscious only of parts of a great uniform "State"; he was aware of only one monarchy with a single monarch; and just as certainly perceptible was his rejection of Greater Germany, of the Paulskirche, of the "Constitution of the German provinces of Austria under the house of Meran." The new Austria of Kaiser Franz Josef shattered the Frankfort Regency of Archduke Johann. Franz had been the name of the new young Emperor's grandfather, the last Emperor of the Holy Roman Empire, the first Emperor of Austria; it was wise and clever to add to the name of the desiccated absolutist the name of the Emperor whom the people of the Imperial State had never forgotten, the noble Emperor Joseph. "Franz Josef" was in itself a programme, the programme of the eternal compromise, of "this, but also that," the forced companionship of opposites, the alliance between God's help and the Will of the People—in fact, a very Austrian programme.

The princely youth upon whom so many hopes were set, was a very remarkable phenomenon among so many eccentric, arrogant, foolish, intriguing, cavalier, militarist members of the old dynasty; there was something perfectly normal about him. He might have been the son of a provincial manufacturer —a good, decent lad, an obedient son, and a good scholar; slender and athletic, not handsome, with irregular features, without any special interests, devoid of imagination, inartistic, but tactful, unassuming, chivalrous, orderly, dutiful in a rather bored and melancholy fashion; early ripe and then visibly developing no more; quietly running on in the traces of a Roman Catholicism which he had never heard disputed nor believed that there could be any doubt about—rather the Spanish grandee, lacking in humour, without many ideas, unshakeable and matter-of-fact. In a word, he was the distinguished descendant of positive absolutists, but actually the very pattern of a decent citizen ruler who in Württemberg or Saxony-Altenburg supported by a moderate parliamentarism, would have been the happy ruler of a happy people. But this Austria was given into his hands, torn and shattered, just pieced together again by force into an Imperial State, product of the life-history of a dynasty over whose future even a genius of statesmanship might well have come to grief. What was this uninteresting average man, without the good fortune of a warm heart or power to rouse enthusiasm, without any ideas of his own, to make of it?

To begin with, to be sure, he had the inestimable advantage of youth; not that he was especially friendly or modest—perhaps a decided tendency to issue peremptory commands was already visible. Although he had little military talent, he at once took upon himself high rank as an officer; the public were told that he was "decorated with fresh laurels, plucked from the battlefields of Italy"; as a matter of fact, he had been with Radetzky. For Austria this was a warlike epoch, all citizen's battles for freedom and parliamentary rights paled before the banners of war, the uniform was the most popular attire. The young Emperor's first act was to issue a number of military promotions. He had shared the trials and dangers of the

337

wars with the army, it was said, and in the army he would find a support in times of storm.

Count Luxburg, Bavarian envoy, also bore witness to the young Kaiser's love for the army: he was far more Bavarian than Austrian, he said, and in his monosyllabic utterance, but well-considered words, and his self-possessed bearing was the true grandson of the Bavarian King Maximilian I, whose second Christian name was also Joseph.

The Future sat upon the Austrian Imperial throne.

## CHAPTER TWELVE

# THE PRUSSIAN *COUP D'ÉTAT*

THE OCTOBER Revolution in Austria was over, with its shedding of blood, its executions and all its cruelties, buried in the days before the young Emperor. The events in Austria had been important enough in themselves; but only in their repercussion upon Germany, especially Prussia, were they seen in their full historical proportions. The counter-revolution in Vienna gave the Prussians courage for the November *coup d'état*; since so much blood had flowed in Vienna in October, the revolution in Prussia could take place without any bloodshed at all. Frederick William IV might never have been elected Emperor in Frankfort if the accession of Franz Josef had not secured the victory for the combined Austrian State. Austrian "constitutionalism" naturally invited imitation. The popular will found expression in the Reichstag. The popular will had manifested itself in the Viennese October Revolution. The Crown, the Army, both claimed to be organs of the popular will. Where were the real people, what was their real purpose? There were whole complexes of opinion. But moods are prone to change and to change quickly, as the overwhelming majority of the citizens of Vienna now proved with astonishing clarity. The Austrian Reichstag was still suffered, but voices, ever louder, were heard to say that it was no longer the expression of the true will of the people, and should be sent about its business. The painful

part of this for the idea of liberty and for the popular movement was that in the main, these voices were quite right.
The dynasty and the army were successful in Austria; the mass
of the people took the winning side. The Austrian Reichstag,
the Prussian National Assembly, the Frankfort Parliament were
all results of the success of—yesterday. The masses remained
true to them only as long as they continued to fight and to win.

The Austrian Counter-Revolution meant the re-awakening
of the Austrian State idea as against Greater Germany, and the
appeal of the old powers to "true" popular opinion against
the March Revolution and its organs. As early as summer, a
similar process had been going on in Prussia. The 6th of
August, the day of the obligatory parade of honour for the
Vicar Imperial in Frankfort, revealed the might of the opposing
forces to the public eye, perhaps for the first time. About a
thousand peasant farmers from the Teltow district marched
with black and white flags, led by their clergy and a couple
of landowners, and sang the loyal anthem "Heil Dir im
Siegerkranz" in front of the monument of the Wars of Liberation. But two hours later, twelve thousand men of Berlin, but
with only one thousand men of the citizen army among them,
assembled at the same place and covered the monument with
black-red-and-golden banners.

There were many publicist utterances of the newly-awakened
Prussian self-consciousness. The anonymous pamphlet on
*German Central Government and the Prussian Army* which
appeared at the end of July made a particularly strong impression and ran into several editions in a short time. Its author,
Lieutenant von Griesheim of the War Office, an influential
and authoritative speaker, belonged to General Staff circles.
In this booklet it was clearly and unmistakeably stated: German
unity is an abstract idea; the object to be achieved is the unity
of North Germany, with Prussia as its core. Prussia must remain
Prussia, Prussia has a right to be measured with a different
measure than a pocket state like Liechtenstein; the attack of

the Frankforters is directed against Prussia, Austria is weak and has Archduke Johann behind her; the fame of the Prussian officers' corps is two hundred years old and it is unexcelled by any other; the Prussian army shall not be destroyed by the civilians of Frankfort and turned into a "National Army"; the "shadow realm" of Frankfort has the audacity to try and deliver Prussia a fatal blow and the ignorance to imagine that its paragraphs can be carried into effect. The organization of the Prussian army was welded to be the sword of Germany in the fires of 1813–15.

The greater Germanism against which Griesheim clatters and rasps in such a lively fashion was also combated by the re-awakened Prussian spirit in another form. In June the "Prussian League for Constitutional Kingship" was formed and in the course of the coming months developed lively activity in gathering together all loyal elements, especially in small towns and in the countryside. Their pompous language, designed to rope in the unwary, was already manifested in their first petition, addressed to the Minister of the Interior and dated July 8th after the storm on the Arsenal.

The special interests of the province were supposed to be served by the "Representatives of the Provinces," whose experimental pamphlet on July 1st expressly promised to publish communications from the provinces. The most important new publication was the *Neue Preussische Zeitung* which bore the device of the Wars of Liberation, *Mit Gott für König und Vaterland* and an "Iron Cross" on its title-page which gave it its popular nickname of the "Kreuzzeitung." The best-known representatives of the old Prussian aristocracy had put money into this venture, including von Kleist-Retzow and von Bismarck-Schönhausen. Baron von Meyendorff, Russian envoy, participated in the founding of the paper and took shares. He proves that the exponents of the "good cause" always complained that no newspaper would take their articles and that they were very anxious to get Russian gold.

"If the Conservatives prove to have intelligence and energy, I shall ask for further funds," he wrote to Chancellor Nesselrode in St. Petersburg. He delighted to note that as anarchy spread, the friends of Russia increased in like measure. The *Kreuzzeitung* now energetically pursued the old Prussian tradition of the days of the Wars of Liberation, which had not been wars of liberty; friendship with Russia was to be a principle of home and foreign policy; all "Germanization" that is, Frankfort ideas and institutions were to be rejected. Above all they tried to organize opposition to parliamentarism in the folk of the countryside and the county towns by awakening agrarian independence, emphasizing the economic dangers of "anarchy," of the red republic, of Jacobinism and of Communism, and to use these feelings once awakened, against the achievements of March and their consequences. On July 20th, for instance, there was published a letter from two hundred and five peasants and peasant-farmers from Pomerania, addressed to their West Prussian colleagues. A Jewish merchant and owner of a printing press, named Behrend, from Cammin, had appealed to the West Prussian countryside in the name of the Pomeranians in the *Allgemeine Pommersche Zeitung*. This new letter was to be a protest in reply. "Those who make trouble shall learn that Pomeranian oxen have strong heads, sharp horns, quite capable of knocking sense into other people's heads! ... Let us once more teach them that Prussia in spite (!) of her constitutional form, is capable of rising once more to her old power and glory . . . so that we can sing the song with pride:

"I am a Prussian, do you know my colours?"

The *Kreuzzeitung* reprinted this article and used it as a propaganda leaflet. The March popular movement thus saw itself forced into a defensive position. The estate owners were in arms against clubs and the peasant farmers' hunger for land. Under Bülow-Cummerow's leadership a society was formed "for the protection of property," promotion of prosperity of all classes consisting predominantly of landowners. It held a general meeting in Berlin in August under the presidency of Kleist-Retzow, whereby it changed its name to "Society for the Protection of the Interests of Landed Property." Here that section of the population organized itself which had come off badly in the elections to the National Assembly. It was the gentlemen and nobles of the United Diet who now showed that they were still alive and had no intention of resigning any part of their political and economic power. The designation "Junker Parliament" fitted this convention exactly; the landed gentry and other interested parties took hold of the new possibilities of press and club with great political acuteness. They were also "the people," they also had their opinions and wished to make them heard. Blood and soil stood up in the lists against ink and intelligence. This general assembly of an economic group had indeed the political effect of a conservative counterbalance to the National Assembly. It is wrong to judge the old Prussian Junkers on the model of Otto von Bismarck. This son of a bourgeois mother acclimatized himself with great energy to the Junker style of paternal tradition and exaggerated it just because he was in reality so different from it. For the old Prussian nobility there existed only a Prussian Fatherland, a Prussian King, and a Prussian God. Their vision of the world and the State had strongly primitive features, but it was a closed unity, supported by its own inward strength. These nobles had little education, they scarcely ever travelled, the outside world existed for them only in uncertain contours; they did not love cities and were especially mistrustful of Berlin. People who lived in rented houses, who did not eat "their own" eggs, the apples from their own trees, and the hares of their own shooting, seemed to them worthy of contempt. The Junkers were real country bumpkins, loved their beech trees, their willow-shaded brooks, their waving fields of rye, considered the varying inhabitants of the State much as the varying races of their hounds and horses, looked after their

343

underlings somewhat pityingly, at once gracious and strict and with an earthy strain of humour, divided up the work to be done like hours of drill on a parade ground and honoured their king as feudal war-lord, a kind of combination of squire and regimental commander. These Prussian Junkers were splendid and intolerable in the same breath, arrogant and good-natured, according to circumstances—arrogant because they had no understanding of interests other or higher than their own and good-natured if they had their own way; in general they were quiet people, phlegmatic to the point of indolence, who never met trouble half way and if anything did not please them, merely clapped down their visors and ignored it. They rejected everything that was not of their own kind; they were seldom angry, but when their fury broke loose it had all the wildness of an elemental catastrophe. The country squire did not boast, he was too proud and left this to the Prussian bureaucrats who did plenty of it, especially in the new Prussia; these nobles liked to call their castle a house and their park a garden; they were comfortable only at home and when they were ruined and sold up they remained homeless and unhappy for the rest of their lives. But woe to the stranger who dared to meddle with their old traditions! Then they were capable of showing what was behind all the country idleness and indifference, behind a sometimes eccentric backwoods behaviour: a wideawake instinct for political command. Of this material were the men who looked after the provinces and exercised their companies for the Prussian King and the Prussian God. They took their kings as they came, more than one "Old Fritz" could hardly be expected, but if necessary they were prepared to knead their monarch into shape; their Prussian God was a dark Being, Old Lutheran in spite of the Union, full of North German reserve, a kind of unapproachable uppermost superior officer who merely demanded punctual fulfilment of duty; the real country Junker seldom had any streak of mysticism, but was often narrowly pious, usually a literal believer in dogma with all his natural obstinacy, and expected that his Prussian God would reward him accordingly. He thought every departure from tradition improper, against class custom, indecent, but the life he led, without regard for criticism or consequences, was earthy and gave full play to the senses, ruled only by the code of honour of the Prussian officer of the Guards, an extraordinary mixture of narrowness and broadness. Taking him all in all, the old Prussian nobleman was a sociological oddity; whether one loves him or not, the fact remains that from him the metallic clang of political determination struck into the revolutionary happenings, cutting with a sharp, shrill note through the soft, dark string-orchestral music of German liberal patriotism.

The great day for Fr. J. Stahl now dawned when his doctrines should come to honour. The *Kreuzzeitung* party stamped petty coin out of the metal of his forging; he himself one of the most energetic helpers: all living reality, said they, has its positive rights, and needed super-subjective sanction and surety, the State is a legal body and an ethical community; the people are an abstraction; classes are a reality. Based on these principles, the judgment of the political opponent followed with a sharpness that must wound; Liberalism was antireligious, was emancipation of man from God, insurrection against His order and revolt against His laws; liberalism is only half a creed, the revolutionary principle ended in socialism; after equality before the law comes equality of fortune; State and Church are divine ordinances; and so are social and economic order; first faith declines, then morality, then prosperity. It is remarkable to note that industrial capitalism was at first regarded by the *Kreuzzeitung* as an enemy, until Wagener drew a distinction between sacred and immoral industry. But their conservative sympathies were plainly and very significantly with the able artisan. Above all they were anxious to uphold the right of primogeniture in the name of justice and true freedom; nobility, it was said, was distinguished by highmindedness, courage and determination; the nobleman wishes not only to conserve tradition, but would sacrifice himself for his class and for the State: "His back against his dunghill, his front towards the foe."

Good, loyal old Prussia! Was it dead, or would it yet revive? How touchingly Emperor Nicholas was wont to write to his Prussian brother-in-law on the subject! If the old Prussian banner were to gather the old Prussians under its folds—but not the Germans under the barricade flag—then the Russian eagle would be at its side. This would have its effect upon "good Germany"; the King of Prussia would be able to lead them together again under the old Prussian flag.

The Guards, the primogeniture of the Junkers, Greater Prussia at the side of Russian absolutism: they were only single facets of a many-sided totality.

General Wrangel was a joy to the people of Berlin, and as true citizens of a world city, they showed him gratefulness from the very first. He was sixty-four at this time, anything but an important general, not even a gifted leader of troops. Moltke rightly condemned his bad strategy. But Wrangel's muddy brain was poised on top of a very stiff neck. He was a cavalryman of the kind that would take his horse to bed with him if he could. In youth he had been bold and wild enough and owed his success to his inborn artfulness; he was, however, still more sly than artful, still more cunning than sly; serious military learning was strange to him, as were political and intellectual interests of any kind; he had great acting talent and rapidly acquired the Berlin dialect, which he had never spoken before; this Pomeranian rascal set to work to imitate Blücher, the Mecklenburger, and translated that legendary figure of the Wars of Liberation by ways of his own clown-like personality into the revolutionary Berlin of 1848. His success with the man in the street and in the inn-parlour was immediate, especially after the Prussian *coup d'état*. There were so many solemn, all-too-learned, leathern writing-table faces, and now, as relief, a man who made coarse and hearty jokes, an irrepressible buffoon and dressed, into the bargain, in a glittering curassier's uniform!

Was Prussia's only path that of particularistic counter-revolution? We know the sharply Prussian feelings of the Berlin National Assembly; now the Democratic Congress also turned against the Frankfort Regency. These aspects throw light upon Prussia's peculiar situation. The Viennese Counter-Revolution turned away from Frankfort and made an end of Archduke Johann's ambitions at home. Was it not the moment for Prussia to strike—together with the popular movement? At the beginning of October, Stockmar and Count Schwerin appeared in Berlin to discuss the withdrawal of the special embassies, but received an unfavourable answer. Alexander von Humboldt said to Baron von Aretin: "You may rest assured that the King sees through the whole matter and that we shall not fall into the trap. My friend Bunsen is also one of them—but one knows these gentlemen's intrigues." There was one person in the Cabinet, however, who was ready to listen to Stockmar: Count Dönhoff, Minister for Foreign Affairs, whom his Undersecretary of State, Count Bülow, tried in vain to restrain. Dönhoff imagined himself as Imperial Minister of Foreign Affairs at Frankfort. At this moment his views were supported by the arrival of Prince Wilhelm Löwenstein, legation secretary from London, as Bunsen's emissary to encourage the fusion of Prussian and Imperial diplomacy. Count Dönhoff was greatly in favour of unity, he declared the legitimate governments to be powerless and the central executive in Frankfort to be a great moral power. A plan was worked out in the Prussian foreign office for delivering up the entire Prussian consulates to the Imperial executive. The King's assent had not yet been attained and would probably not be easy to obtain. For the moment the Prussian government did not wish the legations coalesced, but was prepared to put the central power at the disposal of the Prussian envoy. This was just what Bunsen was working for.

Thus under the influence of happenings in Austria, the idea of setting Prussia quickly at the head of things took more and more hold in Frankfort. Prussia had turned coldly aside in summer, after the choice of the Vicar imperial, but now there was a movement in Berlin, principally represented by Count Dönhoff, to make the most of the favourable situation. But the Prussian National Assembly was a thorn in the side of the Frankfort Parliament. The mutual relations of the two bodies had always been critical. Could not the Prussian National Assembly be set aside altogether and the Prussian Government work together on this basis with the Frankfort Parliament? The Austrian and Bavarian envoys watched the re-awakening of hegemonic ideas in the Prussian Cabinet with great mistrust. Count Lerchenfeld carefully noted when the abolition of the Vicariate was mooted anywhere in Berlin. On October 19th he depicted the situation as follows: Frankfort was approaching Berlin, Austria was drawn away from Frankfort by the occurrences in Vienna; arguments were going on in the Prussian Foreign Office: Austria must either disintegrate or save itself by means of her Slav elements, *ergo*, Prussian hegemony was secure. "As a good Bavarian I have never had any affection for Austria; but I am forced more and more to the conviction that at the present moment, there is more to be hoped from her than from Prussia. . . . Austria's interest is a league of states, Prussia's interest, a centralized Germany. It is plain enough which is most advantageous for us."

Thus Prussia could launch the *coup d'état*, which was being prepared for the end of October, in two extremely opposite directions. Either centralistic-German: by taking over the Vicariate, carrying out mediation, combining with the Frankfort Parliament, occupying North Germany and keeping off any attempt of Austria or Russia to interfere by means of the army; or she could launch a Prussian-particularistic *coup d'état*: could draw the old Prussian core of the State together by means of landowners and the Guard and so force the uncertain provinces, particularly Silesia and the Rhineland, to give up Frankfort and German supremacy, could stand side by side with Russia and the Austrian Counter Revolution. The Prussian National Assembly would be the victim in any case; it was as much a hindrance to German centralism as to Prussian reaction.

The Camarilla and the military party had long been agitating against the National Assembly. It had certainly greatly irritated the Old Prussians by the refusal to acknowledge the formula of Divine Right, by its resolutions against the class and economic policy of the nobility. But it is not as if the majority of the National Assembly had ever taken up the idea of a fresh revolution and desired an alliance with the street mob and the clubs. Most of these popular representatives wanted what all popular representations want: to carry on their work in peace. The National Assembly believed very strongly in itself, its mission and its rights; but in its majority it had expressly declared itself for agreement with the Crown; the last work had not been spoken in any of the constitutional questions. One can imagine that there might have been an energetic ministry under wise leadership which could have achieved a large measure of understanding with a well-intentioned Crown.

Count Brandenburg, the new Prussian Presiding Minister, the son of Frederick William II and Countess Dönhoff, was very handsome: that was his inheritance from his beautiful mother. In common with his half-brother, King Frederick William III, he had a subaltern nature and a phlegmatic temperament; he was now fifty-eight, had been York's adjutant in Russia, and had probably retained from this experience an antipathy to rebellion of any kind. At Eckau he had gained an order Pour le mérite; he was a slim officer of the guards, honest and decent, not troubled by ideas, bored with himself, reminiscent in many ways of his nephew the Prince of Prussia, uncomplicated, a mixture of corporal and petty highness, that is, the true military type of the Hohenzollerns, without acumen, but distrusting the ways of a constitutional State, an enemy of all "confusion"; in April 1848, he had refused to send troops to Posen—he must and would hold "his" province of Silesia. Freedom-loving Breslau was acquainted with the hard hand of this general; he could not really understand the King, and in spite of all loyal respect, could be as harsh with him as with a younger, not quite adult relative; he spoke himself of his dog-like devotion; but there was also in him the foolishness and the elegance of an overbred animal. Count Brandenburg liked to emphasize the dynastic rights as against his underlings—in part at least he was a "bastard of Prussia" by divine right, as the King called him, with a somewhat nervous pride, in remembrance of Schiller's Bastard of Orleans. What he had to do now may have seemed brutal, the Count may have regretted it, but it was not in his power to alter it. It was an agreeable trait in him that he was perfectly well aware of his own limitations and never thrust himself forward. He neither formed his own ministry nor did he ever really direct it. But since no one else would take the risk, he took it, as a loyal uncle and soldier coming to the rescue in time of need. It had become an order, and consequently the duty was done. Endurance, slickness, and goodwill must serve as substitute for other qualities that were lacking; and finally the unfortunate Count Brandenburg was destroyed by the task for which he was not suited, like a loyal cavalry charger in artillery fire.

Intellect in the new cabinet was represented by Baron Otto von Manteuffel—a strangely unjunkerlike apparition, risen slowly from Landrat to Ministerial director in the official machinery of the civil service, an intriguing official nature, solid, proud of his documents, filled with a somewhat subaltern urge to toil, as dry as parchment, reactionary without any

350

conception of what being a German, much less being a European, might mean. This man with his book-keeper's face
behind its genial large spectacles, smiling, wearily, with oily
eagerness, stood ready to provide every twist and crafty turn
that might be needed for the coming *coup d'état*.

The Imperial patriots of Frankfort shared the mistrust of
all their followers and well-wishers of the idea of dictation.
Other factors also came into play. The jealousy between the
Frankfort Parliament and the Prussian National Assembly did
not finally prevent the Frankfort Parliament taking the part
of the badly treated and persecuted National Assembly, out
of a kind of collegial feeling—in spite of the resolution to
refuse taxes on which they disapproved. Dissolution of the
Prussian Assembly would be a blow to the parliamentary idea,
belief in which was the most fervently upheld doctrine of the
age. And now the dictation of a Prussian constitution possibly
"freethinking," was therefore a grave blow to Frankfort,
because it meant that the work of the Frankfort Parliament
was outdated, put in the shade and severely injured in its
political influence. Such influential Frankfort circles as those
of Max von Gagern, Stockmar, Leiningen, had the idea of
"breaking up" Prussia in order that it might be "absorbed"
in the new Germany. The Prussian National Assembly was
therefore inconvenient to these politicians from the beginning;
the premature determination of a liberal Prussian constitution
appeared to them as a fatal endangering of their own political
labours. Heinrich von Gagern was also filled with this thought.
Camphausen reported: "Max von Gagern's old project: Prussia
at the top and alone, but without general diets in Prussia, these
being replaced by provincial diets, will now be represented
by Heinrich von Gagern." In Frankfort, so full of ideas, many
solutions of the problems were discussed; from here to the
representation of such ideas in the sober-sided Berlin of Brandenburg and Wrangel was still a long way.

H. von Gagern's journey to Berlin in November 1848, was

not welcome to the Prussian government. "We believe that Herr von Gagern's presence will be more effective and more necessary in Frankfort than in Berlin," wrote Count Bülow dryly to Camphausen. When Gagern's advent was reported by telegraph, Count Lerchenfeld wrote a report to Munich in which it was said: "The King of Prussia will have to choose whether he wishes to be King by the Grace of God with four hundred thousand bayonets or revolutionary Emperor by the grace of democracy." According to Reichensperger's communication to Count Lerchenfeld—he had just returned from Frankfort—it was the purpose of the Gagern mission "immediately to unite the hereditary Imperial power with the Prussian Crown." No doubt the main stress is to be laid upon the "immediately." Heinrich von Gagern came to Berlin to offer the King of Prussia the Imperial crown—this had often happened before and therefore no longer made much impression. Gagern had brought about the choice of the Vicar; now he thought it time for another bold stroke. In many ways Archduke Johann had been a disappointment to Gagern; to his great disgust he discovered that the man whom he had expected to use as a tool, was following up plans of his own. Now the Austrian Counter-Revolution had broken the Greater German policy of Archduke Johann and Schmerling. Heinrich von Gagern was the coming Imperial prime minister of the smaller German Empire; he desired clarity—not only on the question as to whether the King of Prussia would accept the Imperial crown when it was offered. At this moment of high tension, Gagern desired an *immediate* decision, and from Frederick William IV in person. It is possible that he suggested to the King one idea of the Prussian provincial diets instead of a Prussian National Assembly; but he cannot in his appeal have laid the main stress upon this point. There were three conversations between the King and Gagern; we have reports only of their main content, not of the details. Gagern made two demands. The first was for the dismissal of the Brandenburg ministry. The impression made by Gagern's mission in Berlin was so great that after receiving Reichensperger's information, the ministers offered their resignation to the King. Gagern now demanded a new Prussian ministry quite in the spirit of his Frankfort instructions—a ministry which would naturally be fitted to form a bridge between Berlin and Frankfort. We do not know for certain whether he mentioned the names of Beckerath and Vincke, but it is possible. It was natural to think of Gagern himself as President of a Prussian ministry, Vincke and the Imperial commissioners E. Simson and Hergenhahn, who were sent to Berlin, may have proposed him. King Frederick William IV, however, defended his ministers against Gagern's onset. Thus the success of Gagern's second demand was seriously in doubt. He told the King that the choice now lay between a permanent overlord and the republic and pleaded with the King to accept the Imperial crown at once. We do not know how Gagern envisaged the details of this move—probably he desired an immediate election by the Frankfort Parliament and then, as a matter of course, the retirement of Archduke Johann. But the King again rejected the Imperial crown. He was in the midst of lively negotiations with the princes of South Germany. Frederick William IV already saw himself as president of a Triad of Kings.

In November he repeatedly received the envoy of the King of Württemberg, councillor Klindworth, and allowed proclamations to be composed for him. His ministers to be sure, would not have anything to do with this doubtful personage. In the second half of November, Count Lerchenfeld received an extensive open document of instructions for his negotiations with Prussia, accompanied by a secret one. Prince Karl of Bavaria also appeared at Potsdam at the beginning of December to negotiate about the triple agreement (Trias). Baron von Verger, a particularly lively supporter of the triad, played the accompaniment from Karlsruhe. In showing coolness to Heinrich von Gagern, therefore, Frederick William IV felt

M

that he had plenty of support behind him. To the remark that Austria had become impossible, he returned the reply that he, as King, wished to preserve Austria, he could accept supremacy in Germany only at the hands of the reigning German princes. Gagern noted only the word "accept" and caught it up at once: "Then I will take it upon myself to persuade the princes to undertake the election and will go from one court to another, from State to State." The King resented Gagern's prophecies of a coming republic and of civil war—Silesia in revolt, Rhineland restless, the whole south only kept quiet by the power of the bayonet; but Gagern was certainly right when he spoke of these dangers; the events of 1849 confirmed his fears. But the King was wounded, he had got over March 18th and wished to hear no more of such things. It was Gagern's solemn way to impart a touch of tragedy to everything; he had come to Berlin charged with authority from the Frankfort National Assembly; and he knew that in these conversations with the King he was fighting for his life's work.

Yet he was not the man who could have ripened such ideas into deeds. Finally, Frederick William embraced his "tempter." He was moved, inspired by so much manly earnestness, such patriotism; he was impressed, but also irritated and annoyed. In his womanish fashion he surrendered, enchanted and over-powered, to the mighty impressiveness of Gagern's eloquence; but, sly and obstinate as he was, he at once thought that he would get his own way in spite of him, and secretly enjoyed his own superior power. Gagern was perfectly frank, he could not be otherwise, he was no intriguer. The King had no such delicacy; he glittered with brilliant epigram and appeared to mean what he said; keener-witted men than Heinrich von Gagern were carried away by him. No one really knew what lay behind the torrent of words. The duet between these two Germans presents a remarkable picture; both were born orators, both deeply related to the movements of the age, both really willing to understand one another, both at once attracted and repelled by one another. Neither considered the other to be the great statesman of whom the age had need; and unfortunately both were right. But Gagern was finally more deceived in the King than the King in him. Gagern was in Berlin for the first time and as a true West German he saw this Prussian great power, patched together out of two incompatible states, as an unfortunate formation. He believed that he could open up the greatest possibilities of development to Prussia by his project of a Little-German Empire. Gagern never comprehended the tough Prussian core of this European great power. The fate of the Prussian National Assembly was to Gagern a matter of secondary importance. Let the King do as he liked about it—if only the Frankfort Parliament attained its goal. He simply would not understand the King's "No," he would not believe it to be the final word. Had not the King often enough said "No" or "Never!", only to do exactly what he had so strictly declined to entertain the possibility of doing? The periodicity of the United Diet, denied several times in 1847, was granted in March 1848; the German Parliament had been determinedly rejected, then the King had proclaimed it in person; the black-red-golden flag, shot at by the troops on March 18th, had been carried through the streets of Berlin by Frederick William IV himself three days later; a piece of written paper should never force itself between him and his people—and now he was about to dictate a constitution for Prussia. Matters actually stood thus: whenever this monarch passionately rejected a matter, it might safely be assumed that later he would enthusiastically support it. Would not it also be thus in the matter of the Imperial crown? Gagern imagined Frederick William's refusal to be a kind of coquettishness, which would be overcome at the proper time. Thus he retired from the conference with the King without any sense of having suffered a definite defeat. To be sure, the King wished to keep his government and persist in his Prussian policy, he could not make up his mind to reverse the tiller and make common cause at once with Frankfort. In Prussian matters he referred Gagern to his ministers. Gagern had purposely demanded more than he expected to get, thinking himself all the more certain to interest the King later in Germany's affairs. Gagern therefore held to his plan of hereditary Emperor for Prussia, he now planned to influence the German princes and prove the trustworthiness of the Frankfort assembly by "conservative" laws (election law, press law and limitation of the right of assembly); thus Gagern's intentions were described by one of his close followers, probably Simson, to the Bavarian envoy; to further relieve Bavarian anxiety it was added that Gagern might not want a triad, but he also wished no "Prussian hegemony," no "imperial despotism." "We desire a Crown Council in which Bavaria would have a permanent presidency so that the Emperor could pass no resolution of importance without her consent." Remarkable was Count Lerchenfeld's impression: "Gagern mainly took care to bring nothing to a point, so that the Left in Frankfort should not resort to extreme measures." Gagern must have regarded it as a measure of success due to his visit that there was no break between the Brandenburg government and Frankfort. Gagern appeared to think that hope could still be placed in Frederick William IV; Prince Karl, the Princess of Prussia, with whom he had spent two hours, and various other dignitaries were not at all inclined to refuse Frankfort's proferred hand. Camphausen gave similar declarations in Frankfort. The Prince of Prussia was more reserved. At dinner on November 27th, he said: "With regard to Herr von Gagern's insinuations, there is nothing to be feared, the King is more determined than I am, and that is saying a good deal." But in consequence of the Gagern mission, sharp procedure against Frankfort, such as Vienna would have liked, no longer came into question for Prussia. Frankfort held possibilities which must be kept in reserve.

To a very large extent the Prussian National Assembly was

its own destroyer. It could never compete in brilliance with the Frankfort parliament—it was a sober, objective, industrious, and somewhat pedantic body. It remained always the creation of the March Revolution which had given it life. But historically speaking it is completely incorrect to regard the Prussian National Assembly as being dominated by the decided Left, the democratic Republicans and therefore useless as a parliamentary body. The majority were definitely monarchistic, they desired an honest parliamentary monarchy after the Western European pattern. The principal weight of the National Assembly lay in the middle; if this block had been united, quite other ends might have been attained. But the two centre parties were the fiercest enemies of all. The lack of unity of the bourgeois-liberal parties condemned them to infertility. The Right Centre pushed the Left Centre into the arms of the Left, and the Right was too weak for collaboration of Right Centre and Right to lead to any results. This disintegration of parties, this contest of fractional cliques, largely dictated by personal ambitions, had already soured the life of the Camphausen government and made work completely impossible for the more sensible sections of the Hansemann-Auerswald government. The majority of the National Assembly had certainly realized that the old military state of Prussia could only be modernized if influence could be exercised upon the executive. The actual means of power must be subordinated to the spirit of self-government. From the very beginning there was a particular interest in the army, as a consequence of the 18th of March: "Scharnhorst wanted to create a popular force," said Jung in the sitting of May 30th, "But Prussia today has the most unpopular military." It was one of the main ideas, not only of the decided Left but also of the Liberal reformers in the centre, to create a people's army in the sense of the old Landwehr. The right of petition and assembly was claimed for the soldier, there was opposition to cadet barracks, to military courts. Again and again the deep-seated opposition to the old spirit of blind command was evident; it was not in the least a pacifistic atmosphere; the members of this assembly were in their way extremely conscious of being Prussians and many assented with full conviction to the spirit of 1813—but it was a battle against the old arrogant and commandeering spirit which was felt to be unbearable as applied to a modern citizen. The Schweidnitz incident—where many civil guards were killed by soldiers, had far-reaching consequences. The fight for the citizen army law furnished new proofs. Johann Jacoby, for one, saw in the contemplated definitive form of the citizen army a third independent body to stand by the side of the army of the line and the *Landwehr*, a realization of the universal arming of the population which according to his idea, would form "the most certain, indeed the only, guarantee of freedom for the citizen." When, in the September troubles in Cologne, General Kaiser and Colonel Engels proclaimed martial law and also suspended the Press, the Centre and the Left in that National Assembly raised a storm of protest—it was an attempt on the freedom of the people. Similar debates were raised over the proclamation of martial law in Posen. The mistrust felt by these parliamentary groups for the military organizations thus went far into the moderate Centre; they rightly felt the unbroken obstinacy of these old powers and showed their dismay by passing resolutions and making interpellations, which often appeared eccentric and merely a disturbance of routine, but were prompted by the haste felt to be necessary, by the uncertain feeling of a battle for existence fought by those who were not in possession of the necessary means of power. The instinct for "power" was there, but not the energy to seize it ruthlessly. Eight of the twelve laws which the National Assembly passed after debate, were confirmed by the King, among them the so-called Habeas Corpus Act and the inhibition of negotiations as to the regulation of conditions between landowners and peasant farmers; four laws were not sanctioned

by the King—among them the law abolishing capital punishment and that abolishing peasant taxation. Twenty-two contemplated laws had gone through the individual departments
and been revised by the central departments; a new Prussia
would have risen from these plans—the Prussia that only after
two generations, quite gradually and finally began to be built
up only by the Revolution of 1918. There should be studied,
for instance, the plans for laws regulating freedom from class
taxation, fatherhood of illegitimate children, the laws relating
to servants and farm hands, etc. In addition to these the Prussian
National Assembly issued a number of other statutory com-
ments and went through several thousand petitions. Their
resolutions as to the constitution of the Prussian State awaited
consultation, had no legal binding power, but merely constituted a project, as to which the Crown was to have its say.
The attacks which were levelled against the National Assembly
on account of the particularly striking resolutions respecting
the Grace of God formula and the abolition of the predicate
of nobility, ignored this state of things, frequently with intent.
The National Assembly itself had by no means spoken its last
word. Now it was dissolved, its work destroyed.

The dictated constitution of December 5th was supposed,
in the words of Count Lerchenfeld "to combine the new freedom of 1848 with the authority of Crown and Law." The
formula, familiar to us from Austria, was to be "constitutional
monarchy." The Brandenburg-Manteuffel ministry claimed
not to be reactionary. But the first impression must vanish
on closer inspection, the dictated constitution was not quite
what it appeared to be. A not very flattering remark of the
Belgian envoy Nothomb hit the nail on the head: "Ce n'est
pas avec des caporaux et des commis qu'on fait un coup d'état."
The corporal was Count Brandenburg, the employé was Otto
von Manteuffel. The flooding of Berlin with military had
made any opposition impossible. But the parliamentary
monarchists and republicans in Prussia felt that the time had

come for a new, second revolution, to be made legally, loyally, as it were, by the help of the dictated constitution. The fresh elections would give them the opportunity of showing that they had the support of the majority of the people. The right to vote had not been abolished, and the democratic possibility of voting must secure them the victory. What an illusion! Their March Revolution had broken the chain of law. The National Assembly had taken pains to build up a new positive law upon the basis of the Revolution; the Assembly was the daughter of the Revolution and desired to legalize it. But the Counter-Revolution also claimed—a natural right; and its organs, its classes, its military and bureaucratic institutions still stood in all their power. The dynamic force of the Revolution, which in Prussia had so very quickly become rationalized, was now faced by the dynamic force of the Counter-Revolution.

Under these conditions, the preparations for the January elections must be made. A proclamation by the Democratic-Constitutional club of Thorn expressed a widespread feeling: "We desire the monarchy as a whole and also the freedom of the people as a whole."

Nothing went further to calm the people of Berlin than the simple fact that in spite of the state of martial law, Wrangel permitted the open-air Christmas Fair to take place as usual. German comfortable good-nature could spread itself again after so much madness, confusion, and noise.

Old Prussianism had survived the 18th of March and imagined that the Revolution was now over.

## CHAPTER THIRTEEN

# THE WORK OF THE FRANKFORT PARLIAMENT

THE BOLDEST ideas that were mooted in Frankfort were concerned with the existence of the Austrian Imperial State, the existence of Prussia as a Great Power; but the full force of political will was never concentrated upon these. They retained a temporary quality, the realities of Vienna and Berlin imposed themselves so decisively that even Frankfort was forced to become aware of them. Thus the crushing of the German Great Powers and their absorption into lands of a new Empire of Germany remained an idea only. More essential to actual happenings was another plan which attacked the problem of the rebuilding of the German State from below instead of from above: this was the plan to mediatize the dwarf states and beyond this to achieve a thorough clean-up in the world of the petty states.

The men of 1848 still stood, either personally or indirectly under the full impression of the work done by the Imperial deputation's main conclusion (1803) and by the Vienna Congress. The Napoleonic period had thoroughly kneaded the old German territories and formed them anew; what was left over and what had arisen anew must be regarded rather as the result of the accident of political hazards than as the fruits of "organically" necessary and justifiable construction. Freiherr vom Stein and Ernst Moritz Arndt had levelled all their thunders

M*

against the "chieftains" with their overweening arrogance. "The land and the people should be immortal and eternal, but the lords and princes with their honour and dishonour are but mortal," wrote Arndt. Görres demanded a natural division of Germany into geographical-ethnically circumscribed "dukedoms," Wilhelm von Humboldt wished at any rate to see her divided into four provinces, in the interests of a proper administration of military affairs and of justice. Since then determined unitarians such as Friedrich von Gagern, defenders of a strong Federal State such as Paul Pfizer, hesitating federalists and conservative particularists had all wrestled together for a generation to formulate the plan of the new German Empire. Prince Leiningen, Queen Victoria's half-brother, the first Prime Minister of the Empire, himself a mediatized sovereign, had experienced the "sovereignty and legitimacy swindle" of the dynasties at first hand and developed under the influence of such impressions into one of the most embittered exponents of far-reaching mediatization. The question of mediatization was raised for the first time in the Paulskirche in June, during the discussion over the setting-up of a provincial central governing power. Vincke and Radowitz fought for the preservation of the individual states and emphasized the attachment between dynasty and subjects; but Moritz Mohl described in moving terms the miseries attendant on the old German splitting up into petty sovereign states, and von Wydenbrugk of Weimar, with special regard to Thuringia, advocated the conglomeration of the small fragmentary states into larger, more efficient state bodies. Public opinion now began to be aroused to the problem; discussion did not die down again, particularly in Thuringia. During the debate on the reservations made by the King of Hanover concerning the acknowledgment of the Vicar Imperial, Wesendonck and even Bassermann spoke strongly in favour of centralization and the right of the National Assembly to crush all resistance to unity; that is to say, by mediatization.

Even previous to this (on July 4th), Römer, March minister from Württemberg, had written to his king about mediatization. He advised him to endear himself to public opinion by resigning a part of the civil list and supporting the plan of a German fleet, in order that he might secure a choice portion of the spoils when partition time came. But to Römer's surprise the King received the suggestion very coolly. When King William was in Frankfort in July, the question came up in a conversation with Heinrich von Gagern at which Römer was present. The King's indifference, even antagonism, to possibilities of increase of territory, surprised von Gagern. But the King of Württemberg was much too clever to accept any gifts from the popular movement which might compromise him in the eyes of his princely compeers. He was very well aware of the Emperor of Russia's opinion on such matters. When princes mediatized as had been done formerly—that was the will of Providence and no one could complain; but mediatization by a popular government—that was a revolutionary crime! Emperor Nicholas said to General von Pfuel in St. Petersburg that he was determined never to recognize a new condition of things which should be brought about in Germany by direct or indirect mediatization of the reigning houses.

But the Imperial ministry in Frankfort had pursued the idea of mediatization with lively interest even after Leiningen's resignation from office. He quite rightly regarded the dwarf states as foci of unitarian republicanism. Saxony-Altenburg and Anhalt-Köthen were particularly eager. Here the popular movement had completely paralysed the governmental powers. Similar manifestations occurred in Hohenzollern and even in Nassau. After the defeat of the September Revolution in Frankfort, new revolutionary cells began to be formed everywhere. The simplest and most thorough cure seemed to be the union of the dwarf and petty states with their nearest great neighbour. But representations made by the Imperial ministry to this effect, culminating in the proposal that the rulers in question should apply to the Central Government, had no effect. The petty princes had far too much dynastic independence not to turn a cold shoulder to the idea. Several states, however, supported mediatization in their own interests. Thus Hesse-Darmstadt proposed to amalgamate with Electoral Hesse; thus Saxony-Weimar proposed to unite Thuringia under her wing, but aroused the jealousy of Gotha, which hoped to obtain English sympathies for carrying out a similar plan. Saxony kept watch in hopes of gaining something for herself. The dwarf states in danger of mediatization conceived the idea of a defensive league. But the central power in Frankfort saw in the plan, not only a means of weakening the republican party, but also a promising way of strengthening the states of medium size and thus providing a counter-weight against the Great Powers. The Frankfort patriots had no idea of enlarging Prussia, rather the contrary. Their aim was to form a number of countries, approximately equal in size, economically and technically capable of supporting an ordered government, but dependent upon a strong Central Imperial government to hold them together. Camphausen certainly realized what this movement meant and advised the Berlin government to win the sympathies of the threatened small powers and protect their position.

In August 1848, the then Prussian Prime Minister von Auerswald had himself designated the existence of the small German principalities as the greatest evil; it was impossible for them to continue in their present degree of sovereignty; he had deplored the fact that these small states would rather let themselves be "wholly mediatized" than "connect themselves with a great State, sacrificing a part of their governmental rights." But in the meantime things had taken a rather different course. Pfuel being prime minister, Camphausen now received word that Prussia would take no active part whatever in plans for mediatization; it would take its stand upon loyalty and law.

In times of political decline, economic powers usually push to the fore and aspire to direct the course of national life. The revolutionary period had deeply shaken the power of established authority; the new powers had still to win prestige and acknowledgment. The economic distress immediately before the outbreak of the revolution was generally regarded as one of the main causes of the outbreak. Every epoch is accustomed to simplify the immediate past, in order to attain to a clear perspective of its own conditions of life. From a higher point of view of historical determination, the economic transformation in Germany was in any case one of the fundamental facts of contemporary happenings. The new economic types pressed into politics—merchants, farmers, master artisans, workmen, got together just as everyone else got together, discussed their professional interests in parliamentary fashion, decided on motions, and passed resolutions. The young science of national economy claimed to influence economic and even political practice, and respect for the German professor permitted no contradictions. Jurists and philosophers of history were now thrust back into second place; they were too nearly related to the old State, their work had too often served the purposes of the old, fallen powers. In the proceedings of the *Paulskirche* one clearly distinguishes the deep impression made—at least at first—by the economic theoreticians and practical experts. The economic committee, known as the "Committee of Labour, Trade and Commercial Relations" made the most demands and was the most industrious of all the committees. It always felt itself to be more or less in competition with the Constitutional Committee and often increased its work while making its accomplishment more difficult, although the Constitutional Committee was of far greater immediate importance.

Its endeavour was to solve the German problem by means of economics; but like all great practical tasks, this had to be tackled politically, that is by means of concrete action, and only after this had been done could it be juristically built up and economically underpinned. It is always healthier for political economy to obey than to command. But the national economic committee was obsessed by the prevailing diseases of the age—the itch for sovereignty. It did not wait for problems to be presented to it—it saw problems thrusting up from every side. There was no such thing as an all-German economic plan, knowledge of economic problems, directions of them. The members of this committee, half of them professors, had the great happiness of contemplating a strip of virgin territory. They began their researches, instituted inquiries and formed resolutions. It was the curious factor of the Frankfort events that a German empire was being constitutionally formed and its laws settled, and at the same time was already actively exercising its political functions.

As long as the Imperial unitarianism of the Central Power called forth resistance from Prussia, a Prusso-Bavarian rapprochement was extremely possible. But as soon as the danger of an agreement between Prussia and the Frankfort Parliament appeared on the horizon, Bavaria turned against Prussia, against the Little-German group in the Frankfort Parliament and approached the newly strengthened Austrian Imperial State. King Max would not allow Prussia to assume chairmanship even in his beloved Directorium—if only in order that the diplomatic corps, which had to be accredited to the Central Power, might be forced to come to Munich. Such points were of great importance to a monarch who took such delight in etiquette. Maximilian was a weak character, who wished to stand well with everyone. Just because his wife was a Prussian, he was insistent upon his own Bavarianism; just because, hungry after things of the intellect, he stood for high cultural interests, above creeds and confessions, he left the New

Teutons a free hand; he listened to a great many advisers and then followed the advice of the last one heard. Anyone who was clever could easily gain the confidence of the responsive and always interested monarch; but it was a difficult matter to maintain the relation with a ruler so distrustful and so fond of change; once Prince Wallerstein was the oracle of Nymphenburg, then Count Armansperg with his Greek experiences, then Count Degenfeld, the envoy of Württemberg, who received direct instructions from his king as to the influencing of Maximilian. According to the Russian envoy, Frankfort was the "chauchemar" of the Bavarian ruler; the timid man received little support from his ministers, who had been accustomed to the tyranny of his father. Count Bray, minister of foreign affairs, was a man of high character and principles, but mediocre talents and, in addition, exceedingly indolent. He let things take their course, did everything in an amateurish fashion, was not at all well-informed of current events, never had independent ideas, but did not suffer in the least from these defects; he always found a way out thanks to his sunny disposition, trick of making suitable general remarks and neat witticisms. Thus the King and government never knew their own mind, especially in the German question; their only idea was to get over momentary difficulties as best they could, always with an eye to special advantages for Bavaria.

Even as a raw youth, King Maximilian had always wanted to know everything, to get at deeper meanings, to bring about a happy compromise. An industrious student at Göttingen, he had learned to live with learned men without possessing any learning of his own; he was a tireless, sometimes rather eccentric, questioner; he believed in education and wished to make up for much lost time in Bavaria. He would like to have published his own poems, but took Geibel's advice and returned them to his desk; his nature, rather that of Faust's famulus, Wagner, was now forced jealously to play the sovereign. The former King Ludwig still lived in the old royal chambers of the residency, regretting his abdication more deeply from day to day; burdening the young court with his endless demands for money and souring his already too self-critical son's attempts at kingship by malicious and sarcastic remarks. At the beginning, King Maximilian wanted to see everything and decided everything himself and thus, tiring easily and unequal to thorough debates, he arrived in spite of his decided constitutional leanings, at a Cabinet government which sometimes, strangely enough, took on the form of despotic impatience and capriciousness; it was a style of government which was already familiar in Bavaria, but was not at all in accordance with the gentle, fine nature of this particular ruler. Once a week King Max went to Castle Berg, accompanied only by an adjutant, to receive in all secrecy the most unpleasant visitors. He developed a liking for secret agents and publicists, arising from a not unreasonable mistrust of his official assistants, also from a certain modern-minded preference for independent and original talent, but still more from his fancy for mysterious workings of monarchical favour. Thus the King liked to work with Klindworth, the well-known private diplomat of the King of Württemberg and discussed with him a project for a Directorium of Five, in which Prussia and Bavaria were to take an equal place at the head before the other states; Württemberg was to be compensated by being given command of the Federal alliance, Saxony by command of the Thuringian contingent. The King of Hanover, to be sure, refused to enter into negotiations with the "notorious" Klindworth. The Bavarian king enjoyed making just such indefinite plans; he had nothing like a leading political idea. Thus he arrived at an unreliability, even falsity; his character, which had such good foundations, was destroyed by its own weakness. His popularity already began to suffer. Many of his subjects began to long for old King Ludwig who at least had been thoroughly German in his feelings. Thus unfruitful Bavarianism was logical only in negation; never, no never, said King Max to the Prussian envoy, would he agree to the Frankfort idea of an Emperor, with all his powers he would resist; if it was insisted on, civil war in Germany could be the only result. He wished to go hand in hand with Prussia on the principle of peaceful agreement, and the King told the Saxon chargé d'affaires that his whole people stood behind him in rejecting Prussia's claims to hereditary empery. The Prussian envoy justifiably called King Max's attention to the fact that the desire to collaborate in some way with Prussia found no echo in the Bavarian Press.

Austria and Bavaria therefore came together; they at least agreed in rejecting this Prussian claim to hereditary empire. But the work of the Frankfort Parliament reached its apex precisely in this idea. Sober thinkers, hoping to achieve results by way of pure negotiation, must also note in Frankfort that since the dissolution of the first March Revolution, only a Federal Directorium could be achieved. Gagern's ministry therefore thought it necessary to achieve this measure of sobriety, and in spite of all visible hindrancess and opposition, succeeded in taking the majority of the Frankfort Parliament along this road. The idea of the Directorium was thoroughly discussed in the constitutional committee; only Schreiner, member for Graz supported it—he also composed an exact plan for such a Directorium of five. But the plan only received 84 votes at a plenary session, whereas 120 votes were cast for the Republican head of affairs, that is, to leave the office open for any German to be chosen. Schüler, Wigard, and Heinrich Simon supported this point of view in the Constitutional Committee. Some wished to restrict the president's term of office to six years, others supported twelve years. Welcker's motion to alternate the centre of power every six years between Austria and Prussia was defeated at a full session by 377 votes to 80. The majority of the committee had agreed to the idea of a life-long hereditary "Emperor of the Germans." The title of emperor for the chief ruler was won by a small majority

(214 to 205), but the hereditary character of the sovereign was rejected by the plenum at the first reading, the majority not being very great, but clear enough (263 to 211). The decisive votes were taken on January 19th, 23rd, and 25th. The Imperial council, which was to unite the representatives of the various states only received a majority of 11 votes, but no decision could be arrived at as to the number of its members and the states which were to have the right to appoint them (January 26th). So imperfect, even problematic, did the work of the Frankfort Parliament appear only five weeks after the taking over of its affairs by Heinrich von Gagern! The best-intentioned observer must needs begin to doubt whether it would ever be able to arrive by its own strength at any useful results. The German governments began to go feverishly to work. The race was coming to an end. Decisions were about to be made.

The Imperial candidate of the Gagern Empire, King Frederick William IV of Prussia, now stood once more at the control switch of German destiny. What hopes and expectations were based upon this man! How he put his contemporaries to the test, even to the torture, as, tireless and never dismayed, energetic and sparkling, he surprised and entertained the political world of the day with continually new twists and turns. Yet in all of them there was the same unfruitfulness. Austria, he thought, should again claim the old Imperial crown of the Holy Roman Empire of Germany, while Prussia, as Hereditary Marshal of the Realm, should rule with the other kings over the newly-divided Germany of six Imperial provinces. If this were Prussian ambition, it was a singularly blind and modest ambition. The three federal alliances—the great alliance with all of Austria, the German alliance of states with the German-Austrian countries and the Federal State under the council of kings, of which Frederick William IV babbled in his memorandum of December 21st, harmonized oddly enough with the ideas of Schwarzenberg and King Maximilian. Frederick

William IV was in fact the best ally of the sworn enemies of the Prussian State. For the result of such a monstrous system of boxed compartments would certainly have been the strengthening of Austria's position in Europe and improved status for Prussia's most dangerous rival, Bavaria and the smaller kingdoms.

On March 28th, the day of the voting for the emperor, the Imperial Constitution and the Imperial election law were officially proclaimed. The Frankfort Parliament had finished its work, very tardily and very painfully, as it was well aware. It believed in its work, stoutly as it had always believed in itself. If we consider this work, this Imperial Constitution as it finally came about, once more in its entirety, we are struck by the manner in which all compromise, which only becomes comprehensible when we remember the tactical necessities of parliamentary procedure, fades and disappears behind its main features of a free and proud dignity. The boldness of the March spirit of 1848 revives again with remarkable vigour in the seven sections, worked out with so much difficulty. This Imperial Constitution was a daughter of the revolution, dowered with the best that had come to light in this very German revolution. It made no compromise with the actual situation in March 1849—with defiant courage, the great beginnings, the spirit of the Raveaux motion, the Soiron word of "one and only," the bold grip of Heinrich von Gagern were carried on to a conclusion. With simple clarity, still full of the conscientiousness in words that distinguished the great literary epoch, with a feeling for form which was at once juristically correct and philosophically responsible—so this Imperial Constitution built up the Imperial power upon Imperial territory, fitted out this power with the trappings of diplomatic representation, the right to conclude international treaties, to decide upon questions of peace or war, to control the movements of the army and navy, to supervise traffic and the post; this Imperial power was then to be personified in the person of the ruler of the realm, the Emperor of the Germans, the hereditary incumbent of the highest dignity, with a civil list and responsible ministers, with a highest command and the right to dissolve the Reichstag which was to consist of a house of states and a house of the people; the Emperor was to be a mighty, unitary factor as against the individual states, as against the Reichstag, which was also unitary, but limited by the veto, which had merely a procrastinating force. Finally, the Imperial court of justice took its place as the third unitary factor, a political executive court and guarantor of a unity of law and justice for the entire realm. This unitary basis of the Frankfort Imperial Constitution is, however, weakened in the final form by a number of compromises, in consideration of the wishes of the individual governments. The governments were to give up the right to envoys and consuls, but to maintain representative bodies under the head of the empire, whose members they were to choose for themselves; Imperial lawgiving was under certain restraints and a further extension was to be considered as a constitutional change; the Imperial budget was built upon the presumptive profits of customs dues and imposts; Imperial taxes were only to be levied in case of need; the alteration of the form of government in the separate states was dependent upon the assent of the Imperial power and thus the transition to a republic was made as good as impossible. The Imperial court of justice was also to be the seat of proceedings when separate states had complaints to level against the central power. The house of states was conservative and federalist, both on account of the way it was composed and of its functions. It was well adapted to smooth away any abruptness which might arise from decisions of the people's house, elected by universal, equal and secret vote. This right of franchise, which so greatly disquieted contemporaries by its revolutionary character, was thus corrected in the very Imperial Constitution itself. Certainly one cannot deny that there were weaknesses in the work of the Frankfort Parlia-

ment, especially in the fundamental laws; but seen as a whole·
it was an achievement of equally high value, whether regarded
politically or intellectually, a statement of principle and a demand, daring and yet well-balanced, victoriously rising over all
the early plans of its creators in the Constitutional Committee;
not one of them, nor any of their parties had wished to create
the Constitution as it appeared in its final form; it was in truth
the creation of an inward, truly democratic united spirit; the
princes and their underling officials, all the powers of particularism and the counter-revolution might take offence and
be enraged at the document; but the German popular movement of 1848 recognized in it all that was best in the German
spirit and was once more to take fire at its flame.

Once more in these days Prussian statesmen experienced the
humiliating spectacle of a monarch who alternately raged,
shouted, whined and complained, who interlarded sentimental
babblings with coarse abuse, who always thought less of
Germany than of his own person. Several times he demanded
a congress of princes as a proper organ of franchise and
threatened abdication, if he were to be forced to accept a
crown from the people; Germany was not to have so much
happiness. In Frankfort this abdication was desired, the Austrian
envoy slyly whispered to the King, thereby telling him something which he knew would be pleasant hearing. In speaking
to Prokesch Frederick William IV referred to the Imperial
crown of Frankfort as a "pig's crown"; in a letter of March 7th
to the Grand Duke of Hesse he spoke of it rather more jokingly
as a "sausage sandwich," no divinely ordained crown but a
gift "from Master Butcher and Baker." Thus the Imperial
crown was the most important thing to the King; for him
personally the Constitution already proclaimed receded quite
into the background. The Ministry of State had to make the
best of this fact. In the minutes of April 2nd there is a statement which means a great deal though saying little; right
at the end as point 4: "His Majesty the King considers the

assumption of the Imperial title to be unacceptable under any conditions." As meaning and aim of the message to the Imperial deputation it was established: The first thing to attempt is to achieve an understanding with Austria over the proposed Federal State under Prussian leadership; this Federal State as the Frankfort Imperial Constitution saw it, could only succeed if the German kings agreed to it; if they did not agree, then Prussia would conclude its protective arrangement with the North German petty states, just as Camphausen had already prepared it.

The King's answer was a curious mixture of yes and no, of phrases for and against. There was nothing about the narrower Federal State, no recognition of the work that had been done, no encouraging and positive statement of assent. But, in conclusion, we have a thoroughly banal word of comfort, put in a most offensive form:

"If there should be need of a German sword and shield against danger at home and abroad, I shall not fail, even without being called upon. I shall then cheerfully take the path of German honour and loyalty."

But in its language and content, this proclamation was a most unhappy product of Prussian government wisdom; it expressed but feebly the ministerial intention to express a qualified assent; by wrong intonations in reading, Friedrich Wilhelm IV turned the inadequate assent into a poorly concealed negation. Ungrateful and arrogant in his disarmingly charming manner, he joyfully declined the people's Imperial crown; the offer was treated so contemptuously that it was not even found worthy of express mention. The Russian envoy who was present with Countess Lerchenfeld at the reception to the deputation which brought the offer, must have rejoiced. This was the last stroke of royal revenge for the 18th of March, 1848: Frederick William shattered the work of Frankfort and rattled his Prussian sabre. The deputation was entirely in the right when, in spite of the doubts of Dahlmann, Riesser, and

Biedermann, who wished to allow fourteen days for consideration, they sent a written acknowledgment of this answer as a refusal, and returned home. Let the Prussian government see what it could do with such a king and with the work of the Frankfort Parliament. Frankfort Imperial patriotism had finished with Frederick William IV. It was its gravest, but also its noblest error, ever to have offered the people's Imperial crown to this monarch at all. It was too good for him. In the heads of Heinrich von Gagern and his friends, Max von Schenkendorf's verse, quoted by Wurm of Hamburg in the *Paulskirche* during the debate on the election of an emperor, may long have been ringing:

> O, do at last grow wiser,
> Sheep by no shepherd kept,
> And choose yourselves a Kaiser
> And force him to accept.

They tried to force the King of Prussia to accept. Anyone who had so often changed his mind might also give in this last time. But the calculation was false. Frederick William IV certainly did not become a consistent statesman because he refused the Imperial crown; he was only once more consistent in his inconsistency. What was now to become of the German revolution remained to be seen. How the King of Prussia had run after the popular movement only a year before! Now he poured scorn upon it. Perhaps the revolution would now begin over again? One thing was certain: a crown would not again be offered to a people's Kaiser in Germany.

CHAPTER FOURTEEN

# THE SAVING OF PARTICULARISM

THROUGH the perfecting of the Constitution and the choice of the Emperor, the Frankfort Parliament had once more aroused the attention of the German nation. It had come into being out of a movement which shook all Germany—the unforgettable March storm of 1848. It was meant to create a permanent political form for the national unity which had been felt at that time; and now it had in reality presented the German people with a German Empire. People remembered the Frankfort Parliament again—for it was unfortunately true that already it had nearly been forgotten. The focal point of political events had again shifted to the individual states. Near and immediate troubles thrust aside distant interests. Like every thing in German history, this first great popular movement had split up into fragments. The old German historical principle might be adapted in bitterness; *cuius regio eius—revolutio*. The Frankfort Parliament could, to be sure, create its provisional central power, Imperial regent, and Imperial ministers, argue about mediatization and resolve upon Imperial statutes. Since the autumn of 1848, the situation had changed and not only in the two great powers. But had not the idea of the empire been welcomed most glowingly in the world of the petty states? There came a singular development. The princes with their apparatus of officials and armies had been a heavy and senseless burden upon the all-too-many fragmentary principalities; now there came about in these artificial formations a body of public opinion, an excitable grouping of parties, bitter battles in parliamentary corporations; local ambition was awakened and threw itself into local work. Persons of real significance sat in the Frankfort Parliament and took thought for the great affairs of the nation; the little masters, the busybodies, the chieftains of clans, clubs, and cliques, also wished to achieve something and found in the petty states a welcome field of activity. Whereas the patriciate of money and titles devoted themselves in over-whelming measure to the national idea and encouraged every-thing which led out of the narrow bounds, a new kind of comfortable particularism took its rise in the upper middle class. Here there were fears that strong centralization might bring disadvantages to business, there were fears that oppor-tunities might be lost of playing a part and exercising influence. The suffering middle-classes and the lower levels, sinking into proletarianism, to whom the blessings of the revolution did not in the least extend, were all the more inclined to become sharply unitary as against this new form of particularism, but in the sense of a German Republic which should be one, and with a social-revolutionary programme. There could be no better constellation for the old powers in the German petty states. Dynasties and bureaucracies formed an alliance with the local solid burghers, who felt themselves honoured and at last recognized at their true worth; but supporters of the national Imperial idea and republican revolutionaries were all cast into one pot by these united forces of particularism and duly cursed in the name of all revered traditions. Anyone who is inclined to ask why the great impulse and impetus of the March Revolution so soon faded away, finds his question answered by a study of these relationships. All new forms of political life were used too energetically, were distorted into caricature, turned into their own masks of misery in the Germany of the petty states. The Frankfort Imperial idea had not the courage and the power, probably also no longer the practical possibility of making a clean sweep here: the petty states were robust enough to cast suspicion upon everything, even the moderately unitarian, everything that was national and central; in short, everything truly German that proceeded from Frankfort, and to render it valueless. In greater Austria and greater Prussia important historical powers were at least collected together; the idea of Germanism knew what it had to reckon with there. Bavaria's particularism and that of the petty states, however, represented something overwhelmingly negative— a mixture of ill-will, fear and idle chatter, only apparently harmless, but really foolish, obstinate, and self-satisfied. There was not one German revolutionary movement, not one grouping of parties, not one national aim; oh, no—there were the Lübeck, Anhalt, Mecklenburg, and many another revolution and petty revolt, there were parliaments, large, medium, small, and dwarf, parties according to religions, constitutional, monarchic-dynastic, economic, family and all sorts of other points of view. There were very numerous aims, aims to be achieved by the nation as a whole, but also aims of groups, of interested parties, of the upstarts, and of those who still hoped to arrive. Thus revolutionary and counter-revolutionary presented a particularly lively and tangible picture of the confusion of a political-intellectual goose fair, too much education and energy, too little tact and consideration. Next to true prophets, noble leaders, serious warners, well-meaning and lightened men who blew the trumpets to battle, there were jugglers, money-makers, swindlers, chatterers, gushing spirits, rogues, and fools. Germany was once more poor in its richness, small in its greatness, yet great in pettiness, rich in wretchedness.

Particularism was the true curse of Germany. Bavaria was its classic home, since here the weight of popular feeling ran rampant—because the power of the State was comparatively abrogated and compelled to cling to the Catholic idea. There was no natural centre of interest for all Bavaria, all the separate clans strained apart from one another, the more fervently, the stronger their own racial life was accustomed to express itself. For in Germany, one kind of particularism was eternally getting the best of another. The dynasties were up in arms against an overlord, the Imperial cities against the residences, the various tribes against the domination of any one of them—which in the State of Bavaria was precisely the one that was most backward.

The Frankfort Parliament wished to bring German history to perfection; but German history must first be made. Everything truly national remained a purpose to be attained; the reality was the anti-national rule of each petty state for itself. The princes sulked and trembled for their thrones; the worst pre-March tyrants cooed sweetly and waited for better times; the Crown Princes of yesterday were not a whit better than their royal fathers—they intrigued, made separate alliances, tried to reconstruct the Rhine alliance, made a great many promises, kept very few, rattled their small and rusty sabres, and kissed the Czar of Russia's boots. Between the princes and the most humbly devoted subjects there sprang up a bitter quarrel about money and land. The revolution, it was said, was expensive—but the princes were certainly no cheaper. If there were any prince prepared to compromise, his own nobles forced him back into the old path. Want sat sighing in every alley, it was difficult to help the working class in city and country; neither was there much time to spare for them, for speeches had to be held in clubs, articles written for the Press and debates held and resolutions passed in all the little parliaments. Precisely the hard work done in these assemblies, served to intensify particularism. The new particularism of the many city assemblies, the numerous parties, the thousands of clubs, split up the new Germany almost more thoroughly than old Germany had been split by the old particularism. The worst enemies of the Revolution were the many baby revolutions. Almost every individual State had a franchise system of its own. Everywhere there was grabbing for positions; the smaller the State the more surely personal rivalry, vanity, and envy ruined the life of the communities, large and small. Proletarians shouted for education; parsons preached of a socialistic future; a "Constituent Assembly" was the cure for all evils; even the soldiers began to talk of their human rights. Imperial commissioners from Frankfort travelled all over Germany, tried to create order and quiet and earned nothing but rebuffs. Imperial and other troops marched from one State into another; all the curious frontiers of 1815 were no longer secure; the system of the petty states was cracking and rotten at the core; a strong blow from the shoulder and it would have gone to pieces. But there was no one who dared to strike the blow. German particularism saved itself once more.

## CHAPTER FIFTEEN

# THE CIVIL WAR FOR THE CONSTITUTION

THERE WERE three schools of thought beside and above the particularistic splitting-up of Germany: the national, the clerical and the socialistic-communistic. But the national and socialist-communist schools of thought were also seized by the passion for sub-division which characterized all Germany at this time; Catholicism alone was uniform in its essential being as a new factor in the formation of a political will.

The neo-Roman spirit was everywhere as a potent factor—in Hildesheim, Münster, Cologne, Freiburg, Munich, Vienna. What is the aspect as a whole? In the first place, the episcopate rejoiced over the overthrow of the police state by the Revolution, for it was supposed that the antiquated national church system would now disappear. There were people to defend it, such as Dean Kuenzer of Constance in the Frankfort Parliament. But Geissel, Archbishop of Cologne, who was later to wear a cardinal's hat, attacked all "Liberal" Catholicism with clever and ruthless energy. In May he collected his suffragan bishops about him; the policy to be followed by the Church was developed: free communications of the bishops with Rome, the schools to be directed by the Church according to her own canonical law. The Neo-Roman idea found an extremely effective exponent in Professor Buss of Freiburg: he founded newspapers and societies, roused the masses, and demanded that the new freedom should also apply to the life of the Church. The Münster society was the first to proclaim as election slogan the motto: "For Truth, Freedom, Right!" Many Catholic newspapers took up the cry. Mainz became the natal city of Catholic democracy. The Pius society came to life here, a society "for the protection of religious and ecclesiastical freedom," as early as May 23, 1848; here in October, the first German Catholic Day was convened under Buss's chairmanship, its avowed object being to weld the Pius societies into a "Katholischen verein Deutschlands." The quick-eared Prussian minister in Karlsruhe, von Arnim, spoke in warning tones of "a mighty power" that was being built up and of the Catholic societies that "overran all Germany." When, however, he said that the Catholic clergy were concluding "an open alliance with the Imperialists and Republicans of the *Paulskirche*," he was taking rather too simple a view of matters. The Catholic people's party which was now coming into being was in many ways a most peculiar case. The party finally opposed not only the imperialists, but also the republicans in the Frankfort Parliament, although their ways were the same for a time. It was a power and a class in itself. The significance of the clubs was decreasing, wrote Riederer, Bavarian chargé d'affaires in Karlsruhe; only the "Catholic Society" in Freiburg continued to grow; the population there had never felt any sympathy for Baden; now they openly showed a preference for Catholic interests; everywhere on the Rhine, the hierarchic aspirations of the Catholic party were watched and commented upon by the Press.

In Mainz, Buss and Baron Wilhelm von Ketteler first met in person; Catholicism took up the social problem. Kolping's apprentices' club was augmented by the Vincentius club; a stand was to be made against pauperism; commercial and factory life put on a sound basis; those unable to work should receive support, those out of work must be housed, an attempt made to find jobs for them. Ketteler, one of the mightiest figures of this rising world, was one day to bring these things to fruition. He was a proud nobleman of old Westphalia, who as a youth had had no love for Prussia; who had led a cruel, frivolous hunter's life, and then, reforming, began to read de Maistre and Fénélon and allowed himself to be led into the priesthood by his friend, Count von Reisach, Archbishop of Munich and Freising. He became a belligerent monk, full of the unction of the born commander, physically impressive, pious-hearted, impetuous, despotic; without any of the sentimentality of the aesthetic older Catholic romanticism, lacking the elegance of the prelate; neither a scholar nor a diplomat, but a true working-man's bishop; clever, practical above all, energetic, swift, candid and intent upon getting things done.

Archbishop Geissel sat in person in the Berlin National Assembly and kept his Catholic parliamentary colleagues together by holding regular consultations, without forming a separate faction of his own. Peter Reichensperger and Professor Walter, the Bonn defender of ecclesiastical rights, were his nearest colleagues. Geissel also influenced Diepenbrock, Prince-Bishop of Breslau, who sat very unwillingly and also unsuitably in the Frankfort Parliament; he advised and brought about communications between the Catholic members of the Frankfort and Berlin assemblies; neither did the "Catholic Society" in the Frankfort Parliament which had thirty or forty members, was led by Radowitz and much influenced by the warm-hearted, "Gothic-natured" August Reichensperger, its vice-president, ever become a party, but remained a society of those who thought alike and worked to preserve Catholic interests in each individual case, especially in cultural matters: the Church was to be independent of the State, but to be preserved as a public and legal corporation; the members often opposed one another in purely political matters, and aroused distrust precisely on this account. Radowitz, acting on well-considered tactical grounds, opposed the admission of the

Jesuit Order into Germany in the name of the society. Simultaneously, Geissel was inviting the first Jesuits to Cologne. Within the Society itself, there were many grades; the Catholics thought they could not be satisfied with the conditions of fundamental law which had been down for church and school. Numerous petitions from the Catholic societies all over the country flooded Parliament in support of the Catholic members. After the second discussion of the basic laws, the Catholic Society of the Paulskirche, the club of the "Stone House" was dissolved.

For several reasons, the Neo-Romans did not enter into open battle with the Frankfort Parliament. The first resolution passed by the Bishops' conference at Würzburg in October 1848, which was Geissel's work, gave as a reason that the Frankfort National Assembly was almost the only existing authoritative body in Germany and the last guarantee of the preservation of order and of the future. Geissel, however, allowed Döllinger's proposal to found a German national church to vanish into the archives—it would have been a move against Rome, and the Vatican was already displeased at the idea of this conference of twenty-two German bishops. Geissel was for, not against, Rome. Episcopal authority was to be established, together with the movement of the faithful, as against the State; the public discussion of the bishops on November 11th was based on the principles of the Tridentinum and on the words of St. Irenaeus, that the eyes of Christendom must be turned to Rome and Rome alone. Princes and powers must be obeyed, the manifesto went on; but the Church demanded a share in the new order of the State: "She will once more achieve the independence which is hers by right and which was so long withheld from her, veritably in ill-accord with the best interests of the community. Above all, she will maintain her sacred right of education and instruction, and, as founder of schools for the people, will never permit the child to be torn from the mother's heart." In conclusion, the revolution was declared to be a punishment sent from heaven—the present generation was to return to Mother Church. A manifesto of the bishops addressed to the government demanded the suspension of the concordate, the placet of the landed nobility, etc.; that is, that the Church be independent of the State and the laws with regard to dissolution of the ecclesiastical rights of property should be suspended.

All vital powers of German Protestantism were turned against ecclesiastical fetters in the revolutionary era, and the movements of free communities brought about struggles and activities informed by a truly religious spirit. Such a development, to be sure, had nothing to do with political development —the existing ecclesiastical organs found it all the easier to harness the orthodox immobility of official churchmanship to the service of the old powers. The princes were none other than the provincial bishops. How different were conditions in German Catholicism! Here the bishops felt a great sense of freedom in respect to the provincial rulers; predominantly Catholic Baden protected the bishop with his popular interests as against the princely house. In Saxony, which was almost entirely Protestant, the Neo-Romans took their support from the Catholic Court. In provinces with Protestant ruling houses and a Protestant majority in the population, the Catholic People's party supported criticism and the opposition in order to further its own interests; but in Bavaria and Austria, all Catholic authorities supported the Catholic dynasty and suppressed the minorities of a religious and political character.

German disunion especially contributed to the strengthening of the new political Catholicism. German Catholicism seeped away powerless in the total movement of liberation of the revolutionary year; the profane group formations swamped it; in the Catholic districts, especially, it strengthened the fighting spirit of the Roman Church. The Catholic party that now came into being was at once conservative, liberal, social, and democratic—it was very German in its universal reach, its foundations in general philosophy; it was championed by feudal and aristocratic interests; it was middle class and a friend of the workers, it helped the artisan against the factory, the proletarian against capitalism, the peasant-farmer against the middleman; but it was thoroughly opposed to the social-revolutionary movement, to all violence, to bloodshed of any kind, on account of its Irenian spirit, springing from its religious roots; Diepenbrock disagreed with the resolve of the Berlin National Assembly to refuse payment of taxes; disorder and the adventure of civil war were sinful. Thus the Catholic party had a conservative effect, even though it gladly made use of all the modern forms of life intrinsic in the general popular movement. The Neo-Romans were national, in spite of their religious and ecclesiastical-organizatory connection with Rome; but it was in a contemplative fashion, dictated by old and sacred traditions, friendly to all that was provincial, bound up with small-town, agricultural and family life, rooted in the soil and in purity of ancestry, instinctively opposed to centralistic, Protestant-Prussian popular and hereditary empery, approving of Greater Germany ideals out of a large and warm heart and therefore disposed to cling to the house of Habsburg and the Austrian Imperial State.

The world of clerical thought had gained, rather than lost, by the failure of the revolution. The Neo-Romans had saved the idea of freedom as a vital source of strength, transplanting it into the post-revolutionary era. The general assembly of all Catholic societies at Linz in 1850 showed the power attained by the political-ecclesiastical awakening; the Borromaeus society numbered three hundred and eighty branch societies and distributed two hundred thousand pamphlets; the Society of the Holy Child, devoted itself to the interests of the young, the Vincent Society held ninety-six conferences in Prussia alone; the Conservative-Catholic Press Society attacked Protestantism so violently that it was forbidden in Prussia;

new monastic houses sprang up everywhere; monastic missions, processions, pilgrimages, enriched ecclesiastical life. The priests' seminary founded by the Bishop of Mainz destroyed the Catholic theological faculty at Giessen, the Bishop of Fulda forced the Electoral Hessian ministry to submit to him, the Archbishop of Freiburg forbade a funeral service for the dead Protestant Grand Duke to be held in his cathedral.

The most incisive clerical will of the revolutionary period had been manifested in Cologne, which had also been the headquarters of Karl Marx and Friedrich Engels. After the September crisis, the *Neue Rheinische Zeitung* did not appear for a short time in consequence of the proclamation of martial law. The demand raised by Marx and Engels that there should be a concerted resistance to the Berlin *coup d'état*, that payment of taxes should be refused, the military reserve organized, weapons and munition provided, brought them and their publisher, Korff, before a Cologne jury. Ferdinand Lassalle was arrested in Düsseldorf. But they were all acquitted. The *Neue Rheinische Zeitung* fought on; it ridiculed the parliaments and ministries, triumphed over the battles of the Viennese and Hungarians, demanded a revolutionary war against Russia, declared the necessity of revolutionizing England, so that world markets might be shaken and the world revolution be born of the world at war. The election of an emperor at Frankfort was treated only with ridicule, and the historical significance of the new Constitution was not understood. The witty and impudent Georg Weerth treated Frankfort's efforts as pure farce in a series of light articles. Marx and Engels clearly perceived the coming alliance of the constitutional reform party of the money and title patriciate with the old powers of the separate states; their own ideas of striking revolutionary flame into the whole democratic opposition now attained a certain practical possibility. It is the more remarkable that on April 15th, Marx, Schapper, Wolff, Hermann Becker, and Anneke should have announced their resignation from the democratic district committee—on the grounds that there were too many heterogeneous elements and a closer alliance of working-men's societies was preferable. The working-men's society of Cologne with branch groups in the provinces turned aside to Stephan Born's organization—a very tardy manoeuvre and therefore fated to ineffectiveness.

Stephan Born, sober-minded, cautious, practical, had founded his Central Committee for German Workmen in Leipzig without any of the bitter joy in ruthless polemics which was at once Marx's strength and his weakness. Since October he had been publishing the *Verbrüderung* (Brotherhood), at first printed by Brockhaus, later, from January 1, 1849, by the workmen's league, the Leipzig Vereinsdruckerei; Born wrote most of the paper himself; it appeared twice a week; in a quiet way he tried to instruct his readers in social-political thinking, once he reprinted Heinrich Heine's *Weber*, and in freedom-loving Saxony he had good-natured quarrels with the judicial authorities. A great number of district societies came into being, Born gave lectures and presided at meetings, his organization spread as far as Königsberg and Frankfort. Economic and trades-union questions were entirely to the fore. Born had little talent for the actual politics of the day, much less for questions of world policy and world history, and he guided his readers past these shoals, which was also in the tactical interests of his work. Working women also joined up —Luise Otto proclaimed her allegiance in warm and powerful phrases. To be sure, when the Berlin November crisis arose, Born also demanded that the working classes be armed—the resolution passed by the Prussian National Assembly must be supported. This was unsuccessful. Born was more effective in his efforts to arrange jobs. The Berlin Artisans' Committee were to be consulted in practical matters by the communal officials in the matter of workmen's employment offices. Co-operative companies were founded; linen was purchased wholesale from the indigent weavers of Silesia and made by seamstresses into shirts for the members of the association; in January 1849, a wholesale purchasing society was founded in Berlin; it was followed by similar leagues for the purchase of clothing and cigars. This was all on a very modest scale, the turnover was small, participation entirely voluntary; more interest was taken in the trades-unions themselves; in and around Berlin in the summer of 1849, nineteen such groups had joined the "brotherhood of the workers." In the whole of Germany, there were as many as 12,000 members.

Born and his followers soon perceived that they needed State co-operation if their success were to be permanent. As result of a Saxon local congress at the end of 1848 in Leipzig, the central committee submitted a petition to the parliamentary representatives of the separate provinces, in which it was declared to be the duty of the State to provide financial assistance to those who had nothing but the ability to work in building up their associations; four million thalers were demanded as a beginning from the Kingdom of Saxony for this purpose; a second petition demanded that the unconditional right to vote should be granted to all persons over twenty-one. Thus in Saxony, economically the most progressive province in Germany, quite modern demands of a later development were simultaneously anticipated. At the end of January 1849, the lively Heidelberg provincial congress followed, bringing a programmatic discussion between the socialistic trades-unionist Stephan Born, and Winkelblech. Julius Froebel, the republican social-revolutionary, was in the chair. Born won; the Leipzig and the Frankfort central committee were amalgamated. The *Verbrüderung* was declared to be also the organ of the South German societies. Born spoke in the Mainz Democratic Society and visited Karl Marx and his circle at Cologne. The differences were great, both humanly and objectively speaking; Marx, the Communist of Cologne, a fanatic in the grand manner, full of the arrogance of the thinker and the impatient thoroughness of the man with a system; Engels, proud, bold journalist and politically a man of action: Born, on the contrary, only a modest man, industrious, with solid qualities, a petty master artisan in everything he did, but extremely reliable in his daily tasks and contented with the small successes that offered themselves. He found the men of Cologne too stormy and enthusiastic; they found him too much the schoolmaster, too full of the modest virtues of the petty citizen; no love was lost between them, but they respected each other, made use of one another and helped each other's work. In February, the north German societies had a Workers' Day, presided over by a member of the Leipzig central committee; the simultaneous Thuringian conference in Altenburg was led by Born himself. The Württemberg societies met in March at Göppingen, formed the "Central Workmen's League for Württemberg" and got into touch with Leipzig; their Press organ was called *Sunlight*. Here the main point of discussion was the foundation of a fund for supporting those on the move in search of work.

At the beginning of April, Born took part in the Bavarian workmen's congress. Thus the "workmen's fraternity" had made a most promising beginning in the whole of Germany, outside of Austria, as a socialist trades-union organization. In many places the proletarians had thus already become a proletariate, professional interests were awakened and with them the consciousness of belonging to a class. This had awakened tribally in response to local conditions and extended into something nationally German; whether it could become a political power in times of strife remained to be seen. The "workmen's fraternity" sent petitions to the Frankfort Parliament, like many others, without being able to exercise immediate influence. They regarded the granting in the Constitution of universal and equal franchise, limited only by a condition of three years' minimum German citizenship, as a triumph. They were always very critical of the Prussian hereditary emperor; they rejected all mediation and negotiation, but demanded that the refusal of the Imperial crown should be followed by a "fresh, but this time a decisive, revolution."

As against the mighty organization of the growing Catholic People's Party, these beginnings of awakening a professional sense and an interest in politics in the German working-classes were completely lacking in uniformity. The Communists of Cologne followed a near, perfectly attainable goal, but tactically they were not equal to the political demands of the day. The centres at Cologne and Leipzig worked far more aside from and against one another than they either noticed or desired. How strange that Bisky, Berlin chairman of the workers' fraternity, should have had no communication with the shoemaker Haetzel, who as a member of the Communists' League, encouraged his Berlin "groups" in preparation for a "united, indivisible, social-democratic republic." In the battle for the Constitution, communists, trade-unionists, members of the workmen's fraternity and quite unorganized 'prentice artisans and factory hands all fought against the particularism of the dynasties; but there was no united national proletarian party in Germany.

More significant than the internal split in the growing German proletariat was the lack of clarity in its relations to the "bourgeois" social-republicans and the social-revolutionaries. Men like Friedrich Hecker, Gustav von Struve, Julius Frœbel, deliberately deserted the "middle-class" sphere; to be sure, as socialists of the pre- and non-Marxian era, they were later reproached by Marxian orthodox circles with being "lower middle class," and their ideas were rejected. But these men had a better political grasp of the situation than the Communists of Cologne; the second March Revolution, as the slogan went, could only succeed if once more the entire middle and lower middle classes made common cause with the rising proletariat in striking a united blow—democratic and national. The March programme of 1848 could only be realized in 1849 if it proved possible to re-awaken the popular movement to carry out a clearly-defined patriotic purpose. International, socialist-communistic ideas were quite unsuitable in the Germany of that day; they were rejected by the overwhelming majority as being purely Utopian. But the national idea might perhaps be able to achieve this; it was the strongest motive force in Germany for a generation; the election of the Emperor and the formation of the Constitution meant its final fulfilment. Germany's future must be democratic and national—democratic in the old, all-embracing sense of the negation of the authoritative State; national in the immortal sense of the rejection of provincialism, separate states, particularism, and the acceptance of a uniform German Empire in a rejuvenated Europe. The strongest expression of this democratic nationalism was the "Zentralmärzverein" (Central March League) which was founded at the end of November by members of the Left in the Paulskirche: Simon von Trier, Raveaux, Eisenmann, von Trützschler, Wesendonck; the chairman was Julius Froebel.

The object of the Central March League was to create what the democratic conferences in Frankfort and Berlin had failed to achieve—the united Left front in the battle against the Right wing; its leaders watched with growing anxiety the failure of the Frankfort Parliament, the delays, the lack of clarity, the compromises; they watched with the keenness of political opponents the increasing dependency of the liberal-constitutional reform party upon the growing power of the separate states; in the founding of a uniform German State they saw the real vital problem of the nation, and however much they might respect the patriotism of the party for a hereditary emperor, they most strongly distrusted Prussia and Prussia's king; they believed in the greatness of the revolutionary idea, they wanted to uphold it, to establish it in the course of a fresh struggle; most of the men of the March League were republicans because they despaired of the German type of ruler, many wished to see the great states destroyed and the small and dwarf states combined to create the united republic, consisting of tribal states. Others wished to see a people's emperor at the head. In the March League there was much less clarity as to the positive aims than as to the negative condemnation of the egoism of the dynasties. The Central March League was excellently organized, directed in "absolutistic" fashion and soon spread over all Central and South Germany. Every branch society chose a committee, in every province, every separate State, the branch leagues combined to form a central committee. The lithographed reports of the head office in Frankfort went out to the provincial committees in as many copies as there were local societies. All the leagues already existing under the most various names were amalgamated. Thus the Jena league of the "Colourless" at once joined up with the Central March League.

The popular clubs of Württemberg with their numerous auxiliary organizations joined up to the Central March League all over the State. Its influence penetrated even to the smallest villages and hamlets; many of the countryfolk thought of the "preservation of the March achievements" not only as the elimination of feudal burdens, but simply as abolition of the taxes. As early as February, the preparations for revolt in Württemberg were complete, according to the views of the Prussian envoy; on account of its "anarchistic frame of mind," the Black Forest was known as "Hecker Island." Prussian journeymen in remarkable numbers travelled through Stuttgart, demanding *visas* to Strasburg. The Patriotic League in Stuttgart published a special anonymous defensive pamphlet *Left Party Forces in Frankfort and the March Society* (*Die Linken in Frankfurt und der Märzverein*, Stuttgart, Metzler). The author was Gustav Pfizer. Books and weapons were given out by the Zentralmärzverein; it became a veritable centre, wisely combining everything local and fragmentary, and at the end of March 1849 it comprised nine-hundred and fifty branch societies with nearly half a million members. The rejection of the Imperial crown by the King of Prussia at last provided it with the national slogan which it needed as a spur to action. Counter-Revolution was everywhere raising its head; but could not Germany once more be roused to revolutionary self-help in defence of this Frankfort Imperial Constitution, as to which the Left and the Reform Party had finally come to an agreement? Could not the national patriotic societies unite with the March League? Could the revolutionary idea extend to the Right Centre of the Frankfort Parliament, to the liberal-minded patriciate of money and titles, for the sake of a great, united Germany?

The Central March League put this question, and was destroyed by it. No uniform national party came into being in Germany.

In his day, Prince Metternich had feared nothing more fervently than an alliance of Prussia with the national German movement. This alliance had repeatedly become possible since the outbreak of the revolution. Now came the last opportunity. Schwarzenberg put his whole weight behind it. "In the final instance, the nation looks to where strength and dignity are to be found. Prussia has neither. It is therefore to be anticipated that Austria will prevail. Out of a German problem of organization there has grown up a problem of transforming the whole system of the Central European states, other great powers will not fail to keep these formations and their relation to Prussia under observation," Baron von Linden wrote as early as March, after an interview with Schwarzenberg. The prince regarded the German position from the European point of view. Austria was to overthrow revolutionary Italy, accepted assistance from the Russians in Transylvania would call Emperor Nicholas to aid against revolutionary Hungary, which was proclaiming itself a republic. Schwarzenberg thought he could prevent an alliance of Prussia with revolutionary Germany. The smaller states already began to suspect that changes were to occur upon the European continent which would threaten their own existence; Belgium feared to become the victim of Prusso-French negotiations as to a closer alliance —to become compensation for France! "Prussian ideas of usurpation," as Prokesch expressed it, were thus disturbing Europe; in the name of European peace, Prussia was to be prevailed upon to retreat—thought Schwarzenberg. Through Count Rechberg, the new Austrian plenipotentiary, he caused Archduke Johann to be handed a message from the Emperor, begging him to cling to the post of Vicar; Johann sent an officer to Vienna to convey an affirmative answer in general terms. Prokesch received a commission to justify these decisions in Berlin in honeyed words as the expression of loyal allied feeling, in keeping with the statutes of faithful alliance. At the same time the Austrian members were recalled from Frankfort; Schwarzenberg broke off relations with the Frankfort Parliament, since in its majority it had broken with Austria.

Prussia's dilemma increased; the Vicariate for Frederick William IV could no longer be counted upon; the Ministry of State calmly discussed the Imperial Constitution and established proposals for alterations—preservation of the nobility; retention of the death penalty; no free instruction for the needy; limitation of the franchise; abolition of the oath of loyalty to the head of the empire by the troops; restoration of the veto absolute and of the Imperial Council. This was asking a good deal and certainly showed no surplus of goodwill towards an understanding with the Frankfort Parliament. Camphausen no longer expected it and recommended that the King of Prussia should by way of a proclamation propose to the Frankfort Constitution a "Volkshaus" or people's chamber to consist of members of the Frankfort Parliament and a house of states in Weimar or Gotha to be elected in accordance with the Frankfort Imperial Constitution. It is very probable that these parliamentary bodies had been to some extent conservative in trend, and therefore a revision of the

395

Constitution was the more easily possible. Thus a certain continuity of Federal reform would have been guaranteed. But Heinrich von Gagern did not yet feel that he was conquered. When Camphausen was absent, he invited the plenipotentiaries to a full sitting of the ministry, handed them the Constitution, which had already been proclaimed as Imperial law, and asked for their opinions. Austria and Bavaria made excuses and reservations, so, at first did Saxony and Oldenburg, but Württemberg, Baden, Electoral Hesse, the Grand Duchy of Hesse and others declared their unreserved appreciation, and the others followed, Lippe last of all. A few plenipotentiaries offered assistance in the practical execution of the concept, the representative of Electoral Hesse declared that changes in the Imperial Constitution were only possible in the manner laid down in the Constitution itself. Twenty-eight governments handed the united Imperial ministry a note in common in which they expressed their agreement with the choice of an emperor, their satisfaction with the reservation expressed by the King of Prussia, their unreserved acceptance and recognition of the Imperial Constitution in spite of a few doubts. In accordance with a suggestion by Baden, the agreement of the four kingdoms was finally declared to be obligatory for the binding liability of this declaration. The answer to Prussia's note of April 3rd had arrived—though it was not exactly in agreement with the question that had been put: the resolution of the Frankfort Parliament was now legalized by twenty-eight governments; there was an end to the reservations made by the King of Prussia—the governments had gone into the matter and given their consent. Prussia now had the Parliament and these twenty-eight governments as a united front. Camphausen was not satisfied with the new trend of things, as he openly told Heinrich von Gagern; the plenipotentiaries of the collective declaration refused to negotiate over modifications of the Constitution—Prussia was to accept without reservations.

Prussia therefore needed only to stretch out a hand; Bavaria and Hanover could also be won over with a little effort—but Prussia would not do it. Count Arnim explained to the very satisfied Prokesch that in spite of everything, Prussia would not accede to the Imperial Constitution; the Prussian minister expressed the personal hope that nothing at all would come of all the confusion in Frankfort! King Frederick William IV commissioned Count Trautmansdorff, as he received him in a farewell audience, to report his views by word of mouth to Emperor Franz Joseph and Prince Schwarzenberg: The Frankfort deputation, said he, brought me a collar of untanned leather and expected to chain me up to the Revolution by it; Saxony, Bavaria, and Württemberg are against me; Central Europe must become a great political power; after the victories in Italy, the Emperor of Austria ought to have himself crowned in Aix-la-Chapelle or Rome (!) as Roman Emperor; Prussia wishes to be the Imperial Constable; many princes wished for military posts in the Prussian army. When Count Lerchenfeld attempted to justify the negative attitude of the King of Bavaria, Frederick William IV replied: "No excuses! Your King is acting just as I should wish. I owe him gratitude. Your King is the only one who has really understood me. He recognized that I could not refuse unconditionally, but that this would only be possible with the support of other kings and princes. It was my hope that all the kings would spring to my side with a decided negative, and make it possible for me to break with Frankfort. If I had been set by the princes at the head of Germany as regent, I would have turned out Gagern and company quite independent of my cabinet and ministers, formed a secure ministry and would have forced the National Assembly in Frankfort either to dissolve or to submit. Now we must wait and leave the rest to chance."(!). To Beckerath who had tendered well-meant advice and had come to Berlin on behalf of the Imperial Cabinet, the King said: "Even if the Constitution were any use, I would not accept it, since I desire to remain King of Prussia."

The Saxon chambers dissolved amidst applause for the legal Frankfort Imperial Constitution. They were sure of the country's approval. However energetically the majority in the Chamber may have proceeded and plunged the government into one embarrassing situation after another by battles or questions of principle, interference into administration, and floods of petitions—this still did not suffice to satisfy the agitators in the clubs.

The majority in Saxony belonged to the Left, but the Left was divided against itself. There were parliamentary democrats, social-republicans, social-revolutionaries, social-democrats —there is contemporary evidence even of the last-named party. The patriotic societies demanded "deeds" from the members. In their Dresden assembly of April 22nd, the extremists had a marked preponderance—two hundred and nineteen societies were represented, out of a total of two hundred and eighty with about seventy-five thousand registered members. The majority demanded that the Chamber should agree to refusal of taxes, the minority was stigmatized as "reactionary" and separated from the others. The "German patriotic societies" were confronted by the "Democratic patriotic societies." It was the second division of this kind, and exercised the greatest influence upon the revolutionary events of the next few days. Nowhere was there more open or lively talk of the great outbreak of the second March Revolution than in Saxony; at the very moment when it was due to erupt, the final rupture occurred. The municipal Councillors, the aldermen, the city guard and the officials of the Leipzig university appealed to the King; urging him to proclaim recognition of the Constitution immediately and to summon a fresh ministry which would be loyal to the Constitution, while there must be immediate elections for the new Landtag. The officials and societies of Dresden declared all opposition to the Constitution to be a revolutionary act and that the government must be responsible for all consequences. Encouraged by Berlin, the King definitely declined to recognize the Constitution. After even the former minister von Carlowitz had vainly advised the King to submit, the wholly non-political high court judge Geheimrat Zschinsky was declared chairman of the council of ministers and minister of justice. This was on May 2nd. The other posts were to be filled later. No one knew what to make of this. All the public could see was a reactionary government under Baron Beust.

Patriotic and workmen's societies shouted in placards from the walls of Dresden on the morning of the same day, mentioning the activities of Württemberg, Bavaria, Silesia, and Hanover, speaking of the sacrifices to be made in property and life itself, in defence of the sovereign rights of the people and of the Constitution. But the party of peace was in the majority among the communal guard; they held a parade in honour of the Constitution and sent an address to the King. Glauchau, Zwickau, and Freiberg sent deputations to the capital; the Governments pasted bills urging the populace to have confidence and patience: as long as Prussia had not recognized the Constitution, they said it was impossible for Saxony, with the best will in the world, to do so. This was irritating rather than soothing; the moderates asked themselves why Saxony could not act as so many other states had acted and by decisive support of Frankfort, influence Prussia, which was evidently in two minds? But the crown and ministry clung desperately to Prussia; they were thinking far less of the Constitution, with which they might have borne for the moment, than of the opportunity of making a decided stand against a democratic movement which had already become most burdensome. But the greater part of the Saxon army was away fighting in Schleswig-Holstein; still about eight hundred men were at command in Leipzig, Dresden, and Chemnitz; therefore Beust sent a petition to the Prussian government by courier, asking that several battalions might be sent at once to Dresden to the rescue. This was done as early as the morning of May 3rd before any act of violence had taken place. This step became known and aroused great indignation; the Dresden city council demanded that a provincial committee of defence against inroads of stranger troops should be formed in answer: it took up its duties as a "committee of security." Unfortunately local patriotism crept in in addition to the large patriotic motive; the rising in Dresden was directed at once against reaction and against the Prussians. The social-revolutionary aspect entered in more strongly than had hitherto been the case in Germany. The conflict about the Constitution was used only as an excuse to attack an opponent, both by the Crown and by Michael Bakunin. The personality, the driving power of this man lent a world-wide significance and tension to the Saxon revolutionary struggles.

He had lived in Leipzig since the end of December 1848, and in addition to such German democrats as Hexamer and d'Ester, he kept up relations with young Czechs and Poles; he had hopes of extending the German spring revolt to the Austrian Slavs; since the Slavonic Congress in Prague, he had realized the significance and the possibilities of Bohemia; from Bohemia, where the Counter-Revolution had won victories, he thought the decisive blow for the revolution in Eastern Europe might also take its rise. He thought that in this feudal country there might be a violent social movement of the oppressed Czechs against the German landowners; destruction of castles and documents, annulment of mortgages—a revolution of small peasant farmers which would draw Germany into its whirlpool and turn the predominantly urban movement into a true popular revolt. Bakunin had no opinion of bands of volunteers, or of the "tattling anarchy" of the clubs and magazines; what he wanted was a dictatorship and a regular army of factory-workers, artisans and young unemployed. Neither had he any opinion of the German-Slavonic congress, which d'Ester and Hexamer proposed to convene at Leipzig. He had so much political influence upon the "Slavische Linde" in Prague that the members declared themselves in favour of Kossuth. To think that the Hungarian revolution should be supported by a Czechian national revolt! It might well have been the end of the Austria of Schwarzenberg and Franz Joseph. Bakunin was well aware of the lack of unity and particularistic preoccupation of the German democrats, the powerlessness of the Leipzig central committee, the lack of preparation, organization, arms, above all, the lack of decisive leadership in Germany, but he thought the Saxon revolution might support the revolutionizing of the East, which he had in mind—and so, all at once, he was to be found among its leaders: this mighty man, a giant in physical stature, but far more impressive in the energy of his spirit, the tremendous vigour of his speech, torrential as the Volga. To the young he was irresistible, but older men were also carried away by the blind, impersonal will power of the man, who was always glowing with the leaping flame of his enthusiasm, devoured by the tremendous tensions of his far-flung personality. He was open-hearted and wicked, brutal and ingratiating; he thundered and he whined, cooed and shouted; he wished to be humble and exclude his own personal feelings, yet he longed for the highest power. He thought only of one end, yet often frittered away his days, he was critical to the point of maliciousness, yet sunk in fantastic dreams; he borrowed money only to fling it away, he begged for trifles and felt them to be beneath his notice; he was pathetically helpless in everyday matters, but confident that to him alone grace had been given to give its new form to the world. He lost himself a hundred times for the sake of an idea, only to find himself again with all the glowing passion of a majestic self-assertion. He was neither a fool nor a genius, neither a hero nor an adventurer; no saviour of the world, no criminal, no statesman, but so much a part of all of these that, child and monster at once, he must grasp again and again with all his magic power of entrancement, at the strings of events, playfully destructive, like a being fallen from another planet, rejoicing in destruction, yet the humbly devoted missionary of a grandiose future of which the outlines were entirely uncertain.

The King of Saxony fled, a provisional government was set up, Prussia offered help to subdue the popular movement, and it was accepted as unavoidable. In a civil war lasting three days, the Saxon revolution was crushed. Evil days fell upon Saxony; it was treated as semi-annexed. The troops usually took no prisoners, they simply mowed down the fighters for freedom like so many vermin. Nine thousand prosecutions were instituted. The most famous victim was Richard Wagner, who went into exile for many years.

The North German petty states supported the Imperial Constitution and, dependent as they were upon Prussia, reluctantly participated in the transition to a policy of unity. In West and South Germany, things were different. Nassau, Hesse-Darmstadt, Baden, accepted the Constitution, because they hoped to conciliate the popular movement. In Bavaria, the second chamber even voted for acceptance, although the first chamber protested; the strongest impression was made by events in Württemberg.

The Rump Parliament which had been formed in Stuttgart out of the remnant of the Frankfort Parliament (104 members were present, 50 had excused themselves) was allowed to use the assembly hall of the Württemberg chamber; since no other solution had been found, a provisional Regency took the place of the former central executive: it was composed of Franz Raveaux, Karl Vogt, Friedrich Schüler, Heinrich Simon, August Becher. Their proclamation on June 7th called upon all Germans to stand up for the Constitution and to fight "the unavoidable battle between absolutism and freedom" with all their strength. The Regency at once began to issue orders to the Württemberg government.

Römer did not resign from the National Assembly until June 13th. But his ministry at once protested against the procedure of the Rump Parliament and the Regency—also in the name of the Constitution, which must achieve recognition by legal channels! Römer had no desire to become a revolutionary regent; but to see revolutionary regents in Stuttgart, four of them strangers to the province and the other Becher, the Swabian, whom he had always disliked, was too much for his feelings as a minister of the State of Württemberg. In the Rump Parliament and in the Württemberg chamber the battle would be fought on parliamentary lines, perhaps by the same persons. Who would have the right to put the Constitution into practice? What central power would be legal? Would the regency lay claim to the finances and military power of the Kingdom of Württemberg? Would the Württemberg chamber support the Römer ministry in refusing to co-operate with the regency? The last point was decided in the negative by 60 votes to 14, twelve members abstaining. The break between the National Assembly and Württemberg was complete.

It was a matter that concerned Württemberg and Germany alike. Prince Wittgenstein, president of the new Imperial Cabinet at Frankfort, directed a communication to the Württemberg goverment, in which he demanded that the National Assembly be transferred to Stuttgart and the Regency declared illegal. Legality had been done away with, anarchy had set in. The whole procedure "amounted to revolt." Unless the Württemberg government proceeded at once to strong measures, the central executive must at once do what was necessary. Prussia's procedure was still sharper. The Prussian envoy at Stuttgart was directed to declare that the Prussian government was astonished that the Württemberg government should not have done something to prevent such a state of things from occurring at all. Did they intend to put up with the nonsense or to proceed against it with all the means at command? Otherwise the Prussian envoy was directed to break off all official relations: "since it did not correspond to the dignity of the

Prussian government to send representatives to a country which countenanced such doings." The note which General von Thun, the envoy, handed over on June 14th, contained an offer to send troops if the Württemberg government should have no suitable force available. If no satisfactory explanation were to follow, the Prussian government would consider taking suitable steps on its own accord in conjunction with its allies. This was the answer to King Wilhelm's outburst against the Hohenzollerns, and the refusal of the Römer ministry to take part in the Berlin Union negotiations! Römer had never been friendly to Prussia: now, in a morbid state of irritation, he declared in the Chamber that Württemberg would never make common cause with Prussia: "We now have a central executive in Frankfort, one in Stuttgart and perhaps next thing, one in Berlin," he said, bitterly. Duvernoy, minister of the interior, sent a confidential messenger to the Prussian envoy, to minimize the effect: Württemberg could not yet join the "North German League," but perhaps events might force her to do so later on. In any case, Römer wanted as little to do with Prussia as possible: the Württemberg Foreign Ministry thanked the Prussian government for the offer of troops, but declared that it had sufficient forces of its own and reserved all its rights as against any undesired interference from abroad. Römer much preferred to find a friend in Bavaria. "His feelings are quite Bavarian," the Bavarian envoy wrote approvingly to Munich. Since North Germany was combining, the South Germans also thought of making themselves secure.

Württemberg was in the throes of a grave national crisis. The King refused to return to Stuttgart as long as the Rump Parliament and the Regency were in existence. But he sent out decisive military commands from his secret cabinet in Ludwigsburg; at length the Römer ministry had to recant openly. Römer himself, suffering physically and spiritually from a materialized bad conscience, hesitated and dallied to the last; he took despairing refuge in juristic niceties and sought help in choleric abuse. The Rump Parliament was no longer allowed to use the assembly room. The Regency demanded five thousand Württemberg troops in order to protect Rastatt and Landau against the Prussian onset. The Römer ministry refused and ordered the Regency to remove its seat to another country on account of the danger of revolution and in its own interests. The Regency insisted on its demands; Württemberg should raise all her troops and openly put them at the service of the legal executive, it was necessary for this to retain its seat where the National Assembly was to be found. The Rump Parliament declared the Vicariate of Archduke Johann to be extinguished.

But the Württembergers wished to remain masters in their own house, and at least on this point all official instances were agreed. The existence and appearance of the Imperial Regency awakened the Swabian spirit of contradiction to a quite remarkable degree; the revolution might perhaps have broken out in earnest in Württemberg if the National Assembly had remained in Frankfort or gone to Baden. But as it was, particularization killed loyalty to the Constitution; the Römer ministry had found its golden bridge in the necessity which had arisen to preserve the authority of the State of Württemberg.

Among the people, to be sure, divisions grew wider and confusion increased. The Stuttgart citizens declared that their militia, eleven hundred men strong, would stand by the National Assembly, and all citizens should help. Many popular clubs, many parishes added their support; from Bavarian Swabia, from Central Germany, the Rump Parliament received assurances of sympathy. In Heilbronn, the militia appeared in the market-place and declared itself with great determination in favour of the National Assembly. They wanted to protect the State "against princes and treacherous governments." The government now prepared a counter-attack. All General Miller's troops had been withdrawn from the frontiers and scattered over the country. The King behaved like an old soldier. Miller had told the Regency that he would not respond to their orders, whereupon he was deposed from his post as a general of the Empire. He now marched troops to Heilbronn in order to disband and disarm the militia. But this was not so easy. The militia, which was very well organized and the best in Württemberg, ordered a general march, assembled in the market-place and marched to the Frankenbach Hill outside the city. Joined by recruits from the villages, their numbers swelled to four thousand men. Mayer, a chemist, a leading member of the People's Party, called for self-help. In the meantime, the crowd stormed the town hall in Heilbronn and captured eighty-eight rifles. In Löwenstein, the strategically correct point for a defensive against the military, the militia from all over the country were to assemble; but next morning there was great discouragement and at sight of an approaching cavalry patrol, they began to dissolve. Only sixty men under Mayer reached Wimpfen and joined in the battles in Baden.

The events in Heilbronn were a prelude to those in Stuttgart. The Regency summoned the German people to arms. But there was no money. The amount sent by the provisional government, the sums collected voluntarily in Stuttgart, lasted only a few days. The German revolutionary government was staggering to its doom. It was willing to fight to the last; but not to starve. President Löwe-Calbe received a communication from Römer in the name of the entire ministry demanding an end of the session of the National Assembly and retirement of the Regency and accusing both of revolutionary aims; if these demands were not acceded to, force would be used.

On the morning of June 18th, infantry occupied the town hall: General Miller in person demanded the keys; nineteen sappers were ordered to turn everything out; they went to work with axes and demolished everything, benches, flags, draperies, patriotic inscriptions. An officer of the General Staff directed this vandalism, a civil commissioner expressed his satisfaction.

Schoder spoke words of farewell to the German National Assembly in the Württemberg chamber: "The National Assembly will disappear to-day; perhaps for a time, the German cause will be trodden in the dust; but its spirit, gentlemen, you will not tread its spirit in the dust, and it will soon break away for itself again, in spite of all bayonets. The German people has at least had an opportunity to learn which are the men who did not desert the cause of freedom in the moment of danger. I tell you, gentlemen, the men of the National Association, whom you have driven out to-day, will go forth with their heads erect."

Römer had uttered these final words a year before when his March ministry retired. That shot went home.

Ludwig Uhland, who, impassioned by his sense of justice and moral purpose, had become far more prominent during the last few days than he had ever been in Frankfort, had proposed that the members should assemble at their place of meeting, the Hotel Marquardt; from thence the procession set out, the president at its head, Uhland on his right hand, Schott, Römer's father-in-law, on his left, then all the others, four abreast, solemn, slow and steady—as they had marched to the Paulskirche a year before. Most of these marchers were no longer with them. But the idea of a German nation strode beside them. They took the road to their new place of assembly but they knew that they would never reach it.

"Though all desert, yet will we keep the faith"—the poet's word, so often repeated during the past few weeks, had now a living witness in these men of Germany.

Many a call came from the crowd to greet the silent procession. Then, as Uhland later put it, violence had its way with it. Infantry blocked the corner of the street. The soldiers approached the members. A civil commissioner, his white badge of office on his arm, stepped forward, demanded that the members retire, and renewed the prohibition to hold further meetings. President Löwe demanded in the name of the German nation that the troops should give way; he, Uhland and two others approached close to the soldiers. They were about to penetrate the phalanx. There was a roll of drums. Löwe attempted to speak again, to protest against this high treason. Then came the command: "Fix bayonets!" The soldiers hesitated to obey the order. It was man against man, uniform against frock coat. Uhland cried out in passionate anger: the mercenaries might pierce his German heart. The civil commissioner made an attempt to draw him forth and rescue him; but Uhland remained where he was. Then General Miller, who was watching the scene through his lorgnette, ordered the cavalry out of the side street. Things now went quickly. The command to strike rang out, but the military advanced only at walking pace and struck only with the flat of their swords. The members stood back to back, so that they might not be ridden down. It was of little avail: the procession was completely broken up, many were thrown down, dirtied, wounded by the horse's hoofs; Uhland's hat was struck from his head. "Several members of the National Assembly were not inconsiderably injured," wrote the Russian chargé d'affaires. Some of the members fled into houses, others back to the Hotel Marquardt. One of them attempted to speak to the crowd from the balcony. A cavalry officer, who had followed at the head of his division, threatened immediate arrest if he did not desist. Through the whole disgusting spectacle the militia stood immovable. Their artillery had, to be sure, offered protection to the Rump Parliament and had been requested to drive on ahead to the place of assembly; but unfortunately the government had previously confiscated their cannon. The Regents, except Becher, who had gone to Esslingen for reinforcements, arrived in a carriage at their inn, wished to proceed to their assembly hall, were forced to descend, were threatened that they would be fired upon, turned back and were taken in by the proprietor of the Hotel Marquardt, who was not of their way of thinking, but was indignant at so much violence. The National Assembly now held its very last session undisturbed at the Hotel Marquardt. They took cognizance of the state of things, accepted explanations, but could not pass resolutions as they had no quorum, only ninety-eight members being present. Many wished to proclaim Römer a traitor to the nation and level a public accusation against General Miller, many wished to reassemble the Rump Parliament in some other city. Illusions and confusion prevailed; they had to be prepared for banishment and arrest. Finally, it was agreed to continue meeting informally every day for the present at Werner's restaurant.

As early as June 19th, the minister of the interior demanded the banishment of all members who were not natives of Württemberg: Römer, to be sure, took care that milder measures were applied. President Löwe summoned the next session for June 26th at Karlsruhe. But this session never took place. The play was over.

Baden is the only country in which the greater part of the military seceded to the Revolution. Since the Spring, a fresh revolution had threatened, and now it began as a military revolt. The Offenburg Provincial Assembly resolved upon a radical programme. A provincial committee, which also included soldiers, was set up. Baden took steps to become a republic, and, as such, a centre of European revolution.

The main body of the Badensian troops in the following weeks stood firm behind the revolution, many probably hesitatingly and with inward doubts, but driven onward by those who were more determined. A rise in pay and officers appointed by election combined to make the new regime thoroughly popular. The civil servants also made no difficulties, and, intimidated and fearing to be beggared by the loss of their posts, they took the oath almost without exception "reserving their obligations to the Constitution" which might mean anything. Only the judges refused to take the oath, but nevertheless continued their official duties. For the first time a German state went through the revolutionary process of transformation from monarchy to republic—and it was simpler than most of them had imagined. The government which had fled had made things very easy for their revolutionary successors by leaving all the money in the national funds. The State Committee began work with four million gulden in ready money. The bureaucratic machine therefore ran on without any friction. Brentano acted with great moderation, soon won the confidence of the well-to-do citizens, who had already begun to tremble for their money-bags, took great pains to prevent irregularities, avoided the use of the word "republic" and was evidently delighted to have achieved power. He worked himself unmercifully as if he had been in a lawyer's office, and discovered to his horror that he was a leader who had no idea who his followers were. So unimaginative a grand-ducal Badensian republic was not at all to the taste of most people; they wished to see Baden become to Western Europe what Hungary wished to be for Eastern Europe—the germinal cell of an all-embracing movement.

Many professional revolutionaries now appeared in Karlsruhe: Struve and his followers, Willich, whose socialistic propaganda had caused him to be regarded as "a most dangerous anarchist" and transported from one station to the next on the way to the Swiss frontier with an iron halter round his neck. There were Karl Blind, Bornstedt, Tzschirner, a refugee from Saxony, Dr. Oppenheim—and many Poles, French, Swiss, Hungarians. Poles and Hungarians formed their own legions; one volunteer corps called itself "Robert Blum's Legion." Johann Philip Becker was there too—after difficulties with his German-Swiss legion on account of Swiss neutrality, he had made his way with his revolutionary companions to Baden. The victory of the revolutions in the Palatinate and Baden seemed epochal to the refugees in Switzerland and France. The German revolutionaries assembled in Geneva decided to issue a "Manifesto of the German Democrats Abroad." Here they first decried the "semi- and seeming-democrats," among whom they classed "national politicians, republican, bourgeois, philosophic politicians and petty citizen socialists." Their own programme proclaimed: The State is organized society, the power of the State transcends all economic and social relations; not only production on a grand scale, but all and every production should be a matter for the State, yet no mechanical barracks-like life must ensue and destroy individuality; the German Constitution and the victory of the Hungarians were the two points to which the movement in Germany could cling; revolution was a time for heroes—it let loose the passions of men and redoubled their strength. "The proletarians would take over the revolution, a legacy, from the dying-middle-classes"; humanity must tread "new paths." Basle was full of refugees. The banks refused to take any further deposits of valuables, fearing for their own safety. Agents appeared from Baden, trying to win over Swiss officers to the revolution, especially artillery officers.

In Paris, too, a fresh revolutionary committee had been organized, among its members were Hochstetter, Wilhelmi, Sass, Hentze, formerly a Prussian officer, Beust, formerly an officer of the Viennese revolutionary general staff. Many German refugees left Paris with false passes, under assumed names; some went to Thuringia and Saxony, in order to establish connections for the revolutionary movement between Berlin, Bohemia, and Vienna. Some went to Munich and to the Rhine. Among the principal leaders were: Dr. Eichler of Berlin, Bem's one-time wing adjutant, Niederhuber, Hauf, the former captain of the Viennese academic guards. There was a special committee for the consideration of Hungarian and Austrian affairs—Teleki at its head. Savoye collected sub-scriptions in Alsace and sent arms to Germany. "The great battle is about to be fought which will decide the fate of society," he said. The most intelligent and energetic of the middlemen between French and German social-revolutionaries was Dr. Hermann Ewerbeck, Cabet's translator, a member of the Paris League of Just Men. In his papers, confiscated in Paris, the final aim of the group is most plainly defined: formation of a Rhine Republic, consisting of Baden, the Palatinate, and Alsace. The idea was to proclaim this republic on May 10th and then allow the revolutionary flood to spread over the whole Rhineland to Cologne and Elberfeld. What Jochmus, minister of the realm, said, was perfectly true: that if the Vicar had retired in the middle of May, had the Frank-fort Parliament remained in Frankfort instead of moving into the Stuttgart blind alley, then the prospects of the revolu-tionary movement of carrying with it the whole of the Rhenish west country, at least for a time, would have been much better.

The German revolutionaries must be defended against at least *one* reproach: very few of them had any idea of colla-borating with official French policy—it would, indeed, have been quite useless. Prince Louis Napoleon, President of the French Republic, knew what he was about when he deplored the sad occasion which had forced the Grand Duke of Baden to take refuge on French territory and that he was unable to offer him adequate hospitality, and he added: socialism was the last word—"sinon l'expression instantanée de la révolu-tion." The idea of including Alsace in the Rhine Republic as planned, already disclosed the profound gap between its pro-moters and the national conservatism that prevailed in the growing Second Empire; hence it is false to characterize this movement in the slogan: revolutionary Rhenish League. Naturally the German revolutionaries would have liked to be recognized by France; but only the fall of Louis Napoleon, brought about by the socialists, could have opened up any such possibility. At that time, too, the sending of Schütz, a member of the Frankfort Parliament, as chargé d'affaires for the Palatinate to Paris was a purely ineffective gesture; he was able neither to open up diplomatic relations with France, nor to arrange for French protection or even active help by the "despatch of munitions and generals." The idea of persuading France, as it was phrased in his instructions, "to send troops to march against Prussia" was completely childish. The Badensian State Committee never contemplated such nonsense, either verbally or on paper, in spite of all their brotherly revolutionary enthusiasm for France. Brentano sent Karl Blind to Paris, because he wished to get rid of him in Karlsruhe—but he was far too sober-minded a man to participate in the Palatinate's fantastic dreams. Louis Napoleon's government ignored the Baden-Palatinate deputation completely as far as official attention was concerned, its association with the French extreme Left wing made it such an object of suspicion that Karl Blind was arrested and Schütz narrowly escaped the same fate. The Badensian movement, which broke out on account of the Constitution, was wrongly suspected of anti-national feeling. It was, to be sure, the cheapest and most effective propaganda for their particularistic-dynastic opponents to represent republicans, national patriots and socialists alike as a company of traitors.

Prussia was now on the march against revolution in the Palatinate and in Baden, and it was therefore on the march against all revolution; an example was to be made. The Prince of Prussia wished to accomplish in South-West Germany what Windischgrätz was doing in Prague and in Vienna and Emperor Nicholas in Hungary; and it was he who was put in command. Thus Berlin's Eighteenth of March received its final expiation. Prussia had desired this task and accomplished it as a German and a European Great Power. Tocqueville, the distrustful French minister for foreign affairs, had to be assured by Count Hatzfeld, the Prussian chargé d'affaires, that it was no question of an intervention in a foreign country, but rather of the help offered in brotherly fashion by one ally to another, and Tocqueville, who had just returned from a journey through Germany, thought that the feeling for a greater unity in Germany was also shared by the men of the German Right wing. France would not only not be disturbed by, but would actually welcome, a state of unity under Prussian leadership. Lord Normanby, the British envoy in Paris, thought, to be sure, that Prussian armaments were not in proportion to her momentary task. And the *National* wrote that Prussia was proceeding on the Rhine in agreement with Austria and Prussia, would march into Switzerland and conquer Neuenburg! The poor German revolutionaries posted up bills in the French eastern provinces, hoping thus to win the sympathies of the French army. But the Buonapartist France of 1849 assented whole-heartedly to the crushing of the German revolution in South-West Germany. Count Hatzfeld pleaded urgently and in strict confidence that Prussia might avoid any hint that the French government, even indirectly, had shown itself prepared to assist in crushing the revolt.

Austria's jealousy was already raising its head; in occupying Baden, Prussia would acquire the whole Rhine frontier and thus a dangerously powerful position in Paris. Baden was a veritable cancer in the German body politic.

There was a number of small battles, others, more serious, on the line of the Neckar. The Prussians had to buy their victory dear, in spite of their superior numbers. But these numbers told. Their columns swept like a steam-roller over the roads of Baden. The government in Karlsruhe collapsed. The battle for the Constitution was soon at an end.

About six thousand revolutionary combatants were shut up in the fortress of Rastatt—an infantry regiment, the remnants of four others, fragments of cavalry and field artillery—but only the artillery belonging to the fortress was full strength; there were remnants of the Polish and Hungarian legions, the students' legion from Freiburg, the Swabian legion, even the Robert Blum legion—two-thirds of them soldiers, one-third volunteers and militia.

It was clear to a military eye that this remnant of the revolutionary army could not long continue to hold the fortress against the overwhelming masses of Prussian and Imperial troops. The high command of the Prince of Prussia had no interest in speeding-up the inevitable submission by means of a great sacrifice of troops. In addition, Prince Wittgenstein appealed to Count von den Gröben, commander of the besiegers. A formal siege and cannonade of the fortress of Rastatt was not in the interests of the State, which must bear the expenses of both attack and defence; it was undesirable that an artillery attack should be levelled at the walls, only recently completed at great cost, since the badly provisioned fortress would very soon be forced to capitulate.

The governor of the fortress was Gustav Nicholas Tiedemann. He was the son of a Heidelberg professor, in his youth a lieutenant of dragoons in Baden who had risen to the rank of lieutenant-colonel during the Greek War of Liberation, had married a Greek woman, been retired from the Greek army on account of being a foreigner, and on a visit to his parents in Heidelberg in 1849, was delighted to be given a chance by the Republican Badensian government of playing the soldier once again. He was thus a soldier of fortune, not a revolutionary out of political conviction, a soldier with no special talents, a man of restless nature, personally brave and fond of adventure, good-natured to his subordinates, but touchy, hot-tempered and rather affected; a man in the fifties, going grey, with carefully trimmed moustache, he stalked proudly about the fortress in his dark blue, coquettishly simple uniform, trailing his curved sword behind him. A complete contrast to Tiedemann was Ernst von Biedenfeld, an honest old retired Badensian major of infantry, who had won his spurs in the Napoleonic wars and had been living quietly in Bühl, taking no interest in politics. He had allowed himself to be persuaded to take command of the third regiment of infantry and had thus become a colonel as he had always hoped; he showed, too, that he could be a good commander, maintained order and discipline and was much respected and even beloved by troops and inhabitants on account of his quiet, honourable sense of just dealing. When Tiedemann exploded and fussed about, at once confused and petty, then all peaceful souls appealed to old Biedenfeld to put an end to it and take his place. But Biedenfeld was not capable of such a trick. It was a mixed company in Rastatt; von Corvin and Böning, Mnievski the Pole, Jansen, head of the Workmen's Club at Cologne, Ernst Elsenhans, the writer, son of a Swabian parson and himself originally a theologian, then a decided freethinker and eager prophet of freedom, a member of the club of Extreme Progressives and directing the Rastatt "Festungsboten" in this spirit; a thick-headed man of convictions, with an astonishing zest for life. Finally, there was Karl Schurz.

This son of a schoolmaster and grandson of a peasant farmer from the Cologne district, who had grown up in a castle belonging to Count Wolff-Metternich, was not a type of the times, but one of its happy exceptions. Long before he had ever seen America, he bore the spirit of the New World about with him in his heart. He was a true German student, but there was a good deal of the cowboy about him. The best of the whole man was that he knew no such thing as pose, self-importance, vulgar ambition, sentimental sugariness; they were not only alien, but abhorrent to his nature. This young man of nineteen was therefore in remarkable contrast to the prevailing style of the 1848 generation. He had no opinion of big, solemn speeches, and so he never developed into a sly conspirator or a greasy, roaring, tavern orator. Clear and free, quick and spirited, bold and sparkling—so he went his way as a people's fighter for truth and justice, reliable, steady, inwardly well balanced, an honest man through and through.

Women fell in love with his handsome, boyish face, men were fond of him and prophesied a great future for him. He did not know the meaning of difficulties. Whoever did not succumb to the charm of his amiable nature, or withstood the Rhenish lilt of his delightful speech, was overcome by the freshness and inventiveness of this master of many arts. Many Germans know his sparkling reminiscences—memories of a splendid life, lived to the full, in a spirit of daring adventure. There was nothing ponderous about him, but also nothing of the charlatan, seeking adventure for its own sake, his flaming enthusiasm was always for a great idea. The storms of March never died down in this man's heart. The German revolutionary will, eternally young, took form in him, appealing and convincing as in no other exponent. Certainly he, too, had begun shyly as a modest little German citizen of the middle classes. As a student in Bonn he overcame all his reservations and became filled with the spirit of the student rising. He was merry and chivalrous, gay and excited, keen to join in everything and not especially patient with outworn tradition and pedantry. Such a full-blooded personality could have nothing to do with empty phantasies. No wonder he cherished the idea of writing an "Ulrich von Hutten" drama. He was a good fighter, brilliant, versatile, but never reckless. His heart never got the better of his brain, which remained master. His flight from Rastatt through the water conduits was a vivid film, long before there were such things as films. Even as a schoolboy, he had written about the unity of the German nation—his teacher had doubts as to the expediency of the matter, but patted his promising pupil approvingly on the head. Could anyone have been angry with him? A genial Rhenish quality and the bright fire of the Yankee were marvellously blended in this objectively glowing patriot.

After the fall of the fortress, Gottfried Kinkel was condemned by the Rastatt court martial to life imprisonment in a fortress and the loss of the national cockade. At first he had been condemned to death, like the commanders and so many of his fellows after the capitulation of the fortress. His sentence was not based only upon his participation in the Baden-Palatinate war; he had been secretary to the provisional government of the Palatinate, fought in the "Besançon" company under Willich's leadership, and was wounded and taken prisoner at Durlach. He came before the Cologne assizes on account of the storm on Siegburg as late as 1850, but was acquitted. On August 4th, General von Hirschfeld refused to confirm the sentence, having doubts of its legality, and sent it to Berlin. The general auditoriate there ordered it to be quashed, since sentence of death should have been passed. Kinkel's brave wife, Johanna, now roused a storm—inventive, untiring, brilliant as ever, somewhat violent in her motherliness, a truly free and fearless person, so clever that she seemed beautiful. Bettina von Arnim and the Princess of Prussia used their influence upon the King, who became soft-hearted after his own fashion and declared that all depended upon Kinkel's repentance. Finally, he acceded to a unanimous petition handed to him by the Ministers of State, and graciously converted the life-long imprisonment in a fortress into "civil punishment," that is, confinement in a convict prison.

This "gracious act" of the King's was felt at the time by Kinkel himself and later by public opinion to be nothing more than a cruel and senseless increase of the punishment of a sensitive intellectual; even the conservatives joined in the indignation. The matter was universally felt to be a scandal and therefore Kinkel rose by the side of Robert Blum to the position of a popular martyr for the Revolution. In reality the court martial's sentence had not merely implied plain confinement in a fortress, but the more dishonourable fortress imprisonment. In Prussia of that day, fortress prisoners were treated much worse than convicts; as many as twenty men were herded together in one room, they had only a mattress to lie on and were occupied in groups with the most menial and disgusting tasks and also subjected at the least excuse to corporal punishment. In contrast to this, solitary confinement in a convict prison was really to be considered as a merciful alternative.

Kinkel was neither a powerful writer nor an important political leader. Carried on and upward by his ever-energetic wife, however, he became one of the most remarkable fighting figures of the revolutionary era. He was leader of the democratic club at Bonn, president of the artisans' cultural league for labourers and mechanics, editor of the democratic *Bonner Zeitung* and of the strange publication *Spartakus*, a pamphlet designed to inspire artisans and discuss and further their interests. He was also a member of the Prussian Second Chamber (February-April, 1849)—a man of warm feeling, bewailing the lot of the poor and oppressed in lyric and eloquent strains and battling valiantly to improve their lot. He was a democrat in the all-embracing and deeper sense of the term; no Marxist, but a convinced socialist and republican on principle; most effective, perhaps, as a writer of leading articles, in which his inner nature, which had preserved the religious character of the one-time theologian, could expand itself in lay sermons. Religion, art, and socialism all grew in him from the same root. Kinkel had been one of the first to secure university status for the study of the history of art and literature; he was the most important pioneer of popular higher school education. This gentle, noble-natured man, strong only in his beliefs, impelled by the purest humanitarian motives, politically harmless if only on account of his naïvely egocentric self-consciousness, was now winding wool in Prussian convict-prisons—at first in Naugard, afterwards in Spandau! Karl Schurz got him out by an outrageously bold enterprise—to the joy of all decent-thinking men.

419

Prussia had murdered German patriotism, of which she herself was the finest flower. Politically, she had gained nothing. Everywhere opposing forces rose up. Austria contemplated exercising her right of occupation in Rastatt and sought Bavarian co-operation. In Vienna no objection was raised to the Prussians' North German League, because nothing could be done to prevent it. As a counterweight, however, Bavaria had become head of a South German League, in closest connection with Imperial Austria, rendered still more intimate by a customs union. In any case, Prussia was not to lay hands on South Germany. When the Prince of Hohenzollern-Hechingen came to visit Munich and spoke of the proposed family agreement as to the principality—the Märzverein had tried to detain him in Friedrichshafen! King Max said in great excitement: "Do not do it on any account, for Heaven's sake, otherwise Prussia will have a firm hold in South Germany!" Prussia, thought Prince Schwarzenberg, "had undoubtedly done good service in Baden to the cause, but these services gave her no right to play the master and victor, much less the conqueror."

Prussia's "services" were long remembered in Baden, and the *Badensian Cradle Song* was heard for many a day.

> Sleep, my child, don't cry,
> The Prussian's going by.
> He killed your father at his door,
> He made your wretched mother poor.
> Keep very still, if you'd be wise,
> Or he'll find ways to shut your eyes.
> Sleep, my child, don't cry,
> The Prussian's going by.
>
> We must be quiet and behave,
> Still as your father in his grave.

The last verse runs:

> Sleep, my child, don't cry,
> The Prussian's going by.
> God only knows how long he'll reign
> Before our freedom rise again,
> But where your father lies, my dear,
> There's room for many a Prussian bier.

## CHAPTER SIXTEEN

# FINIS, RESULTS AND AFTER

T HE GERMAN Revolution of 1848–49 falls into five sections: the period of preparation, the first outbreak and apparent victory, social revolutionary and nationalistic threats, consequently the beginning of the counter-revolution, second outbreak, and finally the victory of the counter-revolution.

The pre-history of the Revolution naturally stretches back to the popular movement of 1830, even back to the Napoleonic Era and the Wars of Liberation. I have confined myself to the actual "period of preparation," the 'forties, in which we already find all the elements of the democratic movement of 1848–49: the decay of Metternich's system and the movement of the classes in Austria, the Prussian constitutional question and the United Diet, the Bavarian State crisis provoked by Lola Montez, the oddities and vitality of the petty states, the insufficiency of the German Confederation, and of German National efforts at reform, the splitting-up of the classes, the unemployment and under-nourishment of the lower classes, the yeasty thinking, the urge, the unrest in intellectual and artistic creation: these all point with certainty to the eruption; feeling and inward tension, the sharpness of tone and ruthless consistency of the final demands were already entirely revolutionary.

"The first outbreak and apparent victory" embraces the

period of the March–April Revolution of 1848 and the developments up to June. The democratic movement met with brilliant success everywhere; the men who had been in opposition were called to responsibility; fighting only occurred at a few points, in the end the new ideas achieved a political victory, in Berlin the authoritarian and militaristic state was unquestionably humiliated; the newly-awakened national will was to have strong executive organs created for it to express German political being in its entirety; this national feeling swamped everything, it turned against Denmark, against Poland and Russia, and in internal matters, firmly trusting in the honesty and vitality of the royal power-complex and its will to reform, it collected patriotic ideas and masses together as a barrier against violently revolutionary, socialistically minded republicanism. The apparent victory ended with the assembling of the German National Assembly at Frankfort and the formation of a provisional executive. A Vicar of the Empire with responsible Imperial ministers guaranteed legal transition to a final national form of life, the formation and carrying-out of an Imperial Constitution for the new Germany. Many saw in the Imperial Vicariate the beginning of a centrally built-up Greater Germany under the Lorraine-Meran dynasty.

The "social-revolutionary and national threat, consequently the beginning of the counter-revolution" comprises the period from June to November 1848. The bearers of the revolutionary idea were deeply dissatisfied. The new era was not new at all. The advisory assemblies in all German residencies and especially in Frankfort did not touch the country's real needs. Workmen's leagues came into being, artisans' and trade congresses. The *Neue Rheinische Zeitung* raised the complaint of communism. Democratic congresses in Frankfort and Berlin sought to prepare the continuance of the Revolution. There was much resentment at the alliance of the higher and middle classes of the citizens with the old powers, and their optimism, so easily satisfied. The old March revolutionary front was exploded. March ministers were seen to be powerless and behind them was the old all-powerful phalanx of the bureaucracy, there was militia, there were popular assemblies, and behind them the old military power; people read newspapers and listened to speeches—but in the separate states the princely and aristocratic will to rule was as dominant as ever. Others besides the Germans acquired nationalistic ideas. The Poles hammered at the doors of Prussia; Slavs, Hungarians, and Italians threatened to break up the Austrian Empire. In addition to all this, the idea of a strong, all-embracing Germany went against the idea of the Prussian State, its traditions of a great power, its conditions of life, its territorial form—but just as much against that Napoleonic creation, Bavaria, and all the individual dwarf and petty states.

The new central executive and the Frankfort Parliament, needed to produce national strength and much outward success. Their failure in the matter of the Malmö armistice roused both the nationalistic and social-revolutionary elements to violent effort. The Austrian army defeated the nationalities at Cracow and Prague; the September revolts in the Rhine and Main territory forced the new authorities to make use of the old measures of force.

The Viennese October Revolution fought despairingly for a liberated Greater Germany against the fettered Greater Austria of dynasty, feudalism, clericalism, and military power. Then the Prussian monarchy also ventured to strike a blow against the constitutional National Assembly, which, in defiance of landed proprietors and regiments of guards, was endeavouring to turn Prussia into a democratic State amenable to law. Frankfort and Berlin, which should have joined forces, while Austria was weak, did not, however, come together.

"The second outbreak" covers the period from November 1848 to April 1849. Austria displayed with increasing acerbity the will to become a centralized Imperial State, the "rebels" in Italy and Hungary were suppressed, the realization of a united German Empire was frustrated, but also the so-called Little-Germany solution which continued the Gagern programme. Bavaria and all the petty states were shaken by unrest and trouble of every kind. This particularism was intimately allied with the patriotism which was striving everywhere in Germany to bring about a free and national State. The Frankfort Constitution was actually adopted by all German popular representatives except in Austria and Liechtenstein. The refusal of the King of Prussia to accept the Imperial crown at the hands of the people, and still more the refusal to accept the Constitution, even in a modified form, caused the popular movement to flame up again all over Germany. This rising had been in preparation for months. Once more there was a combination of national and social-revolutionary motives, and these contradictions doomed the whole movement to failure.

The fight for the Constitution was more than a last despairing attempt to bring the work of the Frankfort Parliament to some sort of positive conclusion. It also meant a last bold attempt to seize upon all that the March Revolution of 1848 had failed to achieve. The "Victory of the Counter-Revolution" in Germany lasted from April to July 1849. Outwardly it includes the civil war in Saxony and Baden, the movements in Bavaria, Württemberg, Thuringia, and the Rhineland. The European great power, Prussia, deliberately and consciously threw her military strength into the balance on the side of Austria and Russia. The battle against the Revolution had become a great question of foreign policy. The war with Denmark had already shown that Prussia had no conception of such policy. She repeatedly gave way to Russian pressure; English favour and French friendship could not be counted on; but much more might have been made of them, for the Western Powers delighted in the quarrel between the two Germanic powers. Prussia overpowered the patriots under the name of rebels, and thought to replace them by a lukewarm policy of "Union." The more modest goal of a North German Confederation might have been attainable if well prepared beforehand. But Prussia grasped at South Germany and the end of the revolutionary period shows a totally different picture. Prussia, hope of all progressives, had disappointed everybody, had become an executioner of the Counter-Revolution, without any gain to herself. Austria was maintaining herself with astonishing vitality against all comers and had every prospect of gaining the sympathies in South and West Germany that Prussia had thrown away.

The German Revolution was over, but its spirit was not dead. Revolution had already laid latent in the preparatory era, as Counter-Revolution in the Revolution itself; and in Counter-revolution again the later period of reform lay latent, which was to lead to the foundation of the Empire in 1871. But this was not all; the victory of the Counter-Revolution in Germany was also a victory of the party of constitutional reform over parliamentary and social-revolutionary democrats; the communists, who had warned against half-measures, above all against trustfulness, were shown to have been in the right. The moderates sank wounded and fainting into impotence; the extremists confronted one another in bitterest enmity; dictatorial authority, with its militarist-capitalistic idea of a Great Power—and Marxism.

The victory of the Counter-Revolution in Germany bankrupted the previous revolutionary methods and ideas. Politics became materialistic, intellect, and culture too. The active revolution had been imbued with ideas. The reaction was avowedly exactly the reverse. The naïve pleonasm *Realpolitik* was born at this time. Authoritative power policy, natural-scientific over-assertion of self and Marxian socialism equalled each other in materialism. Nothing proves more saliently the actual importance of the idea in history than the embitterment with which it was opposed and the often unconscious hypocrisy with which it was used as an excuse.

Many observers of the German Revolution of 1848–49 have refused to permit the name of revolution to be applied to it. Certainly, Latin and Slavonic revolutions have exhausted the last possibility of revolutionary action; the English revolution of the seventeenth century was full of stronger tension, although it had one curious characteristic in common with the German revolution, which was, to return to a new legitimacy as rapidly as possible. Every nation makes revolution in accordance with its inner nature. War and foreign policy produce an absolute measure of the best super-national achievement: revolutions are an individual revelation of a people's soul. Revolutions that are choked down are apt to be indigestible; the Revolution of 1848–49 was not able to develop itself to the full, and the German people are still suffering for it today. The Counter-Revolution has shaped German destiny all the more energetically since. The attempt at revolution had been made, with its apparent successes. Since then, all German princes and statesmen have reckoned with revolution and taken counter-measures against it. The fissure had opened, innocence was no more. Experience raised a strident voice. One might say that it took the Counter-Revolution in Germany to demonstrate the full historical existence of the Revolution.

The old powers had now perceived what was in the wind. Police organs had proved inadequate; this had made it necessary to use troops so often. All was now changed. Care of the poor, organization of news, traffic facilities, the censorship, had often failed; the old organization of the State was not equal to the new demands made upon it, and broke down under the pressure of its new content, the subject had begun to look after himself. The badly-paid and socially oppressed middle and lower-class officialdom was almost everywhere on the side of the popular movement. The new authoritative State no longer intended to put up with this state of things; it demanded from every servant of the State that self-confidence and discipline which the higher officials in Prussia, as well as in most of the petty states, had never abandoned. It was determined to have no more patience with illegal organizations, the idea of every man in arms, or revolutionary leagues which undertook their own political salvation. The authoritative State was fighting for itself and therefore knew no mercy. Revolution had meant disorganization of existing institutions in favour of talent; the Counter-Revolution meant the organization of the will to self-preservation by people of moderate ability. The main object to be attained was to educate the subject to a new loyalty. He must be taught to enjoy being led; those who obeyed and worked hard, would come to the top. The man of the world, the travelled genius, the sovereign satirist on Heinrich Heine's model, went out of fashion; the period of Anton Wohlfahrt (the hero of Gustav Freytag's novel *Soll und Haben*) dawned, the day of the industrious burgher, the man who makes profits, because he understands the laws of loss. The authoritative State had won the victory, and with it the right to scribe the history of the popular movement of 1848–49. It had all been no more than silliness and folly, unripe dreams, philistinism, childishness, absurdity; pedagogues laid the blame upon inadequate education, professors upon lamentable ignorance; officials complained of so much insubordination, army officers of the lack of discipline, diplomats of the naïve clumsiness of the form; the aristocratic thought the Revolution vulgar, the prosperous saw in it a new form of begging or even of highway robbery; the German has no talent for politics, it was said; he would do better to leave the government in trained official hands.

It was the true master-stroke of the Counter-Revolution to implant in the German people a widespread belief in its own political inefficiency. Before 1848 they were convinced of the contrary: the national free State was the last, the only thing lacking to the Germans, now that they had attained the highest levels in philosophy and art. This final perfection of our historical destiny was to be denied to us, because—we were not ripe for it!

The good-natured German actually believed his masters, thought "the people" had done everything very foolishly and so brought about all the misfortune; they believed that parliamentarism and democracy were foreign articles of import, not really proper for a true German; they believed that a benevolent Constitution could offer everything that could not be done without in the way of constitutionalism; the good-natured Germans again became worshippers of the military and devotees of the aristocracy. They learned to respect money, especially a great deal of money; they crammed knowledge into themselves, especially petty details; independent political thinking soon came to be regarded as a kind of impudence; writers were again considered to be unrestrained, immodest persons, democrats to be rogues, men of the world to be blind worshippers of foreign ways, patriotic Germans to be traitors to Prince, State, and Diet. Creative civic service was replaced by the order from above and the blind obedient response. The "mad" year was over and everyone went soberly about his duty. Germans had wanted to be great, free, and strong, and now everything was just as it had been before. Why should the good Germans be dissatisfied? They could become a people of thinkers and word-spinners as they had been before, spinning out a thin thread of logic and dancing on it. But there was a new uncertainty in the air. Since 1848, Germans have suffered from political inferiority complexes. They had lost confidence in themselves and never found it again. It was not reason, but force, which had succeeded. Many now worshipped force. Many turned away resigned, composed Persian lyrics, fled to the sagas of the Middle Ages, or back to the old Germanic gods or to Buddha. Hegel had not been right after all. The last great German synthesis was a failure. The day of Schopenhauer dawned.

But things were not as they had been. There was something

429

to be made good, a crime to be wiped out. The next decades were obsessed by this feeling. Something had been broken and crippled in the innermost heart of the German. The wound had never closed—it is not closed today.

Had all been in vain—daring and hope, enthusiasm and fire? Had all these ideas, feelings, urges been spent in vain? Such sacrifices of happiness, blood and property? About five thousand persons may have perished during the revolutionary period, including the troops killed in the civil wars, about twelve million gulden's worth of property may have been lost. A moderately important battle in the Franco-Prussian War spent more blood, a single day of the World War more money. But this is a false standard to apply. The importance of the destruction wrought by the Revolution of 1848–49 must be measured by the standard of life in the 'forties. This period, so rich and fecund, was the fulfilment of a long period of peace, the values which it creates were bourgeois and peaceful, human life was precious and people were persuaded that happiness could be attained by accumulation of property and creative participation of all in a reasonable and harmonious development of the State. The psychical effect of street fighting far exceeded the effect produced by military events. Any serious, especially any fatal, injury sustained in the midst of peaceful citizen life had a widespread and exaggerated inflammatory influence. But as the Revolution proceeded, this effect became less and less marked; sensitiveness and bitterness increased again during the fresh confusions of the civil war of 1849. Industry had developed so rapidly and accumulated such reserves that normal production had naturally sunk ever since 1846, producing a slump and considerable unemployment in the factories and among artisans. Agricultural products, on the other hand, fetched higher prices than formerly. Property owners were best off during the revolutionary era; they were the Counter-Revolution in person. It was the misfortune of the urban bourgeoisie to be plunged into an economic crisis just at the moment when they were at last attempting to assert themselves as a political factor. Purchasing power had greatly decreased, receipts sank, credit was over-strained, securities low. Lack of money corresponded to super-fluity of human material. Mercenaries could be had cheap, so could demonstrators, agents and spies. By the side of serious statesmen and reformers stood the spinners of plans, the fantastic prophets of a more splendid world.

Bruno Bauer called the Revolution of 1848–49 "the bourgeois revolution" and thus helped to found a conception which, although completely erroneous, has prevailed to this day.

The designation "bourgeois" has been commonly used for the Revolution of 1848–49 in opposition to "proletarian" or "socialistic." Certainly the urban middle-class, though in process of decay, stood in the forefront of the movement and its main objective was the reform of the Constitution. But the fate of the population was decided by auxiliary factors, working beside and behind the scenes—the agrarian revolts, the associations of artisans and workmen, the striving after new forms and conditions of social intercourse in Germany, often with a strong undercurrent of philosophic principles, a sharply critical tendency, a revolutionary inspiration. The battle for a new Constitution was in itself by no means hopeless, and would perhaps have met with success had it not been for the radical minorities whose existence rendered it easier for the forces of counter-revolution to split up and weaken the bourgeoisie. Apart from the sociological development which sought, not to consolidate, but to separate and build up anew —the intellectual spirit of the popular movement was as determinedly bourgeois in the one camp as it was deliberately revolutionary in the other. It is these contrasting and conflicting forces which make the aspect of the time so contradictory. Counter-revolutionaries pointed mockingly to many philistine and puritan elements among the new forces; but far more marked was the spirit of youthful enthusiasm which informed the movement to the last. The young were glad to be young, they were proud of their youth; they called things fearlessly by their right names and the very boldness and uncompromising spirit of their youth awakened confidence and won them followers from among the simple hearts of the lower classes who did not want to be pedantically instructed, but led with enthusiasm. Sometimes a little foolishness is both subtle and more fruitful than too much wisdom; the rising classes were all for emotion and sentiment; their strongest feature was a blind natural urge and they sought passion at which they could take fire. They believed because they wished to believe and had need of sacrifice, often the sacrifice of their very lives. It has rightly been said that revolutions bring about outbreaks of both sensual and religious emotion. Something absolute arose and masks were laid aside. Nature demanded her eternal rights. It was the task of the leaders to find an ethical and reasonable justification in opposition to everything conventional. Everything in reason was supposed to be attainable. No doubt the last great battle for the Constitution was beset by stupidities; nothing is easier than to prove this; but it is quite unimportant. The new, free, strong, just Germany was sought after with passionate heroism by the blinded, excited, newly-awakened combatants; they, too, wished for better times; why not, indeed? Every true fighter battles for himself and for his cause at the same time. The two things should not be separated. In any case it was anything but bourgeois to possess so much imagination, such a capacity for sacrifice. It was these qualities which made the conquered of 1849 into pioneers for the eternal revolution of humanity.

Naturally there were fanatics and quacks in this German revolution, as in every other. The masses were too enraptured by what was new for its own sake to distinguish the charlatan and the profiteer at first sight. This condition of things most bitterly affected the old guard of 1848; their seriousness and experienced knowledge was suddenly challenged and overwhelmed by unbalanced hysteria; disgusted, the former opposition either retired altogether from the scene or sought alliance with the older powers, being usually unable to discern the element of strength in the new, young oppositional spirit.

This procedure meant something decisive in German social history and in the later development of the German party system. Before 1848 there were many signs that a new lower-class might be formed in Germany on a broad basis, consisting of artisans, employees, servants, working-men, peasant-farmers, and small shopkeepers; a class that would have been democratic in the widest sense of the word; that is, national, parliamentary, and social, and which would not have been disinclined to acknowledge a democratic emperor. The Counter-Revolution prevented the development of this class and thus the evolution of such a party. The very name of "democratic" vanished for a time. In South Germany, it was replaced by "People's Party" (Volkspartei). The name and conception "social-democratic," which we have seen appearing in Baden, Saxony, and Electoral Hesse, was destined to a splendid career later.

The opposition to social oppression is an essential factor of the formation of parties in the revolutionary year. There was still an insulting differentiation between the "Fräulein" and the "demoiselle," between a young woman and a young lady; schoolmasters were often considered unworthy to be addressed as "Mr."; soldiers were spoken to in the third person singular. As late as 1847, an order of the Prussian ministry of the interior directed that "corporal punishment should be administered only to persons of the lower classes." The attempt to introduce the address "Citizen" at the beginning of the democratic movement must not be regarded as a slavish imitation of the great French Revolution, but as a reform of the class differentiation in common speech as well as of the abuse of titles.

It may be maintained in general that humanitarian ideas, logically enough, were represented only in the Left or radical groups, whereas the Old Liberals made shamefaced reservations. A man was no longer to become a human being only from a Baron upwards; instead, humanity now began as low as the professor and the factory-owner. Old Liberalism showed that enlightenment and romance with all metaphysical contradictions lay in its tenets. Its greatness was its critical attitude towards orthodoxy, absolutism, class tyranny, economic conjunctions, individual eccentricities and prejudices. Now came the hour of creation, of constructiveness; it appeared that Old Liberalism, which was so just and understanding, also had its dogmas, that it moved within limits and wanted to erect barriers, and that in spite of all its belief in goodness and reason, nothing was left as residue but intolerance, force and the employment of all the national instruments of power.

We must make an attempt to understand the bitterness roused in the lower classes against the moneyed and titled patriciate by their experiences in time of revolution. It was this patriciate which had demanded the leadership of the popular movement and which had now abandoned the struggle. The arrogance of the nobles had been offensive to the small man; but pride of purse and professional pompousness were still worse. The piteous end of the Revolution tended to widen differences between classes and parties in Germany. The Conservatives rejoiced when the Liberals were reproached with having deserted the poor devils on the barricades and in the street fighting and left them to shed their blood alone. It is one of the strangest consequences of the Revolution that the lower middle classes were politically put to death in Germany. The Revolution had disintegrated them, and as a class they could not coalesce again. It was better, people said, to respect your betters in school, army, and civil authorities, then at least you got on in the world. Intellectual and economic aspects played into each others' hands, to build up a counter-revolution founded on the primal instinct for stability and inaction in the artisan and yeoman.

434

The revolutionary parties spread confusion among their own followers by their lack of unity, the quarrels among the leaders and the incomprehensible attenuation of their programme. The worst disagreement was between the evolutionary Democrats and the Social Revolutionaries. Often the two parties cancelled one another out on proposed motions, so that nothing at all happened. Discussion was especially fiery in the early days, for it was the new political way of life. German talent for the theoretical, celebrated orgies; printed paper guaranteed the immortality of every shade of opinion. The reaction to all this frothiness was the worship of positive power, the "saving deed," everything authoritative which should effectually balance one's own weakness and indecision. The bankruptcy of the Revolution was also a bankruptcy of fine speaking. Oratory had done nothing to alter facts. Nobody had any faith left in sounding phrases. The Prussian spirit of self-assertion again and again called upon the memory of Frederick the Great as a barricade against German-National and liberty-loving demands. A copy of the proposed German Constitution was burnt by its most violent opponents on the site Unter den Linden where a monument to Frederick the Great was to be erected. But the Reform Party was determined not to let the Old Prussians have the great old man, with all the magic power of his genius. An opposing pamphlet contained an imaginary letter of Frederick the Great to his "dear Berliners" in which he spoke of having seen the first gleams of dawning freedom and urged them to serve the name of Prussia by becoming devoted *Germans*. This battle over the bones of Frederick the Great was a battle over the interpretation of the Prussian tradition. The Conservatives, who were excellent business men and never scrupled to use more power than they really had, never understood the true depths of the Christian religion, of Prussian history or of German statesmanship. Once outside their own sphere, they failed in matters requiring firm decision and were almost helpless. They regarded an individual right to vote as a positively revolutionary conception and the beginning of democracy, socialism, and communism. Equal incomes had equal rights, the root of all disorder was sin against the God-given principles of State and Church. At first, industry and the money market were regarded entirely with enmity by the Prussian Conservatives. Later Hermann Wagener drew the delicate distinction between moral and immoral industry.

The 'fifties are a strange contradiction to the previous decade—anaemic, weary. Work was done with dogged determination; politics left to those directly concerned. Later, the reactionaries took credit for the economic revival. What might it not have meant had it been accompanied by a little political and intellectual freedom!

Like a man just before the death agony, the democratic movement rallied, and the moment of its death resembled its most vital period. The counter-revolutionary forces were not blind to this, and with all their brutality, they were afraid. It was no longer as it had been. Even the type of ruler changed.

Germany kept all her Stuarts and Bourbons; but that European event, the Revolution, left trembling echoes for a long time in royal hearts. There were moody and jealous despots like the rulers of Hanover and Electoral Hesse, fantastically confused absolutists like Ludwig of Bavaria and Friedrich Wilhelm of Prussia. Such personalities could but further the republican idea. But most of the princes showed such utter lack of character, granting at once everything that they had already refused a hundred times, only in order to retain their power, that this at first disarmed the democratic movement. Examples of personal courage were as rare as examples to the contrary were common. False and genial, the rulers quietly prepared for the Counter-Revolution. Some, like Grand Duke Frederick I of Baden, its most successful representative, evolved a new type. They became respectable and middle-class, emphasized their family life, kept their love affairs more carefully out of sight, patronized art and learning as far as respectable and often supported constitutionalism and even German freedom—as long as their royal rights were respected—in a word, they presented the industrious and loyal German of the 'fifties and 'sixties with the very picture he desired to see, since it resembled himself.

Much more serious than the battle against the princes in 1848 was the battle against the petty states. Energetically, and supported by many good reasons, all the frontiers of 1815 were called into question. A caricature very aptly showed the thirty-eight potentates of the Deutsche Bund as cobbling tailors, busily putting patches in the old cloak of the Holy Roman Empire. German Michael was advised to pulp up the old cloak and tailor himself a new one in modern style. There were many beginnings in this question of mediatization, but no end. The idea of the democratic emperor, closely related to the dream of the unified German Republic, really sprang from despair at the realization that particularism was a disease ingrained in the German nature, which broke out afresh in the era of the Revolution and could only be cured by force either of a social-revolutionary or an Imperial character.

All kinds of plans were made, there were even defenders of the petty states. The discussion could not be brought to any logical conclusion. There were as many kinds of particularism as there were types of state in Germany, and they all proclaimed their right to liberty. Austria and Prussia maintained that their units had European character and precluded any idea of a uniform German State. Bavaria roused up all the diplomacy of Europe to maintain her claim to be the largest purely German State. She was a classic example of anti-national particularism, too small to be the bearer of a national Union, but large enough to be a serious hindrance, and to feel the separate entities of the Palatinate, Franconia, and the former Imperial cities as a danger to her own individual existence. But the real danger was the weak dynasty, the much neglected army and the most bureaucratic officialdom in Germany.

In the petty states, tribal and local patriotism struggled oddly with princely particularism. All the German states behaved in the revolutionary period like a family of blood-relations, eternally quarrelling and making up, not only because they needed each other, but because a certain attachment existed. Quarrels were continual and inevitable, but complete estrangement unthinkable.


National cohesion, a national way of life existed in Germany long before there was a strong national form of existence. Hence the devouring longing of the progressives; they were ashamed to be so rich and yet so unripe. The idea of a strong German nation which was to create its strong empire, filled and pervaded all leading Germans, from Radowitz to Robert Blum, thrusting every other consideration into the background —perhaps too much. The men of the Frankfort Parliament called again and again upon the unfinished Cathedral of Cologne as symbol of the German Empire of the future: one day both would be finished and soar proudly upward. In these days, the belief still prevailed that the German spirit would have the power to break down all opposition.

It was once said most appositely in the Frankfort Paulskirche that it must be feared that the Prussian Diet would prove the iron wheel in the golden repeater watch of the empire. One could scarcely find an apter metaphor for the unsolved and probably insoluble Prusso-German problem.

It can be precisely observed how the national idea, the great, all-embracing experience of the outbreak of the Revolution, coarsened and lost its ideal character in the course of events. There was something in the idea and in its aims which carried people away and united them; but the paths of accomplishment ran in different directions and even crossed one another.

The embitterment over the Danish encroachments and Prussian weakness was probably the most permanent feeling of the period. Mistrust of Russia continued in Western and Southern Germany in spite of all assurances from Berlin. Attempts were made to distract attention by fomenting an anti-French patriotic outbreak, but without success. Yet public feeling was very sensitively against any suspicion of direct connection with a foreign country. The agitation against Prussia was nurtured by the argument of the dependency of Prussia's policy upon Russia—and since there had been a particularly confidential relation ever since the Wars of Liberation and Prussia would probably have disappeared altogether but for Russia—at least, she would never again have grown into a European Great Power—this was in accordance with historical truth. A broadsheet once lampooned Berlin's near future in the style of the reports of Napoleon's return from Elba. At the beginning, it was said that the Russians, the most cannibal people in Europe, were lying in wait at the frontier, and at the end: "The noble Czar Nicholas insists on strictest discipline; a friendly nation, the magnanimous Russians, are our welcome guests." The Counter-Revolutionaries, for their part, purposely identifying democracy and communism, reproached both with internationalism. There was certainly a communistic International, though it was only the dream of a small group of conspirators. Certainly middle-class evolutionaries such as Venedey and Robert Blum reposed too much confidence in the humanitarian policy of the second French Republic. But a really serious political connection between the two countries existed far less on both shores of the Rhine than inside the princes' trust, which was fighting the popular movement.

In reality, the Revolution of 1848–49 was something thoroughly German, as a whole and in detail; foreign prototypes were only a masquerade, in a deeper sense, an inspiration; it was precisely an entirely German trait to measure oneself against the rounded and already complete national figures of neighbour nations and so gather courage and strength for a path of one's own.

Montesquieu, Rousseau, Sieyès, Mirabeau, were cited in the Frankfort Parliament. Their words were quoted as proofs; there were arguments as to their meaning. Several pamphlets were published about Mirabeau; the great French Revolution was still such a living thing as the contemporary history of their fathers' generation, that even the names of leaders and parties were transferred to the present-day, often misleadingly; a "German Gironde," "the German Danton." The great Napoleon still cast his mighty shadow over the German democratic movement of 1848. The magic of a name pointed the way to overcome the Revolution by substituting the monarchic State controlled by arbitrary power.

At the beginning, many people hoped that this might be avoidable. They pointed warningly to the English critics of the great French Revolution, especially Edmund Burke and also Adam Smith and Macaulay. The battle of the German Revolution sometimes resolved itself into a struggle between historical parliamentary discipline, orderliness, and freedom in the English style and intellectual radicalism in the French style. Even Arndt, in agreement with his master, Freiherr vom Stein, pointed to the model of English political self-control. English example greatly influenced the practical work of the Frankfort Parliament. Lassaulx described the basic formation of the British Constitution as the ideal for all constitutional monarchies; examples from English policy were cited to clinch arguments; Vogt compared the superfluous numbers of German officials with the economical English self-administration. Mittermaier proclaimed the masterly character of the English law of official responsibility, first and most excellent of its kind in all Europe. "We could not do better than simply translate it."

On July 23, 1848, Arnold Ruge proposed a motion in the Paulskirche to summon an international congress to discuss

European disarmament, "since armed peace with its standing armies imposes an intolerable burden upon the peoples of Europe and endangers civil freedom." Ruge pointed to Lamartine's pronouncements, to English efforts to bring about European disarmament, to America's rejection of a standing army: the three great nations of Europe, Germany, England, and France, must unite—Russia could not then remain isolated; this was the only possibility of a new democratic and republican order. But the motion did not get a majority.

The embittered battle, fought with absolute hatred on both sides, between the Greater Germans and the Little Germans was founded upon an inversion and perversion of over-sensitive national feeling; at the end of the revolutionary period this hatred outweighed every other feeling in Germany, even that against foreign tyranny, and keen observers thought that a warlike settlement was unavoidable.

In pointing to the example of the United States, Ruge and Sepp were appealing to one of the most effective motives in the political thought of the time. The German-Americans themselves were always directing their former countrymen's attention to the institutions of their new country. A pamphlet circulated along the Rhine and Main in 1847 and dated from New York, warned Germany against faith in hollow declamations, military service to the princes, the self-seeking clergy, the bureaucrats and despots who had broken all their promises; Germany should arise, should achieve the republic by force of arms; if she were practical, she would also gain her freedom. After the outbreak of the Revolution, mass assemblies in the three centres of German-Americanism, the Middle West, Pennsylvania, and New York, sent addresses of sympathy to the German democratic movement. "Chase away all the princes and create perfectly free Republicans!" cried the Germans of Philadelphia in their address. The "Address of German Brothers in the free United States of America to the German People" of April 1848, signed by four hundred and ninety-four German-Americans, was brought to Bremen by the ship *Washington* together with a donation of three thousand five hundred dollars. She had hoisted two flags, the American Stars and Stripes and the German black-red-and-gold. On May 29th, this address was communicated to the Frankfort Parliament, where the assembly rose to cheer its authors—the only case of this kind. The German-Americans did their best to awake understanding for the German democratic movement among their compatriots of other ancestry. The refugees after the first Revolution, Hecker at their head, kept up a tireless agitation, above all with the object of collecting money.

Germany's answer to America was serious and strong, borne on the wings of a great longing. The Constitution of the United States was again held up as a very model of perfection. It was reproduced in one Stuttgart pamphlet, together with those of Pennsylvania and Texas and the constitutions of Belgium, Norway, and Switzerland.

Many other authors wrote on the subject, some designing plans for a State similar to the United States, and this was directly demanded by the extreme Left in the Paulskirche in their first party report. It was to be no mere slavish copy, but adapted to German needs. Much goes to show that in the Frankfort Parliament there was a feeling of community of life and destiny with the peoples of North America. The president of the United States was the only foreign ruler who sent a direct greeting to the German National Assembly.

At the beginning of the Revolution there appeared in Dresden a broadsheet by Dr. S. Reissmann with the high-sounding title: "Documentary Exposition of the Effectiveness of the German Federal Assembly, with regard to the Representation, Defence and Preservation of the Rights of the German People against the Forced Measures of the German Governments since its Inauguration up to the Present Day." There was nothing behind this title-page but a sheet of blank paper. It was a joke, but with a bitter sting. Deep shame was felt that those responsible had done nothing at all for the rights of the German people. The basic idea of the democratic movement was the longing for freedom from oppression, from arrogance, from exploitation. More respect for the rights of man, instead of the claims of princes. The soul of the Germany of that day was in revolt against the conceit, sluggishness and malicious caprice which they encountered in the ruling classes. Wrong had been done them too often and too severely. Most people of this generation had lost their sense of humour. The Germans of the Wars of Liberation had hoped to build up a better world, an ethically more valuable form of existence. The majority no longer believed in this in 1848. People no longer demanded the maximum of ethics, but the minimum of rights; guarantees, order, a lawful State. In its deepest sense, the Revolution in Germany was a fight for right. Lothar Bucher, regretted that the many professional lawyers in the National Assembly tended to cause long-winded arguments, pointed out that the unexampled task before them was to bring about the consequences of an unfinished revolution by peaceful methods of jurisdiction.

A Revolution that was still unfinished! This was the moot point: the politicians had been content with an apparent victory and now the lawyers had to erect a building where no site had been cleared: the instinct of the Germans was to demand something legitimate; they wished to see the Revolution settle down as soon as possible into something orderly. Berlin never finished; but in Frankfort the result was a new positive lawfulness, very cautious, more conservative than revolutionary. The counter-revolutionaries were not so scrupulous; they swept away parliaments and constitutions with all their legal correctness and set up a new written code, based only upon historical authority and unwritten law.

Everyone knows how important the historians were in the revolutionary struggles of 1848–49; it seemed natural that

443

those who studied and taught history should be the people who helped to make it. But the part played by the jurists is much less well-known. The battle for the word was matched by the battle for the idea. The philologists confronted the verbal interpretation and the ideological universality with the best they had; the living German being, explained in the being and meaning of the language itself with a right to its own development into the form natural and valuable to itself alone. Thus a battle royal of the faculties ensued and often enough they reproached one another with lack of practical sense and overmuch devotion to theory. Yet it must be said that often university professors were among the few who really knew their German Fatherland from their own experience.

German women also felt the revolutionary period to be the opening-up of new possibilities. When Malvida von Meysenbug brought a poor woman a pamphlet explaining the basic rights of the German people, she received it with eyes filled with tears and the words: "Well, if that's the way it is—if my children will see better days than I have, then I don't mind having suffered." The social oppression and deep injustice which whole generations suffered in Germany also implied the greatest humiliations of their mothers, sisters, and wives. Perhaps the years about 1850 represent the first great heroic period of the German housewife. Later the type of the motherly woman who kept house, turned her hand to anything, and yet found time to read Schiller's poems to her children and correct her husband's proofs or keep his accounts, became rarer. Malvida von Meysenbug came from another class; she sprang from a diplomatic family and grew out of her caste, both intellectually and spiritually; she had the courage to be herself, a womanly woman, intensely human, a splendid personality, with a courageous heart, untiringly looking for good; a true incorporation of that humanitarian idealism which was to dissolve before the Bismarck generation like a morning mist. Malvida was enthusiastic but careful, silent and energetic, always learning, and a firm stay to many good friends with everything fine and decent, shy and estranged from the loud posterings of the worldly and conventional. She was truly a free being, because she remained fettered to the pure essence of her true self and therefore, strong as were few others, melancholy yet prophetic, she bore the message of the "International Battle of the Spirit" of 1848 into the later, more understanding epoch of the grandchildren.

Louise Otto-Peters had a sturdier, more practical nature. The great year of revolution aroused her from novel-writing to organizing work, to the battle for independent duties and therefore independent rights for women. The woman's old calling as teacher was to be broadened, deepened, fixed firmly on a scientific basis and economically secured. Froebel's Kindergarten offered new opportunities, simple but suitable work. The clever daughters of so many learned fathers aspired to the higher schools. Here they encountered the greatest hindrances. Emilie Wüstenfeld now founded a special higher school for women at Hamburg. Woman's deep desire for recognition and appreciation also became emancipated; detached from the sphere of housewife and mother, a special eagerness to learn and to teach developed, an untiring energy which usually remained in gracious forms. The German woman's talent for systematic building-up, for instinctive and determined penetration into higher and more important spheres of life awoke and insisted on recognition.

Woman's part in political life was still indirect. Women of the Rhine sent forth the most proclamations. The wife of Professor Walter of Bonn wrote her husband such clever political letters that he was accustomed to read them to the King and his ministers in Berlin. Most women were only spectators, but absorbed ones. Many were enthusiastic republicans; the new State offered both men and women fresh possibilities of rising to honour and esteem. Young men came to the fore; Pegasus replaced the ox-wain. Wit, oratory, temperament, and brilliant ideas carried the day. Women loved this state of things, especially those who were young and beautiful. Clothilde Koch-Gontard, wife of the English consul at Frankfort, showed the world that a political salon was possible, indeed, especially at home in a republican, parliamentary world. We have this lady's letters and diaries which reveal her as a woman of by no means exclusively feminine cleverness and unforgettable charm.

Comparison with all other revolutions in modern history shows the German Revolution of 1848–49 to have had the smallest percentage of deeds of violence, also of crimes against property. During his revolt, Friedrich Hecker ran along the ranks, urging his men to take nothing without paying for it on the nail, since the villagers were already lamenting as if a band of robbers were approaching. When, during the Berlin March Revolution, certain people threatened to take a fancy to the silver vessels in the Jerusalemer Church, Wolff the sculptor, who had marched to revolution in his dressing-gown, girt with a sabre and crowned with a flapping broad-brimmed hat, pretended to be seized with revolutionary fury, bore the vessels off and secreted them in his house until things quieted down. There was no organized revolutionary terror; a couple of isolated acts such as the tearing down of the Dresden opera house were mere individual excesses. But there is much evidence that the soldiers beat their prisoners, and the treatment of political prisoners in convict prisons was often purposely harsh.

The German Revolution of 1848 erected no guillotines and held no extraordinary courts of a purely political nature. No one except Prince Metternich was banished; there was no confiscation of fortunes, no holding-up of salaries, no refusal of pensions. No one in Germany thought that in order to combat the past, its representatives must be made personally defenceless and economically impotent. Outwardly it was nothing more than a purely political reversal, borne aloft by representatives of pure humanitarianism; a humane revolution is necessarily a semi-revolution. This was probably the deepest error of the men of 1848. Revolution is battle and carries the principle of force into the formation of the State. The princes had always made their wars ruthlessly without regard either to other peoples or to their own. The German democratic movement of 1848 wished to achieve a gentle victory. No historian will reproach the leaders with shedding too little blood; there are other ways of removing opponents. The Revolution of 1848 did not perceive them or took no note of them. The leaders must have known their opponents well enough, but did nothing to cripple their activity or to replace them in their posts by followers of the new order. The Frankfort central power could have chosen people in whom they could have confidence; but the old particularistic bureaucratic machine continued to rattle untroubled on its way. There were martyrs enough from the Revolution of 1830 and the Wars of Liberation. Certainly they were elected to the Frankfort Parliament—Ernst Moritz Arndt, Jahn, Uhland, Eisenmann, Sylvester Jordan—but they had very little voice in affairs. The young revolutionaries suffered from the German fault of over-trustfulness. They took no revenge; the patriotic and liberty-loving citizens saw the principal danger in the Jacobins, Social-Revolutionaries, and Communists.

Naturally, there was much malicious joy over the fall of the mighty; the lack of talent for quick, sharp action was compensated for by a tremendous gift for scolding: grumbling, criticism, speculations as to how it could have been better done, frittered away the urge to action. Curiously enough, this quarrelsome criticism rapidly turned from the old to expend its force against the new leaders. The new men may have had their weaknesses; but they were mercilessly exposed. The moment anyone rose to the top, he was attacked with embittered jealousy; Welcker, Heinrich von Gagern, Robert Blum, Friedrich Hecker—the same fate overtook them all. This was the reverse side of the medal of the conscientious revolution of 1848; it destroyed its own children. The Revolution had practically talked itself to death by the time the Counter-Revolution was on the march. The people's leaders had only a momentary authority; they had continually to fight for it; their weaknesses were those of the people themselves and therefore unforgivable. Public opinion was particularly resentful if the new men profited economically from their work. Anyone who accepted a government position with a fixed income, like Karl Mathy or Wilhelm Jordan, was already half a traitor. Heinrich von Gagern was so sensitive on this point that it was necessary absolutely to force upon him the salary accompanying the post of President of the Frankfort Parliament by passing a law that there could be no refusal of this salary. A healthy desire to see clean hands in public affairs was thus so exaggerated as to lead to pure absurdity. For the bureaucratic apparatus remained, just for this reason, practically unchanged.

Thus the humanitarian State, as the March movement dreamed of it, could not come into being. Men longed for action and feared it at the same time. When the big speeches were over, there was remarkable modesty in deeds and also a certain hesitation. The old layer of officialdom presented a very solid front in comparison. It did not glitter, it did not trifle, it was something in itself and had no need to become anything different. When these people accused the democratic leaders of wanting to snatch office, of vanity and who knows what else, there was scarcely anyone who thought to rebuff the questioner by asking where these noblemen, these property-owners, these manufacturers had come by their fortunes. Most of the new people were poor and suffered from poverty; they therefore hesitated between shyness and excited claims; they had talent, good sense, patriotism, a feeling for what was right;

448

they turned everything into debate, believed they could convince the majority and carried motions; they thought they
could alter German realities by a new Constitution, by new
laws. It was an honourable undertaking, but unfortunately
the mass of the public soon grew tired of it. There was not
enough going on, it was not rapid, not dramatic, not wild
enough. The loud-mouthedness which sprang up by the side
of the noble pioneers of a new justice, awakened in the mass
of the public a respect for what had been; pity and sympathy
for fallen greatness is also a good trait of the German nature;
only a clever twisting of contemporary events was necessary
to weld a new loyalty, in exercising which the people thought
themselves mighty fine fellows and true as steel. It was just
those who had always been despised and ill-treated by the
old powers who now made use of the opportunity to get a
little nearer to the throne, without running any great danger
and so to gain social and economic advantages. The nobles
had always had a certain independence; unquestioning devotion was to be the characteristic of this new class of citizen.

The Reform movement had tried to be just to everyone,
a political point of view must never anticipate the judgment
of history. Will to righteousness made these men self-righteous.
This roused their political opponents to absolute hatred. The
Republicans, the Social-Revolutionaries, the Communists had
the active courage to be unjust; but only minorities followed
their lead.

The Counter-Revolution certainly had more courage to be
unjust. There was no question of asking whether blood might
be shed or property destroyed; there was no need to seize
the means of power; the Counter-Revolution had all that was
necessary. If the popular movement in North Germany, except
in Berlin, seemed somewhat lacking in temperament, the
Counter-Revolution was undoubtedly more emotional. Religion, patriotism, morality, loyalty to the traditional ruling
house, proceeded to the attack. The Revolution had branded

only Metternich as a criminal; the Counter-Revolution branded a whole social class as rogues and vagabonds. When the vanquished marched out of Rastatt, the Prince of Prussia turned away. He did not want to see "such people." The Revolution had built up a legend of its own pre-history; the Counter-Revolution now wrote the legend of the nature of this democratic movement and thus exercised a decisive influence upon two German generations. The Revolution had taken care to make no martyrs; the Counter-Revolution had no such scruples. Ordinary courts competed with courts-martial. The feeling of justice, so sensitive at this time, was once more deeply wounded by a whole series of political trials.

Jacob Burckhardt said power was an evil thing. There is something worse than power. Power is, above all, fickle. It must be won and manifested afresh from day to day. Only use can keep it bright and keen. It serves only those who grasp it firmly. Woe to them who possess it and do not use it, for it will turn against them. This was the experience of the German citizen of 1848; the measure of logical retribution which he had not in himself, was visited upon him with interest by the Counter-Revolution. The humanitarian, the decent citizen, the cosmopolitan dialectician, had no more to say. The world had shown that it was not beautiful and pure as the classic form, nor joyous and brightly-coloured like an intellectual romantic play. A dashing age usurped the scene, impudent and coarse, unashamed, inclined to mockery and brutality. Certainly no political movement could be suppressed entirely by police and the courts; there were more subtle measures and these had a decisive effect. The "people," it was said, had proved themselves to be insolent, avaricious, rough, and treacherous; they needed control and they should have it. Arrogance and contempt of mankind, the ancient vices of ruling classes, now went disguised as the art of protective government.

The reaction in Germany was all in browns and greys. How

450

picturesque the Revolution had been! Now the best thing was to say nothing more about it; the very recollection was to be buried. Few of the painters of the time have preserved its gay aspect; the green sharpshooters with their hunting-knives; the blue militia with light or dark trousers worn with their wide coats, feathers in their hats, cockades, sashes, often broader than necessary, sabres, halberds, old rusty rifles as weapons; everywhere the daring, energetic young men, usually in gymnast's dress, with white, frogged blouses, older men in caps, with long beards, a few gentlemen in blue frock-coats, hunting-rifle slung on their arms, people in all kinds of odds and ends of military uniforms, and finally a sprinkling of Polish frogged tunics. Hosemann's sketches are about the best.

The best of this generation acclaimed a new legal State at once, as a logical and moral postulate and as a work of art. Thus the Paulskirche changed from a sober Lutheran church into a timeless sacred temple, eternal home of the German idea. On the faces of the men who assembled in Frankfort in May 1848, there was the brightness of such fulfilment of destiny. We can still perceive it to this day. But even in this National Assembly, men of such calibre could be only a minority. Next the seers were pedants and fools. Just because the new politicians took themselves with such extreme seriousness, the rebound was sure to follow. Before the tragedy was at an end, the farce began.

In its depths, the eloquence of Heinrich von Gagern was akin to that of Robert Blum—it called forth the cynicism of Detmold and Karl Vogt, so different from one another, but united by their sceptical attitude towards all heavy-browed solemnity. Poor Germany, which was also so rich! Beautiful and rich in its landscapes and talents, poor in the results of all this richness, happy in its individuals, and therefore longing for the final depth of individualization, luckless as a whole, confused and put out of countenance by the superfluity, yet tempted again and again to try and master it!

The distance between the two poles of the German being caused the development of that malady which is perhaps the German's especial curse. Georg Friedrich Daumer considered the events of the European revolution of 1848 to be so monstrous that he believed the "old slavish conditions" under which the German spirit had lived, were now gone for ever and the time had come for a completely new conception of the world in place of the Christian, for the "Religion of the New Age of the World," affirmative, natural, the truly good, and wholesome conception of life and eternity. Thus the German spirit again swept forth into the ether at the moment when the practical day's work was most urgent. It strove from the relative to the absolute, it was at once bound to the past and filled with the future, but somewhat estranged from its immediate present. German political creation therefore grew rampantly in space, missing the clear and logical formation of the new, as in France, not drawn to unity by an irresistible popular leadership, as in Italy, nor capable of simple sensible action, wise for the next day to come, as in England, and a Russian intoxication of destruction and creation was equally impossible to it. German political work in 1848 was at once too universal and too specialized—the old powers made the most of this weakness. It is remarkable how the experience of the unity of the German people, the witnesses of which can be seen to-day in any Provincial Museum, could so rapidly recede again, even be almost forgotten. The German's old inferiority complex was still greater after the Revolution than before. Each kept strictly within his social and professional sphere, the judge consorted only with judges, the professor with professors. Closer than all party formations were the bonds of the clique and the *Stammtisch*, the familiar table at the inn, always frequented by the same few friends. The people broke apart again. There was a temporary end, too, of the self-admiration of the 'forties. Many had grown humble and willing to be impressed. The Revolution had come to a halt before the thrones and the money-bags—another reason for these two powers to become allies. The immediate future belonged to middle-class militarism. People had seen where a multiplicity of talents led. The superfluity of talents had seized upon everything and with spirit and thoroughness had accomplished all that intelligent patriotism can bring about. There was no strong man, whose personality could have held the thing together. Ideas are good and there had been no lack of ideas, enough to last for two generations. Ideas are splendid, but men are better.

The German Revolution of 1848–49 stands between Freiherr vom Stein and Otto von Bismarck. Stein's idea had an immediate influence upon the democratic movement, through Arndt, Gagern father and sons, Stockmar, Prince Leiningen. After 1850, Stein's memory was revived, his figure set up to point to a better German future. But this future was little in accordance with the will of the great leader, whose aim had been to set justice in the place of authority. It is much more proper to say that the destiny of the German Democratic Movement of 1848 coincided in one decisive point with the destiny of Freiherr vom Stein: both were finally wrecked on the northeast German agrarian class and the dynamics of foreign policy.

Prince Schwarzenberg and Louis Napoleon taught Bismarck how domestic policy can be mastered by means of foreign policy, how the danger of a revolutionary state, which arises from reshuffling of classes, can be averted by military power, foreign wars, growth of power, and territory. The greatness of Bismarck's foreign policy becomes really apparent when it is regarded from the point of view of Revolution and Counter-Revolution. European and particularistic restrictions made the work of Frankfort difficult to the point of impossibility. General Cavaignac had already said as early as the summer of 1848 that the Franco-Russian alliance was certain if Germany were united on a democratic basis. England supported the Little-German solution because it was directed against Austria, but this favour soon came to a standstill over the question of the dukedoms. Bismarck is a complete contrast to the democratic movement of 1848: the popular movement wanted to win the dukedoms of Schleswig and Holstein as a German petty state—Bismarck simply annexed them. The democratic movement wished to free the Poles, or at least to secure the rights of the Polish people within the Prussian State—Bismarck sacrificed the idea of Polish independence for the sake of Prussian friendship and began the Prussianization of the Poles; the 1848 movement wished as a majority to see the Little-German democratic empire of the King of Prussia preserving the petty states, suppressing Prussian State egotism, and, as a minority, wished for decided unitarism in place of particularistic federalism—Bismarck created a Great-Prussian Empire firmly bound to authority, he annexed a number of Central German states, but left the South Germans to themselves, especially Bavaria; he took over universal suffrage for the empire, but in Prussia and therefore also in a number of allied states, he prevented free development, in the interests of the dynasties and the ruling classes. The restoration of the old Diet served to restore German unity, if only in a very modest form; Prussia drew back from England, Russia, and France, one after the other. Nothing much could be done with French friendship. Bismarck's life-work can be plainly seen to be founded upon this constellation: he used Russian and French friendship to squeeze Austria out of Germany, the Austria of Franz Josef, which had far more friends in Germany than post-revolutionary Prussia. Bismarck founded the North German Confederation and prevented a similar formation in South Germany. The German Empire of 1871 was thus the enlarged North German Confederation—Greater Prussia united with a Bavaria which could not become Greater Bavaria, and soon also allied with the Austro-Slav-Hungarian monarchy which after the loss of Italy and Germany could turn only to the Balkans. The 1848 movement had sought to dissolve the Austrian Imperial State.

Our pre-history of the 1848–49 Revolution needed a great deal of detail: the post-history of the Revolution can be pressed into one great name—Bismarck. His work wiped out the democratic movement of 1848–49; Königgrätz, the 18th of March, and the *Paulskirche*. As a personality, too, Bismarck belongs entirely to the Counter-Revolution. The really creative part of his achievement lies in the fact that for a certain time he combined the Revolution and the Counter-Revolution. As a statesman, he completely outgrew the dogmatic repressions of the Christian-Germanic reactionary; there lived in him the spontaneity, the unrestrainedness, the originality of revolutionary energy; he was no man of yesterday, but seemed—although not permanently—really to promise a bright morning. The cultural struggles and the break with the National Liberals brought the turn of the tide, and in domestic policy the beginning of a rigidity which the ageing great statesman could no longer throw off. The Constitution of 1871 was a masterpiece of statesmanship according to the state of things at the time; knowledge of the true inner history of 1848–49 makes it comprehensible that it should have taken the form and come about in the way that it did. Bismarck's work and achievement had the eternal justification of a practical and bold historical action, in which the right moment was seized and used.

But was it necessary that Bismarck should, in a deeper sense, have prevented his successors from carrying on his work? He never ceased to worry about the Reich; he was succeeded by men full of careless self-confidence. One can imagine a generation, this very generation of 1860, trained by Bismarck, which would have been proud and independent enough to found the German Empire anew after Bismarck's departure, to enable the parties and classes, till then suppressed, to take part in the life and work of the State and thus to create the free democratic nation with a strong democratic emperor which the first German popular movement of 1848–49 had envisaged with such longing. This did not happen—but it is not our task here to explain the why and wherefore.

The Spain of Philipp II, the England of Elizabeth, the France of Louis XIV, the Austria of Maria Theresia, produced a unity of state, culture, and religion which could no longer come about in Germany as a whole since the division in religion. The great French Revolution gave France vital strength. Enlightenment, the ideal of humanity, the idea of the lawful State, organic conceptions of State and of history, socialism, materialism, are all nothing more than partial manifestations in Germany, which affected the entire people, but neither thoroughly shook them, nor gave a new form to their lives.

The new never entirely destroyed the old. The German is not good at destruction. Even after the founding of Bismarck's empire, German unity was a foreign political and economic reality, but not a spiritual experience of the people as a whole. This is still more true of the political forms of the Weimar republic period. The demands arising from them will always lead us back to 1848. He who is not certain what to do will certainly not find that history informs him. But he whose will is clearly set to certain aims ahead can search the past and find an answer there. Every century since the sixteenth has brought severe civil struggles in Germany. The old German lust of battle found vent in wars between the individual states every time a quarrel arose. Not until the German Confederation of 1815 was there any peacefulness, at the cost of freedom. When the people of 1848 arose, everyone once more fought against everyone else; but the struggle did not come fully to a head. To this extent the year 1866 represents the late realization of everything that had been neglected or could not be achieved by the better way of understanding. The year 1866 is a secular epoch—it was thrust into the background by the brilliance and fulfilment of the year 1870–71, but historically speaking, it weighed almost more heavily.

Nations have the primeval right to throw off foreign oppression. They also have the primeval right so to shape the State that it is ruled by a class of leaders so fitted for the task that the working people are taught to be contented. A great deal of force has been used in Germany—formerly it was mostly the slaves, peasants, citizens, working-men, who bore the brunt. The peace-loving cosmopolitan, too, may be turned into a world-revolutionary by the narrow-minded opposition of those in power. Revolution is not a sin. With the year 1848, a new era of revolutions began, which is not yet at an end. Fichte already sought the Revolution which Napoleon had ruined. Just as Bismarck in 1866 asked an indemnity from the Prussian people's representatives, so should the whole military-bureaucratic epoch of Imperial Germany have begged a timely indemnity from the idea of the free democratic State. The right to revolution finds its only limitations in the degree of talent available to carry it through and create a new State. Formerly revolutions and wars were strictly divided. The danger of revolution was parried by declaring war, and lost wars usually ended in revolution. Today pointing of war and revolution is seen as an identical threat, pointing in different directions, achieved by the same means. Every revolution, too, is a technical fighting problem. In 1848, fighting was done simultaneously with antiquated weapons, such as the barricade system and the volunteer principle, and with very modern weapons, such as the utilization of means of transport and the organization of news. Wars and revolutions seem to be growing more and more to resemble one another; the revolutions have learned from the wars the idea of universal arming of the people, as was repeatedly done in 1848. War learnt terrorism from revolution. We know that the reform of the Prussian Army in the 'sixties can be traced back to the attitude of the Prussian Landwehr or reserve troops,

457                                             P*

in 1848–49, which, in many places, felt themselves as militia rather than as tools of authority.

The popular movement of 1848, the strongest motive in which was the national urge, ended with the conviction that nationalism and internationalism are contrary poles. But always, ever since the days of feudalism, Europe has been a unit. Have not Kant and Goethe influenced England; Hegel, France; Nietzsche, Italy; Marx and Engels, Russia, to the greatest extent? There is no isolation. Today we see very plainly that a fruitful and peaceful international life is only possible between democratic nations, ripened, grown peaceful, nationally satisfied. The history of Germany as a nation and as a form of State and society is not yet complete. It may be carried on by fresh revolutions, but not necessarily. There is no danger of revolution which cannot be banned by reforms and wise statesmanship. The Revolution of 1848, trodden underfoot by the Counter-Revolution, was not dead. It sat in the Eternal Paulskirche of Greater Germanism and waited for the hour of re-birth. Doubtless it is still sitting there to this day. The old cannot and will not return. But the patriotism of 1848, in its purity and its resolve, is the immortal ally in all future struggles of the German nation.

# INDEX

465

# NAME INDEX

v. Abel, Karl, Bavarian Prime Minister, 74, 75, 79, 80–82, 87
Aegidi, Ludwig, student, 203
Albert II, Archbishop of Bremen, 125
Albert, Prince Consort, 60–61, 62, 63, 161, 168, 303
Albrecht, Archduke of Austria, 81
Albrecht, the Naughty, 113
Albrecht, Wilhelm Eduard, Professor, representative, 242
Alexander I, Emperor of Russia, 91
Alexander II, Emperor of Russia (Grand Duke Alexander Nikolajewitsch), 64, 320
v. Alvensleben, Count, landed proprietor, 196
Ancillon, J. P. F., Prussian Foreign Minister, 34
v. Andlaw, Baden envoy, 299
v. Andrian-Werburg, Victor, Baron, publicist, representative, 19, 20
Anneke, Fritz, former lieutenant, revolutionary, 388
Arese-Visconti, Franzesco, Count, Italian politician, 249
v. Aretin, Karl Maria, Baron, Bavarian *chargé d'affaires*, 294, 347
v. Armansperg, Josef Ludwig, Count, Bavarian politician, 367
Arndt, Ernst Moritz, poet, representative, 43, 361, 362, 440, 447, 453
v. Arnim, Bettina, authoress, 59, 134, 418
v. Arnim-Boitzenburg, Count, Prussian Prime Minister, 18, 19, 47, 195, 198, 211, 224, 229, 230, 243, 247, 382, 397
Arthaber, manufacturer, 189
v. Auersperg, Anton, Count (Anastasius Grün), poet, 251, 269
v. Auersperg, Count, Austrian general, 325
v. Auerswald, Alfred, Prussian Minister of the Interior, 195
v. Auerswald, Hans, General, representative, 309
v. Auerswald, Rudolf, Prussian Prime Minister, 357, 364
August, Director of a grammar school, 203
Augusta, Princess of Prussia, 356, 418
Augustenburg, Duke, 316
Avenarius, printer, 321

v. Baader, Franz Xavier, philosopher, 76
Bach, Alexander, Austrian Minister of Justice, 189
Bakunin, Michael, Russian revolutionary, 298, 321, 322, 400, 401
Barbarossa, *see* Emperor Friedrich I

467

468

474

477